William Robertson Smith

The Prophets of Israel and their place in history to the close of the eighth century B.C.

Eight Lectures

William Robertson Smith

The prophets of Israel and their place in history to the close of the eighth century B.C.
Eight Lectures

ISBN/EAN: 9783744735773

Printed in Europe, USA, Canada, Australia, Japan

Cover: Foto ©Lupo / pixelio.de

More available books at **www.hansebooks.com**

THE

PROPHETS OF ISRAEL

AND

THEIR PLACE IN HISTORY

TO THE CLOSE OF THE EIGHTH CENTURY B. C.

Eight Lectures

BY

W. ROBERTSON SMITH, LL. D.

NEW YORK
D. APPLETON AND COMPANY
1, 3, AND 5 BOND STREET
1882

PREFACE.

THE Lectures contained in this volume were delivered last winter to large popular audiences in Edinburgh and Glasgow, at the invitation of an influential committee of gentlemen interested in the progress of Biblical study. The Lectures were to some extent planned as a sequel to a course delivered in the same cities in the previous winter, and published last year under the title of *The Old Testament in the Jewish Church*. The primary design of that course was to expound, in a manner intelligible to persons unacquainted with Hebrew, the problems and methods of modern criticism of the Old Testament, and so to enable the laymen of Scotland to follow with intelligence the controversy then occupying the Courts of the Free Church as to the right of criticism to assert itself within the Churches of the Westminster Confession. So far as the Church Courts are concerned, that controversy has for the present been abruptly terminated, by what may fairly be called an act of violence, and without a legal decision being obtained from the General Assembly of the Church on questions which certainly cannot be permanently disposed of until they have been exhaustively considered in their relation to the doctrine of the Protestant Churches on the one hand, and to the laws of scientific inquiry and the evidence of historical fact upon the other. Ecclesiastical leaders have always been prone to flatter themselves that questions of truth and Christian liberty can be set at rest by an exertion of authority; but those who love truth for its own sake cannot acquiesce in this easy method; and not in Scotland alone, but in all Protestant Churches of English tongue, it is becoming yearly more manifest that thoughtful and earnest students of the Bible will continue to examine the history of revelation for themselves, and will not rest satisfied with conclusions that do not commend themselves to the scientific as well as to the religious consciousness.

For the popularisation of science in all its branches, which is so characteristic of our age, has accustomed men to examine the foundations of current beliefs, and to acquiesce in no results that have been reached or are defended by methods which science condemns. Historical science in particular has made vast strides; in every part of history traditional ideas have been upset, and old facts have been set in a new light. Even schoolbooks are no longer content to transcribe ancient sources, but seek to interpret them on scientific and critical principles. The records of our religion are historical documents, and they claim the same treatment which has been so fruitfully applied to the other sources of ancient history. They claim it all the more because the supreme religious significance of this history gives it an interest to which no other part of ancient history can pretend.

In point of fact the Bible has not been neglected in the general progress of historical study. A vast amount of genuine work has been done in this field, and, though much still remains for future research, many new results of the highest importance have been reached on which scholars are practically agreed. But unhappily the fruits of modern Biblical study are still very little accessible to the general reader. Many of them are only to be found in learned books, encumbered with technicalities and written in foreign languages, or, if translated, translated into that peculiar jargon which only translators venture to call English. And in general the best results of modern research must be sought in so great a variety of books, and are often expressed in so controversial a form, that it is difficult for the ordinary reader to follow them and combine them into an intelligible whole. It is far easier for the English reader to gain a just view of the present state of inquiry in Greek or Roman history and literature than to learn what modern scholarship has done for the history and literature of the Hebrews. And yet it is manifestly absurd to think that the very best use of the Bible can be made by those who read it for the nourishment of their religious life, so long as the history of the revelation which it contains is imperfectly understood. In the interests of religion, as well as of sound knowledge, it is of the highest importance that everything which scholarship has to tell about the Old and New Testaments should be plainly and fully set before the intelligent Bible reader. The timidity which shrinks from this frankness, lest the untrained student may make a wrong use of the knowledge put into his hands, is wholly out of place in Protestant Churches, and in modern society, which refuses to admit the legitimacy of esoteric teaching.

The Lectures now laid before the public are designed as a contribution to the popularisation of modern Biblical science. They cover but a small part of the Old Testament field, and they purposely avoid the tone of theological controversy. There are, indeed, many questions relating to the prophets and their work on which controversial feeling is still keen; but the most hotly discussed of these lie in great part outside the period, closing with the end of the eighth century B.C., which the present volume deals with; and where this is not the case I have sought to keep my discussion as close as possible to the historical facts, without raising dogmatic issues, which for the most part have really very little to do with the proper function of the historical interpreter. It is impossible to deal frankly with any Biblical problem without saying many things which may challenge opposition; but where the purpose is to give real help to Bible students, and not to advance the interests of a theological party, the controversial method should always be avoided, for the questions of modern controversy are generally derived from mediæval rather than Biblical thought.

The period with which this volume deals is that of the earliest prophetic literature, and therefore presents the prophetic ideas in their least complex form. Some readers may be surprised at the very small amount of developed theology which these ideas contain; the elements of prophetic religion in the eighth century before Christ are marvellously simple in comparison with the range of conceptions with which the modern theologian is accustomed to operate, and which are often traced back to the earliest Old Testament times. It must, however, be remembered that the theological thought of the Hebrews underwent a great development after the time of Isaiah; the principles of the oldest prophecy are germinal principles, which unfolded themselves gradually and led to results which, though now familiar to every one, were not contemplated by the earlier teachers of Israel. It would have been easy to pause from time to time and point out the line of development connecting the truths of the earliest prophetic religion with New Testament doctrine; but to do so within the space of a single volume would have unduly straitened the exposition of what the first prophets actually taught, and were understood to mean by their contemporaries. If occasion offers I hope to be able at a future time to continue the history through the subsequent stages of prophetic teaching; but to mix all stages together and read later views of truth into the earlier teaching is not likely to produce anything but confusion. There is a religious as well as an historical gain in learning to read every part of the Bible in its original and natural sense. Much unnecessary exacerbation of dogmatic controversy would be avoided if theologians were always alive to the fact that the supreme truths of religion were first promulgated and first became a living power in forms that are far simpler than the simplest system of modern dogma.

The habit of reading more into the utterances of the prophets than they actually contain is partly due to dogmatic prepossessions, but partly to a lack of historical criticism. The notion which has proved most fatal even in modern times to a right understanding of the prophets is the notion of the later Jews that all the prophets are interpreters of the Pentateuch, which either as a whole or at least in its most essential parts is supposed to be older than the oldest prophetical books. This opinion has only of late years been radically subverted by the demonstration—for such I venture to call it—that the Priestly Legislation did not exist before the Exile. I know that this conclusion of criticism is not universally received among scholars, but it makes way daily, and at least it can no longer be disputed that the ideas of the prophets do not presuppose those of the priestly parts of the Pentateuch. So much will be admitted even by scholars like Nöldeke, who do not accept the whole results of that construction of the history of the Pentateuch which is generally associated with the name of Graf, and has been mainly worked out and established in detail by Kuenen in Holland and Wellhausen in Germany. That I accept the leading critical conclusions of the newer school of criticism will be evident to the reader of this volume; my reasons for doing so are already before the public. But I trust that it will be found that what I have to say with regard to the progress of the prophetic teaching is not dependent on any evidence or argument that lies outside of the prophetical books themselves, and the indisputable attention to works that are indispensable or might easily be overlooked, and to indicate where full discussions may be found on questions that I am obliged to treat perfunctorily. Besides such references the notes contain a good deal of illustrative matter of a somewhat miscellaneous kind, including some things specially designed to make the book more useful to academical students and a few observations which may, I hope, be of interest to fellow-workers in Biblical science.

I have only to add that the Lectures, as now printed, are considerably expanded from the form in which they were originally delivered.

W. ROBERTSON SMITH.

EDINBURGH, 3d *April* 1882.

CONTENTS.

LECTURE I.

ISRAEL AND JEHOVAH 1

LECTURE II.

JEHOVAH AND THE GODS OF THE NATIONS . . 47

LECTURE III.

AMOS AND THE HOUSE OF JEHU . . . 90

LECTURE IV.

HOSEA AND THE FALL OF EPHRAIM . . . 144

LECTURE V.

THE KINGDOM OF JUDAH AND THE BEGINNINGS OF ISAIAH'S WORK 191

LECTURE VI.

THE EARLIER PROPHECIES OF ISAIAH . . . 235

LECTURE VII.

Isaiah and Micah in the Reign of Hezekiah . 279

LECTURE VIII.

The Deliverance from Assyria . . . 317

Notes and Illustrations 375

Index 441

LECTURE I.

ISRAEL AND JEHOVAH.

THE revelation recorded in the Bible is a jewel which God has given to us in a setting of human history. The love of God to His people now is the continuation of the love which He showed to our fathers; and Christianity, like all else that is of value in the spiritual possessions of mankind, is an inheritance the worth and permanence of which have been tried by the experience of generations. Such treasures are not won without effort and battle. What is appropriated easily is as easily lost, and the abiding possessions of humanity consist of truths that have been learned by laborious experiences, relations that have been knit and strengthened by long habit, and institutions that have been shaped and polished by the friction of practical use. A religion fit to be a part of actual life cannot be exempt from this law, and revelation itself has become a force in human conduct only by first becoming a factor in human history. It was not enough that God should declare His will and love to man. The declaration required to be incorporated with the daily lessons of ordinary life, to be woven into the personal experience of humanity, to become part of the atmosphere of moral and intellectual influences which surrounds every man's existence, of which he is often as little conscious as of the air he breathes, but without which spiritual life would be just as impossible as physical life is under an exhausted receiver.

It is often remarked upon as a strange thing that Jesus was born so late into the world, that Christianity has been permitted to spread through slow and imperfect agencies from so narrow a centre as Judæa, and that the divine wisdom deemed it fitting to prepare the way for the world-wide religion of Jesus by that long series of rudimentary revelations, addressed to a single nation, of which the Hebrew Scriptures form the record. The slowness of the moral process by which God's will for our salvation realises itself on earth, the incomplete establishment of the moral kingdom of God in the midst even of professing Christians, and the fact that for long ages the power of revealing love seemed to pass by the greater mass of mankind altogether, and to deal very tardily and partially even with the chosen nation of Israel, appear hard to reconcile with the sovereignty of the divine purpose and the omnipotence of the divine working. It would serve no good purpose to deny that there is a difficulty in understanding these things, but the difficulty lies less in the facts to be explained than in the limited point of view from which finite creatures contemplate the work of an infinite and eternal being.

That the eternal and infinite God has anything to do either in the way of nature or of grace with the finite world of time is a mystery which we cannot hope to comprehend; but in itself it is not more surprising that revelation follows the laws of historical progress than that a law of continuity runs through the succession of physical phenomena. The difference between nature and grace is not that nature follows fixed laws and that grace breaks through them; there are laws in the moral world as well as in the material cosmos, and the sovereignty of revealing grace does not lie in the arbitrary quality of the acts in which it is manifested, but in its dominion over the moral order of things to which the physical order is subservient. In revelation God enters into personal relations with man; but these personal relations would not be spiritually valuable unless they were constituted, maintained, and perfected by the same methods as the personal relations of a man to his fellows. According to the doctrine of the Old Testament the whole work of revelation and salvation rests on the fact that man was created in the image of God, and so is capable of entering into intelligent moral relationship with his heavenly father. But even in the sphere of ordinary human life the filial relation is one that has a gradual growth. The mere physical fact of parentage is but a small element in the meaning of the words father and son; the greater part of what these words involve, as used between a loving father and son, lies in the relation of affection and reverence, which is not of mere physical origin, but grows up with the growth and training of the child. Thus the analogies which the Bible itself presents as our guides in understanding the work of divine grace lead us to expect that revelation must have a history, conformed to the laws of human nature, and limited by the universal rule that every permanent spiritual and moral relation must grow up by slow degrees, and obey a principle of internal development.

The older theology was not sufficiently attentive to this truth. It had indeed learned from the parables of the Gospel that the growth of the kingdom of God is similar to the development of a great tree from a small seed; but it did not fully realise that this analogy not only affirms the contrast between the small beginnings and ultimate world-wide scope of the kingdom of grace, but teaches us to look on the growth as subject to an organic law similar to the physical law of development in a living germ. The very idea of law as applied to the course of history has been clearly grasped and fruitfully worked out only in recent times, and therefore it is not surprising that even those theological schools which made a serious effort to understand the successive stages of God's saving dealings with man did not get much beyond the notion of a mechanical series of covenants or dispensations.[1] And in particular almost all speculation on this topic, down to quite a recent date, fell into the cardinal mistake of over-estimating the knowledge of divine things given to the earliest recipients of revelation. The fact that the work of salvation is one from first to last, that Christ is the centre of all revelation and the head of all redeemed humanity, led to the idea that from the first the faith of the Old Testament believers looked to a personal Messiah as distinctly if not as clearly as the faith of the New Testament Church.

This assumption involved the study of the old dispensation in extraordinary difficulties. The Old Testament contains no explicit declaration in plain words of the cardinal New Testament truths about Christ, and it was therefore necessary to suppose that the men of the Old Covenant possessed, in addition to the written Word, certain traditional conceptions about the coming Saviour, which gave them a key to the symbolism of the sacred ordinances, and enabled them to draw a meaning from the language of the Prophets and the Psalms which does not lie on the surface of the words of Scripture.[2] This theory arose naturally enough in the ancient Church, which held that a similar state of things continued under the Christian dispensation, and that the help of ecclesiastical tradition was still necessary to understand the mysteries which formed the really valuable teaching of the New Testament as well as of the Old. But when the Protestant Church broke with the doctrine of ecclesiastical tradition, and sent every man to Scripture to edify himself by the plain sense of the holy oracles, it was a strange inconsistency to continue the figment of a hidden sense and a traditional interpretation as applied to the old dispensation. Far from reading in the words of the prophets a profounder sense that lay beneath the surface, the Hebrews, as their history abundantly proves, could hardly be taught to accept the simple and literal lessons inculcated upon them line by line, and enforced by providential discipline as well as by spoken words. It is plain that the very elements of spiritual faith were still but half learned by a nation that made continual relapses into crass and immoral polytheism, and the elementary character of much of the prophetic teaching is not to be explained as vailing a hidden sense, but simply by the fact that the most elementary teaching was still not superfluous in the spiritual childhood of the people of God.

This is the true state of the case, and perhaps the chief reason why people are still unwilling to admit that it is so is a fear that, by stripping the prophecies of their supposed mysteriousness, we shall destroy their interest and value for the Christian dispensation. Such a fear is altogether groundless. It would be absurd to expect to find in the Old Testament truth that is not in the New. The real use of the record of the earliest stages of revelation is not to add something to the things revealed in Christ, but to give us that clear and all-sided insight into the meaning and practical worth of the perfect scheme of divine grace which can only be attained by tracing its growth. A mechanism is studied by taking it to pieces, an organism must be studied by watching its development from the simplicity of the germ to the final complexity of the finished structure. Or, to put the thing under a more familiar analogy, the best way to understand the full-grown man is to watch his growth from childhood upwards, and the childhood of the Church shows us in simple and elementary expression the same principles which are still active in the full manhood of the Christian dispensation.

It would be easy to illustrate this argument by additional analogies, but it will be more profitably elucidated in the actual study of the prophets and their work, to which we are to proceed during the hours we spend together. In these Lectures I propose to adopt the simplest and most straightforward historical treatment. I shall take up the prophetic writings in the order of their date, and look at them in connection with what is known of the prophet and his times, just as one does with any other ancient book. Instead of asking at the outset what the prophet has to teach us, I shall inquire what he desired to teach his own contemporaries to whom his message was directly addressed. In this way we shall get at the plain meaning of his words, and what is still more important, we shall learn something of his place and function in the unity of the divine work of revelation. We shall see the principles of revealing and redeeming grace shaping themselves from age to age in living contact with the life and needs of successive generations, and thus I hope we shall attain a more reasoned assurance of the consistency and supernatural wisdom of God's saving dealings in all ages, while at the same time the study of each divine word as it first came home to the immediate necessities of the people of God will make it easier for us to apply the same word to the support of our own spiritual life. The details of this practical application of course belong to the preacher or to the devotional reader, and not to the expositor of the Old Testament history. On the province of the preacher I do not propose to trench, but I hope that we shall be able to reach the point of view, and appreciate the methods and principles, from which the study of the prophecies can be profitably undertaken with the design of personal edification.

There is, however, one question of a general nature to which it may be well to devote a few words before we enter on this course of historical inquiry. The justification of the general conception of the method of revelation which I have just indicated must ultimately lie in the proof that it is consistent with historical facts. The doctrine of an organic development in the plan of revelation and redemption, analogous to the gradual education of a son by his father, can be established or refuted only by inquiring whether the analogy is justified by the actual course of history in the pre-Christian childhood of the people of God. But the whole conception of a progressive revelation worked out in special dealings of God with the people of Israel is often represented by modern thinkers as involving something inconsistent with the universality of the divine purpose. There is a large and thoughtful school of modern theologians, fully possessed with the idea of a divine education of mankind, and ready to do sincere homage to the teaching of Christ, which yet refuses to believe that God's dealings with Israel in the times before Christ can be distinguished under the specific name of revelation from His providential guidance of other nations. They contend, and so far they are undoubtedly right, that God prepared all nations, and not the Jews alone, for the reception of the truth as it is in Jesus; but they also maintain that there was no specific difference between the growth of divine truth in Israel and the growth of truth among other nations. The prophets who were the organs of God's teaching in Israel appear to them to stand on the same line with the other great teachers of mankind, who were also searchers after truth, and received it as a gift from God.

In one point of view this departure from the usual doctrine of Christians is perhaps less fundamental than it seems at first sight to be. For, as a matter of fact, it is not and cannot be denied that the prophets found for themselves and their nation a knowledge of God, and not a mere speculative knowledge, but a practical fellowship of faith with Him, which the seekers after truth among the Gentiles never attained to. This, at least, is sufficiently proved by the fact that the light which went forth in Christ Jesus to lighten the Gentiles did proceed from the midst of the Old Testament people. But behind this there appears to lie a substantial and practical difference of view between the common faith of the Churches and the views of the modern school of which I speak. The difference is generally expressed by saying that the modern theologians deny the supernatural; but I do not think that this phrase expresses the real gist of the point at issue. The practical point in all controversy as to the distinctive character of the revelation of God to Israel regards the place of Scripture as the permanent rule of faith and the sufficient and unfailing guide in all our religious life. When we say that God dealt with Israel in the way of special revelation, and crowned His dealings by personally manifesting all His grace and truth in Christ Jesus the incarnate Word, we mean that the Bible contains within itself a perfect picture of God's gracious relations with man, and that we have no need to go outside of the Bible history to learn anything of God and His saving will towards us,—that the whole growth of the true religion up to its perfect fulness is set before us in the record of God's dealings with Israel culminating in the manifestation of Jesus Christ. There can be no question that Jesus Himself held this view, and we cannot depart from it without making Him an imperfect teacher and an imperfect saviour. Yet history has not taught us that there is anything in true religion to add to the New Testament. We still stand in the nineteenth century where He stood in the first; or rather He stands as high above us as He did above His disciples, the perfect Master, the supreme Head of the fellowship of all true religion.

It is a bold thing, therefore, to affirm that we have any need to seek a wider historical foundation for our faith than sufficed Him whose disciples we are. And I apprehend that the apparent difficulty of the supposition that the whole course of revelation transacted itself in the narrow circle of a single nation is not so great as it appears at first sight. For it is not necessary to suppose that God gave no true knowledge of Himself to seekers after truth among the Gentiles. The New Testament affirms, on the contrary, that the nations were never left without some manifestation of that which may be known of God (Rom. i. 19; Acts xvii. 27); and the thinkers of the early Church gave shape to this truth in the doctrine of the λόγος σπερματικός—the seed of the Divine Word scattered through all mankind.

But, while all right thoughts of God in every nation come from God Himself, it is plain that a personal knowledge of God and His will—and without personal knowledge there can be no true religion—involves a personal dealing of God with men. Such personal dealing again necessarily implies a special dealing with chosen individuals. To say that God speaks to all men alike, and gives the same communication directly to all without the use of a revealing agency, reduces religion to mysticism. In point of fact, it is not true in the case of any man that what he believes and knows of God has come to him directly through the voice of nature and conscience. All true knowledge of God is verified by personal experience, but it is not exclusively derived from such experience. There is a positive element in all religion, an element which we have learned from those who went before us. If what is so learned is true we must ultimately come back to a point in history when it was new truth, acquired as all new truth is by some particular man or circle of men, who, as they did not learn it from their predecessors, must have got it by personal revelation from God Himself. To deny that Christianity can ultimately be traced back to such acts of revelation, taking place at a definite time in a definite circle, involves in the last resort a denial that there is any true religion at all, or that religion is anything more than a vague subjective feeling. If religion is more than this, the true knowledge of God and His saving will must in the first instance have grown up in a definite part of the earth, and in connection with the history of a limited section of mankind. For if revelation were not to be altogether futile it was necessary that each new communication of God should build on those which had gone before, and therefore that it should be made within that society which had already appropriated the sum of previous revelations. Some true knowledge of God might exist outside of this society, but at all events there must have been a society of men possessed of the whole series of divine teachings in a consecutive and adequate form. And under the conditions of ancient life this society could not be other than a nation, for there was then no free communication and interchange of ideas such as now exists between remote parts of the globe. Until the Greek and Roman empires broke up the old barriers of nationality, the intellectual and moral life of each ancient people moved in its own channel, receiving only slight contributions from those outside. There is nothing unreasonable, therefore, in the idea that the true religion was originally developed in national form within the people of Israel; nay, this limitation corresponds to the historical conditions of the problem. But at length a time came when the message of revelation was fully set forth in Christ. The coming of Christ coincided under divine providence with the breaking down of national barriers and the establishment of a cosmopolitan system of politics and culture under the first Roman emperors, and so Christianity was able to leave the narrow field of Old Testament development and become a religion not for one nation but for all mankind.[3]

It would seem, then, that the distinctive character claimed by the Biblical revelation, and expressed in the creed of the Churches by the doctrine that the Bible is the supreme and sufficient rule of faith and life, ultimately resolves itself into something which is quite capable of verification. It will not be denied that the knowledge of God reached by Gentile nations was fragmentary and imperfect, that there was no solid and continuous progress in spiritual things under any heathen system, but that the noblest religions outside of Christianity gradually decayed and lost whatever moral power they once possessed. If the religion of the Bible can be shown to have run a different course,—if it can be shown that in it truth once attained was never lost and never thrust aside so as to lose its influence, but that in spite of all impediments the knowledge of God given to Israel moved steadily forward till at last it emancipated itself from national restrictions, and, without changing its consistency or denying its former history, merged in the perfect religion of Christ, which still satisfies the deepest spiritual needs of mankind,—then, I apprehend, the distinctive claims of the Bible and the religion of the Bible are set upon a broad and safe basis, and the revelation of the Old and New Testament may fairly claim to be the revelation of God to men in a special and absolute sense. It is not necessary to encumber the argument by comparing the way in which individual divine communications were given to Israel with the way in which the highest thinkers of other nations came to grasp something of spiritual truth. The mode of God's communication to man is a matter of detail; the essential advantage claimed by the religion of the Bible does not lie in details, but in the consistent unity of scheme that runs through its whole historical development, and gives to each part of the development a share in the unique character that belongs to it as a whole.

To thoughtful minds it has always been a matter of

supreme interest to realise what proof of the truth and sufficiency of the Christian religion can be adduced apart from the internal impress of genuineness which it produces on the believing mind. The external evidences of religion have been very variously set forth, and perhaps no one statement of them has ever been quite satisfactory. In recent times the whole question has assumed a new and startling aspect, through the attacks that have been made on the old favourite evidence from miracle. Instead of accepting the miracles as a proof of Christianity, a large number of men, who are neither unthoughtful nor irreverent, have come to regard the miraculous narratives of the Bible record as a chief difficulty in the way of its acceptance. It is felt that the reality of these miracles is the very thing in the teaching of Scripture which it is most difficult to prove; and, so long as no deeper evidence can be offered of the truth of the Christian religion than is given by the old argument that it is attested by miracle, the objection is ready that this, far from being a distinctive peculiarity of one religion, is a prerogative to which all religions lay claim. Indeed, most of the arguments which make men unwilling to allow to the Bible the character of the record of a special revelation resolve themselves into objections to the idea that the narratives of a supernatural character which the Bible contains are different from the miraculous narratives found in other ancient histories. And in like manner it is contended that it is impossible to prove that the truths preached by the prophets came to them in any other way than the truths proclaimed by Gentile teachers.

I am not prepared to deny that these objections may be put in a form which has great force against many current apologetical arguments, but they do not go to the root of the matter. There is an external evidence of the truth of the Biblical revelation which lies behind the question of the supernatural as it is usually stated, an evidence which lies, not in the miraculous circumstances of this or that particular act of revelation, but in the intrinsic character of the scheme of revelation as a whole. It is a general law of human history that truth is consistent, progressive, and imperishable, while every falsehood is self-contradictory, and ultimately falls to pieces. A religion which has endured every possible trial, which has outlived every vicissitude of human fortunes, and has never failed to re-assert its power unbroken in the collapse of its old environments, which has pursued a consistent and victorious course through the lapse of eventful centuries, declares itself by irresistible evidence to be a thing of reality and power. If the religion of Israel and of Christ answers these tests, the miraculous circumstances of its promulgation need not be used as the first proof of its truth, but must rather be regarded as the inseparable accompaniments of a revelation which bears the historical stamp of reality. Occupying this vantage-ground, the defenders of revelation need no longer be afraid to allow free discussion of the details of its history. They

are not bound to start, as modern apologists too often
do, with preconceived notions as to the kind of acts
by which God made His presence and teaching known
in Bible ages—they can afford to meet every candid
inquirer on the fair field of history, and to form their
judgment on the actual course of revelation by the
ordinary methods of historical investigation.

It is on these lines that I ask you to join me in the
inquiry on which we are about to enter,—not in a spirit
of controversy, or with preconceived notions as to what
must be the course and manner of a true revelation,
but with a candid resolution to examine the documents
of the Old Testament religion, and see whether they
actually possess that evidence of consistent, progressive,
and indestructible truth which entitles them to be received as embodying a scheme of Divine teaching. In
a brief course of lectures our attention must necessarily
be confined to one corner of this great subject, to a brief
period of the history of Revelation and a very small
part of the Old Testament documents. But the period
and the books with which we shall be occupied are, in
many respects, the most important that the Old Testament student has to deal with. They are very little
understood by ordinary Bible readers, and yet they form
the key to all the chief problems of Old Testament study,
and without understanding them no one can hope to make
real progress in the knowledge of the Old Testament as a
whole. The work of the prophets of the Assyrian and
Babylonian periods falls in the most critical stage of the

history of the religion of Israel,—when, humanly speaking, it seemed far from improbable that that religion would sink to the level of common Semitic heathenism, and perish, like the religions of other Semitic peoples, with the political fall of the nation that professed it. It was the work of the prophets that averted such a catastrophe, drawing forth with ever-increasing clearness the elements of moral and spiritual truth which were well-nigh lost in the corruptions of the popular worship, holding up a conception of Jehovah's holy purpose and saving love to Israel in which even the utter ruin of the Hebrew state appeared as part of a gracious plan, and so maintaining the faith of Jehovah unbroken and victorious when every other part of the inheritance of Israel was swept away by the ruthless tide of Assyrian and Chaldæan conquest. Nowhere in the Old Testament history is the victory of true religion over the world, its power to rise superior to all human vicissitudes and bestow a hope and peace which the world cannot take away, so clearly manifested as in this great achievement of the prophetic word. In the long struggle with the empires of the East the Word of Jehovah was tried as gold in the furnace, and its behaviour under this crucial test is the best demonstration of its incorruptible purity and enduring worth. But there is another reason which gives this part of the history of the Old Covenant a central importance to the Biblical student. The Assyrian and Babylonian period is the age of written prophecy, the only age in which the whole movements of Israel's spiritual life can be closely studied in the writings of the very men who directed them. The period between Amos and the return is the golden age of Old Testament literature, which stands before us in contemporary records more clearly and fully than any other considerable period of Hebrew history. And for this period, too, we now possess in the Assyrian inscriptions a most valuable mass of contemporary illustration from the records of the foreign nation with which Israel's history was most closely involved,—a new source of light which, by a singular and admirable providence, has been put at our command at the very moment when the progress of Biblical study has concentrated the prime attention of all scholars on the prophets and their times.[4]

And now I trust that enough has been said to justify the choice of our subject, to give at least an initial conception of its importance, and to define the point of view from which I design to consider it. Let us turn without further preface to the matter in hand, and begin by assuring ourselves in a rapid historical survey that we possess a sufficiently clear conception of the field in which the prophets laboured, and the political and religious condition of the people to whom they spoke.

We have already had occasion to note that the conception of a personal revelation of God to man, which underlies the scheme of Biblical religion in both Testaments, implies that God approaches man in the first instance in the way of special dealing with chosen individuals. According to the Old Testament prophets, the circle chosen for this purpose is the nation of Israel, the only nation, as Amos expresses it, among all the families of the earth which Jehovah knows in a personal way (Amos iii. 2). To the prophets, then, the nation of Israel is the community of the true religion. But it is important to observe how this is put. Amos does not say that Israel knows Jehovah, but that Jehovah knows or personally recognises Israel, and no other nation. The same idea is expressed by Hosea in figures drawn from domestic life. Israel is Jehovah's spouse (chaps. i. to iii.), or His son (chap. xi. 1). Thus the basis of the prophetic religion is the conception of a unique relation between Jehovah and Israel, not, be it observed, individual Israelites, but Israel as a national unity. The whole Old Testament religion deals with the relations between two parties—Jehovah on the one hand, and the nation of Israel on the other. Simple as this conception is, it requires an effort of attention to fix it in our minds. We are so accustomed to think of religion as a thing between individual men and God that we can hardly enter into the idea of a religion in which a whole nation in its national organisation appears as the religious unit,—in which we have to deal, not with the faith and obedience of individual persons, but with the faith and obedience of a nation as expressed in the functions of national life. We shall have frequent opportunity as we proceed to familiarise ourselves with this fundamental Old Testament conception in its practical aspects. For the present it may suffice to illustrate it by a single example. In the New Testament dispensation every believer is regarded as a son of God. Under the Old Covenant it is the nation of Israel that is Jehovah's son. There are two questions, then, which lie at the root of all study of the prophetic teaching— Who is Israel? and who is Jehovah?

The history of the ancient world, so far as it exists for us, was transacted within a narrow strip of the earth's surface, running eastward from the Atlantic to the Pacific, so as to include the lands easily accessible from the Mediterranean waters and the countries of Southern Asia as far as India and China, but excluding the great mass of Africa and the northern parts of Europe and Asia. Even this small world was again cut in two by the great mountains and deserts that divide Eastern and Western Asia, and the far East which lay beyond these boundaries was practically an isolated part of the globe. The geography of the Bible, as contained in the tenth chapter of Genesis, extends from Tarshish in the West— the Spanish settlements of the Phœnicians in the region of Cadiz—to the Eastern lands of Persia and Media lying between the Caspian and the Persian Gulf. And here again we have a further limitation to make. The nations of Europe had not yet begun to play an independent part in the drama of universal history. To the Hebrews the lands that gird the Northern and Western Mediterranean were known as the Isles or rather Coasts of the Sea—a vague designation, derived, no doubt, from the Phœnician mariners who skirted their shores without penetrating into the interior. Thus, at the epoch with which we are concerned, the main movements of Western civilisation lay between the mountains of Media and the Libyan desert, the shores of the Levant and the Persian Gulf. In the eastern and western quarters of the region so defined lie two great alluvial countries, fertilised by mighty rivers, and producing the means of life in such abundance that they not only sustained a teeming population, but supplied their inhabitants with that superfluity of natural wealth which is the first condition for the growth of material civilisation. Egypt on the Nile, Babylonia and Assyria in the Euphrates and Tigris valleys, were marked out by nature as the seats of populous cities and great empires, strong enough to defy or subdue their neighbours, and rich enough to cultivate the arts of life. The bridge between these two great civilisations was the land which we call Syria, extending from the Euphrates to the Egyptian frontier, from the Mediterranean to the deserts of Northern Arabia. Syria, as well as the huge peninsula of Arabia, which bounded it on the south-east, and which in its northern parts was habitable only by nomads, was occupied by branches of the great family which we call Semitic. In language, and presumably also in race, the Semites of Syria and Arabia were closely related to the main stem of the Assyrians and Babylonians. They had also many kinsmen in the

Delta of Egypt, but the Egyptian civilisation acknowledged no brotherhood with them, and held itself aloof from its Eastern neighbours (Gen. xliii. 32).

The natural features of Syria were not favourable to the growth of a great and united nation fit to meet on equal terms with the empires on each side of it. For a time, indeed, a powerful people, called Hittites in the Bible, but better known from the Egyptian and Assyrian monuments, where they appear as Khita and Khatti, occupied the part of Syria between the Orontes and the Euphrates, and from their capital of Carchemish (Jirbâs on the Euphrates) seem to have extended their influence far into Asia Minor.[5] But the prime of the Hittite monarchy was earlier than the period with which we are immediately concerned, perhaps indeed earlier than the settlement of the Hebrews in Canaan. It is possible that they were not of Semitic stock, and they hardly come within the sphere of the Biblical history. Apart from this mysterious people, the inhabitants of Syria (I still use the word in the ordinary English sense, including Palestine) were broken up into a multitude of small nations, as was natural from the deserts and mountains that divided the land. By their language these nations can be arranged in two groups, according as they spoke Aramaic or dialects belonging to the Hebrew stock. In the English Bible Aramaic is called Syriac (2 Kings xviii. 26 ; Dan. ii. 4 ; Ezra iv. 7), and when Syria or Syrians are mentioned we are not to think of modern Syria, but of the land and people of

Aramaic tongue. The Aramæans of the Bible were partly settled in Mesopotamia, partly west of the Euphrates as far as Damascus and the borders of Canaan. They formed a number of small states, of which Damascus was from the time of Solomon the most important, at least in relation to Israel, exercising the hegemony over a considerable district to the north-west of Canaan.

Between the Aramæans and Egypt, again, we find a number of small nations speaking a language distinct from Aramaic, in several dialects sufficiently close to one another to be mutually intelligible, — Canaanites, Philistines, Ammonites, Moabites, Edomites, and finally Israelites, all gathered in the narrow isthmus of habitable land between the Mediterranean and the Desert, which, from Damascus and Hermon southwards, forms the only passage between the two great seats of civilisation and empire on the Euphrates and the Nile. The whole habitable area of this isthmus, which on the south is separated from Egypt by a tract of desert, is very small. It may be roughly compared in length and breadth with Northern England from the Humber to the Scottish border, but even this measurement includes great tracts either wholly desert, or, like the wilderness of Judæa, capable of supporting only a scanty population of herdsmen. From north to south it is split up the centre by the great natural depression of the Jordan valley and the Dead Sea, the surface of the latter lying a quarter of a mile below the Mediterranean. To the east of this valley, or rather trough, lies a tableland gradually merging into wild desert; to the west are the mountains of Palestine, intersected by fertile valleys, which in the north are wide and numerous, and slope westward in long glades towards the Mediterranean, while further south the maritime plain is wider, but the mountains are stony and sterile, and the valleys often narrow defiles, till at length the cultivable land passes into bare steppe, and finally into absolute desert.

Even in its geographical features this narrow region has a singular interest. It is almost an epitome of the ancient world, where the ocean and the desert, the pastures of the wilderness and the terraced vineyards of sunny hills, the cedars, fir-trees, and rhododendrons of Lebanon, the cornfields of Jezreel and the oak-clad glades of Tabor, the shores of the Lake of Galilee bright with shrubbery of oleander, the hot cane brakes and palm groves of Jericho, represent in brief compass almost every variety of material condition which enters into the development of Eastern antiquity. But a more important influence on the history of Palestine lay in the fact that it was the bridge between the East and the West. Before the opening up of the Red Sea and the Indian Ocean as a water-way, all the through traffic of the world necessarily crossed it, or passed along the edge of the adjoining deserts. And, in close connection with this, the cities of the Phœnician coast became the central emporia of the world. It was Phœnician sailors who opened up the Western waters, extending their voyages as far as the tin mines of Cornwall, and tapping the trade of inland Europe by their stations on the Gulf of Lyons, and at the mouths of the great rivers of Russia. How Tyre was the very centre of the world's commerce, drawing riches on all sides from the furthest lands, we still read in Ezekiel xxvii.

The Phœnicians of Tyre and Sidon, who held so important a place in the ancient world, were only one branch of the so-called Canaanites or Amorites (the two names are practically interchangeable),[6] who at the earliest date for which we have precise information not only occupied Palestine west of the Jordan, but had extensive eastern settlements in Bashan and Gilead. Their language, which was nearly the same as the Hebrew of the Bible, marked them off alike from the Aramæans who lay to the north and from the Arabs of the southern and eastern desert. They were an agricultural and trading people, with walled towns and considerable material civilisation, but politically weak from their division into a multitude of petty states, each with its own kinglet or aristocratic senate, and morally corrupted by a licentious religion, in which drunken carousals and the grossest sexual excesses were practised in honour of the gods. These gods, which were worshipped under a multitude of local forms, had a twofold type—male and female. The male god of any community was its Ba'al (lord or owner); the corresponding female deity was 'Ashtōreth. The one was often identified with the sun, the other with the moon. In

general terms it may be said that the Canaanites looked
on their deities as productive powers—givers of life,
fertility, and increase. Just as physical life is divided
into two sexes, they thought that the divine productive
power was male and female; and, assigning to this sexual
analogy a great and literal prominence in all the observances of worship, their religion easily ran into sensuality, and lent its countenance to every form of immorality, if only performed at the sanctuary and the sacred
feasts. Instead of affording a sanction to sobriety and
domestic purity, the exercises of Canaanite religion gave
the rein to the animal nature, and so took the form of
Dionysiac orgies of the grossest type. Through the
Phœnicians the practices of Canaanite worship were
carried across the sea and introduced to the Western
nations, and wherever they came they formed an element
of pollution, a blacker spot even in the darkness of
heathenism.

The situation of Palestine naturally exposed it to
invasion from different sides. The early campaigns of
the Egyptians in this quarter do not concern our present purpose, and the western movements of Babylonia
and Assyria were later than the Canaanite period. But
apart from these, the Aramæans from the north, the
Arabs from the south and east, were constantly pressing
on the land. The relation of the Northern Arabs to
Palestine has been much the same in all ages. Their
hordes make periodical descents on the cultivated land,
which are easily repelled by a good and strong govern-

ment, but prove successful when the settled inhabitants are weakened by division and misrule. So, in ancient times, the Midianites, Amalekites, and other tribes overran the land from time to time. The Amalekites seem at one time to have ranged freely as far as the mountains of Ephraim; and the population of the east, but especially of the south, in the wilderness or steppe of Judæa, contained an important Arab element in Biblical times. Indeed the large population of Judah, which gave that tribe such a preponderance in the time of David, was due, as can still be proved from the Biblical genealogies, to a fusion between the pure Judæans and other families of nomad origin.[7]

More lasting in their results were the migrations of a group of small nations which came from the direction of Aram, and acknowledged kindred to one another. They were four in number—Ammon, Moab, Edom, and Israel. The Ammonites and Moabites settled to the east of the Dead Sea, on the verge of the great desert, taking the place of the aboriginal Zamzummim and Emim (Deut. ii. 10, 20), but not interfering with the Canaanites proper. The Edomites found a seat to the south of the Dead Sea, where they conquered or absorbed the early troglodyte inhabitants (Horim). They were a wilder, less settled race than their northern cousins, and appear to have approached much more closely to the Arabic type. Their land, as it is described in Gen. xxvii. 39, was "far from the fat places of the earth and from the dew of heaven above."

They lived by their sword—that is, by robbery—and the importance of their position lay in the fact that the caravan routes from Arabia and the Red Sea to Gaza and the other mercantile towns of the coast passed through their territory.[8] The fourth nation, Israel, found no fixed abode, and, crossing the southern desert, dwelt for a time on the borders of Egypt, where they continued to live a pastoral nomadic life, and, though acknowledging a certain dependence on the Pharaohs, never came into close contact with Egyptian culture.[9] Their most intimate relations at this time were with Arab tribes, and, when the Egyptians oppressed them and tried to break them to forced labour on public works, it was among the Arabian Kenites that Moses, the leader of Israel's flight, found help and counsel.[10] Once more crossing the desert, the tribes of Israel appeared after long wanderings on the eastern frontier of Palestine. It was only by the sword that they could win a place of rest; but, respecting their cousins in Edom, Moab, and Ammon, they fell on the Amorites, east of the Jordan, and, after occupying their seats, crossed the river and established themselves in Western Palestine, not by one sustained and united effort, but by a multitude of local campaigns, in which each tribe generally fought for its own hand.[11] A war of emigrants for the possession of territory is always bloody, and this war was no exception to the rule. Whole communities of Canaanites were exterminated in the long struggle, for the Israelites, as well as their foes, were fighting for existence, and the "ban" by which a hostile community was devoted to utter destruction was an institution of Semitic warfare which the Israelites had in common with the kindred nations—for example, with Moab.[12] But the Canaanites were not exterminated. On the Phœnician coast their force was unbroken, and many strong places even in the centre of the land remained unsubdued till the time of the Davidic kingdom. Such were the mountain fastness of Jerusalem, long esteemed impregnable, and a whole series of walled cities on the edge of the fertile plain of Jezreel, where, in fact, after the first tide of victory was stayed, the tribe of Issachar sank into the condition of a tributary (Gen. xlix. 15). The struggle lasted for generations before all the Israelites found a fixed abode; the Danites, for example, are still found ranging the land as an armed horde in the days of the grandson of Moses (Judges xviii.), when they at last found a settlement at the base of Mount Hermon. In the days of Deborah and Barak the Canaanites were near re-establishing their mastery at least over Northern Palestine, and the tribes of Israel were too little at one to make common front against them. But, on the whole, Israel maintained its superiority, and the large Canaanite population which still survived in all parts of the land was gradually reduced to vassalship. To a certain extent the two nationalities began to fuse and form intermarriages, as was not difficult, since both spoke one language. Once at least we find an attempt to form a mixed Hebrew and Canaanite

state, for Shechem, which was then a Canaanite city with
a Canaanite aristocracy of the Bnê Hamor family, was
the centre of the short-lived kingdom of Abimelech,
who himself apparently was a Canaanite on the mother's
side. Though the adventurer Abimelech failed to establish a dynasty, the temporary success of the experi-
ment shows how far the original antagonism of race had
been softened, and the condemnation pronounced by
the moral sense of the Hebrews on the slaughter of the
tributary Gibeonites by Saul proves that the Israelite
aristocracy and their Canaanite subjects began to feel
themselves united by the bonds of common humanity.
And so, in the age of the Judges, it might readily
appear that this invasion was to run the same course
as so many other incursions from the desert into a land
of higher civilisation, and that the conquerors would
gradually become assimilated to the conquered, from
whom the Hebrew nomads on their first introduction to
settled life and agricultural pursuits had everything to
learn. At the close of the period of the Judges the
greater part of the Israelites had quite lost their pastoral
habits. They were an agricultural people living in
cities and villages, and their oldest civil laws are framed
for this kind of life. All the new arts which this complete change of habit implies they must have derived
from the Canaanites, and as they learned the ways of
agricultural life they could hardly fail to acquire many
of the characteristics of their teachers. To make the
transformation complete only one thing was lacking—

that Israel should also accept the religion of the aborigines. The history and the prophets alike testify that to a great extent they actually did this. Canaanite sanctuaries became Hebrew holy places, and the vileness of Canaanite nature-worship polluted the Hebrew festivals. For a time it seemed that Jehovah, the ancestral God of Israel, who brought their fathers up out of the house of bondage and gave them their goodly land, would be forgotten or transformed into a Canaanite Baal. If this change had been completed Israel would have left no name in the world's history; but Providence had other things in store for the people of Jehovah. Henceforth the real significance of Israel's fortunes lies in the preservation and development of the national faith, and the history of the tribes of Jacob is rightly set forth in the Bible as the history of that divine discipline by which Jehovah maintained a people for Himself amidst the seductions of Canaanite worship and the ever-new backslidings of Israel.

To understand who Jehovah was, and what He was to Israel, we must return to the deliverance of the Hebrew tribes from Egyptian bondage, to which later ages looked back as the birth of the nation. In the land of Goshen the Hebrews had not even a vestige of national organisation. The tribes into which they were divided acknowledged a common ancestry, but had no institutions expressive of the unity of race; and, when Moses called them to a united effort for liberty, the only practical starting-point for his work was an appeal to the name of Jehovah, the God of their fathers. It is not easy to say how far the remembrance of this God was a living power among the Hebrews. The Semitic nomads have many superstitions, but little religion. The sublime solitudes of the desert are well fitted to nourish lofty thoughts about God, but the actual life of a wandering shepherd people is not favourable to the formation of such fixed habits of worship as are indispensable to make religion a prominent factor in everyday life. It would seem that the memory of the God of the Hebrew fathers was little more than a dormant tradition when Moses began his work; and among the Israelites, as among the Arabs of the desert, whatever there was of habitual religious practice was probably connected with tribal or family superstitions, such as the use of teraphim, a kind of household idols which long continued to keep their place in Hebrew homes. The very name of Jehovah (or Iahwè, as the word should rather be pronounced) became known as a name of power only through Moses and the great deliverance.

At any rate it would be a fundamental mistake to suppose that the traditional faith in an ancestral God, round which Moses rallied his brethren, included any developed metaphysical conceptions such as we associate with the idea of a spiritual God. Not the nature of the Deity, but His power and will to help His people were the points practical to the oppressed Hebrews. A living God, according to a conception never fully superseded in the Old Testament, must have a kingly seat on earth where He showed Himself to men, and this seat, it would seem, an ancient tradition placed on Mount Sinai, which still appears in the Song of Deborah as the place from which the divine majesty goes forth in thunderstorm and rain to bring victory to Israel. It would be a profitless task to attempt to analyse this conception, and seek a symbolic meaning in the poetic language in which it is clothed. The Israelites thought in poetic figures, and we must take their thoughts as they themselves present them. The storm that broke on the mountains of Sinai and rolled across the desert in fertilising showers made the godhead of Jehovah real to them; the thunder was His voice of majesty, the voice of the same God who wrought the great deliverance at the Red Sea, and beyond this they did not care to go. The new message that Moses brought to his brethren was not an abstract revelation of Jehovah's spiritual attributes, but an assurance of His personal interest in Israel, and a promise of effectual help. The promise was fulfilled in a marvellous display of Jehovah's saving strength; and, when the proud waters rolled between the Hebrews and the shattered power of the Egyptians, Israel felt that it was a nation, the nation of Jehovah.

I have explained in a former course of lectures [13] that the ordinances of the Pentateuch, in which tradition has accustomed us to seek the forms under which the great idea of Israel, the people of Jehovah, was organised during the wilderness wanderings, are really of very

various dates, and that the law of Israel did not take
final shape till after the Babylonian captivity. The Pentateuch as we now have it is not the immediate record
of the institutions of Moses, but the last codification of
the divine teaching begun by Moses, and carried on and
perfected through many centuries by the discipline
of history and the word of the prophets who took up
Moses' work. The sacred writers of the Old Testament
were so deeply convinced of the unity and consistency
of all Jehovah's teaching that they did not attempt to
leave an historical record of its several stages. In
every age their one concern was to set forth a clear
testimony to the whole truth of God as they themselves
knew it. It did not seem important to them to distinguish the very words of Moses from the equally
authoritative additions of later organs of revelation.
Thus it is difficult for us to determine with precision
how far Moses in person carried the work of giving to
Israel divine ordinances fitted to express the new-born
consciousness that Israel was the nation of Jehovah.
We may be sure, however, that his work was carried
out on practical lines. The ordinary judges of the
people were still the elders, or, as an Arab would call
them, the sheikhs of the several tribes and sub-tribes;
and this fact implies that Moses did not cancel the old
customary laws which already existed as the basis of
tribal justice.[14] But the new circumstances of Israel,
and, above all, the new sense of national unity, which
was no longer a mere sentiment of common ancestry,

created a multitude of new questions. On these Moses had to decide, and he sought the decision from Jehovah, whose ark now led the march of Israel. It is only on the march and in time of war that a nomad people feels any urgent need of a central authority, and so it came about that in the first beginnings of national organisation, centering in the sanctuary of the ark, Israel was thought of mainly as the host of Jehovah. The very name of Israel is martial, and means "God (El) fighteth," and Jehovah in the Old Testament is *Iahwè Çebâôth*, the Jehovah of the armies of Israel. It was on the battlefield that Jehovah's presence was most clearly realised; but in primitive nations the leader in time of war is also the natural judge in time of peace, and the sanctuary of Jehovah, where Moses and the priests, his successors, gave forth the sacred oracle, was the final seat of judgment in all cases too hard for the ordinary heads of the Hebrew clans.

It must, however, be observed that the idea of executive government as we understand it is quite unknown to the inhabitants of the desert. The business of a judge, among the Hebrews as among the Arabs, was to declare the law when consulted, not to enforce it, or even to offer a decision that was not asked. This principle held good alike in criminal and civil cases, and the foundation of what we call criminal law was the right of self-help on the principle of exact retaliation.[15] Thus Israel entered Canaan without any developed system of national government. As the tribes moved off from the central camp where the ark stood, and won themselves dwelling-places in different quarters of the land, often separated by districts which the Canaanites still held, their feelings of national unity ceased to find any regular expression, the Hebrew federation became weaker and weaker, and there was no central authority to enforce the duties of political and religious unity.

Now, it followed from the circumstances of the Exodus that these two unities necessarily went together. Jehovah was essentially the God of the whole nation, not of individual families; every act of worship to Jehovah, every approach to the sacred judgment-seat at the sanctuary, was an expression of national feeling, which lost the best part of its meaning when the Israelite forgot the bonds of national unity that had been knit at the Red Sea and in the wilderness. But, in fact, the Mosaic sanctuary soon lost much of its central importance. It was fixed on the first entrance into Canaan at the headquarters of the armed force of Israel, originally at Gilgal, afterwards at Shiloh, in the land occupied by the strongest and most martial of the Hebrew clans, the great tribe of Ephraim. The dispersion and isolation of the tribes, therefore, brought it about that Shiloh became the local sanctuary of Ephraim, and was not regularly visited by the more distant tribes. This, indeed, did not imply that the other tribes ceased to do sacrifice to Jehovah, whose altars of earth or unhewn stone were seen in all corners of the land, while in many places a priesthood claiming kinship with Moses administered the sacred oracle as his successors. But such local worship necessarily came into contact with the Canaanite service of Baal; and, apart from the fact that the luxurious festivals of the latter had a natural attraction for the sensuous Semitic nature of the Hebrews, there was a more innocent motive which tended to assimilate the two worships. The offerings and festivals of Jehovah were acts of homage in which the people consecrated to Him the good things of His bestowing. These were no longer the scanty products of pastoral life, but the rich gifts of a land of corn and wine, which the Canaanites had taught the Hebrews to cultivate. Thus the religious feasts necessarily assumed a new and more luxurious character, and, rejoicing before Jehovah in the enjoyment of the good things of Canaan, the Israelites naturally imitated the agricultural feasts which the Canaanites celebrated before Baal. It is not therefore surprising that we find many indications of a gradual fusion between the two worships; that many of the great Hebrew sanctuaries are demonstrably identical with Canaanite holy places; that the autumn feast, usually known as the Feast of Tabernacles, has a close parallel in the Canaanite Vintage Feast; that Canaanite immorality tainted the worship of Jehovah; and that at length Jehovah Himself, who was addressed by His worshippers by the same general appellation of Baal or Lord which was the ordinary title of the Canaanite nature-god, was hardly distinguished by the masses who worshipped at the local shrines from the local Baalim of their Canaanite neighbours.[16]

The growth of this religious syncretism not only threatened to sap the moral strength of the Hebrews, but boded entire extinction to the national feeling which had no other centre than the religion of Jehovah. And so in the providence of God it was by a series of imperious calls to united national effort that Israel was prevented from wholly forgetting Jehovah. Every invasion which woke the dormant feeling of patriotism woke at the same time something of the old faith. There was no patriotic fire in the religion of the Baalim, which had not even stimulated the Canaanites to united struggle against their Hebrew conquerors. In battle and in victory Jehovah was still the ancestral God, shaking the earth and dissolving the mountains as He marched from the desert of Seir to deliver His people (Judges v.). Hence it is that in the time of the Judges every revival of the religion of Jehovah is connected with the wars in which the Hebrews succeeded in maintaining their ground against numerous invading foes.

It is plain, however, that the religion of Jehovah could not always stand still at the point which it had reached in the wilderness. It was not enough to have one religion for times of patriotic exaltation, and another for daily life. A God who dwelt afar off in Sinai and only came down to Canaan in the day of battle was not sufficient for human needs. It was necessary that the old religion should become master of the new and altogether changed life of the Hebrews in their new seats. Jehovah and the Baalim had to contend for sovereignty in the ordinary existence of the Hebrews, when the simplicity of the desert had inevitably given way to the progress of material civilisation in a rich and cultivated land.

And here we must ask what was the essential difference between Jehovah and the Baalim, which had to be preserved amidst all changes of circumstances if Jehovah was still to maintain His individuality? In the first place, as we have seen, Jehovah represented a principle of national unity, while the worship of the Baalim was split into a multitude of local cults without national significance. But this would have been an empty difference if there had been nothing behind. National unity is a meaningless thing unless the nation feels that it is united for some common task. Now Jehovah represented to Israel two of the greatest blessings that any people can enjoy, blessings for which it is well worth while to unite in sustained and strenuous effort. The first of these was *liberty*, for it was Jehovah that brought Israel forth from the house of bondage; the second was *law, justice*, and the *moral order* of society, for from the days of Moses the mouth of Jehovah was the one fountain of judgment. So in the Ten Words, the fundamental document of the religion of the Old Testament, the claim of Jehovah to the exclusive worship of Israel is based on the deliverance that made Israel a free people, and issues in the great laws of social morality. The cause of Jehovah in Israel was the cause of national freedom and social righteousness, and the task of the religion of Jehovah was to set these fast in the land of Canaan in a society which ever looked to Jehovah as its living and present head.

The idea of *righteousness* is of course familiar to every one as a cardinal Old Testament conception. The idea of *liberty* may sound less familiar, but only because it has two aspects, which are covered by the conceptions of *deliverance* and *peace*. Thus, when the Psalmist speaks of *righteousness* and *peace* kissing each other (Psalm lxxxv. 10), he expresses precisely the ideal of the religion of Jehovah which we are now considering. At the very close of the Old Testament dispensation the same ideal meets us in the song of Zachariah, " That we being delivered out of the hand of our enemies might serve Him in holiness and righteousness before Him all our days." Here indeed we have one more idea, that of *holiness*, which will come prominently before us as our argument advances, but which it would be premature to dwell on at present. The holiness of Israel is in fact a summary expression for the conception that the whole national vocation of Israel is a religious vocation discharged by a worshipping people, inasmuch as the Judge, Lawgiver, and King of Israel is none other than Israel's God.

Every true thought contains a deeper meaning and involves more important consequences than can be seen at once. And this is especially the case with religious truth, which presents itself in the first instance in the form not of general propositions but of direct personal experience. The early Hebrews did not think about Jehovah; they believed in Him, and experienced the reality of His sovereignty in the great things which He did for His people. Thus it was only by slow degrees and in connection with the historical experiences of the nation that the whole meaning of His religion, the full difference between Him and the gods of the nations, came to be realised, or that the Israelites learned all that was implied in their vocation as the people of Jehovah. In the first generations after the conquest the great practical question, as we have already seen, was whether Israel would continue in any sense to retain that consciousness of national unity which, in the absence of all political centralisation, had no other rallying-point than the faith of Jehovah. We have seen, too, that the struggle for freedom against successive attacks of powerful enemies was the means used by Providence in the age of the Judges to preserve at once national feeling and national faith in Jehovah. Jehovah in this period appears pre-eminently as the champion of Israel's freedom, the divine King to whom Israel owes national allegiance, and whose majesty is dishonoured when His servants pay tribute and homage to other nations and their gods. The foreign invaders of Israel encroach on Jehovah's sovereignty, and thus are His enemies too. So He goes forth and rallies His armies, the armies of Israel, around Him, calling them to help Jehovah against the mighty (Judges v. 23). And when the victory remains with Israel the song of triumph ends with the prayer, "So let all thine enemies perish, O Jehovah; but let them that love Thee be as the sun when he goeth forth in his might."

At this stage of Israel's religion, pictured most clearly in the Song of Deborah, the presence of Jehovah with His people was quite fully realised only in the hour of battle and victory. The ark itself, the visible token of the angel, or rather embassy of Jehovah, sent by Him to direct the march of His people and subdue the Canaanite before them (Exod. xxiii. 20 *seq.*; Num. x. 33; Judges ii. 1), was rather the sanctuary of the host than of the settled nation, and after it was fixed at Shiloh became, as we have seen, little more than the local shrine of the tribe of Ephraim. In the Song of Deborah Jehovah has not yet a fixed seat in the land of Canaan, but goes forth from Sinai to help His people in their distress. Hence the establishment of local sanctuaries of Jehovah, at Dan, at Ophrah, and at other points throughout the land during the period of the Judges, must not be looked upon as essentially a retrograde movement. It is true that these local shrines exposed Jehovah-worship to the great danger of taking up Canaanite elements and assimilating itself to the worship of the Baalim, and thus it is easy to understand that from one point of view the age of the Judges may be represented as one of continual backsliding. But, on the other hand, these local shrines brought Jehovah nearer to the daily life of the people. He came down, as it were, from Sinai and took possession of Canaan as the suzerain to whom the people in every corner of the country did homage for the good things of Jehovah's land. At the close of the period of the Judges the religion of Jehovah is thoroughly identified with the possession of Palestine. "They have driven me out this day," says David, "from being attached to the inheritance of Jehovah, saying, Go serve other gods." In other words, banishment from Canaan is now conceived as banishment from the service of Jehovah, and the religion of Jehovah has become part of daily national life. Thus we see that the long struggle that was inevitable when the religion of Jehovah went forth from the desert and came into contact with the life of the larger world was not in vain. The crisis was sharp, and Israel had not passed through it unscathed; but in the end Jehovah was still the God of Israel, and had become the God of Israel's land. Canaan was His heritage, not the heritage of the Baalim, and the Canaanite worship appears henceforth, not as a direct rival to the worship of Jehovah, but as a disturbing element corrupting the national faith, while unable to supplant it altogether. This, of course, in virtue of the close connection between religion and national feeling, means that Israel had now risen above the danger of absorption in the Canaanites, and felt itself to be a nation in the true sense of the word. We learn from the books of Samuel how this great advance was ultimately and permanently secured. The earlier wars recorded in the book of Judges had brought about no complete or lasting unity among the Hebrew tribes. But at length a new enemy arose, more formidable than any whom they had previously encountered. The Philistines from Caphtor, who, like the Israelites, had entered Canaan as emigrants, but coming most probably by sea had displaced the aboriginal Avvim in the rich coastlands beneath the mountains of Judah (Deut. ii. 23 ; Amos ix. 7), pressed into the heart of the country, and broke the old strength of Ephraim in the battle of Ebenezer. This victory cut the Hebrew settlements in two, and threatened the independence of all the tribes. The common danger drew Israel together. They found a leader in the Benjamite Saul, whom Jehovah Himself designated as the king of Israel by the mouth of the prophet Samuel. The resistance which Saul first organised in the difficult hill country of his native tribe was conducted with varying fortune, but not without success. Saul himself fell in battle, but his work was continued by Abner in the north, while in the south David consolidated his power as king of Judah without disturbance from the Philistines, whose suzerainty he was content to acknowledge till his plans were ripe. When David was accepted as king of all Israel, and by a bold stroke found a capital in the centre of the land in the strong fortress of Jerusalem, till then deemed impregnable, Israel met the invader on more than equal terms, and the Hebrews became masters where a few years before they had been servants.

It was Jehovah who had given them this victory,

and, what was more than any victory, had at length given permanent expression to the unity of the nation by placing at their head a king who reigned as the anointed of the Lord. The first crisis was past, and thenceforward Israel could never forget that it was one nation, with a national destiny and a national God.

LECTURE II.

JEHOVAH AND THE GODS OF THE NATIONS.

In last Lecture we followed the history of Israel and Israel's religion down to the consolidation of the state under Saul and David. Throughout the period of the Judges, neither the nationality of Israel nor the religion of Jehovah stood on a sure footing. The tribes of Israel were broken up into isolated fractions, and often seemed on the point of absorption among the Canaanites; and the religion of Jehovah in like manner, which lost the best part of its original meaning when divorced from the idea of national unity, threatened to disappear in the Canaanite Baal worship before it could succeed in adapting itself to the change from nomad to agricultural life. Both these dangers were at length surmounted, and, whatever physical and political circumstances may have conspired towards the result,[1] it was the faith of Jehovah that united the Hebrews to final victory, and Jehovah who crowned His gift of the goodly land of Canaan by bestowing on Israel a king to reign in His name, and make it at length a real nation instead of a loose federation of tribes.[2] And so the religion of Jehovah was not only a necessary part of the state, but the chief cornerstone of the political edifice. To Jehovah Israel owed, not only the blessings of life, but national existence and all the principles of social order; and through His priests, His prophets, but above all His anointed king, He was the source of all authority, and the fountain of all law and judgment in the land.

In principle, this paramount position of Jehovah the God of Israel was never again disputed. The kingdom of David was torn asunder, and new dynasties reigned in Northern Israel. But the kings of Ephraim, not less than the house of David, reigned in Jehovah's name, and derived their authority from Him (1 Kings xi. 31 *seq.*; 2 Kings ix. 3). The sanctuaries founded by Jeroboam were sanctuaries of the God who brought up Israel out of the land of Egypt (1 Kings xii. 28); and even Ahab, who provoked so bitter a religious conflict by making room in Samaria for the Baal of his Tyrian queen, did not give up the religion of his ancestors; for it was Jehovah's prophets whom he consulted in time of need, and Jehovah was the God whose sustaining help and loftiness he acknowledged in giving names to his sons. In the north not less than in the south to forsake Jehovah was a crime against the state, and the technical expression for treason was to abjure God and the King (1 Kings xxi. 13).

In virtue of their common religion the Israelites of the north and south retained a sense of essential unity in spite of political separation and repeated wars; and it was felt that the division of the tribes was inconsistent with the true destiny of Jehovah's people. We shall have repeated opportunity to observe how this feeling asserts itself in the teaching of the prophets, but it was a feeling in which all Israelites participated, and which had at least as great strength in Ephraim as in Judah. The so-called Blessing of Moses (which does not itself claim this name, but on the contrary bears clear internal marks of having been written in the kingdom of Ephraim) remembers Judah with affection, and prays that he may be strengthened against his enemies, and again restored to union with his brethren (Deut. xxxiii. 7).

But while the religion of Jehovah had thus acquired a fixed national character, it would be a great mistake to suppose that it already presented itself to the mass of the people, as it did to the later Jews, as something altogether dissimilar in principle and in details from the religions of the surrounding nations. The Jews after the exile not only had a separate religion, but a religion which made them a separate nation, distinct from the Gentiles in all their habits of life and thought. In old Israel it was not so. The possession of a national God, to whom the nation owed homage, and in whose name kings reigned and judges administered justice, was not in itself a thing peculiar to Israel. A national religion and sacred laws are part of the constitution of every ancient state, and among the nations most nearly akin to the Hebrews these ideas took a shape which, so far as mere externals were concerned, bore a close family likeness to the religion of Jehovah. Among the Semitic peoples it is quite the rule that each tribe or nation should have its tribal or national God. This of course does not imply a monotheistic faith; the Ammonite who worshipped Milcom, the Moabite who ascribed his prosperity to Chemosh, did not deny the existence of other supernatural beings, who had power to help or hurt men, and were accessible to the prayers and offerings of their worshippers. But the national god in each case was regarded as the divine lord, and often as the divine father, of his nation, while other deities were either subordinate to him, or had the seat of their power in other lands, or, in the case of the gods of neighbouring nations, were his rivals and the enemies of his people. He was therefore the god to be looked to in all national concerns; he had a right to national homage, and, as we learn expressly, in the case of Chemosh, from the stone erected by Mesha to commemorate his victories over Israel, national misfortune was ascribed to his wrath, national success to his favour.[3] It was he too that was the ultimate director of all national policy. Mesha tells us that it was Chemosh who commanded him to assault this or that city, and who drove out the king of Israel before him, giving him to see his desire on all his enemies. The parallelism with the Old Testament extends, you see, not only to the ideas but to the very words. But the parallelism is not confined to such near cousins of the Israelites as the Moabites. Equally striking analogies to Old

Testament thoughts and expressions are found on the Phœnician monuments. As the kings of Israel ascribe their sovereignty to the grant of Jehovah, so the king of Gebal on the great monument of Byblus declares that it was the divine queen of Byblus who set him as king over the city. As the psalmist of Ps. cxvi. says, "I take up the cup of salvation, and call upon the name of Jehovah," so this heathen king is figured standing before the goddess with a cup in his hand, and exclaiming, "I call upon my lady the sovereign of Gebal, because she hath heard my voice, and dealt graciously with me." And just as the prayer for life and blessing to the king of Israel in Psalm lxxii. is a prayer for a king judging in righteousness, the Phœnician goddess is invoked to bless Iḥawmelek, king of Gebal, and give him life and prolong his days in Gebal, because he is a just king, and to give him favour in the eyes of gods and men.[4]

It would not be difficult to add to these analogies even from the scanty materials at our command, consisting mainly of a few weather-worn inscriptions hewn by the command of ancient kings. But it is not necessary to do so; I have quoted enough to show that the characteristic conception of Jehovah as the national God of Israel is reproduced with very similar features, expressed in very similar language, in the religions of the surrounding nations. The most important point to carry with us is the bearing of these observations on the current conception of the Hebrew theocracy. The word theocracy, which has had such vogue among Christian theologians, is the invention of Josephus, who observes in his second book against Apion (chap. xvi.) that, while other nations had a great variety of institutions and laws, some states being monarchies, others oligarchies, and others again republics, Moses gave to his nation the unique form of a *theocracy*, assigning all authority and power to God, teaching the Israelites to look to Him as the source of all blessings to the nation or to individuals, and their help in every distress, making all the virtues, as justice, self-command, temperance, and civil concord, parts of piety, and subjecting the whole order of society to a system of divine law. Nothing gives so much currency to an idea as a happy catchword, and so people have gone on to this day using the word theocracy, or God-kingship, to express the difference between the constitution of Israel and all other nations. But in reality, as we now see, the word theocracy expresses precisely that feature in the religion of Israel which it had in common with the faiths of the surrounding nations. They too had each a supreme god, whose favour or displeasure was viewed as the cause of all success or misfortune, and whose revelations were looked to as commands directing all national undertakings. This god was conceived as a divine king, and was often invoked by this name. Moloch, or Milcom, for example—the name of the god of the Ammonites—is simply the word king, and the Tyrian sun-god in like manner was called Melkarth, "king of the city." The human king reigned by the favour and gift of his divine Lord, and, as we see from the stone of Gebal, the exercise of kingly justice was under the special protection of the godhead. Perhaps the most characteristic expression of the theocratic idea is the regular payment to the sanctuary of tithe, or tribute, such as human kings claimed from the produce of the soil (1 Sam. viii. 15, 17); for this was an act of homage acknowledging the god as the sovereign of the land. But the tithe is not confined to Israel. It is found among other nations, and in Tyre was paid to the divine king Melkarth.[5]

The religious constitution of Israel, then, as laid down by Moses and consolidated in the institution of the kingship, was not the entirely unique thing that it is frequently supposed to be. Indeed, if Moses had brought in a whole system of new and utterly revolutionary ideas he could not have carried the people with him to any practical effect. There was a great difference between the religion of Israel and other religions; but that difference cannot be reduced to an abstract formula; it lay in the personal difference, if I may so speak, between Jehovah and the gods of the nations, and all that lay in it only came out bit by bit in the course of a history which was ruled by Jehovah's providence, and shaped by Jehovah's love.

From these considerations, we are able to understand what is often a great puzzle to Bible readers, the way, namely, in which the Old Testament, especially in its earlier parts, speaks of the gods of the nations. Jehovah is not generally spoken of in the older parts of the Hebrew literature as the absolutely one God, but only as the one God of Israel; and it is taken to be quite natural and a matter of course that other nations have other gods. The prophets, indeed, teach with increasing clearness that these other gods are, in point of fact, no gods at all, mere idols, dead things that cannot help their worshippers. But this point of view was not clearly before the mind of all Israelites at all times. Another and no doubt an older habit of thought does not say that there is no god except Jehovah, but only that there is none among the gods like him (Exod. xv. 11). According to the words of Jephthah (Judges xi. 24), the natural order of things is that Israel should inherit the land which Jehovah has enabled them to conquer, while the invader who attempts to encroach on this inheritance ought to be content with the lands which Chemosh his god has given him. And David takes it for granted that a man who is excluded from the commonwealth of Israel, "the inheritance of Jehovah," must go and serve other gods (1 Sam. xxvi. 19). In truth, the great deliverance which manifested Jehovah to the Hebrews as their king and Saviour did not necessarily and at once compel them to deny the existence of other superhuman beings capable of influencing the affairs of mankind. A man might believe firmly in Jehovah, Israel's God, and feel secure in His strength and love, without being drawn into the train of reflection necessary to carry the conviction that those who were not the people of Jehovah had no divine helper at all. It was not every one who could rise with the prophet Amos to the thought that it was Jehovah's supreme providence which had determined the migrations of all nations just as much as of Israel (Amos ix. 7). It is not therefore surprising that the mass of the people long after the time of David held the faith of Jehovah in a way that left it open to them to concede a certain reality to the gods of other nations. The ordinary unenlightened Israelite thought that Jehovah was stronger than Chemosh, while the Moabite, as we see from the stone of Mesha, thought that Chemosh was stronger than Jehovah; but, apart from this difference, the two had a great many religious ideas in common, and, but for the continued word of revelation in the mouths of the prophets, Israel's religion might very well have permanently remained on this level, and so have perished with the fall of the Hebrew state.

We see, then, that it was not the idea of the theocracy that gave to the religion of Israel its unique character. It is well to observe that the same thing may be said of the sacred ordinances which are so often thought of as having been from the first what they undoubtedly became after the time of Ezra, a permanent wall of separation between Israel and the Gentiles. To discuss this subject in detail it would be necessary to trace the history of the ritual laws of the Pentateuch. This I have done, to a certain extent, in a previous course of lectures, and I shall not repeat what I then said. But in general it must be observed that to the ordinary Israelite the most prominent of the sacred observances previous to the exile must have seemed rather to connect his worship with that of the surrounding nations than to separate the two. Israel, like the other nations, worshipped Jehovah at certain fixed sanctuaries, where He was held to meet with His people face to face. The method of worship was by altar gifts, expressive of homage for the good things of His bestowal, and the chief occasions of such worship were the agricultural feasts, just as among the Canaanites.[6] The details of the ceremonial observed were closely parallel to those still to be read on Phœnician monuments. Even the technical terms connected with sacrifice were in great part identical. The vow (*néder*), the whole burnt offering (*kālíl*), the thank-offering (*shélem*), the meat-offering (*minḥath*), and a variety of other details appear on the tablet of Marseilles and similar Phœnician documents under their familiar Old Testament names, showing that the Hebrew ritual was not a thing by itself, but had a common foundation with that observed by their neighbours.[7] And no hesitation was felt in actually copying foreign models. When Ahaz took the pattern of a new altar from Damascus, he simply followed the precedent set by Solomon in the building of the temple. The court with its brazen altar and lofty columns (Jachin and Boaz), the portico (2 Kings xxiii. 11—not suburbs, as the Authorised Version has it), the ornaments, chased or embossed in gold, the symbolic palm-trees, and so forth, are all described or figured on Phœnician inscriptions and coins.[8]

Again the approach of the worshipper to his God in sacrifice and offering demands, as its necessary complement, a means by which the response of the deity can be conveyed to His people. Among the Hebrews the answer of Jehovah to the people's supplications was given by the priestly lot and the prophetic word. But here again the vast difference between the revelation of Jehovah and the oracles of the nations lies in what Jehovah had to say, rather than in the external manner of saying it. The holy lot is of constant occurrence in ancient religions;[9] there were prophets of Baal as well as prophets of Jehovah; and the official prophets, connected with the sanctuary, were, according to the testimony of Jeremiah and Micah, often not distinguishable from sorcerers—a fact quite inexplicable if there had been a broad acknowledged difference in externals between their functions and those of the prophets of the heathen. In point of fact, we find Saul and his servant going to Samuel with a trifling present, just as in other early nations.

In every way, then, the attempt to reduce the difference between the early religion of the Hebrews and that of other nations to broad tangible peculiarities that can be grasped with the hand breaks down. It was Jehovah Himself who was different from Chemosh, Moloch, or Melkarth; and to those who did not *know*

Jehovah, to use the expressive prophetic phrase, there was no insurmountable barrier between His worship and heathenism. Even the current ideas of the Hebrews about unseen things were mainly the common stock of the Semitic peoples, and nothing is more certain than that neither Moses nor Samuel gave Israel any new system of metaphysical theology. In matters of thought as well as of practice, the new revelation of Jehovah's power and love, given through Moses, or rather given in actual saving deeds of Jehovah which Moses taught the people to understand, involved no sudden and absolute break with the past, or with the traditions of the past common to Israel with kindred nations. Its epoch-making importance lay in quite another direction — in the introduction into Israel's historical life of a new personal factor — of Jehovah Himself as the God of Israel's salvation. Jehovah, as the prophet Hosea puts it, taught Israel to walk, holding him by the arms as a parent holds a little child; but the divine guidance fitly characterised in these words is something very different from such a course of lectures on dogmatics as is often thought of as the substance of Old Testament revelation. Again to borrow the language of Hosea, Jehovah drew Israel to Him by human ties, by cords of love; the influence of His revelation in forming the religious character of the nation was a personal influence, the influence of His gracious and holy character. It was from this personal experience of Jehovah's character, read in the actual history of His dealings with His people, that the great teachers of Israel learned, but learned by slow degrees, to lay down general propositions about divine things. To suppose that the Old Testament history began with a full scheme of doctrine, which the history only served to illustrate and enforce, is to invert the most general law of God's dealings with man, whether in the way of nature or of grace.

Unless we keep this principle clearly before our minds, the whole history of the divine teaching contained in the Old Testament will be involved in hopeless confusion; and therefore it will not be amiss to devote a few sentences to show in detail how impossible it is to place the original peculiarity of Israel's religion in anything of the nature of abstract theological doctrine. For this purpose I may select two principal points, which are always held to be cardinal features in a spiritual theology, the doctrine of the unity and absolute spiritual being of God, and the doctrine of the future state and retribution in the world to come. No question has been more discussed by writers on the Old Testament than the monotheism of the Hebrews. Was the doctrine of monotheism an inheritance from the patriarchs? or was it introduced by Moses? or did it come to the front for the first time in the days of Elijah? or was it, in fact, not precisely formulated till the time of Jeremiah?

That these questions can be asked and seriously argued by scholarly inquirers is, at any rate, sufficient proof that the older parts of the Bible do not give to the abstract doctrine of monotheism the importance that it possesses to our minds. To the early Hebrews the question which we view as so fundamental, and which was, in fact, felt to be fundamental by the later prophets, seems hardly to have presented itself at all. For the practical purposes of religion, the thesis that there is no god who can compare with Jehovah appeared as sufficient as the more advanced doctrine that there is no god except Him. As long as the Israelites, with Jehovah at their head, were absorbed in the conflict for freedom against other nations and their gods, there was no practical interest in the question whether the foreign deities had or had not metaphysical existence. The practical point was that Jehovah proved Himself stronger than they by giving Israel victory over their worshippers. And, in fact, it required a process of abstract thought, not at all familiar to early times, to deny all reality to deities which in many cases were identified with actual concrete things, with the sun, for example, or the planets. Even in the latest stages of Biblical thought the point of view which strictly identifies the heathen gods with the idols that represented them, and therefore denies to them all living reality, varies with another point of view which regards them as evil demons (1 Cor. viii. 4 *seq.*; x. 20 *seq.*).

Nor is it at all clear that in the earliest times the difference between Jehovah and other gods was placed in His spiritual nature. The Old Testament word which we translate by spirit (*rū̇ḥ*) is the common word for wind, including the "living breath" (*rū̇ḥ* of life,

Gen. vi. 17), and so used of the motions of life and the affections of the soul. Now, observation of human life taught the Hebrews to distinguish between man's flesh, or visible and tangible frame, and the subtile breath or spirit which animates this frame. It was in the fleshy body that they saw the difference between man and God. "Hast Thou eyes of flesh," says Job, "or seest Thou as man seeth" (Job x. 4). "The Egyptians are men and not God, and their horses flesh and not spirit" (Isa. xxxi. 3). These passages are the clearest expressions of the spirituality of the godhead which the Old Testament contains, and you observe that they are not directed to distinguish between the true God and false gods, but to characterise the godhead in its difference from human nature. It is, in fact, the divine working, rather than the divine nature, that the Hebrew Scriptures regard as spiritual—that is, as possessing a subtile and invisible character, comparable with the mysterious movements of the wind. The common doctrine of the Old Testament is not that God is spirit, but that the spirit of Jehovah, going forth from Him, works in the world and among men. And this is no metaphysical doctrine; it simply expresses that difference between divine and human agency which must be recognised wherever there is any belief in God, or at least any belief rising above the grossest fetichism. That the early Israelites possessed no metaphysical doctrine of the spirituality of Jehovah, conceived as an existence out of all relation to space and time, is plain from the fact

that the Old Testament never quite stripped off the idea
that Jehovah's contact with earth has a special relation
to special places—that the operations of His sovereignty
go forth from Sinai, or from Zion, or from some other
earthly sanctuary, where He is nearer to man than on
unconsecrated ground. It is true that this conception
generally takes a poetical form, and did not to the
prophets appear irreconcilable with the thought that it
is impossible to escape from Jehovah's presence (Amos
ix. 1 *seq.*; Ps. cxxxix. 7), that heaven and the heaven
of heavens cannot contain Him (1 Kings viii. 27); that
He sits on the circle of the earth, and its inhabitants
are as grasshoppers (Isa. xl. 22). But the figures of
early poetry express the actual thoughts of the people
who use them; and there can be no question that, by
the ordinary Israelite, the local relation of Jehovah to
the land and sanctuaries of Israel, the idea of His march
from Sinai in the thunderstorm that announces His
approach, were taken with a degree of literality that
would have been impossible if Moses had already
given to the people a metaphysical conception of the
divine being. As for the common notion that the name
Jehovah expresses the idea of absolute and unconditioned
existence, that is a mere fiction of the Alexandrian
philosophy, absurdly inconsistent with the whole language of the Old Testament, and refuted even by the
one phrase Jehovah of hosts—the Jehovah of the armies
of Israel.[10] Even the principle of the second commandment, that Jehovah is not to be worshipped by images,

which is often appealed to as containing the most characteristic peculiarity of Mosaism, cannot, in the light of history, be viewed as having had so fundamental a place in the religion of early Israel. The state worship of the golden calves led to no quarrel between Elisha and the dynasty of Jehu ; and this one fact is sufficient to show that, even in a time of notable revival, the living power of the religion was not felt to lie in the principle that Jehovah cannot be represented by images.

It was as a living personal force, not as a metaphysical entity, that Jehovah was adored by Israel, and so a living faith was possible in spite of much vagueness and vacillation upon the very points in the conception of the Godhead which, to our habit of mind, seem most central. In truth, metaphysical speculation on the Godhead as eternal, infinite, and the like, is not peculiar to the religion of revelation, but was carried by the philosophers of the Gentiles much further than is ever attempted in the Old Testament.

The other point to which I have referred, the views of the Hebrews as to the state after death and future retribution, may be disposed of more briefly. Apart from the doctrine of the resurrection, of which nothing is heard till the later books of the Old Testament, the religion of the Hebrews has to do with this life, not with a life to come, as, indeed, was inevitable, seeing that the religious subject, the object of Jehovah's love, is, in the first instance, the nation as a whole, individual Israelites coming into relation with their God as members of the nation sharing in His dealings with Israel *quâ* nation. After death man enters the shadowy realm of Sheôl, where the weak and pithless shades dwell together, where their love, their hatred, their envy are perished, where small and great are alike, and the servant is free from his master (Eccles. ix. 4 *seq.*; Job. iii. 13 *seq.*), where there is no more remembrance of God, and none can praise His name or hope for His truth (Ps. vi. 5; Isa. xxxviii. 18). There is nothing in these conceptions which partakes of the character of revelation; they are just the same ideas as are found among the surrounding nations. The very name of shades (Rephâîm) is common to the Old Testament with the Phœnicians; and, when the Sidonian king Eshmunazar engraved on his sarcophagus the prayer that those who disturbed his tomb might "find no bed among the shades," he used the same imagery and even the same words as are employed in the books of Isaiah and Ezekiel in describing the descent into Sheôl of the kings of Babylon and Egypt (Isa. xiv. 9, 18 *seq.*; Ezek. xxxii. 25).[11] In accordance with this view of the state of the dead, the Hebrew doctrine of retribution is essentially a doctrine of retribution on earth. Death is itself a final judgment; for it removes man from the sphere where Jehovah's grace and judgment are known. Here, then, even more clearly than in the other case, it is plain that the religion of the Hebrews does not rest on a philosophy of the unseen universe. The sphere of religion is the present life, and the truths of religion are the truths of an everyday experience in which to Hebrew faith Jehovah is as living and personal an actor as men are. His agency in Israel is too real to invite to abstract speculation; all interest turns, not on what Jehovah is in Himself, or what He does beyond the sphere of the present national life, but on His present doings in the midst of His people, and the personal character and dispositions which these doings reveal.

Now, to all early nations religion is an intensely real thing. The primitive mind does not occupy itself with things of no practical importance, and it is only in the later stages of society that we meet with traditional beliefs nominally accepted by every one, but practically regarded by none, or with theological speculations which have an interest to the curious but are not felt to have a direct bearing on the concerns of life. In the earliest stages of the religion of any nation we may take it for granted that nothing is believed or practised which is not felt to be of vital importance for the nation's wellbeing. There is no remissness, therefore, in religious duty, no slackness in the performance of sacred rites. This principle holds good for ancient Israel as well as for other ancient nations. The prophets themselves, amidst all their complaints against the people's backsliding, bear witness that their countrymen were assiduous in their religious service, and neglected nothing which they deemed necessary to make sure of Jehovah's help in every need. The Israelites, in fact, had not reached the stage at which men begin to be indifferent about religion, and if Jehovah had been such a god as Baal or Chemosh, content with such service as they exacted from their worshippers, there would have been no ground to complain of their fidelity to His name or their zeal for His cause.

But here we come back to the real difference between the religion of Jehovah and the religion of the nations, which, as we have just seen, cannot be sought in the external forms of the Old Testament worship, or in a system of abstract monotheistic theology. That difference lies in the personal character of Jehovah, and in the relations corresponding to His character which He seeks to maintain with His people. Properly speaking, the heathen deities have no personal character, and no personal relations to their worshippers. They were, indeed, conceived as a kind of persons, as capable of anger and of pleasure, as hungering and fed by sacrifices, as showing affection to their worshippers, who were often looked on as their sons and daughters, and so forth. But character in the sense of a fixed and independent habit of will was not theirs. The attributes ascribed to them were a mere reflex of the attributes of their worshippers, and what character they had was nothing else than a personification of the character of the nation that acknowledged their lordship. Heathen religions were by no means without moral value in giving fixed expression to national character, and adding a sacred sanction to the highest national conception of right and wrong. But they had no effect in developing character. The god always remained on the same ethical level with his people. His virtues were their virtues, and their imperfections were his also. The god and the people therefore never parted company. It was not difficult to worship and serve him aright, for he asked no more than popular sentiment approved. The heathen nations, says Jeremiah, never gave up their gods, which yet are no gods (Jer. ii. 11). In point of fact, there was no motive to give up a religion which had no higher moral standard and no higher aims than those of the worshippers themselves. The god and the people kept together because they formed a natural unity, because the deity had no independent will, and at most was conceived as being sometimes temporarily estranged from his people for reasons not clearly distinguishable from the caprice of an Eastern despot.

Not so Jehovah. He approved Himself a true God by showing throughout the history of Israel that He had a will and purpose of His own—a purpose rising above the current ideas of His worshippers, and a will directed with steady consistency to a moral aim. Jehovah was not content to receive such service as it was easy and natural for the people to perform, and to give them such felicity as they themselves desired. All His dealings with Israel were directed to lead the people on to higher things than their natural character inclined towards. To know Jehovah and to serve Him aright involved a moral effort—a frequent sacrifice of natural inclination. It was an easy thing to acknowledge the Divine King of Israel in the day of battle when He led His armies on to victory; and it is not difficult to understand that in the prosperous days of David the Hebrews could rejoice before Jehovah, and find nothing burdensome in His service. But very different experiences awaited the nation in the ages that followed—when Israel was divided against itself, when its rulers were drawn into the larger stream of politics by the forward movement of the great empire on the Tigris, and when the old social system, based on peasant proprietorship, began to break up and left a dangerous gulf between the rich nobles and the landless or impoverished classes.

Every change in the old national life, every disorder in society or in the state, opened a new religious problem—a new question, that is, as to the reason why Jehovah suffered such evils to befall His people. To the unthinking masses these things were only a proof that Jehovah was temporarily estranged, and did not lead them to doubt that He could be won back to them by greater zeal in acts of external worship which might with advantage be made more effective and splendid by taking hints from their heathen neighbours. But though the sacrifices were redoubled and the feasts thronged with eager worshippers, all this brought no help to Israel. The nation sank continually lower, and Jehovah still stood afar off; to the common judgment He seemed to have forsaken His land.

Under such trials a heathen religion which was capable of no higher hopes than were actually entertained by the mass of the Hebrews would have declined and perished with the fall of the nation. But Jehovah proved Himself a true God by vindicating His sovereignty in the very events that proved fatal to the gods of the Gentiles. Amidst the sceptical politics of the nobles and the thoughtless superstition of the masses He was never without a remnant that read the facts of history in another light, and saw in them the proof, not that Jehovah was powerless or indifferent, but that He was engaged in a great controversy with His people, a controversy that had moral issues unseen to those who knew not Jehovah and neglected the only service in which He was well pleased. When Jehovah seemed furthest off He was in truth nearest to Israel, and the reverses that seemed to prove Him to have forsaken His land were really the strokes of His hand. He desired mercy and not sacrifice, obedience rather than the fat of lambs. While these things were wanting His very love to Israel could only show itself in ever-repeated chastisement, till the sinners were consumed out of His land and His holy will established itself in the hearts of a regenerate people. Jehovah's purpose was supreme over all, and it must prove itself supreme in Israel though the Hebrew state perished in hopeless conflict with it. He who redeemed His nation from Egypt could redeem it from a new captivity; and, if Israel would not learn to know Jehovah in the good land of Canaan, it must once more pass through the desert and enter the door of hope through the valley of tribulation. Such is the prophetic picture of the controversy of Jehovah with His people, the great issues of which are unfolded with increasing clearness in the successive prophetic books.

I am afraid that this long discussion has proved a somewhat severe tax on your attention, but the results to which it has led us are of the first importance, and will help us through all our subsequent course. Let me repeat them very briefly. The primary difference between the religion of Israel and that of the surrounding nations does not lie in the idea of a theocracy, or in a philosophy of the invisible world, or in the external forms of religious service, but in a personal difference between Jehovah and other gods. That difference, again, is not of a metaphysical but of a directly practical nature; it was not defined once for all in a theological dogma, but made itself felt in the attitude which Jehovah actually took up towards Israel in those historical dealings with His nation to which the word of the prophets supplied a commentary. Everything that befell Israel was interpreted by the prophets as a work of Jehovah's hand, displaying His character and will—not an arbitrary character or a changeable will, but a fixed and consistent holy purpose, which has Israel for its object and seeks the true felicity of the nation, but at the same time is absolutely sovereign over Israel, and will not give way to Israel's desires or adapt itself to Israel's convenience. No other religion can show anything parallel to this. The gods of the nations are always conceived either as arbitrary and changeful, or as themselves subordinate to blind fate, or as essentially capable of being bent into sympathy with whatever is for the time being the chief desire of their worshippers, or, in some more speculative forms of faith, introduced when these simpler conceptions broke down, as escaping these limitations only by being raised to entire unconcern in the petty affairs of man. In Israel alone does Jehovah appear as a God near to man, and yet maintaining an absolute sovereignty of will, a consistent independence of character. And the advance of the Old Testament religion is essentially identified with an increasing clearness of perception of the things which this character of the Deity involves. The name of Jehovah becomes more and more full of meaning as faith in His sovereignty and self-consistency is put to successive tests in the constantly changing problems presented by the events of history.

Now, when we speak of Jehovah as displaying a consistent character in His sovereignty over Israel, we necessarily imply that Israel's religion is a moral religion, that Jehovah is a God of righteousness, whose dealings with His people follow an ethical standard. The ideas of right and wrong among the Hebrews are forensic ideas; that is, the Hebrew always thinks of the right and the wrong as if they were to be settled before a judge. Righteousness is to the Hebrew not so much a moral quality as a legal status. The word "righteous" (*çaddîḳ*) means simply "in the right," and the word "wicked" (*rāshā'*) means "in the wrong." "I have sinned this time," says Pharaoh, "Jehovah is in the right (A.V. righteous), and I and my people are in the wrong (A.V. wicked)," Exod. ix. 27. Jehovah is always in the right, for He is not only sovereign but self-consistent. He is the fountain of righteousness, for from the days of Moses He is the judge as well as the captain of His people, giving forth law and sentence from His sanctuary. In primitive society the functions of judge and lawgiver are not separated, and reverence for law has its basis in personal respect for the judge. So the just consistent will of Jehovah is the law of Israel, and it is a law which as King of Israel He Himself is continually administering.[12]

Now, in every ancient nation, morality and law (including in this word traditional binding custom) are identical, and in every nation law and custom are a part of religion, and have a sacred authority. But in no other nation does this conception attain the precision and practical force which it has in the Old Testament, because the gods themselves, the guardians of law, do not possess a sharply-defined consistency of character such as Jehovah possesses. The heathen gods are guardians of law, but they are something else at the same time; they are not wholly intent on righteousness, and righteousness is not the only path to their favour, which sometimes depends on accidental partialities, or may be conciliated by acts of worship that have nothing to do with morality. And here be it observed that the fundamental superiority of the Hebrew religion does not lie in the particular system of social morality that it enforces, but in the more absolute and self-consistent righteousness of the Divine Judge. The abstract principles of morality—that is, the acknowledged laws of social order—are pretty much the same in all parts of the world in corresponding stages of social development. Heathen nations at the same general stage of society with the Hebrews will be found to acknowledge all the duties of man to man laid down in the decalogue; and on the other hand there are many things in the social order of the Hebrews, such as polygamy, blood revenge, slavery, the treatment of enemies, which do not correspond with the highest ideal morality, but belong to an imperfect social state, or, as the gospel puts it, were tolerated for the hardness of the people's hearts. But, with all this, the religion of Jehovah put morality on a far sounder basis than any other religion did, because in it the righteousness of Jehovah as a God enforcing the known laws of morality was conceived as absolute, and as showing itself absolute, not in a future state, but upon earth. I do not, of course, mean that this high view of Jehovah's character was practically present to all His worshippers. On the contrary, a chief complaint of the prophets is that it was not so, or, in other words, that Israel did not know Jehovah. But the higher view is never put forth by the prophets as a novelty; they regard it as the very foundation of the religion of Jehovah from the days of Moses downwards, and the people never venture to deny that they are right. In truth they could not deny it, for the history of the first creation of Israel, which was the fundamental evidence as to the true character of Jehovah's relations to His people, gave no room for such mythological conceptions as operate in the heathen religions to make a just conception of the Godhead impossible. Heathen religions can never conceive of their gods as perfectly righteous, because they have a natural as well as a moral side, a physical connection with their worshippers, physical instincts and passions, and so forth. The Old Testament brings out this point with great force of sarcasm when Elijah taunts the prophets of Baal, and suggests that their god may be asleep, or on a journey, or otherwise busied with some human avocation. In fact, all this was perfectly consistent with the nature of Baal. But the Hebrews knew Jehovah solely as the King and Judge of Israel. He was this, and this alone; and therefore there was no ground to ascribe to Him less than absolute sovereignty and absolute righteousness. If the masses lost sight of these great qualities, and assimilated His nature to that of the Canaanite deities, the prophets were justified in reminding them that Jehovah was Israel's God before they knew the Baalim, and that He had then showed Himself a God far different from these.

But religion cannot live on the mere memory of the

past, and the faith of Jehovah had to assert itself as the true faith of Israel by realising a present God who still worked in the midst of the nation as He had worked of old. No nation can long cleave to a God whose presence and power are not actually with them in their daily life. If Jehovah was Israel's God, He must manifest Himself as still the King and the Judge of His people, and these names must acquire more and more full significance through the actual experience of deeds of sovereignty and righteousness. Without such deeds no memory of the days of Moses could long have saved the God of the Hebrews from sinking to the level of the gods of the nations, and we have now to see that such deeds were not wanting, and not without fruit for the progress of the Old Testament faith.

Before the time of Amos, the father of written prophecy, the record of Israel's religious life is too fragmentary to allow us to follow it in detail. Of the history of religion between Solomon and Ahab we know next to nothing. In the greater Israel of the North, which in these ages was the chief seat of national life, a constant succession of revolutions and civil wars obscures all details of internal history. The accession of the powerful dynasty of Omri, which regained in successful war a good part of the conquests of David—it was Omri, as we know, that reduced Moab to the tributary condition spoken of in 2 Kings iii. 4[13]—restored the northern kingdom to fresh vigour; and it is characteristic of the close union between national life and the religion of Jehovah which was involved in the very principles of the Hebrew commonwealth that the political revival was the prelude to a great religious movement. We know from the stone of Mesha that the war of Israel with Moab appeared to the combatants as a war of Jehovah with Chemosh. The victory, therefore, could not fail to give a fresh impulse to the national faith of the Hebrews. Now Omri, who imitated the conquests of David, followed also the Davidic policy of close union with Tyre, so obviously advantageous to the material interests of a nation which was not itself commercial, and could find no market for its agricultural produce except in the Phœnician ports. The marriage of Ahab with a Tyrian princess was also a direct imitation of the policy of Solomon's marriages; and in building and endowing a temple of Baal for his wife Ahab did no more than Solomon had done without exciting much opposition on the part of his people. But now there were men in Israel to whom every act of homage to Baal appeared an act of disloyalty to Jehovah, and Elijah openly raised the question whether Jehovah or Baal was God. There was no room for two gods in the land.

As Ahab had no intention of giving up the worship of Jehovah when he gratified Jezebel by establishing a service of Baal, we may be sure that to him the conflict with Elijah did not present itself as a conflict between Jehovah and Baal. Hitherto the enemies of Jehovah had been the gods of hostile nations, while the Tyrian

Baal was the god of a friendly state. To the king, as to many other persecutors since his day, the whole opposition of Elijah seems to have taken a political aspect. The imprisonment of Micaiah shows that he was little inclined to brook any religious interference with the councils of state, and the prophetic opposition to Jezebel and her Baal worship was extremely embarrassing to his political plans, in which the alliance with Tyre was obviously a very important factor. On his part, therefore, the severe measures taken against the prophets and their party simply expressed a determination to be absolute master in his own land. The previous history of the northern tribes proves that a strong central authority was not at all popular with the nation. Ancestral customs and privileges were obstinately maintained against the royal will, as we see in the case of Naboth; and the same case shows that the Tyrian influence encouraged the king to deal with this obstinacy in a very high-handed way. Elijah did not at first find any sustained popular support, but no doubt as the struggle went on, and especially after the judicial murder of Naboth sent a thrill of horror through the land, it began to be felt that he was pleading the cause of the ancient freedoms of Israel against a personal despotism; and so we can understand the ultimate success of the party of opposition in the revolution of Jehu, in spite of the fact that only a small fraction of the nation saw the religious issues at stake so clearly as Elijah did. From the point of view of national

politics the fall of the house of Ahab was a step in the
downfall of Israel. The dynasty of Jehu was not nearly
so strong as the house of Omri; it had little fortune
in the Syrian wars till Damascus was weakened by the
progress of Assyria, and Hosea, writing in the last days
of the dynasty, certainly did not judge amiss when he
numbered the bloodshed of Jezreel among the fatal sins
of the people, a factor in the progress of that anarchy
which made a sound national life impossible (Hosea i. 4;
vii. 7). In this respect the work of Elijah foreshadows
that of the prophets of Judah, who in like manner had
no small part in breaking up the political life of the
kingdom. The prophets were never patriots of the
common stamp, to whom national interests stand higher
than the absolute claims of religion and morality.

Had Elijah been merely a patriot, to whom the state
stood above every other consideration, he would have
condoned the faults of a king who did so much for the
greatness of his nation; but the things for which Elijah
contended were of far more worth than the national
existence of Israel, and it is a higher wisdom than that
of patriotism which insists that divine truth and civil
righteousness are more than all the counsels of state-
craft. Judged from a mere political point of view
Elijah's work had no other result than to open a way
for the bloody and unscrupulous ambition of Jehu, and
lay bare the frontiers of the land to the ravages of the
ferocious Hazael; but with him the religion of Jehovah
had already reached a point where it could no longer be

judged by a merely national standard, and the truths of which he was the champion were not the less true because the issue made it plain that the cause of Jehovah could not triumph without destroying the old Hebrew state. Nay, without the destruction of the state the religion of Israel could never have given birth to a religion for all mankind, and it was precisely the incapacity of Israel to carry out the higher truths of religion in national forms which brought into clearer and clearer prominence those things in the faith of Jehovah which are independent of every national condition, and make Jehovah the God not of Israel alone but of all the earth. This, however, is to anticipate what will come out more clearly as we proceed. Let us for the present confine our attention to what Elijah himself directly saw and taught.[14]

The ruling principle in Elijah's life was his consuming jealousy for Jehovah the God of hosts (1 Kings xix. 14); or, to put the idea in another and equally Biblical form, Jehovah was to him pre-eminently a jealous God, who could endure no rival in His land or in the affections of His people. There was nothing novel in this idea; the novelty lay in the practical application which gave to the idea a force and depth which it had never shown before. To us it seems obvious that Ahab had broken the first commandment in giving Baal a place in his land, but to Ahab and the mass of his contemporaries the thing could hardly be so clear. There are controversies enough even among modern commentators as to the exact force of the "before me" of the first commandment; and, even if we are to suppose that practical religious questions were expressly referred to the words of this precept, it would not have been difficult to interpret them in a sense that meant only that no other god should have the pre-eminence over Israel's King. But no doubt these things were judged of less by the letter of the decalogue than by habitual feeling and usage. Hitherto all Israel's interest in Jehovah had had practical reference to His contests with the gods of hostile nations, and it was one thing to worship deities who were felt to be Jehovah's rivals and foes, and quite another thing to allow some recognition to the deity of an allied race. But Elijah saw deeper into the true character of the God of Israel. Where He was worshipped no other god could be acknowledged in any sense. This was a proposition of tremendous practical issues. It really involved the political isolation of the nation, for as things then stood it was impossible to have friendship and alliance with other peoples if their gods were proscribed in Israel's land. It is not strange that Ahab as a politician fought with all his might against such a view; for it contained more than the germ of that antagonism between Israel and all the rest of mankind which made the Jews appear to the Roman historian as the enemies of the human race, and brought upon them an unbroken succession of political misfortunes and the ultimate loss of all place among the nations. It is hard to say how far the followers of Elijah or indeed the prophet himself perceived the full consequences of the position which he took up. But the whole history of Elijah testifies to the profound impression which he made. The air of unique grandeur that surrounds the prophet of Gilead proves how high he stood above the common level of his time. It is Jehovah and Elijah not against Ahab alone, but against and above the world.

The work of Elijah, in truth, was not so much that of a great teacher as of a great hero. He did not preach any new doctrine about Jehovah, but at a critical moment he saw what loyalty to the cause of Jehovah demanded, and of that cause he became the champion, not by mere words, but by his life. The recorded words of Elijah are but few, and in many cases have probably been handed down with the freedom that ancient historians habitually use in such matters. His importance lies in his personality. He stands before us as the representative of Jehovah's personal claims on Israel. The word of Jehovah in his mouth is not a word of doctrine, but of kingly authority, and to him pre-eminently applies the saying of Hosea: "I have hewed them by the prophets; I have slain them by the word of My mouth: and My judgments were as the light that goeth forth" (Hosea vi. 5).[15]

This view of the career of Elijah, which is that naturally derived from the Biblical narrative, is pretty much an exact inversion of the common representation of the function of the prophets. The traditional view which we have from the Rabbins makes the prophets mere interpreters of the Law, and places the originality of their work entirely in their predictions. In that case Elijah would be the least original of prophets, for he gave no Messianic prediction. But in reality Jehovah did not first give a complete theoretical knowledge of Himself and then raise up prophets to enforce the application of the theoretical scheme in particular circumstances. That would not have required a prophet; it would have been no more than is still done by uninspired preachers. The place of the prophet is in a religious crisis where the ordinary interpretation of acknowledged principles breaks down, where it is necessary to go back, not to received doctrine, but to Jehovah Himself. The word of Jehovah through the prophet is properly a declaration of what Jehovah as the personal King of Israel commands in this particular crisis, and it is spoken with authority, not as an inference from previous revelation, but as the direct expression of the character and will of a personal God, who has made Himself personally audible in the prophet's soul. General propositions about divine things are not the basis but the outcome of such personal knowledge of Jehovah, just as in ordinary human life a general view of a man's character must be formed by observation of his attitude and action in a variety of special circumstances. Elijah's whole career, and not his words merely, contained a revelation of Jehovah to Israel—that is, made them feel that through this man

Jehovah asserted Himself as a living God in their midst.

We had occasion to observe in the course of last Lecture that all genuine religious belief contains a positive element—an element learned from the experience of former generations. And so it will be found that all great religious reformations have their roots in the past, that true reformers do not claim to be heard on the ground of the new things they proclaim, but rather because they alone give due weight to old truths which the mass of their contemporaries cannot formally deny, but practically ignore. And they do so with justice, for all genuine religious truth is personal truth, and personal truth has always a range far transcending the circumstances in which it was originally promulgated and the application to which it was originally confined. So it was with Elijah. The God whom he declared to Israel was the God of Moses—the same God, declaring His character and will in application to new circumstances. Elijah himself is a figure of antique simplicity. He was a man of Gilead, a native of that part of the land of Israel which had still most affinity with the old nomadic life of the age of Moses, and was furthest removed from the Tyrian influences to which Ahab had yielded. It is highly characteristic for his whole standpoint that in the greatest danger of his life, when the victory of Jehovah on Mount Carmel seemed to be all in vain, he retired to the desert of Sinai, to the ancient mountain of God. It was the God of the Exodus to whom he appealed, the ancient King of Israel in the journeyings through the wilderness. In this respect Elijah shows his kinship to the Nazarites, a very curious and interesting class of men, who first appear in the time of the Philistine oppression, and who, some generations later, are mentioned by Amos side by side with the prophets (Amos ii. 11, 12). The cultivation of the vine is one of the most marked distinctions between nomadic and sedentary life. Nomads and half-settled tribes have often a certain amount of agricultural knowledge, raising occasional crops of corn, or at all events of edible herbs. But the cultivation of the vine demands fixed sedentary habits, and all Semitic nomads view wine-growing and wine-drinking as essentially foreign to their traditional mode of life.[16] Canaan, on the contrary, is pre-eminently a land of the grape, and the Canaanite worship was full of Dionysiac elements. Wine was the best gift of the Baalim, and wine-drinking was prominent in their luxurious worship. The Nazarite vow to abstain from wine, which in the earliest case, that of Samson, appears as a life-long vow, was undoubtedly a religious protest against Canaanite civilisation in favour of the simple life of ancient times. This appears most clearly in the case of the Rechabites, who had received from their father Jonadab the double precept never to drink wine, and never to give up their wandering pastoral life for a residence in cities (Jer. xxxv.). We have no evidence that Elijah had a personal connection with the Rechabites; but Jonadab was a prominent partisan of Jehu, and went with him to see his zeal for Jehovah when he put an end to Baal and his worshippers (2 Kings x. 15 *seq.*). We see, therefore, that one element, and not the least popular, in the movement against Baal was a reaction in favour of the primitive simplicity of Israel in the days before it came into contact with Canaanite civilisation and Canaanite religion.

Another seat of the influence of the movement was the prophetic guilds. Elijah himself, so far as we can judge, had little to do with these guilds; but his successor Elisha, who had the chief share in giving political effect to his ideas, found his closest followers among the "sons of the prophets." The idea of "schools of the prophets," which we generally connect with this Biblical phrase, is a pure invention of commentators. According to all the laws of Semitic speech the sons of the prophets were not disciples of a school, but members of a guild or corporation,[17] living together in the neighbourhood of ancient sanctuaries, such as Gilgal and Bethel, and in all likelihood closely connected with the priests, as was certainly the case in Judah down to the extinction of the state (Jer. xxix. 26, cf. xx. 1, 2; Lam. ii. 20, etc.). The prophets of Jehovah and the priests of Jehovah were presumably associated much as were the prophets and priests of Baal. It would be a great mistake to suppose that wherever we hear of prophets or sons of prophets—that is, members of prophetic guilds—we are to think of men raised as high above their contemporaries as Elijah,

Amos, or Isaiah. The later prophets, in our sense of the word, were in constant feud with the common prophets of their day, whose profession was a trade, and whose oracles they condemn as mere heathenish divination implying no true knowledge of Jehovah. The very name and idea of the prophet (*nâbî*) are common to Israel with its heathen neighbours, as appears, not only from the existence of prophets of Baal in connection with Jezebel's sanctuary, but from the fact that the Assyrians had a god Nebo, whose name is essentially identical with the Hebrew nâbî, and who figures as the spokesman of the gods, the counterpart of the Greek Hermes.[18] The first appearance of companies of prophets is in the history of Samuel and Saul (1 Sam. x. 3, 10 *seq.*), where they are found engaged in the worship of Jehovah under circumstances of physical excitement closely parallel to what is still seen among the dervishes of the East, and occasionally among ourselves in times of strong religious feeling.[19] Excitement of this sort is often associated with genuine religious movements, especially among primitive peoples. Like all physical accompaniments of religious conviction, it is liable to strange excesses, and may often go along with false beliefs and self-deluding practices; but religious earnestness is always nearer the truth than indifference, and the great movement of which Elijah was the head found large support among the prophets of Jehovah. Yet we must not forget that physical enthusiasm is a dangerous ally to spiritual faith. The revolution of Jehu, which Elisha set on foot with the aid of the prophetic guilds, used means that were far removed from the loftiness of Elijah's teaching, and under the protection of Jehu's dynasty the prophetic guilds soon sank to depths of hypocrisy and formalism with which Amos disclaimed all fellowship (Amos vii. 14).

One feature in the teaching of Elijah still remains, which was perhaps the most immediately important of all. The divine denunciation of the fall of Ahab's house had its basis, not in the worship of Baal, but in the judicial murder of Naboth (1 Kings xxi.); and Wellhausen has given deserved prominence to the observation of Ewald, that this act of injustice stirred the heart of the nation much more deeply than the religious policy of the house of Omri (2 Kings vi. 32; ix. 25 *seq.*). Naboth's offence was his obstinate adhesion to ancient custom and law, and the crime of Ahab was no common act of violence, but an insult to the moral sense of all Israel. In condemning it Elijah pleaded the cause of Jehovah as the cause of civil order and righteousness; the God as whose messenger he spoke was the God by whom kings reign and princes decree justice. The sovereignty of Jehovah was not an empty thought; it was the refuge of the oppressed, the support of the weak against the mighty. Without this it would have been nothing to declare war against the Tyrian Baal; if Jehovah claimed Israel as His dominion, in which no other god could find a place, He did so because His rule was the rule of absolute righteousness.

It would have been well for the house of Jehu if in mounting the throne of Ahab it had learned this lesson. But the dynasty which began in treachery and bloodshed, which profaned the great work of Elijah by making it the instrument of a vulgar ambition, rooted Baal out of the land without learning to know the true character of Jehovah. The second crisis in the religion of Israel was not without its wholesome issues. The faith of Jehovah was never again assailed from without, but within it grew more and more corrupt. Priests and prophets were content to enjoy the royal favour without remembering that Jehovah's cause was not victorious in the mere extirpation of Baal, and the nation returned to the service of Jehovah without learning that that service was worthless when it produced no other fruits than a constant succession of feasts and offerings. And meanwhile the inner state of Israel became daily more desperate. The unhappy Syrian wars sapped the strength of the country, and gradually destroyed the old peasant proprietors who were the best hope of the nation. The gap between the many poor and the few rich became wider and wider. The landless classes were ground down by usury and oppression, for in that state of society the landless man had no career in trade, and was at the mercy of the land-holding capitalist. It was of no avail that the Damascene enemy, lying as he did between Israel and Assyria, was at length compelled to leave Samaria at peace, and defend his own borders against the forward march of the great Eastern power, or that the last kings of the house of Jehu availed themselves of this diversion to restore the external greatness of their empire, not only on the Syrian frontier, but by successful campaigns against the Moabites. Under Jeroboam II. the outward state of Israel appeared as brilliant as in the best days of old, and the wealth and splendour of the court seemed to the superficial observer to promise a long career of prosperity ; but, with all these outward signs of fortune, which the official organs of religion interpreted as sure proofs of Jehovah's favour, the state of the nation was rotten at the core ; there was no truth or mercy or knowledge of God in the land. A closer view of the condition of Israel at this epoch must, however, be reserved for our study of the prophets who have left the record of it in their written books—Amos of Tekoah and Hosea ben Beeri.

LECTURE III.

AMOS AND THE HOUSE OF JEHU.

THE century during which the house of Jehu reigned over Israel is handled very briefly in the epitome of the history of Ephraim preserved to us in the book of Kings. It was in its first part a time of wars and troubles, in which the house of Joseph maintained itself with difficulty against the power of Damascus. The Aramæans, supported by the Ammonites, devastated the lands east of the Jordan with circumstances of barbarity which were still fresh in the memory of the Hebrews when Amos wrote (Amos i. 3, 13; 2 Kings x. 32 seq.). The frontier land of Gilead, which appears in Genesis xxxi. as the sacred boundary between Jacob and the Aramæan, had most to suffer, but the whole kingdom was more than once in the sorest straits (2 Kings xiii. 3 seq.; Amos iv. 10). The Israelites played a manful part in the unequal struggle, and at length, as we read in 2 Kings xiii. 5, Jehovah "gave to them a deliverer, and they went forth from under the hand of Syria, and the children of Israel dwelt in their tents as beforetime." The "deliverer," as we now know, can be no other than the host of the Assyrians, who began to make expeditions in the direction of Damascus under Shalmaneser II., and received tribute from Jehu in one of the first years of his reign (B.C. 842). To us it seems plain enough that the forward movement of a great empire boded inevitable destruction to all the minor states of Syria and Palestine, and that the advance of the Assyrians could not be checked till they came to measure themselves with the other great power that was seated on the Nile. At first, however, the Hebrews had very little conception of the power and plans of so remote a nation. The earliest historical allusions to the enemy that held Damascus in check are so vague that we are led to suppose that the very name of Assyria was unknown to the mass of the Hebrews;[1] and the tribute of Jehu seems to have been offered to the conqueror of Hazael without being extorted by armed force. Damascus barred the road from the Tigris to Palestine, and till Damascus fell the successes of Assyria served to give Israel a needful breathing time. We cannot follow in detail the wars between the Aramæans and the Great King; but it is plain that they ultimately broke the power of Damascus. The Israelites, so long put on their defence, were able to assume the aggressive, and under Jeroboam II. the old boundaries of the land were restored, and even Moab once more became tributary (2 Kings xiv. 25; Amos vi. 14).[2] The defeat of Moab at this time appears to be the subject of the ancient fragment, Isaiah xv., xvi., now incorporated as a quotation in the book of Isaiah, which represents the fall of the proud and once prosperous nation as a proof of the helplessness of its gods, who can give no answer to their worshippers.[3] To Israel, on the contrary, their victory was a new proof of Jehovah's might, and we learn from 2 Kings xiv. 25 that King Jeroboam was encouraged in his successful wars by the word of Jehovah, spoken through the prophet Jonah of Gath-hepher. It has been conjectured that part of the prophecy of Jonah is preserved in the passage quoted by Isaiah, who expressly tells us (xvi. 14) that it is a word spoken by Jehovah against Moab long ago (A.V. "from that time"). There is, however, nothing in the prophecy which implies that its author belonged to the invading nation. He seems rather to watch the fall of Moab from a neutral position, and the only verses which are not taken up with a description of the calamity suggest rather that the writer was a Judæan. The Moabites are described as fleeing southward and taking refuge in the Edomite capital of Sela, whence they are exhorted to send tokens of homage to the Davidic king in Jerusalem, Edom's overlord, entreating his protection and mediation (xvi. 1, 3, 4), while this exercise of mercy towards the fallen is recommended as a worthy deed, tending to confirm the just rule of the house of David. We must not, however, linger over this prophecy, which is too fragmentary to be interpreted with certainty when we have so little knowledge of its history. The glimpse which it gives us of one sitting in truth in the tent of David, searching out justice and prompt in righteousness, will prove valuable when we come to be more closely concerned with the Southern Kingdom ; but under the dynasty of Jehu our chief interest still lies in the North, whose monarchs overshadowed the Davidic kings as the cedar of Lebanon overshadows the thistle that grows at its foot (2 Kings xiv. 9). After the victories of Jeroboam the house of Ephraim enjoyed external prosperity for a whole generation ; wealth accumulated and luxury increased. It seems, however, that the advantages of this gleam of fortune were reaped almost exclusively by the aristocracy. The strength of old Israel had lain in the free agricultural class, who formed the national militia, and in peace and war gathered round the hereditary heads of their clans as their natural leaders. We must suppose the life of Israel in its best times to have been very similar to what is still found in secluded and primitive Semitic communities, where habits of military organisation are combined with simplicity of manners and steady industry. The Israelites were an isolated people, and became so in an increasing degree as the doctrine of Jehovah's jealousy made it more difficult for them to enter into alliance with other states (Deut. xxxiii. 28 ; Num. xxiii. 9). To maintain their position amidst hostile nations, their superiority over the subjugated Canaanites, it was necessary for them to observe a sort of standing military discipline. Among all Semitic tribes which have successfully asserted their independence in similar circumstances we find an almost ascetic frugality of life, such as becomes men who are half soldiers half farmers. Custom prescribes that the rich should live on ordinary days as simply as their poorer neighbours; there is no humiliating interval between the several classes of society. The chiefs are the fathers of their clan, receiving a prompt and child-like obedience in time of war, administering justice with an authority that rests on custom rather than on force, and therefore obeyed and loved in proportion as they are themselves true to traditional usages. The power of custom is unbounded, and notwithstanding the strong sense of personal dignity common to all free men, which in the oldest Hebrew laws finds its expression in the entire absence of corporal punishments, individual liberty, as we understand it, is strictly confined by the undisputed authority of usage in every detail of life. A small nation so organised may do great things in the Semitic world, but is very liable to sudden collapse when the old forms of life break down under change of circumstances. Eastern history is full of examples of the rapidity, to us almost incredible, with which nations that have grown strong by temperance, discipline, and self-restraint pass from their highest glory into extreme corruption and social disintegration.[4]

Now, in Israel, under Saul and David, the kingship was only the natural development and crown of the old tribal system. But with Solomon the transition to the vices of Oriental despotism began to be felt. In Northern Israel, though not in Judah, Solomon substituted government by officials of the Court for the ancient aristocratic organisation, and his levies of forced labour and other innovations also tended directly to break down the old estate of Israel's freemen. The rebellion under Jeroboam was beyond question a conservative revolution, but with the rise of the house of Omri the policy of Solomon reappears at the Northern Court, and we have seen what deep offence Ahab gave by his high-handed interference with ancient custom and privilege.[5] Under the dynasty of Jehu the old order of things may have had a temporary victory, but certainly not a lasting one. A dynasty founded by bloodshed and perfidy was not likely to be more faithful to ancient law and custom, more jealous of the rights of subjects, than the house of Omri. But, above all, the long unhappy wars with Damascus, with the famines and plagues that were their natural accompaniments (Amos iv.), exhausted the strength and broke the independence of the poorer freemen. The Court became the centre of a luxurious and corrupt aristocracy, which seems gradually to have absorbed the land and wealth of the nation, while the rest of the people were hopelessly impoverished. The old good understanding between classes disappeared, and the gulf between rich and poor became continually wider. The poor could find no law against the rich, who sucked their blood by usury and every form of fraud (Amos ii. 6, 7; iv. 1; viii. 4, etc.) ; civil corruption and oppression became daily more rampant (Amos iii. 9 *seq.*, and *passim*). The best help against such disorders ought to have been found in the religion of Jehovah, but the official organs of that religion shared in the general corruption. Into this point we must look with some fulness of detail, as it is of the first consequence for the understanding of many parts of Amos and Hosea.

We have already seen that the revolution inaugurated by Elijah and Elisha appealed to the conservatism of the nation. It was followed therefore by no attempt to remodel the traditional forms of Jehovah worship, which continued essentially as they had been since the time of the Judges. The golden calves remained undisturbed, though they were plainly out of place in the worship of a Deity who had so markedly separated himself from the gods of the nations ; and with them there remained also many other religious institutions and symbols—such as the Ashēra or sacred pole at Samaria (A.V. "grove," 2 Kings xiii. 6)—which were common to Israel with the Canaanites, and in their influence on the popular imagination could only tend to efface true conceptions of the God of Elijah, and drag Him down again to the level of a heathen deity. Yet the sanctuaries which contained so many elements unfavourable to a spiritual faith were still the indispensable centres of national religion. True religion can never be the affair of the individual alone. A right religious relation to God must include a relation to our fellow-men in God, and solitary acts of devotion can never satisfy the wants of healthy spiritual life, which calls for a visible expression of the fact that we worship God together in the common faith which binds us into a religious community. The necessity for acts of public and united worship is instinctively felt wherever religion has a social influence, and in Israel it was felt the more strongly because Jehovah was primarily the God and King of the nation, who had to do with the individual Israelite only in virtue of his place in the commonwealth. It was in the ordering of national affairs, the sanctioning of social duties, that Jehovah made Himself directly present to His people, and so their recognition of His Godhead necessarily took a public form, when they rejoiced before Him at His sanctuary. The Israelite could not in general have the same personal sense of Jehovah's presence in his closet as when he "appeared before Him" or "saw His face" at the trysting-place where He met with His people as a king meets with his subjects, receiving from them the expression of their homage in the usual Oriental form of a gift (Exod. xxiii. 15, 17), and answering their devotion by words of blessing or judgment conveyed through the priest (Deut. x. 8 ; xxxiii. 8, 10). It was at the altar that Jehovah came to His people and blessed them (Exod. xx. 24), and acts of worship at a distance from the sanctuary assumed the exceptional character of vows, and were directed towards the sanctuary (1 Kings viii.), where in due time they should be supplemented by the payment of thank-offerings. How absolutely access to the sanctuary was conceived as the indispensable basis of all religion appears from the conception that Jehovah cannot be worshipped in foreign lands (1 Sam. xxvi. [?]   [...]se lands are themselves unclean (Amos vii. 1[?];   that the captives in Assyria and Egypt, [...] drink-offerings and sacrifices to Jehovah, are like men who eat the unclean bread of mourners "because their food for their life is not brought into the house of Jehovah" (Hosea ix. 4). So too when Hosea describes the coming days of exile, when the children of Israel shall remain for many days without king or captain, without sacrifice or *maççēba* (the sacred stone which marked the ancient sanctuaries), without *ephod* (plated image), or *teraphim* (household images), he represents this condition as a temporary separation of Jehovah's spouse from all the privileges of wedlock.[6]

While the sanctuaries and their service held this position, every corruption in the worship practised at them affected the religion of Israel at its very core. The worship at the sanctuaries was guided by the priests, whose business it was to place the savour of the sacrifice before Jehovah, and lay whole burnt-offerings on His altar (Deut. xxxiii. 10). The personal interests of the priests lay all in the encouragement of copious gifts and offerings; and, as the people had the choice of various sanctuaries—Bethel, Gilgal, Dan, Mizpah, Tabor,

Shechem, etc. (Amos v. 5; Hosea v. 1; vi. 9, where for *by consent* read *at Shechem*)—and pilgrimages to distant shrines were a favourite religious exercise (Amos v. 5 ; viii. 14), the priesthoods of the several holy places were naturally led to vie with one another in making the services att⸺ ⸱ .⁀ʜ̌ḍ ṁaːses. The sacred feasts were occasi̇οr̥.ˢ᷄ʊ̄! ⸱ᒪn.⸨th and jollity (Hosea ii. 11), where men ᵗ ⸱ᴜ. l᷄˙˙raîtk, ṡaḥg aᵓnd dánced, with unrestrained merriment. The poet of Lament. ii. 7 compares the din in the temple at Jerusalem on a great feast day to the clamour of an army storming the town. It is easy to judge what shape the rivalry of popular sanctuaries would take under these circumstances. The great ambition of each priesthood was to add every element of luxury and physical enjoyment to the holy fairs. The Canaanite ritual offered a model only too attractive to the Semitic nature, which knows no mean between almost ascetic frugality and unrestrained self-indulgence, and Amos and Hosea describe drunkenness and shocking licentiousness as undisguised accompaniments of the sacred services (Amos ii. 7, 8 ; Hosea iv. 14). The prosperous days of Jeroboam II. gave a new impulse to these excesses; feasts and sacrifices were more frequent than ever, for was it not Jehovah, or rather the Baalim— that is, the local manifestations of Jehovah under the form of the golden calves—who had given Israel the good things of peace and plenty (Hosea ii. 5 *seq.*) ? The whole nation seemed given up to mad riotousness under the prostituted name of religion : " whoredom and wine and lust had turned their head " (Hosea iv. 11).

In order, however, fully to appreciate the corrupting influence of these degraded holy places and their ministers, we must remember that in the ancient constitution of Israel the sanctuary and the priesthood had another function even more important than that connected with feasts and joyous sacrifices. Since the days of Moses it had been the law of Israel that causes too hard for the ordinary judges, who decided by custom and precedent, must be brought before God for decision (Exod. xviii. 19). In the oldest part of the Hebrew legislation the word which our version renders "judges" properly means "God" (Exod. xxi. 6; xxii. 8), and to bring a case before God means to bring it to the sanctuary. It was at the door-post of the sanctuary that the symbolic action was performed by which a Hebrew man might voluntarily accept a life-long service; it was God speaking at the sanctuary who was appealed to in disputed questions of property. "If one man sin against another," says Eli, quoting it would seem, an old proverb, "God shall give judgment on him." This judgment was the affair of the priests, who sometimes administered the "oath of Jehovah," which was accepted as an oath of purgation (Exod. xxii. 11); in other cases the holy lot of the Urim and Thummim was appealed to; but in general no doubt the priests acted mainly as the conservators of ancient sacred law; it was their business to teach Jacob Jehovah's judgments and Israel His law (Deut. xxxiii. 10), and in better days it was their highest praise that they discharged this duty without fear or favour, that they observed Jehovah's word and kept His covenant without respect to father or mother, brethren or children (*ibid.* ver. 9). Those days, however, were past. Under the kingship the judicial functions of the priests were necessarily brought into connection with the office of the sovereign, who was Jehovah's representative in matters of judgment, as well as in other affairs of state (2 Sam. viii. 15 ; xiv. 17 ; 1 Kings iii. 28). The priests became, in a sense, officers of the Court, and the chief priest of a royal sanctuary, such as Amaziah at Bethel (Amos vii. 10, 13), was one of the great officials of state. (Compare 2 Sam. viii. 17 *seq.*, where the king's priests already appear in the list of grandees.) Thus the priesthood were naturally associated in feelings and interests with the corrupt tyrannical aristocracy, and were as notorious as the lords temporal for neglect of law and justice. The strangest scenes of lawlessness were seen in the sanctuaries—revels where the fines paid to the priestly judges were spent in wine-drinking, ministers of the altars stretched for these carousals on garments taken in pledge in defiance of sacred law (Amos ii. 8 ; comp. Exod. xxii. 26 *seq.*). Hosea accuses the priests of Shechem of highway robbery and murder (Hosea vi. 9, *Heb.*) ; the sanctuary of Gilead was polluted with blood, and the prophet explains the general dissolution of moral order, the reign of lawlessness in all parts of the land, by the fact that the priests, whose business it was to maintain the knowledge of

Jehovah and His laws, had forgotten this holy trust (Hosea iv.).

The whole effect of the unfaithfulness of the priests upon national morality and the sense of right and wrong cannot be appreciated without some explanation of the point of view under which the early Hebrews looked upon sin. We have already had occasion to see that in early nations the idea of law, or binding custom, is co-extensive with morality, and that, among the Hebrews in particular, right and wrong are habitually viewed from a forensic point of view. This, of course, influences the notion of sin. The fundamental meaning of the Hebrew word *ḥāṭā*, to sin, is to be at fault, and in Hebrew, as in Arabic, the active (causative) form has the sense of missing the mark (Judges xx. 16) or other object aimed at. The notion of sin, therefore, is that of blunder or dereliction, and the word is associated with others that indicate error, folly, or want of skill and insight (1 Sam. xxvi. 21). This idea has various applications, but, in particular, a man is at fault when he fails to fulfil his engagements, or to obey a binding command ; and in Hebrew idiom the failure is a " sin," whether it be wilful failure, or be due to forgetfulness, or even be altogether involuntary. Jonathan's infringement of his father's prohibition and curse in 1 Sam. xiv. was not less a "sin" in this sense because he did not know what Saul had enjoined. In two respects, then, the Hebrew idea of sin, in its earlier stages, is quite distinct from that which we attach to the word. In the first place, it is not necessarily thought of as offence against God, but includes any act that puts a man in the wrong with those who have power to make him rue it (2 Kings xviii. 14). "What is my sin before thy father," says David, "that he seeks my life?" (1 Sam. xx. 1). "That which was torn of beasts," says Jacob to Laban, "I brought not to thee; I bore the loss of it"—literally, I took it as my sin (Gen. xxxi. 39). If David dies, says Bathsheba, without providing against the succession of Adonijah, "I and my son Solomon shall be sinners" (1 Kings i. 21). In the second place, the notion of sin has no necessary reference to the conscience of the sinner, it does not necessarily involve moral guilt, but only, so to speak, forensic liability. In two ways, however, the Hebrew notion of sin comes into relation with religion. In the first place, the lively sense of Jehovah's presence in Israel as a King, who issues commands to His people and does not fail to enforce them, gives prominence to the conception of sins against Jehovah. In by far the greatest proportion of passages in the older parts of the Bible where such sins are spoken of, the reference is to religious offences, to the worship of false gods or of Jehovah Himself in ways not acceptable to Him, to disobedience to some particular injunction—as in the case of Saul's failure to fulfil his commission against Amalek—or neglect to discharge a vow (1 Sam. xiv. 38; Judges xxi. 22). Offences which we should call moral, such as polytheism, stand on the same level with disobedience to purely ritual customs, such as eating the flesh of animals whose blood has not been offered to Jehovah (1 Sam. xiv. 33 *seq.*), or with such an offence against popular feeling as David's numbering of the people (2 Sam. xxiv. 17). In cases like the last the sin is not clearly felt to be such until misfortune follows, and this habit of judging actions by subsequent events, which plainly might give rise to very distorted views of right and wrong if guided only by popular feeling, became, under the spiritual guidance of the prophets, a chief means to produce juster and deeper views of Jehovah's holy will. But, in the second place, offences of man against man came to be viewed as religious offences, inasmuch as Jehovah is the supreme judge before whom such cases come for decision (Judges xi. 27; 1 Sam. ii. 25). The whole sphere of law in Israel is Jehovah's province, and He is the vindicator, not only of His own direct commands, but of all points of social order regulated by traditional law and custom. Thus, in virtue of the coincidence of law and custom with moral obligation, Jehovah, in His quality of judge, has to do with every part of morals, and all kinds of sin in Israel come before His tribunal. Jehovah has many ways of vindicating the right and punishing sinners, for He commands the forces of nature as well as presides over the visible ordinances of judgment in Israel. But it was to the judgment-seat at the sanctuary that the man who felt himself wronged naturally turned for redress, and the man who knew he had done wrong turned for expiation, which was granted by means of sacrifice (1 Sam. iii. 14; xxvi. 19), or on a money payment to the priests (2 Kings xii. 16), the latter being regarded in the light of a fine, which was naturally held to wipe out the offence in a state of society when all breaches of law, except wilful bloodshed, were cancelled by payment of a pecuniary equivalent. When the priests, therefore, began to view the sins of the people as a regular and desirable source of income, as we learn from Hosea iv. 8 that they actually did in the times of that prophet, the whole idea of right and wrong was reduced to a money standard, and the moral sense of the community was proportionally debased in every relation of life.

The shortcomings of the priesthood might, in some measure, have been supplied if the prophets, whose influence with the masses was doubtless still great, had retained aught of the spirit of Elijah. But prophecy had sunk to a mere trade (Amos vii. 12). Hosea brackets prophet and priest in a common condemnation. In the fall of the priesthood the prophet shall fall with him (Hosea iv. 5).

Was everything then lost which Elijah had contended for? Was there nothing in the nation of Jehovah to distinguish it from other peoples, except that pre-eminence in corruption against which Amos calls the heathen themselves as witnesses (Amos iii. 9 *seq.*)? In reading the prophetic denunciations of the kingdom of Jeroboam we might almost deem that it was so; and there can be no question that the inner decay of the state had gone so far that it was impossible to restore new and healthy life to the existent body politic. But, on the one hand, it must be remembered that Amos and Hosea, in virtue of their function as preachers of reformation, and uncompromising exposers of every abuse, necessarily give exclusive prominence to the evils of the state, and, on the other hand, it is to be observed that Amos at least speaks almost solely of the corruption of the wealthy and ruling classes, whose vices in an Eastern kingdom are far from a true index to the moral condition of the poorer orders. Amos by no means regards the sinners of Jehovah's people (chap. ix. 10) as co-extensive with Israel. He likens the impending judgment to the sifting of corn in a sieve, in which no good grain falls to the ground. There was still a remnant in Ephraim that could be compared to sound corn ; and, though all the sinners must perish, Jehovah, he tells us, will not utterly destroy the house of Jacob (ver. 8).

This, it may be at once observed, is a characteristic feature of all Old Testament prophecy. The prophets have much to say of the sins of Israel, sins so aggravated that Jehovah can no longer pass them by ; but they never despair of Jehovah's good cause in the midst of the nation, or hold that all His goodness and grace have been lavished on Israel to no purpose. Amidst the universal corruption there remains a seed of better hope, some tangible and visible basis for the assurance that Jehovah will yet shape from the remnant of the reprobate nation a people worthy of His love. This conviction is not expressed in the language of modern sentimental optimism, which will not give up all hope even of the most depraved men. The prophets were not primarily concerned with the amendment of individual sinners; it was the nation that they desired to see following righteousness and the knowledge of Jehovah, and they were too practical not to know that the path of national amendment is to get rid of evil-doers and put better men in their place (comp. Jer. xiii. 23, 24). But this they feel is not a thing impossible; there is a true tradition of the knowledge and fear of Jehovah in the land, though it has no influence on the actual leaders of the state ; and in appealing to this higher conception of duty and faith they feel that their words are not spoken to the winds, but that they are advocating a cause which, sustained by Jehovah's own hand, must ultimately triumph in that very community which at present seems so wholly given up to evil. So, when Elijah complains that he is left alone in his jealousy for Jehovah God of hosts, the divine voice answers him that, in the sweeping judgment to be executed by the swords of Jehu and Hazael, he will spare seven thousand men, all the knees which have not bowed to Baal, and every mouth which hath not kissed him. (In 1 Kings xix. 18, for "Yet I have left" read "And I will leave," comp. 2 Kings xiii. 7.)

The clearest proof that Jehovah's work in time past had not been without fruit in Israel lies in the high and commanding tone that prophets like Amos assume. When they speak of the omnipotent Jehovah, the

Creator of heaven and earth, the Lord of all nations, to whose supreme purpose of righteousness all nature and all history must bend, they confess themselves to be speaking truths that the mass of their countrymen ignore, but never claim to be preachers of a new or unheard-of religion. If it sometimes appears that they treat Israel as sunk below the level even of heathen nations, it is elsewhere plain that they measure the people of Jehovah by a standard which could not be applied to those who have never known the living God. The keynote of the prophecy of Amos lies in the words of chap. iii. 2, "You only have I known of all families of the earth; therefore I will punish you for all your iniquities." The guilt of Israel is its declension, not from the common standard of other nations, and not from a new standard now heard of for the first time, but from a standard already set before them by the unique Jehovah who had made this nation His own. For the right understanding of the prophets, it is plainly of the highest importance to realise, with some precision, what this standard was.

Up to quite a recent date it was commonly assumed that this question presented no difficulty; the laws of the Pentateuch, fully written out by Moses and continuously preserved from his days, were held to have been the unvarying rule of faith and obedience before as after the Exile. In the present day this easy solution of the problem can no longer be accepted by historical students. The prophets before the Exile never appeal to the finished system of the Pentateuch. The older historical books do not appeal to it; and in fact the several parts of these books can be classed in distinct groups, each of which has its own standard of religious observance and duty according to the age at which it was composed. The latest history in the books of Chronicles presupposes the whole Pentateuch; the main thread of the books of Kings accepts the standard of the book of Deuteronomy, but knows nothing of the Levitical legislation; and older narratives now incorporated in the Kings—as, for example, the histories of Elijah and Elisha, which every one can see to be ancient and distinct documents—know nothing of the Deuteronomic law of the one altar, and, like Elijah himself, are indifferent even to the worship of the golden calves. These older narratives, with the greater part of the books of Samuel and Judges, accept as fitting and normal a stamp of worship closely modelled on the religion of the patriarchs as it is depicted in Genesis, or based on the ancient law of Exod. xx. 24, where Jehovah promises to meet with His people and bless them at the altars of earth or unhewn stone which stand in all corners of the land, on every spot where Jehovah has set a memorial of His name. And in like manner, as I have shown at length in a former course of Lectures, the sacred laws of Israel which the earlier history acknowledges are not the whole complicated Pentateuchal system, but essentially the contents of that fundamental code which is given in

Exod. xxi.-xxiii. under the title of the Book of the Covenant.[7]

The limits of the present Lectures forbid us to enter on a detailed inquiry as to how much of the Pentateuchal law was already known to Amos or Hosea, and it would be unreasonable to ask you to take on trust results of other men's researches which you have had no opportunity to test. We must rather ask whether there is not some broad practical method by which we can get as near the truth as is necessary for our purpose, without committing ourselves to details that must be settled by the minute inquiries of scholars specially equipped for the task. If I have succeeded in carrying you with me in the course which we have already traversed, I do not think that we shall find this to be impossible. We have not hitherto had the help of any detailed results of Pentateuch criticism, and yet by simply concentrating our attention on undeniable historical facts, and giving them their due weight, we have been able to form a consistent account of the progress of the religion of Jehovah from Moses to Elijah. We have not found occasion to speak of Moses as the author of a written code, and to inquire how much his code contained, because the history itself makes it plain that his central importance for early Israel did not lie in his writings, but in his practical office as a judge who stood for the people before God, and brought their hard cases before Him at the sanctuary (Exod. xviii. 19 ; xxxiii. 9 *seq.*). It is this function of Moses, and not the custody of the written word, which appears in the oldest history as carried on by his successors, and Israel knew Jehovah as its Judge and Lawgiver, not because He had given it a written Torah, but because He was still present to give judgment in its midst. So again we have not found occasion to dwell on the legislation at Mount Sinai, as if the covenant ratified there were the proper beginning of Israel's life as the people of Jehovah; for the early history and the prophets do not use the Sinaitic legislation as the basis of their conception of the relation of Jehovah to Israel, but habitually go back to the deliverance from Egypt, and from it pass directly to the wilderness wandering and the conquest of Canaan (Josh. xxiv. 5 *seq.*, 17 *seq.*; Amos ii. 10; Hosea ii. 15; xi. 1; xii. 9, 13; Jer. xi. 4). We are thus dispensed from entering into knotty questions as to the date of the several parts of the Sinaitic legislation, simply because the events of the year spent at Sinai are not those which have practical prominence in the sequel. And so again, when we came to speak of Elijah, we found it unnecessary to ask what novelty his work exhibited in comparison with Pentateuchal laws that may be supposed to have existed in his time, because the practically epoch-making significance of his stand against Baal is rendered clear by the fact that in the time of Solomon the introduction of foreign worships under similar circumstances passed without popular challenge, and that in Judah Solomon's sanctuaries dedicated to heathen gods were left untouched till long after the time of Elijah (2 Kings xxiii. 13), and must therefore have been tolerated even by Ahab's contemporary Jehoshaphat, who passed for a king of indubitable orthodoxy. Facts like these are landmarks in the history which we cannot afford to overlook, and which veracity forbids us to explain away, and such facts, rather than traditional or hypothetical assumptions as to the date of the Pentateuch, are our best key to understand the actual condition of the people to whom the prophets spoke. In truth those who hold the Mosaic authorship of the Pentateuch and yet desire to do justice to the history are compelled to admit that it was practically a buried book, many of its most central laws being quite ignored by the best kings and the most enlightened priests. They were equally ignored by the prophets, as we shall see more clearly in the sequel, and so for the historical study of the prophets and their work we must leave them on one side, and direct our attention to things that can be shown to have had practical place and recognition in Israel. In other words, the history and the prophets are not to be interpreted by the Pentateuch, but they themselves must be our guides in determining what constituted the sum of the extant knowledge of Jehovah in the time to which they belong.

In the first place, then, it is perfectly clear that the great mass of Levitical legislation, with its ritual entirely constructed for the sanctuary of the ark and the priests of the house of Aaron, cannot have had practical currency and recognition in the Northern Kingdom. The priests could not have stultified themselves by accepting the authority of a code according to which their whole worship was schismatic ; nor can the code have been the basis of popular faith or prophetic doctrine, since Elijah and Elisha had no quarrel with the sanctuaries of their nation. Hosea himself, in his bitter complaints against the priests, never upbraids them as schismatic usurpers of an illegitimate authority, but speaks of them as men who had proved untrue to a legitimate and lofty office. The same argument proves that the code of Deuteronomy was unknown, for it also treats all the northern sanctuaries as schismatic and heathenish, acknowledging but one place of lawful pilgrimage for all the seed of Jacob. It is safe, therefore, to conclude that whatever ancient laws may have had currency in a written form must be sought in other parts of the Pentateuch, particularly in the Book of the Covenant, Exod. xxi.- xxiii., which the Pentateuch itself presents as an older code than those of Deuteronomy and the Levitical Legislation. In fact, the ordinances of this code closely correspond with the indications as to the ancient laws of Israel supplied by the older history and the prophets. Quite similar, except in some minor details which need not now delay us, is another ancient table of laws preserved in Exod. xxxiv. These two documents may be taken as representing the general system of sacred law which had practical recognition in the Northern Kingdom, though the very fact that we have two such documents conspires with other indications to make it probable that the laws, which were certainly generally published by oral decisions of the priests, were better known by oral tradition than by written books. Neither Amos nor Hosea alludes to an extant written law (Hosea viii. 12 is mistranslated in A.V.), though this fact does not prove that written laws did not exist, but only that they had not the same prominence as in later times.

Jehovah, however, instructed His people and revealed His character to them quite as much by history as by precept, and the recollection of His great deeds in times gone by forms the most frequent text for prophetic admonition. I have already remarked that the extant historical narratives fall into several groups, each of which is closely akin to the Book of the Covenant, to the Deuteronomic code, or to the finished Pentateuch (or, if you please, the Levitical legislation) respectively. In the Northern Kingdom, where the Deuteronomic and Levitical legislations had no recognition, it may safely be assumed that the parts of the historical books which are akin to these, and judge the actions of Israel by the standard which they supply, were also unknown. This would exclude those sections of the Pentateuch and the book of Joshua which are plainly by the same hand as the Levitical laws, and a considerable number of passages in the Deuteronomic style, chiefly comments on the older narrative or speeches composed in the usual free manner of ancient historians, which are found here and there in the other historical books. The main thread of the books of Kings, as distinguished from the author's extracts from earlier sources, must of course be set aside, since the history of Kings goes down to the close of the Judæan Kingdom, and is written throughout from the standpoint of Josiah's reformation, which took place long after the fall of the kingdom of Ephraim.

It is important to indicate these deductions in a general way, but for our present purpose it is unnecessary to follow them out in detail, because, speaking broadly, they affect the interpretation rather than the substance of the history. In the time of Amos and Hosea the truest hearts and best thinkers of Israel did not yet interpret Jehovah's dealings with His people in the light of the Deuteronomic and Levitical laws; they did not judge of Israel's obedience by the principle of the one sanctuary or the standard of the Aaronic ritual; but they had heard the story of Jehovah's dealings with their fathers, and many of them, perhaps, had read it in books, great part of which is actually incorporated in our present Bible. Take, for example, the history of the Northern Kingdom as it is given in the Kings. No attentive reader, even of the English Bible, can fail to see that the substance of the narrative, all that gives it vividness and colour, belongs to a quite different species

of literature from the brief chronological epitomes and
theological comments of the Judæan editor. The story
of Elijah and Elisha clearly took shape in the Northern
Kingdom; it is told by a narrator who is full of personal interest in the affairs of Ephraim, and has no idea
of criticising Elijah's work, as the Judæan editor
criticises the whole history of the North, by constant
reference to the schismatic character of the northern
sanctuaries. Moreover, the narrative has a distinctly
popular character; it reads like a story told by word of
mouth, full of the dramatic touches and vivid presenta-
tions of detail which characterise all Semitic history
that closely follows oral narration. The king of Israel
of whom we read in 2 Kings viii. 4 was, we may be sure,
not the only man who talked with Gehazi, saying, "Tell
me, I pray thee, all the great things that Elisha hath
done." By many repetitions the history of the prophets
took a fixed shape long before it was committed to
writing, and the written record preserves all the essential features of the narratives that passed from mouth
to mouth, and were handed down orally from father to
child. The same thing may be said of the earlier
history, which in all its main parts is evidently the
transcript of a vivid oral tradition. The story of the
patriarchs, of Moses, of the Judges, of Saul, and of
David is still recorded to us as it lived in the mouths
of the people, and formed the most powerful agency of
religious education. Even the English reader who is
unable to follow the nicer operations of criticism may

by attentive reading satisfy himself that all the Old Testament stories which have been our delight from childhood for their dramatic pictorial simplicity belong to a different stratum of thought and feeling from the Deuteronomic and Levitical laws. They were the spiritual food of a people for whom these laws did not yet exist, but who listened at every sanctuary to Jehovah's great and loving deeds, which had consecrated these holy places from the days of the patriarchs downwards. Beersheba, Bethel, Shechem, Gilgal, and the rest, had each its own chain of sacred story, and wherever the Israelites were gathered together men might be heard "rehearsing the righteous deeds of Jehovah, the righteous deeds of His rule in Israel" (Judges v. 11). A great part of the patriarchal history—almost all, indeed, that has not reference to Abraham and Hebron—is gathered in this way round northern sanctuaries or round Beersheba, which was a place of pilgrimage for Northern Israel (Amos v. 5; viii. 14); and the special interest which the narrative displays in Rachel and Joseph is an additional proof that we still read it very much as it was read or told in the house of Joseph in the days of Amos and Hosea.

There are two chapters in the Bible which can be pointed to as specially instructive for the way in which the Israelites of the North thought of Jehovah and His reign in Israel. One of these is the so-called blessing of Moses in Deut. xxxiii., which plainly belongs to the Northern Kingdom, because it speaks of Joseph as the crowned one of his brethren (ver. 16; A.V. *separated from his brethren*), and prays for the reunion of Judah to the rest of Israel (ver. 7). The other is Josh. xxiv., a narrative connected with Shechem, which speaks without offence of the sacred tree and sacred stone that marked this great northern sanctuary, and is therefore quite ignorant of the Deuteronomic law. The chapter gives a *résumé* of the history of Israel and the patriarchs in the mouth of Joshua, which is in fact the closing summary of a great historical book, known as the Elohistic history, to which large parts of the Pentateuchal narrative are referred by critics; and taken with the Blessing of Moses it shows us better than any other part of Scripture how thoughtful and godly men of the Northern Kingdom understood the religion of Jehovah though they knew nothing of the greater Pentateuchal codes. In the Blessing of Moses the religion of Israel is described in a tone of joyous and hopeful trust—the glory of Jehovah when He shined forth from Paran and came to Kadesh full of love for His people, the gift of the law through Moses as a possession for the congregation of Jacob, the final establishment of the state when there was a king in Jeshurun uniting the branches of the people, and knitting the tribes of Israel together (ver. 5). The priesthood is still revered as the arbiter of impartial divine justice. The tribes are not all prosperous alike; Simeon has already disappeared from the roll, and Reuben seems threatened with extinction; but the princely house of Joseph is strong and victorious, and round the thousands of Manasseh and the myriads of Ephraim the other tribes still rally strong in Jehovah's favour. "There is none like unto the God of Jeshurun, who rides on the heavens for thy help, and in His loftiness on the skies. The God of old is thy refuge and the outspreading of the everlasting arms; He drives out the enemy before thee, and saith, Destroy. Then Israel dwells secure; the fountain of Jacob flows unmixed in a land of corn and wine, where the heavens drop down dew. Happy art thou, O Israel; who is like unto thee, a people victorious in Jehovah, whose help is the shield, whose pride is the sword, and thy foes feign before thee, and thou marchest over their high places."[8] This is still the old warlike Israel, secure in the help of the God of heaven, whose presence is alike near in the day of battle and in the administration of a righteous law. In Josh. xxiv. the picture has another side. The God who has done these great things for Israel is a holy and a jealous God; He will not forgive His people's sins. It is no easy thing to serve such a God, for He must be served with single heart. The danger of departing from Him lies in two directions. On one hand Israel is tempted to fall back into the ancient heathenism of its Aramæan ancestors (vers. 2, 15); on the other hand it is drawn away by the gods of the Amorites. Such were, in fact, the two great influences with which the religion of Jehovah had to contend through all the history of Israel, and both had a strange attraction, for they made no such demands on their worshippers as the holy and jealous Jehovah. "Ye cannot serve Jehovah, for He will not forgive your sins; if ye forsake Him and serve foreign gods, then He will turn and do you hurt, and consume you after He hath done you good." These words might serve as the epitaph of the Hebrew state in the destruction towards which it was hastening in the last days of the house of Jehu, and with them the history of Israel might have closed, but for the work of a new series of prophets, which built up another Israel on the ruins of the old kingdom. The founder of this new type of prophecy is Amos, the herdsman of Tekoa.[9]

The first appearance of Amos as a prophet is one of the most striking scenes of Old Testament history. His prophecy is almost wholly addressed to Northern Israel, and the scene of his public preaching was the great royal sanctuary of Bethel, the chief gathering-point of the worshippers of Ephraim. But he appeared in Bethel as a stranger, and had nothing in common with the prophetic guild which had long had its seat there. His home was in the kingdom of Judah, not in any of the great centres of life, but in the little town of Tekoa,[10] which lies some six miles south of Bethlehem on an elevated hill, from which the eye ranges northward to Bethlehem and the Mount of Olives, while eastward the prospect extends over rugged and desolate mountains, through the clefts of which the Dead Sea is visible, with the lofty tableland of Moab in the far distance. Though it stands on the very edge of the great wilderness, the spot itself is fruitful, and pleasant to the eye. Its oil, according to the Mishna, was the best in the land (*Men.* viii. 3), and in the middle ages its honey passed into a proverb (Yâḳût *s.v.*). But immediately beyond Tekoa all agriculture ceases, and the desert hills between it and the Dead Sea offer only a scanty subsistence to wandering flocks. Amos himself was not a husbandman, but "a shepherd and a gatherer of sycamore figs" (vii. 14 *seq.*), the coarsest and least desirable of the fruits of Canaan. He was nurtured in austere simplicity, and it was in the vast solitudes where he followed his flock that Jehovah said to him, "Go prophesy to my people Israel." It was a strange errand for the unknown shepherd to undertake; for the prophet was not a preacher in the modern sense, whose words are addressed to the heart of the individual, and who can discharge his function wherever he can find an audience willing to hear a gospel that speaks to the poor as well as to the great. Jehovah's word was a message to the nation, and above all to the grandees and princes who were directly responsible for the welfare and good estate of Israel. But the summons of Jehovah left no room for hesitation. "The Lord roareth from Zion, and sendeth forth His voice from Jerusalem, and the pastures of the shepherds mourn, and the top of Carmel withereth. . . . Shall a trumpet be blown in the city, and the people not be afraid? shall there be evil in the city and Jehovah hath not done it? Surely the Lord Jehovah will not do anything, but He revealeth His secret to His servants the prophets. The lion hath roared, who will not fear? the Lord Jehovah hath spoken, who can but prophesy?" (i. 2; iii. 6-8). The call of Amos lay in the consciousness that he had heard the voice of Jehovah thundering forth judgment while all around were deaf to the sound. In this voice he had learned Jehovah's secret—not some abstract theological truth, but the secret of His dealings with Israel and the surrounding nations. Such a secret could not remain locked up within his breast—"the Lord Jehovah hath spoken, who can but prophesy?" And so the shepherd left his flock in the wilderness, and, armed with no other credentials than the word that burned within him, stood forth in the midst of the brilliant crowd that thronged the royal sanctuary of Bethel, to proclaim what Jehovah had spoken against the children of Israel (iii. 1).

Before we examine more fully the contents of this word, it will be convenient to complete the brief record of the prophet's history as it is given in the seventh chapter of his book. Amos had many things to say to the nation and its rulers, but they all issued in the announcement of swift impending judgment. The sum of his prophecy was a death-wail over the house of Israel:—

The virgin of Israel is fallen, she cannot rise again:
She is cast down upon her land, there is none to raise her up.
(v. 2.)

This judgment is the work of Jehovah, and its cause is

Israel's sin. "You only have I known of all the families of the earth; therefore will I punish you for all your iniquities." In the characteristic manner of Eastern symbolism, Amos expressed these thoughts in a figure. He saw Jehovah standing over a wall with a plumb-line in His hand. Jehovah is a builder, the fate of nations is His work, and, like a good builder, He works by rule and measure. And now the great builder speaks, saying, "Behold I set the plumb-line—the rule of divine righteousness—in the midst of Israel; I will not pass them by any more; and the high places of Isaac shall be desolate, and the sanctuaries of Israel shall be laid waste, and I will rise against the house of Jeroboam with the sword." However little the audience understood of the prophet's harangue, the last words were intelligible enough. It was not the first time that a prophet had foretold the fall of a northern dynasty; the conspiracy that set Jeroboam's ancestor on the throne received its first impulse from Elijah's sentence on the murderer of Naboth (2 Kings ix. 25 *seq.*). The priest Amaziah, who was responsible for the order of his sanctuary, at once took alarm, and sent to the king the report of what he concluded to be a new conspiracy. "Amos," he said, "hath conspired against thee in the midst of the house of Israel; the land cannot bear all his words." The audacious speaker must be silenced, but usage and the traditional privilege of the prophets made the priest reluctant to use force against one who spoke in the name of Jehovah. The great man seems, in fact,

to have looked on the Judæan intruder with something
of the same contempt which the captains of the host at
Ramoth Gilead felt for the "madman" that brought
Elisha's message to Jehu (2 Kings ix. 11); the freedom
allowed to the prophets was in good measure due to the
conviction that they could do little harm unless they
had stronger influences at their back. "Get thee hence,
O seer," he says, "flee into the land of Judah, and there
earn thy bread, and prophesy there.¹¹ But prophesy no
more in Bethel, for it is a royal sanctuary and a royal
residence." To Amaziah Amos seemed half an intriguer,
half a fanatic—a man whose prophesying was a trade,
and who had made a bold stroke for notoriety in the
hope, perhaps, that the Court would buy him off. Nay,
says Amos, "I am no prophet, nor a son of the prophets
[that is, no prophet by trade like the *Nebîîm* of Bethel] . . .
Jehovah took me as I followed the flock, and Jehovah
said to me, Go prophesy against my people Israel. Now,
therefore, hear thou the word of Jehovah. Thou sayest,
Prophesy not against Israel, and preach not against the
house of Isaac. Therefore, thus saith Jehovah, thy wife
shall be prostituted in the city, and thy sons and thy
daughters shall fall by the sword, and thy land shall be
divided by the line; and thou shalt die in an unclean
land, and Israel shall surely go into captivity forth of
his land." The judgment denounced on Amaziah com-
prehends only the usual incidents of the sack of a city
in those barbarous times; and Amos, it is plain, does
not hurl a special threat against the priest, but merely

repeats his former prediction of the fall of the nation before the invader, with the assurance that Amaziah shall live to see it accomplished. To so precise an intimation there was nothing to add. Amos, no doubt, was compelled to yield at once to superior force ; and the fact that his book, as we possess it, is a carefully planned composition, in which this historical incident holds the central place, followed as well as preceded by prophecies, shows that he effected his escape, retiring no doubt to Judah, where he placed on permanent record the words of Jehovah which the house of Israel refused to heed. As his prophesying was not a profession, he had not ceased to be a shepherd in fulfilling his divine mission ; and, though the mediæval Jewish tradition which showed his grave at Tekoa was certainly apocryphal, it may be presumed that he returned to his old life, and died in his native place.

The humble condition of a shepherd following his flock on the bare mountains of Tekoa has tempted many commentators, from Jerome downwards, to think of Amos as an unlettered clown, and to trace his "rusticity" in the language of his book. To the unprejudiced judgment, however, the prophecy of Amos appears one of the best examples of pure Hebrew style. The language, the images, the grouping are alike admirable ; and the simplicity of the diction, obscured only in one or two passages by the fault of transcribers (iv. 3 ; ix. 1),[12] is a token, not of rusticity, but of perfect mastery over a language which, though unfit for the expression of abstract ideas, is unsurpassed as a vehicle for impassioned speech. To associate inferior culture with the simplicity and poverty of pastoral life is totally to mistake the conditions of Eastern society. At the courts of the Caliphs and their Emirs the rude Arabs of the desert were wont to appear without any feeling of awkwardness, and to surprise the courtiers by the finish of their impromptu verses, the fluent eloquence of their oratory, and the range of subjects on which they could speak with knowledge and discrimination.[13] Among the Hebrews, as in the Arabian desert, knowledge and oratory were not affairs of professional education, or dependent for their cultivation on wealth and social status. The sum of book learning was small; men of all ranks mingled with that Oriental freedom which is so foreign to our habits; shrewd observation, a memory retentive of traditional lore, and the faculty of original reflection took the place of laborious study as the ground of acknowledged intellectual pre-eminence. In Hebrew, as in Arabic, the best writing is an unaffected transcript of the best speaking; the literary merit of the book of Genesis, or the history of Elijah, like that of the *Kitáb el Aghány*, or of the Norse Sagas, is that they read as if they were told by word of mouth; and, in like manner, the prophecies of Amos, though evidently rearranged for publication, and probably shortened from their original spoken form, are excellent writing, because the prophet writes as he spoke, preserving all the effects of pointed and dramatic delivery, with that breath of lyrical fervour which lends a special charm to the highest Hebrew oratory. Semitic authorship never becomes self-conscious without losing its highest qualities, the old dramatic and lyric power gives way to artificial conceits and affected obscurities. Ezekiel is much more of a bookman than Amos, but his style is as much below that of the shepherd of Tekoa as the rhetorical prose of the later Arabs is below the simplicity of the ancient legends of the desert.

The writings of Amos, however, are not more conspicuous for literary merit than for width of human interest based on a range of historical observation very remarkable in the age and condition of the author. There is nothing provincial about our prophet; his vision embraces all the nations with whom the Hebrews had any converse ; he knows their history and geography with surprising exactness, and is, in fact, our only source for several particulars of great value to the historian of Semitic antiquity. The rapid survey of the nations immediately bordering on Israel—Aram - Damascus, Philistia, Edom, Ammon, Moab—is full of precise detail as to localities and events, with a keen appreciation of national character. He tells how the Philistines migrated from Caphtor, the Aramæans from Kir (ix. 7). His eye ranges southward along the caravan route from Gaza through the Arabian wilderness (i. 6), to the tropical lands of the Cushites (ix. 7). In the west he is familiar with the marvels of the swelling of the Nile (viii. 8 ; ix. 5), and in the distant Babylonian east he makes special mention of the city of Calneh (vi. 2, comp. Gen. x. 10). His acquaintance with the condition of Northern Israel is not that of a mere passing observer. He has followed with close and sympathetic attention the progress of the Syrian wars (i. 3, 13 ; iv. 10), and all the sufferings of the nation from pestilence, famine, and earthquake (chap. iv.). The luxury of the nobles of Samaria (vi. 3 *seq.*), the cruel sensuality of their wives (iv. 1 *seq.*), the miseries of the poor, and the rapacity of their tyrants (iii. 6 *seq.* ; viii. 4 *seq.*), the pilgrimages to Gilgal and Beersheba (v. 5 ; viii. 14), are painted from the life, as well as the ritual splendour and moral abominations of the sanctuary of Bethel. It is obviously illegitimate to ascribe this fulness of knowledge to special revelation ; Amos, we may justly conclude, was an observer of social and political life before he was a prophet, and his prophetic calling gave scope and use to his natural acquirements. The source of Amos's knowledge of nations and their affairs is of secondary consequence, but the critic will observe that his geographical horizon corresponds with those parts of Genesis x. which may plausibly be assigned to that oldest stratum of the Pentateuchal narrative which we have already spoken of as substantially representing the historical traditions of Israel at the time when he lived.[14] The exact details which he possesses as to Israel and immediately surrounding districts point rather to personal observation ; but long journeys are easy to one bred in the frugality of the wilderness, and either on military duty, such as all Hebrews were liable to, or in the service of trading caravans, the shepherd of Tekoa might naturally have found occasion to wander far from his home.

The prophetic work of Amos, forming, as it does, a mere episode in an obscure life, is sharply distinguished, not only from the professional activity of the prophetic guilds which lived by their trade, but from the lifelong vocation of men like Isaiah and Jeremiah, who received the divine call in their youth, and continued their work for many years, receiving new revelations from time to time in connection with the changing events among which they lived. Amos is a man of one prophecy. Once for all he has heard the thunder of Jehovah's shout, and seen the fair land of Canaan wither before it. The roar of the lion, to which he compares the voice that compelled him to prophecy, is the roar with which the beast springs upon its prey (comp. iii. 8 with iii. 4); it is not Israel's sin that brings him forward as a preacher of repentance; but the sound of near destruction encircling the land (iii. 11) constrains him to blow the alarm (iii. 6), and stir from their vain security the careless rioters who feel no concern for the ruin of Joseph (vi. 1 *seq.*).

We have seen from the words he addressed to Amaziah that Amos looked for the fall of Israel before its enemies within his own generation; in the figure of the roar of the lion, which is silent till it makes its spring, he seems to imply that the destroying power was already in motion. What this power was Amos expresses with the precision of a man who is not dealing with vague threats of judgment, but has the destroyer clearly before his eyes. "Behold, I raise up against you a nation, O house of Israel, and they shall crush you from the frontier of Hamath" on the north "to the brook of the Arabah," or brook of willows, a stream flowing into the Dead Sea, which separated Jeroboam's tributary Moab from the Edomites (vi. 14 ; comp. Isa. xv. 7). The seat of the invader is beyond Damascus, and thither Israel shall be carried captive (v. 27). It is plain, therefore, that Amos has Assyria in his mind, though he never mentions the name. It is no unknown danger that he foresees ; Assyria was fully within the range of his political horizon ; it was the power that had shattered Damascus by successive campaigns following at intervals since the days of Jehu, of which there is still some record on the monuments, one of them being dated B.C. 773, not long before the time when, so far as we can gather from the defective chronology of 2 Kings, Amos may be supposed to have preached at Bethel. When the power of Damascus was broken, there was no barrier between Assyria and the nations of Palestine ; in fact, the breathing space that made it possible for Jeroboam II. to restore the old borders of his kingdom was only granted because the Assyrians were occupied for a time in other directions, and apparently passed through a period of intestine disturbance which terminated with the accession of Tiglath

Pileser II. (B.C. 745). The danger, therefore, was visible to the most ordinary political insight, and what requires explanation is not so much that Amos was aware of it as that the rulers and people of Israel were so utterly blind to the impending doom. The explanation, however, is very clearly given by Amos himself. The source of the judicial blindness of his nation was want of knowledge of the true character of Jehovah, encouraging a false estimate of their own might. The old martial spirit of Israel had not died, and it had not lost its connection with religious faith and the inspiriting words of the prophets of the old school. Elisha was remembered as the best strength of the nation in the Syrian wars—" the chariots and horsemen of Israel" (2 Kings xiii. 14). The deliverance from Damascus was "Jehovah's victory" (*ibid.* ver. 17), and more recently the subjugation of Moab had been undertaken in accordance with the prophecy of Jonah. Never had Jehovah been more visibly on the side of His people. His worship was carried on with assiduous alacrity by a grateful nation. Sacrifices, tithes, thank-offerings, spontaneous oblations, streamed into the sanctuaries (Amos iv. 4 *seq.*). There was no question as to the stability of the newly-won prosperity, or the military power of the state (vi. 13). Israel was once more the nation victorious in Jehovah, whose help was the shield, whose pride was the sword (Deut. xxxiii. 29). Everything indeed was not yet accomplished, but the day of Jehovah's crowning victory was doubtless near at hand, and nothing remained but to pray for its speedy coming (Amos v. 18).[15]

We see, then, that it was not political blindness or religious indifference, but a profound and fanatical faith, that made Israel insensible to the danger so plainly looming on the horizon. Their trust in Jehovah's omnipotence was absolute, and absolute in a sense determined by the work of Elijah. There was no longer any disposition to dally with foreign gods. There was none like unto the God of Jeshurun, who rode on the heavens for His people's help. That that help could be refused, that the day of Jehovah could be darkness and not light, as Amos preached, that the distant thunder-roll of the advance of Assyria was the voice of an angry God drawing nigh to judge His people, were to them impossibilities.

Amos took a juster view of the political situation, because he had other thoughts of the purpose and character of Jehovah. In spite of their lofty conceptions of the majesty and victorious sovereignty of Jehovah, the mass of the people still thought of Him as exclusively concerned with the affairs of Israel. Jehovah had no other business on earth than to watch over His own nation. In giving victory and prosperity to Israel He was upholding His own interests, which ultimately centred in the maintenance of His dignity as a potentate feared by foreigners and holding splendid court at the sanctuaries where He received Israel's homage. This seems to us an extraordinary limitation of view on the part of men who recognised Jehovah as the Creator. But, in fact, heathen nations like the Assyrians and Phœnicians had also developed a doctrine of creation without ceasing to believe in strictly national deities. Jehovah, it must be remembered, was not first the Creator and then the God of Israel. His relation to Israel was the historical foundation of the religion of the Hebrews, and continued to be the central idea in all practical developments of their faith. To Amos, on the other hand, the doctrine of creation is full of practical meaning. "He that formed the mountains and created the wind, that declareth unto man what is His thought, that maketh the morning darkness and treadeth on the high places of the earth, Jehovah, the God of hosts is His name" (iv. 13). This supreme God cannot be thought of as having no interest or purpose beyond Israel. It was He that brought Israel out of Egypt, but it was He too who brought the Philistines from Caphtor and the Aramæans from Kir (ix. 7). Every movement of history is Jehovah's work; it is not Asshur but Jehovah who has created the Assyrian empire, and He has a purpose of His own in raising up its vast overwhelming strength and suspending it as a threat of imminent destruction over Israel and the surrounding nations. To Amos, therefore, the question is not what Jehovah as King of Israel will do for His people against the Assyrian, but what the Sovereign of the World designs to effect by the terrible instrument which He has created. The answer to this question is

the "secret of Jehovah," known only to Himself and
His prophet; and the key to the secret is Jehovah's
righteousness, and the sins, not of Israel alone, but of the
whole circle of nations from Damascus to Philistia, which
the advance of Assyria directly threatens. In the first
section of his book Amos surveys each of these nations
in succession, but in none does he find any ground to
think that Jehovah will divert the near calamity. The
doom is pronounced on each in the same solemn formula: "For three transgressions of Damascus and for
four"—that is, according to Hebrew idiom, for the multiplied transgressions of Damascus—"I will not turn it
aside." The "it" is a transparent aposiopesis, for the
picture of the terrible Assyrian is constantly before the
prophet's eyes.

Now, it is plain that the sins for which Damascus,
Ammon, Moab, and the rest are judged cannot be
offences against Jehovah as the national God of Israel.
Amos teaches that heathen nations are to be judged, not
because they do not worship Israel's God, but because
they have broken the laws of universal morality. The
crime of Damascus and Ammon is their inhuman treatment of the Gileadites; the Phœnicians and Philistines
are condemned for the barbarous slave-trade, fed by
kidnapping expeditions, of which Tyre and Gaza were
the emporia. In the case of Tyre this offence is aggravated by the fact that the captives were carried off in
defiance of the ancient brotherly alliance between Israel
and the Phœnician city; and in like manner the sin of

Edom is the unrelenting blood-feud with which he follows his brother of Judah. These are the common barbarities and treacheries of Semitic warfare; and it is as such that they are condemned, and not simply because in each case it is Israel that has suffered from them. Moab is equally condemned for a sin that has nothing to do with Israel, but was a breach of the most sacred feelings of ancient piety—the violation of the bones of the king of Edom.[16]

As Amos teaches that Jehovah's wrath falls on the heathen nations, not because they are heathen and do not worship Him, but because they have broken the universal laws of fidelity, kinship, and humanity, so He teaches that Israel must be judged and condemned by the same laws in spite of its assiduous Jehovah worship. The sinners of Israel thought they had a special security in their national relation to Jehovah, in the fact that He was worshipped only in their sanctuaries. Nay, says Amos, He will make no difference between you and the children of the Cushites, the remotest denizens of the habitable world (ix. 7). Jehovah is the high judge of appeal against man's injustice, and He is a judge who cannot be bribed or swayed by personal influences (iii. 2). "I hate, I despise your feast days; I take no pleasure in your solemn assemblies. Though ye offer me whole burnt-offerings with your gifts of homage I will take no pleasure in them, and I will not look upon your fatted thank-offerings.[17] Take away from Me the noise of thy songs; I will not hear the melody of thy viols. But let justice flow like waters and righteousness as an unfailing stream" (v. 21 seq.). Israel is impartially condemned by the same laws that condemn its neighbours, and for offences patent to the universal moral judgment, as appears particularly at iii. 9, where the grandees of Ashdod and Egypt are summoned to appear before Samaria and bear witness against the disorder and oppression that fill the city.

We see, then, that to Amos the forward march of the Assyrian is a manifestation of Jehovah's universal justice on principles applicable to all nations, the fall of Israel is but part of the universal ruin of the guilty states of Palestine. But, though Jehovah in revealing Himself to Israel does not divest Himself of His supreme character as the universal judge, He has relations with Israel which are shared by no other nation, and these relations involve special responsibilities, and give a peculiar significance to the development of His purpose as it regards His chosen people. It is on this special aspect of the impending judgment that Amos concentrates his attention after the general introduction in chapters i. and ii. of his prophecy. As the fall of Israel is part of the common overthrow of the Palestinian states, Judah and Ephraim are alike involved, Jerusalem as well as Samaria must fall before the destroyer (ii. 4, 5).[18] What Amos has to say to Israel is addressed to the whole family that Jehovah brought up out of Egypt (iii. 1), and they that are at ease in Zion are ranked with the self-confident princes of Samaria

(vi. 1). But the sin and fate of Judah are very briefly touched. The centre of national life was not in the petty state of Judah, but in the great Northern Kingdom. Though the restoration of the Davidic monarchy is the ideal of Amos (ix. 11), as in another sense it had been the ideal of the greatest monarchs of Ephraim (*supra*, p. 76), he does not treat the larger Israel of the north as a schismatic state. Revolt from the house of David and the sanctuary of Jerusalem is no part of Ephraim's sin, and the prophet addresses himself more directly to the house of Joseph, not because the sins of Joseph and of Judah were essentially distinct, but because the house of Joseph was still the foremost representative of Israel.

The fundamental law of Jehovah's special relations to Israel as they bear on the approach of the Assyrian is expressed in a verse which I have already cited. "You only have I known of all the families of the earth; therefore I will punish you for all your iniquities" (iii. 2). To know a man is to admit him to your acquaintance and converse. Jehovah has known Israel inasmuch as He has had personal dealings with it. The proof of this is not simply that Jehovah brought up His people from Egypt and gave them the land of Canaan (ii. 9, 10), for it was Jehovah who brought up the Philistines from Caphtor and the Aramæans from Kir (ix. 7) although they knew it not. But with Israel Jehovah held personal converse. "I raised up of your sons for prophets, and of your young men for Nazarites" (ii. 11). "The Lord Jehovah will not do anything without revealing His secret to His servants the prophets" (iii. 7). This is the real distinction between Israel and the nations—that in all that Jehovah did for His people in time past, in all that He is purposing against them now, He has been to them not an unknown power working by hidden laws, but a God who declares Himself to them personally, as a man does to a friend. And so the sin of Israel is not merely that it has broken through laws of right and wrong patent to all mankind, but that it has refused to listen to these laws as they were personally explained to it by the Judge Himself. They gave the Nazarites wine to drink, and commanded the prophets not to prophesy (ii. 12). And now every good gift of Jehovah to Israel is but a new reason for dreading His judgment, when Israel has refused to hear how He means them to use His gifts. The princes of Zion and Samaria are at ease and unconcerned. What! says the prophet, is not Israel the chief of nations? Is there from Calneh and Hamath to the Philistine border a single kingdom broader or better than your own? "Therefore ye shall go into captivity with the first that go captive" (vi. 1 seq.).

As the privilege of Israel is that all Jehovah's favours are accompanied and interpreted by His personal revelation, the special duty of Israel is to *seek Jehovah*. Thus saith Jehovah to the house of Israel, "Seek me and live" (v. 6). "To seek God" is the old Hebrew phrase for consulting His oracle, asking His help or decision in difficult affairs of conduct or law (Gen. xxv. 22; Exod. xviii. 15; 2 Kings iii. 11; viii. 8); and by ancient usage Jehovah was habitually sought at the sanctuary, though the phrase is equally applicable to consulting a prophet. In fact, the offerings of the sanctuary may be broadly divided into two classes, those which express homage and thanksgiving (*minhah, shélem*), and those which were presented in connection with some request or inquiry. In the latter class the burnt-offering is most conspicuous. But Amos refuses to acknowledge this way of seeking God. "Seek ye not Bethel, and come not unto Gilgal, and pass not over the border to Beersheba; for Gilgal shall go captive, and Bethel shall come to nought. Seek Jehovah, and live; lest He break forth like fire in the house of Jacob, and it devour and there be none to quench it in Bethel" (v. 5, 6). The multiplication of gifts and offerings is but multiplication of sin; the people love to do these things, but Jehovah answers them only by famine, blasting, and war (chap. iv.). He is not to be found by sacrifice, for in it He takes no pleasure; what Jehovah requires of them that seek Him is the practice of civil righteousness.

When Amos represents the national worship of Israel as positively sinful, he does so mainly because it was so conducted as to afford a positive encouragement to the injustice, the sensuality, the barbarous treatment of the poor, to which he recurs again and again as the cardinal sins of the nation. The religion of Israel had become a religion for the rich, the priests and the nobles were linked together in unrighteousness, and the most flagrant scenes of immorality and oppression were seen at the sacred courts (ii. 7, 8). Amos never speaks of the golden calves as the sin of the northern sanctuaries, and he has only one or two allusions to the worship of false gods or idolatrous symbols. The Guilt of Samaria, spoken of as a concrete object in viii. 14, is probably the Ashera of 2 Kings xiii. 6, which had a connection with the moral impurities of Canaanite religion; and in Amos v. 26 there is a very obscure allusion to the worship of star-gods, which from the connection cannot have been a rival service to that of Jehovah, but probably attached itself in a subordinate way to the offices of His sanctuary.[19] Once, and only once, in speaking of leavened bread as burned on the altar, does the prophet appear to touch on a ritual departure, of Canaanite character and presumably Dionysiac significance, from the ancient ritual of Exod. xxiii. 18.[20] But these points are merely touched in passing. The whole ritual service is to Amos a thing without importance in itself. The Israelites offered no sacrifice in the wilderness, and yet Jehovah was never nearer to them than then (v. 25 compared with ii. 10). The judgment of Jehovah begins at the sanctuary (ix. 1 *seq.*; iii. 14), because the sanctuaries are the centre of Israel's religious life and so also of its moral corruption. The palace and the temple stood side by side (vii. 13), and they fall together (iii. 14, 15; vii. 9) in the common overthrow of the state and its religion.

If we ask what Amos desired to set in the place of the system he so utterly condemns, the answer is apparently very meagre. He has no new scheme of church and state to propose—only this, that Jehovah desires righteousness and not sacrifice. Amos, in fact, is neither a statesman nor a religious legislator ; he has received a message from Jehovah, and his duty is exhausted in delivering it. Till this message is received and taken to heart no project of reformation can avail ; the first thing that Israel must learn is the plain connection between its present sin and the danger that looms on its horizon. If two men walk together, says Amos, you know that they have an understanding ; if the lion roars he has prey within his reach ; if the springe flies up from the ground, there is something in the noose ; if the springe catches the bird it must have been rightly set (iii. 3 *seq*.). And so, let Israel be assured, the advance of Assyria and the sin of Israel hang together in Jehovah's purpose, and the man who knows the secret of Jehovah's righteousness cannot doubt that the approaching destruction is a sentence on the nation's guilt. To produce conviction of sin by an appeal to the universal conscience, to the known nature of Jehovah, above all to the already visible shadow of coming events that prove the justice of the prophetic argument, is the great purpose of the prophet's preaching.

That that judgment will be averted by the repentance of those who rule the affairs of the nation Amos has no hope. The doom of the kingdom is inevitable, and the sword of Jehovah shall pursue the sinners even in flight and captivity till the last of them has perished. What Amos means by the total destruction of the sinners of Jehovah's people (ix. 1-10) is of course to be understood from his view of Israel's sin as consisting essentially in social offences inconsistent with national righteousness. He does not mean by the word "sinner" the same thing as modern theology does. The sinners of Israel are the corrupt rulers and their associates, the unjust and sensual oppressors, the men who have no regard to civil righteousness. The total destruction of these is the first condition of Israel's restoration, for even in judgment Jehovah has not cast off His people, and, though He could easily destroy the land by natural agencies or burn up the guilty nation in a sea of flame (vii. 1 *seq.*), He chooses another course, and carries His people into captivity, that He may sift them while they wander through the nations as corn is sifted in a sieve, without one sound grain falling to the ground. And so when all the sinners are consumed His hand will build up a new Israel as in the days of the first kingdom. The fallen tent of David shall be restored, and the Hebrews shall again rule over all those vassal nations that once were Jehovah's tributaries. Then the land inhabited by a nation purged of transgressors shall flow with milk and wine. "And I will restore the prosperity of My people Israel, and they shall build waste cities and dwell therein, and plant vineyards and drink the wine thereof, and make gardens and eat the fruit of them. And I will plant them upon their land, and they shall no more be plucked out of their land which I give unto them, saith Jehovah thy God."

These are the closing words of the prophecy of Amos, and here we must pause for the present, reserving the remarks which they suggest till we can compare them with the picture of the restoration of Israel set forth a little later by his immediate successor Hosea.

LECTURE IV.

HOSEA AND THE FALL OF EPHRAIM.

THE prophetic work of Amos, which we examined in last Lecture, falls entirely within the prosperous reign of Jeroboam II. Hosea began to prophesy in the same reign, as appears not only from the title of his book, but from the contents of the first two chapters. "Yet a little while," says Jehovah in Hosea i. 4, "and I will punish the house of Jehu for the bloodshed of Jezreel"—that is, for the slaying of the seed of Ahab—"and will cause to cease the kingdom of the house of Israel." But Hosea continued his ministry after the prediction of judgment on the descendants of Jehu had been fulfilled, and the latter part of his book contains unmistakable references to the state of anarchy into which the Northern Kingdom fell on the extinction of the last great dynasty that occupied the throne of Samaria. Before we address ourselves, therefore, to the study of his life and prophecies it will be convenient to take a rapid survey of the history of Ephraim after the death of Jeroboam, and in order to gain a clear view of the sequence of events it is indispensable to say a few words on the tangled chronology of the period, which is usually interpreted in a way that does no small violence to the Biblical narrative.[1]

According to the chronology which has passed into general currency from the *Annals* of Archbishop Ussher, and is represented on the margins of most English Bibles, the death of Jeroboam was followed by an interregnum of eleven years, after which his son Zachariah reigned for six months, when he was slain by Shallum. The Bible knows nothing of this interregnum, but on the contrary informs us in the usual way that Zachariah reigned in his father's stead (2 Kings xiv. 29). The coronation of Zachariah must in fact have followed as a matter of course, since his father died in peaceable possession of the throne. Even if revolt broke out immediately on this event, the party which sided with the old dynasty would at once recognise the legal heir as king, and, as it is admitted that Zachariah did mount the throne, if only for six months, we cannot doubt that he would date his accession from the time when he became king *de jure*. And apart from this it is quite inconceivable that an interregnum of eleven years, with the stirring incidents inseparable from a prolonged period of civil war, could be passed over in absolute silence by the Biblical narrative.

Whence, then, do Archbishop Ussher and other chronologists derive their eleven years of interregnum? From the death of Solomon to the fall of Samaria the history of the books of Kings forms a double line.

Dates are determined in the one line by years of the kings of Ephraim, in the other by years of the kings of Judah, and as the author of our present book of Kings used separate sources for the history of the two kingdoms we must assume, at all events provisionally, that the two lines of chronology were originally distinct. In point of fact they are not merely distinct, but of unequal length, as may be shown by the following simple calculation. According to the Judæan line there are just 480 years from the founding of Solomon's temple to the return from Babylonian exile, B.C. 535. According to the Northern reckoning the fall of Samaria took place in the 241st year from the revolt against Jeroboam, or in the 278th year of the temple. Counting then up the Judæan line and down the other we get for the date of the fall of Samaria B.C. 737. On the other hand, if we start from the statement of 2 Kings xviii. 9, that Samaria fell in the sixth year of Hezekiah, remembering that he reigned twenty-nine years in all, and that his death fell 160 years before the restoration, we get for the date of Samaria's fall B.C. 719. In other words, the Judæan line is about twenty years longer than the Northern one. It is in order to get over this discrepancy without admitting any error in the two sets of numbers that chronologists assume the long interregnum after Jeroboam II.'s death, and another period of anarchy somewhat later.[2] But in point of fact to invent an interregnum of which the history does not speak is quite as serious a liberty with the text as

to suppose that there is some error in the numbers.
On the other hand, to suppose that the numbers have
been corrupted in transmission, and to introduce arbitrary corrections—as was done, for example, by the late
George Smith, who gives Jeroboam II. fifty-one years
instead of forty-one, and Pekah thirty instead of twenty
—is thoroughly unsatisfactory. The facts justify us in
saying that the chronology as we have it cannot be right;
but they do not justify us in amending it at our own
hand and by purely conjectural methods. And when
we look at the thing more closely we are led to ask,
not whether this or that particular number is corrupt,
but whether the early Hebrews had a precise chronology
dating every event by the years of the reigning king.
As the history now stands we have an exact date for the
accession of each monarch, but events happening in the
course of a reign are habitually undated. No date of
the Northern history prior to the fall of Samaria is given
by the year of the reigning king of Ephraim, and in
the history of Judah, till the time of Jeremiah, almost
all events, dated by years of the kings of Jerusalem,
have reference to the affairs of the temple (1 Kings vi.
37, 38; xiv. 25, 26; 2 Kings xii. 6; xviii. 13 *seq.*; xxii.
3; xxiii. 23). In the temple archives, therefore, a systematic record of dates seems to have been kept, but the
system did not extend to general affairs; Amos, for
example, does not date his prophecy by the year of
King Uzziah, but says that it was "two years before
the earthquake." Where there is no precise system by

which events are regularly dated, a reckoning by round numbers can hardly be avoided; and on such a system the most natural unit in estimating long periods is not the year but a round period of years taken to represent a generation. Traces of this way of counting are common enough in early history, and among the Hebrews the unit was taken at forty years—forty, in fact, being a common round number in antiquity.[3] The whole early chronology of the Hebrews is measured by this unit. Forty, twenty, and eighty are constantly-recurring numbers; the period from the Exodus to the founding of the temple is 480 years, or twelve forties, and an equal period extends from the latter event to the return from exile, while 240 years is the duration of the Northern Kingdom.

But again, when we analyse the 480 of the Judæan genealogy and the 240 of the Northern Kingdom, we find that each is naturally divided into three equal parts, and in each case the commencement of the second third is given by a date which is not due to the redactor of the books of Kings, but stood in the original sources from which he worked. The second third of the Judæan line begins with the year of Joash's reforms in the temple, and ends with the death of Hezekiah. In the Northern line the second period of 80 years precisely corresponds with the duration of the Syrian wars, which began four years before the death of Ahab. These cannot be mere coincidences; they are part of a system, and, when taken with other details which cannot be dwelt on here, they seem to show that the chronology on each line was constructed on the method of genealogies, and reduced to years by what a mathematician might call a method of interpolation,—that is, by starting with certain fixed dates, which were taken as the great divisions of the scheme, and then filling up the intervals in an approximate way from a rough knowledge of the longer or shorter duration of the several reigns. The scheme as a whole, at least as regards Judah, appears to have been worked out after the Exile, since it reckons back from the date of the return. It has also been shown by a critical argument, supported by observation of the Septuagint text, that the 480 years from the Exodus to the temple were added to the text of 1 Kings vi. after the Exile. Of course a chronology framed in this way can make no claim to be absolutely exact, and it ceases to be surprising that the two lines for Ephraim and Judah are not precisely correspondent. The whole body of dates except the few that are derived from the original sources are to be regarded as nothing more than an approximate and partly conjectural reconstruction of the chronology, which we cannot hope to render more exact without the help of records lying outside of the Bible.

Of late years, however, such external aid has turned up in the records of the Assyrian kings. Unlike the Hebrews, the Assyrians were exact chronologers. They had considerable astronomical knowledge, and thus had learned to keep a precise record of years. As Roman chronology is based on the list of consuls, or as the

Athenians named each year after the so-called Archon Eponymus, so in Assyria there was a high official appointed annually who gave his name to his year of office. The list of these eponyms or date-giving officials has fortunately been preserved in a number of copies, and, as a note of royal expeditions and the like stands opposite each name, it forms, in conjunction with other monuments, a complete key to Assyrian chronology, the accuracy of which has been verified by numerous tests, on which it is unnecessary to enlarge. The lower part of the Eponym Canon runs parallel with the Canon of Ptolemy, which is one of the chief bases of ancient chronology, and in this way it becomes possible to express the Assyrian dates with reference to the Christian era.

Now the Assyrian annals mention Jehu as paying tribute to Shalmaneser B.C. 842, and Menahem is mentioned B.C. 738, 104 years later. It can be shown that this tribute of Jehu must have fallen in one of the first years of his reign, and as the sum of the reigns from Jehu to Menahem inclusive is just 112 years, according to the Bible, the Assyrian records confirm the general accuracy of the Northern line of chronology for this period, and completely justify us in our refusal to allow the eleven years' interregnum of the Ussherian chronology. It ought, however, to be observed that these results do not afford any guarantee that the details of the Bible chronology, even in Northern Israel, are more than approximate, or weaken the force of the argument that the original reckoning was in round numbers. For there is every reason to believe that the old history of the Northern prophets, from which the editor of the books of Kings worked, gave eighty years for the Syrian wars; and, with this datum and a generation of prosperity under Jeroboam II., the editor could not fail to give a tolerably correct estimate of the length of the period in question. For the period between Menahem and the fall of Samaria the Biblical chronologer seems to have had less full guidance from ancient sources. For, according to the monuments, Samaria was besieged *cir.* B.C. 722, so that the reigns of the last three kings of Samaria, which the Bible estimates at thirty-one years, must be reduced by one half.[4] The practical result of this inquiry is that the decline of Israel, after the death of Jeroboam, was much more rapid than appears from the usual chronology, and instead of occupying sixty years to the fall of Samaria, was really complete in less than half that time. This rapid descent from the prosperity of the days of Jeroboam throws a fresh light on the predictions of speedy destruction given by Amos and Hosea.

Let us now, with the aid of the amended chronology, take a rapid view of the successive steps in the fall of the kingdom of Samaria. On the death of Jeroboam II., his son Zachariah succeeded to the throne, but after six months lost his kingdom and his life in the conspiracy of Shallum. The assassin assumed the royal dignity, but was not able to maintain it, for he was immediately attacked by Menahem, and perished in turn. Menahem established himself on the throne after a ferocious struggle (2 Kings xv. 16). The success, however, was not due to his own prowess, but to the assistance of Pul, king of Assyria, to whom he gave a thousand talents, raised by a tax on the great men of the country, "that his hand might be with him to confirm the kingdom in his hand" (2 Kings xv. 19). Menahem reigned, therefore, as an Assyrian vassal, and so within a few months after Jeroboam's death his dynasty was extinguished, and the foe, whose approach Amos foresaw, had laid his strong hand on Israel, never again to relax his grasp. On the death of Menahem, the flame of civil war broke out once more. His son Pekahiah was assassinated after a short reign, and the throne was occupied by a military adventurer named Pekah, supported by a band of Gileadites. Pekah allied himself with Rezin of Damascus, and formed the project of dethroning Ahaz, king of Judah. Ahaz appealed to Tiglath Pileser, who marched westward, led the Damascenes captive, as Amos had foretold, and also depopulated Gilead and Galilee. In this disastrous war Pekah had lost his prestige, and, though the Assyrians seem to have left him in power, he was presently attacked and slain by Hoshea, the son of Elah. He in turn had to reckon with the Assyrian, and had to pay a subsidy and yearly tribute as the price of his throne. But Hoshea was eager to cast off the yoke, and sought help from the king of Egypt, who had begun to bid against Assyria for the lordship of the mountains of Canaan, which formed the natural barrier between the great powers of the Nile and the Tigris. This defection sealed the doom of Samaria. The Assyrians again invaded the land; after a prolonged and desperate resistance, the capital was taken, and the Israelites were carried captive to the far East, new populations being brought from Babylon and other districts to take their place. It appears from the Assyrian monuments that a vassal kingdom existed in Samaria after this deportation, which no doubt was only partial, and it is not improbable that it was ruled by princes of Hebrew race for half a century longer;*⁵ while we know that Jehovah worship did not altogether cease in the land, and was even accepted in a corrupt form by the new colonists (2 Kings xvii. 24 *seq.*; 2 Kings xxiii. 15; Jer. xli. 5). But the distinctive character of the nation was lost; such Hebrews as remained in their old land became mixed with their heathen neighbours, and ceased to have any share in the further history of Israel and Israel's religion. When Josiah destroyed the ancient high places of the Northern Kingdom he slew their priests, whereas the priests of Judæan sanctuaries were provided for at Jerusalem. It is plain from this that he regarded the worship of the Northern sanctuaries as purely heathenish (comp. 2 Kings xxiii. 20 with ver. 5), and it was only in much later times that the mixed population of Samaria became possessed of the Pentateuch, and set up a worship on Mount Gerizim in imitation of the ritual of the second temple. We have no reason to

* See page 439.

think that the captive Ephraimites were more able to retain their distinctive character than their brethren who remained in Palestine. The problem of the lost tribes, which has so much attraction for some speculators, is a purely fanciful one. The people whom Hosea and Amos describe were not fitted to maintain themselves apart from the heathen among whom they dwelt. Scattered among strange nations, they accepted the service of strange gods (Deut. xxviii. 64), and, losing their distinctive religion, lost also their distinctive existence. The further history of the people of Jehovah is transferred to the house of Judah, and with the fall of Samaria Northern Israel ceases to have any part in the progress of revelation.

Hosea, or Hoshea, as the name should rather be written, is the last prophet of Ephraim.[6] Unlike Amos, he was himself a subject of the Northern Kingdom, as appears from the whole tenor of his book, and especially from vii. 5, where the monarch of Samaria is called "our king." Like Amos, he is mainly concerned with the sins and calamities of the house of Joseph; but, while Amos speaks from observation which, with all its closeness, is that of an outsider, whose personal life lay far from the tumults and oppressions of the Northern capital, Hosea views the state of the kingdom from within, and his book is marked by a tone of deep pathos, akin to that of Jeremiah, and expressive of the tragic isolation of the prophet's position in a society corrupt to the very core and visibly hastening towards dissolution.

Amos could deliver his divine message and withdraw from the turmoil of Samaria's guilty cities to the silent pastures of the wilderness; but the whole life of Hosea was bound up with the nation whose sins he condemned and whose ruin he foresaw. For him there was no escape from the scenes of horror that defiled his native land, and the anguish that expresses itself in every page of his prophecy is the distress of a pure and gentle soul, linked by the closest ties of family affection and national feeling to the sinners who were hurrying Israel onwards to the doom he saw so clearly, but of which they refused to hear. And so while the work of Amos was completed in a single brief mission, the prophecies of Hosea extend over a series of terrible years. The first two chapters of his book are dated from the reign of Jeroboam, the gala-days of the nation (ii. 13), when the feast-days, the new moons, and the Sabbaths still ran their joyous round, and the land was rich in corn and wine and oil, in store of silver and gold (ii. 8). But the later chapters of the prophecy speak of quite other times, of sickness in the state which its leaders vainly sought to heal by invoking the help of the "warlike king" [A.V. King Jareb] of Assyria (v. 13), of civil wars and conspiracies, of the assassination of monarchs, of new dynasties set up without Jehovah's counsel, and powerless to better the condition of the nation (vii. 7; viii. 4), of a universal reign of perjury and fraud, of violence and bloodshed (iv. 1, 2). These descriptions carry us into the evil times that opened with the fall of the house of Jehu; but the actual captivity of Israel is still in the future (xiii. 16): even in the closing chapter of his book Hosea addresses a nation which has not come to open breach with the Assyrians, but cherishes the vain hope of deliverance through their help (xiv. 3). Gilead and Galilee, which were depopulated by Tiglath-Pileser in his expedition against Pekah (B.C. 734), are repeatedly referred to as an integral part of the kingdom (v. 1; vi. 8; xii. 11), and it is therefore probable that the work of Hosea was ended before that event, and that the prophet was spared the crowning sorrow of seeing with his own eyes the fulfilment of the doom of his nation.[7]

There is no reason to believe that Hosea, any more than Amos, was connected with the recognised prophetic societies, or ever received such outward adoption to office as was given to Elisha. At chapter iv. 5 he comprises priest and prophet in one condemnation. Israel is undone for lack of knowledge, for the priests whose office it was to teach it have rejected the knowledge of Jehovah, and He in turn will reject them from their priesthood. They shall fall, and the prophet shall fall with them in the night, their children shall be forgotten of Jehovah, and their whole stock shall perish.[8] Thus Hosea, no less than Amos, places himself in direct opposition to all the leaders of the religious life of his nation, and like his Judæan compeer he had doubtless to reckon with their hostility. "As for the prophet," he complains, "a fowler's snare is in all his ways, and enmity in the house of his God" (ix. 8). To discharge his ministry year after year amidst such opposition was a far harder task than was appointed to Amos. Even Amos was constrained to exclaim that in times so evil the part of a prudent man was to hold his peace (Amos v. 13). But Amos at least could shake the dust off his feet and return to his kindred and his home; Hosea was a stranger among his own people, oppressed by continual contact with their sin, lacerated at heart by the bitterness of their enmity, till his reason seemed ready to give way under the trial. "The days of visitation are come, the days of recompense are come, Israel shall know it; the prophet is a fool, the man of the spirit is mad for the multitude of thine iniquity and the great hatred" (ix. 7). The passionate anguish that breathes in these words gives its colour to the whole book of Hosea's prophecies. His language and the movement of his thoughts are far removed from the simplicity and self-control which characterise the prophecy of Amos. Indignation and sorrow, tenderness and severity, faith in the sovereignty of Jehovah's love, and a despairing sense of Israel's infidelity are woven together in a sequence which has no logical plan, but is determined by the battle and alternate victory of contending emotions; and the swift transitions, the fragmentary unbalanced utterance, the half-developed allusions, that make his prophecy so difficult to the commentator, express the agony of this inward conflict. Hosea, above all other prophets, is a man of deep affections, of a gentle poetic nature. His heart is too true and tender to snap the bonds of country and kindred, or mingle aught of personal bitterness with the severity of Jehovah's words. Alone in the midst of a nation that knows not Jehovah, without disciple or friend, without the solace of domestic affection—for even his home, as we shall presently see, was full of shame and sorrow—he yet clings to Israel with inextinguishable love. The doom which he proclaims against his people is the doom of all that is dearest to him on earth; his heart is ready to break with sorrow, his very reason totters under the awful vision of judgment, his whole prophecy is a long cry of anguish, as again and again he renews his appeal to the heedless nation that is running headlong to destruction. But it is all in vain. The weary years roll on, the signs of Israel's dissolution thicken, and still his words find no audience. Like a silly dove fluttering in the toils, Ephraim turns now to Assyria, now to Egypt, " but they return not to Jehovah their God, and seek not Him for all this." Still the prophet stands alone in his recognition of the true cause of the multiplied distresses of his nation, and still it is his task to preach repentance to deaf ears, to declare a judgment in which only himself believes. And now the Assyrian is at hand, sweeping over Canaan like a fatal sirocco. "An east wind shall come, the breath of Jehovah ascending from the wilderness, and his spring shall become dry and his fountain shall be dried up; He shall spoil the treasure of all precious jewels. Samaria shall be desolate, for she hath rebelled against her God : they shall fall by the sword : their infants shall be dashed in pieces, and their women with child shall be ripped up " (xiii. 15).

And yet, when all is lost, the prophet's love for guilty and fallen Israel forbids him to despair. For that love is no mere earthly affection. It is Jehovah's love for His erring people that speaks through Hosea's soul. The heart of the prophet beats responsive to the heart of Him who loved Israel when he was a child and called His son out of Egypt. " How can I give thee up, Ephraim ? How can I cast thee away, Israel ? My heart burns within Me, My compassion is all kindled. I will not execute the fierceness of My wrath; I will not turn to destroy thee ; for I am God and not man, the Holy One in the midst of thee" (xi. 8). How this invincible love shall triumph even in the utter fall of the nation Hosea does not explain. But that it will triumph he cannot doubt. In the extremity of judgment Jehovah will yet work repentance and salvation, and from the death-knell of Samaria the accents of hope and promise swell forth in pure and strong cadence in the last chapter of the prophecy, out of a heart which has found its rest with God from all the troubles of a stormy life. " I will heal their backsliding, I will love them freely : for Mine anger is turned away from him. I will be as the dew to Israel : he shall bud forth as the lily and strike his roots as Lebanon. . . . Who is wise, and he shall understand these things? prudent, and he shall know them? For the ways of Jehovah are right, and the just shall walk in them; but the transgressors shall fall therein."

Hosea is a man of emotion rather than of logic, a poet rather than a preacher, and the unity of his book is maintained through the sudden transitions and swift revulsions of feeling characteristic of his style, not by a well-planned symmetry of argument such as we find in Amos, but by a constant undercurrent of faith in the identity of Jehovah's love to Israel with that pure and unselfish affection which binds the prophet himself to his guilty and fallen nation. Jehovah is God and not man, the Holy One in the midst of Israel. But this does not mean that the heart of Jehovah has no likeness to that of man. His righteousness is not an impersonal unlovable thing with which His reasonable creatures can have no fellowship, and which they cannot hope to comprehend. Where Amos says that Jehovah knows Israel, Hosea desires that Israel should *know Jehovah* (ii. 20; iv. 1, 6; vi. 3; viii. 2; xiii. 4). And this knowledge is no mere act of the intellect; to know Jehovah is to know Him as a tender Father, who taught Ephraim to walk, holding them by their arms, who drew them to Himself with human cords, with bands of love (xi. 1 *seq.*). In chap. vi. 6 the knowledge of God is explained in a parallel clause, not by "mercy," as the Authorised Version renders it, but by a word (*hésed*)[9] corresponding to the Latin *pietas*, or dutiful love, as it shows itself in acts of kindliness and loyal affection. It is quite characteristic of the difference between the two prophets, that in Amos this word *hésed* or kindness never occurs, while in Hosea it not only expresses the right attitude of man to God, but kindness and truth, kindness and justice, are the sum of moral duty (iv. 1; x. 12; xii. 6). Amos in such a case would speak of justice alone; his analysis of right and wrong pierces less deeply into the springs of human action. For the kindness of which Hosea speaks is no theological technicality; it is a word of common life used of all those acts, going beyond the mere norm of forensic righteousness, which acknowledge that those who are linked together by the bonds of personal affection or of social unity owe to one another more than can be expressed in the forms of legal obligation.

In primitive society, where every stranger is an enemy, the whole conception of duties of humanity is framed within the narrow circle of the family or the tribe; relations of love are either identical with those of kinship or are conceived as resting on a covenant. "Thou shalt show kindness to thy servant," says David, "for thou hast brought thy servant into a covenant of Jehovah with thee." And so in Hosea the conception of a relation of love and kindness between man and God goes side by side with the conception of Jehovah's covenant with Israel (vi. 7; viii. 1). Jehovah and Israel are united by a bond of moral obligation,—not a mere compact on legal terms, a covenant of works, as dogmatic theology would express it, but a bond of piety—of fatherly affection on the one hand, and loyal obedience on the other. Jehovah and Israel form as it were one community, and *ḥésed* is the bond by which the whole community is knit together. It is not necessary to distinguish Jehovah's *ḥésed* to Israel which we would term his grace, Israel's duty of *ḥésed* to Jehovah which we would call piety, and the relation of *ḥésed* between man and man which embraces the duties of love and mutual consideration. To the Hebrew mind these three are essentially one, and all are comprised in the same covenant. Loyalty and kindness between man and man are not duties inferred from Israel's relation to Jehovah, they are parts of that relation; love to Jehovah and love to one's brethren in Jehovah's house are identical (compare iv. 1 with vi. 4, 6). To Hosea, as to Amos, justice and the obligations of civil righteousness are still the chief sphere within which the right knowledge of Jehovah and due regard to His covenant are tested. Where religion has a national form, and especially in such a state of society as both prophets deal with, that is necessary; but Hosea refers these obligations to a deeper source. Israel is not only the dominion but the family of Jehovah, and the fatherhood of God takes the place of his kingly righteousness as the fundamental idea of Israel's religion. Jehovah is God and not man, but the meaning of this is that His love is sovereign, pure, unselfish, free from all impatience and all variableness as the love of an earthly father can never be.

This fundamental thought of Hosea, that the relation between Jehovah and Israel is a relation of love and of such duties as flow from love, gives his whole teaching a very different colour from that of Amos. Amos, as we saw, begins by looking on Jehovah as the Creator and God of the universe, who dispenses the lot of all nations and vindicates the laws of universal righteousness over the whole earth ; and, when he proceeds to concentrate attention on his own people, the prophet still keeps the larger point of view before the mind of his hearers, and treats the sin and judgment of Israel as a particular case under the general laws of Divine government, complicated by the circumstance that Jehovah knows Israel and has personal communications with it in which no other nation shares. Hosea has no such universal starting-point ; he deals with the subject not from the outside inwards but from the heart outwards. Jehovah's love to His own is the deepest thing in religion, and every problem of faith centres in it. To both prophets the distinction which we are wont to draw between religious and moral duties is unknown ; yet it would not be unfair to say in modern language that Amos bases religion on morality, while Hosea deduces morality from religion. The two men are types of a contrast which runs through the whole history of religious thought and life down to our own days. The religious world has always been divided into men who look at the questions of faith from the standpoint of universal ethics, and men by whom moral truths are habitually approached from a personal sense of the grace of God. Too frequently this diversity of standpoint has led to an antagonism of parties in the Church. Men of the type of Amos are condemned as rationalists and cold moderates; or, on the other hand, the school of Hosea are looked upon as enthusiasts and unpractical mystics. But Jehovah chose His prophets from men of both types, and preached the same lesson to Israel through both.

To Amos and Hosea alike the true standard of religious life is the standard of conduct. The state of the nation before its God is judged by its actions; and the prevalence of immorality, oppression, and crime is the clearest proof that Israel has departed from Jehovah. The analysis of Amos stops at this point; he does not seek into the hidden springs of Israel's sin, but simply says, Without a return to civil righteousness, which you are daily violating, you can find no acceptance before Jehovah. Hosea, on the contrary, with his guiding principle of a relation of love between Jehovah and Israel, pierces beneath the visible conduct of the nation to the disposition that underlies it. Amos had said, Cease your ritual service, and do judgment and justice (Amos v. 24); Hosea says, " I desire love and not sacrifice, and knowledge of God rather than burnt offerings" (Hosea vi. 6). Amos judges the moral offences of Israel as breaches of universal law aggravated by the possession of special privileges; Hosea judges them as proofs of a heart not true to Jehovah, out of sympathy with His character, and ungrateful to His love. Accordingly, while Amos deals mainly with Israel as a state, Hosea habitually thinks of Ephraim as a moral individual, and goes back again and again to the history of the nation, treating it as the history of a person, and following its relations to Jehovah from the days of the patriarch Jacob (xii. 2, 3, 12), through the deliverance from Egypt onwards (xii. 13 ; xi. 1 *seq*.). He dwells with special interest on the first love of Jehovah to His people when He found Israel like grapes in the wilderness (ix. 10), when He knew them in the thirsty desert (xiii. 5), before the innocence of the nation's childhood was stained with the guilt of Baal-peor, and its early love had vanished like the dew of dawn, or like the light clouds which hang on the mountains of Palestine in the early morning and dissolve as the sun gets high (vi. 4). Hosea's allusions to the past history of Israel are introduced in unexpected ways, and are often difficult to understand. Sometimes he seems to refer to narratives which we no longer possess in the same form (ix. 9 ; x. 9) ; but their general drift is always the same—to vindicate the patient consistent love of Jehovah to His nation, and to display Ephraim's sin as a lifelong course of spurned privileges and slighted love. It is this thought of the personal continuity of Israel's relations to Jehovah that leads the prophet to speak of God's dealings with Jacob ; for Jacob is, in fact, the nation summed up in the person of its ancestor (comp. Heb. vii. 10). And so the whole history, from the days of the patriarchs downwards, is the history of a single unchanging affection, always acting on the same principles, so that each fact of the past is at the same time a symbol of the present (ix. 9), or a prophecy of the future (ii. 15 ; compare Josh. vii. 24). It is worth remembering, in connection with Hosea's frequent use of the early history, that in last Lecture we saw reason to believe that the sanctuaries of Northern Israel, to which he belonged, were the special home of the greater part of the patriarchal history, as it is still told in the book of Genesis ; and it is hardly disputable that some episodes in that history personify the stock of Israel or individual tribes, and so treat them as moral individuals, much in the same way in which Hosea treats Ephraim. The blessing of Jacob ascribes a personal character to Reuben, Levi, and Simeon, which is the character of the tribes, not of individual sons of Jacob, and refers to narratives which there are the very strongest reasons for regarding as allegories of historical events subsequent to the settlement of the Hebrews in Canaan. This consideration enables us to see that the allegorical treatment of Jehovah's relations to Israel in the book of Hosea would appear much less strange and puzzling to his contemporaries than it does to a modern reader. Their current habits of thought and expression made this way of teaching easy and natural.[10]

Since Hosea everywhere concentrates his attention on the personal attitude and disposition of Ephraim towards Jehovah, as constituting the essence of the national sin, he is led to look at the sins of the people's worship much more closely than Amos does. Amos contents himself with noting the acts of injustice and immorality that were done in the name of religion, and with urging that no ritual service can be acceptable to Jehovah where civil righteousness is forgotten. Beyond this he shows a degree of indifference to all practices of social worship which is not uncharacteristic of an inhabitant of the desert. But when Israel's relation to Jehovah is conceived as a personal relation, the intercourse of Jehovah with His people at the sanctuary naturally assumes a much larger significance. Acts of worship are the direct embodiment of the attitude and feelings of the worshipper towards his God, and in them Hosea finds the plainest exhibition of Ephraim's unfaithfulness. It is necessary to look somewhat closely at the way in which this point is developed. In speaking of Ephraim's connection with Jehovah in the language of human relationship, it was open to the prophet to make use of various analogies. Jehovah was Israel's King, but this image did not adapt itself to his idea.[11] He required a more personal relation, such as is supplied by the analogy of domestic life. The idea of a family relation between Jehovah and Israel appears in the book of Hosea in two forms. On the one hand Ephraim is Jehovah's son (xi. 1), and this is the predominant figure in the latter part of the book. But in the first three chapters, which present the prophet's allegory in its most complete and original form, the nation or land of Israel (i. 2; ii. 13) appears as Jehovah's spouse. The two figures are intimately connected, indeed in chapter i. they occur combined into a single parable. For, according to a common Hebrew figure, a land or city is the mother of its inhabitants, or, by a slight variation of the symbolism, the stock of a family or clan is personified as the mother of the members of the clan (2 Sam. xx. 19; Ezek. xix. 2; Hosea iv. 5). The mother is the ideal unity of land and nation, having for her children the actual members of the nation as they exist at any particular time. Jehovah, therefore, is at once the father of His people, and the husband of their ideal mother. We are not to suppose that Hosea invented either form of this image. That the deity is the father of his worshippers, that the tribe springs from the stock of the tribal god, who is worshipped as the progenitor of his people, is a common conception in heathenism (comp. Acts xvii. 28). In Num. xxi. 29 the Moabites are called the sons and daughters of Chemosh, and even Malachi calls a heathen woman "the daughter of a strange god" (Mal. ii. 11). Proper names expressive of this idea are common among the Semites, a familiar instance being Benhadad, "son of the god Hadad." But in heathenism it is to be observed that god-sonship has a physical sense; the worshippers are of the stock of their god, who is simply their great ancestor, and so is naturally identified with their interests, and not with those of any other tribe. In Israel, however, the idea of Jehovah's fatherhood could not take this crass form in the mind of any one who remembered the history of Jehovah's relations to His people. The oldest forefathers of the Hebrews in their original seats beyond the Euphrates were not the people of Jehovah, but served other gods (Josh. xxiv. 2), and Jehovah's relation to Israel is not of nature but of grace, constituted by the divine act of deliverance from Egypt. And so, according to Hosea, Jehovah does not love Israel because he is His son, but took him as His son because He loved him (xi. 1). The same contrast between natural and positive religion is expressed in the conception of Jehovah's covenant with His people; for a relation resting on a covenant is not natural but moral. There was no covenant between Moab and Chemosh, but only a natural kinship quite independent of Moab's conduct. But in Israel the rejection of Jehovah's covenant suspends, and but for sovereign love would cancel, the privileges of sonship. The sonship of Israel, therefore, must find its expression in filial obedience, and from this point of view the sin of the people is that they have ceased to take heed to Jehovah (iv. 10) and hearken to Him (ix. 17). Ephraim is not a wise son (xiii. 13). Jehovah has spoken much to him by the ministry of His prophets (xii. 10), but though He should write for him a myriad of precepts, they would seem but a strange thing to this foolish child (viii. 12).

But though Hosea dwells on the sonship of Ephraim with great tenderness, especially in speaking of the childhood of the nation, the age of its divine education (xi. 1 *seq*.), this analogy does not exhaust the whole depth of Israel's relation to Jehovah. In ancient society the attitude of the son to the father, especially that of the adult son employed in his father's business, has a certain element of servitude (Mal. iii. 17). The son honours his father as the servant does his master (Mal. i. 6.; Exod. xx. 12). Even now among the Arabs the grown-up son and the slave of the house do much the same menial services, and feel much the same measure of constraint in the presence of the head of the house. It is only towards his little ones that the father shows that tenderness which Hosea speaks of in describing the childhood of Ephraim. And so the whole fulness of Jehovah's love to His people, and the way in which Israel has proved unfaithful to that love, can be fitly brought out only in the still more intimate relation of the husband to his spouse.

In looking at the allegory of Jehovah's marriage with mother-Israel, or with the mother-land, we must again begin by considering the current ideas which served to suggest such a conception. Alike in Israel and among its heathen neighbours, the word Baal, that is "Lord" or "Owner," was a common appellative of the national Deity. Instead of the proper names compounded with Jehovah, which are common from the time of Elijah, we frequently find in old Israel forms compounded with Baal which are certainly not heathenish. When we meet with a son of Saul named

Ish-Baal, a grandson Meri-Baal, both names meaning "Baal's man," while David in like manner gives to one of his sons the name of Beeliada, "Baal knoweth," we may be sure that Baal is here a title of the God of Israel.[12] In Hosea's time the worshipping people still addressed Jehovah as Baali, "my Lord," and the Baalim of whom he often speaks (ii. 13 ; xiii. 1, 2) are no other than the golden calves, the recognised symbols of Jehovah. Now, among the Semites the husband is regarded as the lord or owner of his wife (1 Pet. iii. 6), whom in fact, according to early law, he purchases from her father for a price (Exod. xxi. 8 ; xxii. 17).[13] The address *Baali* is used by the wife to her husband as well as by the nation to its God, and so in an early stage of thought, when similarities of expression constantly form the basis of identifications of idea, it lay very near to think of the God as the husband of the worshipping nationality, or of the mother-land.[14] It is not at all likely that this conception was in form original to Hosea, or even peculiar to Israel ; such developed-religious allegory as that which makes the national God, not only father of the people, but husband of the land their mother, has its familiar home in natural religions. In these religions we find similar conceptions, in which, however, as in the case of the fatherhood of the deity, the idea is taken in a crass physical sense. Marriage of female worshippers with the godhead was a common notion among the Phœnicians and Babylonians, and in the latter case was connected with immoral practices akin to those that defiled the sanctuaries of Israel in Hosea's day.[15] It even seems possible to find some trace in Semitic heathenism of the idea of marriage of the Baal with the land which he fertilises by sunshine and rain. Semitic deities, as we saw in Lecture I. (p. 26), are conceived as productive powers, and so form pairs of male and female principles. Heaven and Earth are such a pair, as is well known from Greek mythology; and, though Baal and ʽAshtoreth are more often represented as astral powers (Sun and Moon, Jupiter and Venus), it is certain that fertilising showers were one manifestation of Baal's life-giving power. Even the Mohammedan Arabs retained the name of Baal (baʻl) for land watered by the rains of heaven. The land that brings forth fruit under these influences could not fail to be thought of as his spouse; and, in fact, we have an Arabic word (ʻathary) which seems to show that the fertility produced by the rains of Baal was associated with the name of his wife ʽAshtoreth.[16] If this be so, it follows that in point of form the marriage of Jehovah with Israel corresponded to a common Semitic conception, and we may well suppose that the corrupt mass of Israel interpreted it in reference to the fertility of the goodly land, watered by the dews of heaven (Deut. xi. 11), on principles that suggested no higher thoughts of God than were entertained by their heathen neighbours.

This argument is not a mere speculation; it gives us a key to understand what Hosea tells us of the actual religious ideas of his people. For we learn from him that the Israelites worshipped the Baalim or golden calves under just such a point of view as our discussion suggests. They were looked upon as the authors of the fertility of the land and nothing more (ii. 5); in other words, they were to Israel precisely what the heathen Baalim were to the Canaanites, natural productive powers. We have already seen that a tendency to degrade Jehovah to the level of a Canaanite Baal had always been the great danger of Israel's religion, when the moral fibre of the nation was not hardened by contest with foreign invaders, and that in early times the reaction against this way of thought had been mainly associated with a sense of national unity, and with the conception of Jehovah as the leader of the hosts of Israel. These patriotic and martial feelings were still strong during the Syrian wars; and in the time of Amos, in spite of the many Canaanite corruptions of the sanctuaries, Jehovah was yet pre-eminently the God of battles, who led Israel to victory over its enemies. But a generation of peace and luxury had greatly sapped the warlike spirit of the nation, while the disorders of the state had loosened the bonds of national unity. The name of Jehovah was no longer the rallying cry of all who loved the freedom and integrity of Israel, and the help which Ephraim had been wont to seek from Jehovah was now sought from Egypt or Assyria. Jehovah was not formally abjured for Canaanite gods; but in the decay of all the nobler impulses of national life He sank in popular conception to their level; in essential character as well as in name the calves of the local sanctuaries had become Canaanite Baalim, mere sources of the physical fertility of the land. And that this view of their power was embodied in sexual analogies of a crass and physical kind, such as we have found to exist among the heathen Semites, is proved by the prevalence of religious prostitution and widespread disregard of the laws of chastity, precisely identical with the abominations of ʽAshtoreth among the Phœnicians, and accompanied by the same symbolism of the sacred tree, which expressed the conception of the deity as a principle of physical fertility (Hosea iv. 13 *seq.*).

Thus, in looking at Hosea's doctrine of the marriage of Jehovah with Israel, we must remember that the prophet was not introducing an entirely new form of religious symbolism. The popular religion was full of externally similar ideas; the true personality and moral attributes of Jehovah were lost in a maze of allegory derived from the sexual processes of physical life; and the degrading effects of such a way of thought were visible in universal licentiousness and a disregard of the holiest obligations of domestic purity. In such circumstances, we might expect to find the prophet casting aside the whole notion of a marriage of Jehovah, and falling back like Amos on the transcendency of the Creator and Ruler of the moral universe. But he does not do so. Instead of rejecting the current symbolism he appropriates it; but he does so in a way that lifts it wholly out of the sphere of nature religion and makes it the vehicle of the profoundest spiritual truths. Jehovah is the husband of His nation. But the essential basis of the marriage relation is not physical, but moral. It is a relation of inmost affection, and lays upon the spouse a duty of conjugal fidelity which the popular religion daily violated. The betrothal of Jehovah to Israel is but another aspect of the covenant already spoken of; it is a betrothal "in righteousness and in judgment, in kindness and in love," a betrothal that demands the true knowledge of Jehovah (ii. 19, 20). A union in which these conditions are absent is not marriage, but illicit love; and so the Baalim or local symbols of Jehovah, with which the nation held no moral fellowship, worshipping them merely as sources of physical life and growth, are not the true spouse of Israel; they are the nation's paramours, and their worship is infidelity to Jehovah. There is no feature in Hosea's prophecy which distinguishes him from earlier prophets so sharply as his attitude to the golden calves, the local symbols of Jehovah adored in the Northern sanctuaries. Elijah and Elisha had no quarrel with the traditional worship of their nation. Even Amos never speaks in condemnation of the calves. But in Hosea's teaching they suddenly appear as the very root of Israel's sin and misery. It is perfectly clear that in the time of Hosea, as in that of Amos, the popular worship was nominally Jehovah worship. The oath of the worshippers at Gilgal and Bethel was by the life of Jehovah (iv. 15); the feasts of the Baalim were Jehovah's feasts (ii. 11; 13, ix. 5); the sanctuary was Jehovah's house (ix. 4), the sacrifices His offerings (viii. 13). But to Hosea's judgment this ostensible Jehovah worship is really the worship of other gods (iii. 1). With the calves Jehovah has nothing in common. He is the living God (i. 10), the calves are mere idols, the work of craftsmen (xiii. 2); and the nation which calls the work of its hands a god (xiv. 3) breaks its marriage vow with Jehovah and loves a stranger.

If the prophecy of Hosea stood alone it would be reasonable to think that this attack on the images of the popular religion was simply based on the second commandment. But when we contrast it with the absolute silence of earlier prophets we can hardly accept this explanation as adequate. Amos is as zealous for Jehovah's commandments as Hosea; and, if the one prophet condemns the worship of the calves as the fundamental evidence of Israel's infidelity, while the other, a few years before, passes it by in silence, it is fair to conclude that the matter appeared to Hosea in a much more practical light than it did to Amos. Our analysis of Hosea's line of thought enables us to understand how this was so. Amos judges of the religious state of the nation by its influence on social relations and the administration of public justice. But Hosea places the essence of religion in personal fidelity to Jehovah and a just conception of His covenant of love with Israel. The worship of the popular sanctuaries ignored all this, setting in its place a conception of the Godhead which did not rise above the level of heathenism. The attachment of Israel to the golden calves was not the pure and elevated affection of a spouse for her husband. It was in its very nature a carnal love, and therefore its objects were false lovers, who had nothing in common with the true husband of the nation. Hosea does not condemn the worship of the calves because idols are forbidden by the law; he excludes the calves from the sphere of true religion because the worship which they receive has no affinity to the true attitude of Israel to Jehovah. By this judgment he proves the depth of his religious insight; for the whole history of religion shows that no truth is harder to realise than that a worship morally false is in no sense the worship of the true God (Matt. vi. 24; vii. 22).

As we follow out the various aspects of Hosea's teaching we see with increasing clearness that in all its parts it can be traced back to a single fundamental idea. The argument of his prophecy is an argument of the heart, not of the head. His whole revelation of Jehovah is the revelation of a love which can be conceived under human analogies, and whose workings are to be understood not by abstract reasonings but by the sympathy of a heart which has sounded the depths of human affection, and knows in its own experience what love demands of its object. One of the first points that struck us in Hosea's impassioned delineation of Israel's infidelity, in the inward sympathy with which he mourns over his nation's fall, yet holding fast the assurance that even in that fall the love of Jehovah to His people shall find its highest vindication, was that Jehovah's affection to Israel is an affection that burns within the prophet's own soul, which he has not learned to speak of by rote but has comprehended through the experience of his own life. It is a special characteristic of the Hebrew prophets that they identify themselves with Jehovah's word and will so completely that their personality seems often to be lost in His. In no prophet is this characteristic more notable than in Hosea, for in virtue of the peculiar inwardness of his whole argument his very heart seems to throb in unison with the heart of Jehovah. Amos became a prophet when he heard the thunder of Jehovah's voice of judgment; Hosea learned to speak of Jehovah's love, and of the workings of that love in chastisement and in grace towards Israel's infidelity, through sore experiences of his own life, through a human love spurned but not changed to bitterness, despised yet patient and unselfish to the end, which opened to him the secrets of that Heart whose tenderness is as infinite as its holiness.

In the first chapters of the book of Hosea the faithlessness of Israel to Jehovah, the long-suffering of God, the moral discipline of sorrow and tribulation by which He will yet bring back His erring people, and betroth it to Himself for ever in righteousness, truth, and love, are depicted under the figure of the relation of a husband to his erring spouse. This parable was not invented by Hosea; it is drawn, as we are expressly told, from his own life. The Divine Word first became audible in the prophet's breast when he was guided by a mysterious providence to espouse Gomer, the daughter of Diblaim, who proved an unfaithful wife and became the mother of children born in infidelity (i. 2, 3). The details of this painful story are very lightly touched; they are never alluded to in that part of the book which has the character of public preaching—in chapter i. the prophet speaks of himself in the third person; and as Hosea gave names to the children of Gomer, names of symbolic form, to each of which is attached a brief prophetic lesson (i. 4, 5; 6, 7; 8 *seq.*), it is plain that he concealed the shame of their mother and acknowledged her children as his own, burying his bitter sorrow in his own heart. But this long-suffering tenderness was of no avail. In chapter iii. we learn that Gomer at length left her husband, and fell, under circumstances of which Hosea spares the recital, into a state of misery, from which the prophet, still following her with compassionate affection, had to buy her back at the price of a slave. He could not restore her to her old place in his house and to the rights of a faithful spouse; but he brought her home and watched over her for many days, secluding her from temptation, with a loyalty which showed that his heart was still true to her.[17] These scanty details embrace all that we know of the history of Hosea's life; everything else in chapters i. and iii., together with the whole of chapter ii., is pure allegory, depicting the relations of Jehovah and Israel under the analogy suggested by the prophet's experience, but working out that analogy in a quite independent way.

It is difficult to understand how any sound judgment can doubt that Hosea's account of his married life is literal history ; it is told with perfect simplicity, and yet with touching reserve. We feel that it would not have been told at all, but that it was necessary to explain how Hosea became a prophet, how he was led to that fundamental conception of Jehovah's love and Israel's infidelity which lies at the root of his whole prophetic argument. Those who shrink from accepting the narrative in its literal sense are obliged to assume that Hosea was first taught by revelation to think of Jehovah's relation to Israel as a marriage, and that then, the better to impress this thought on his auditors, he translated it into a fable, of which he made himself the chief actor, clothing himself with an imaginary shame which could only breed derision. But in truth, as we have already seen, the history of Hosea's life is related mainly in the third person, and forms no part of his preaching to Israel. It is a history that lies behind his public ministry ; and we are told that it was through his marriage with Gomer-bath-Diblaim—whose very name shows her to be a real person, not a mere allegory —that Hosea first realised the truths which he was commissioned to preach. The events recorded in chap. i. are not Hosea's first message to Israel, but Jehovah's first lesson to the prophet's soul. God speaks in the events of history and the experiences of human life. He spoke to Amos in the thundering march of the Assyrian, and he spoke to Hosea in the shame that blighted his home.[18]

Apart from the still surviving influence of the old system of allegorical interpretation, which, though no longer recognised in principle, continues to linger in some corners of modern interpretation, the chief thing that has prevented a right understanding of the opening chapters of our book is a false interpretation of chap. i. 2, as if Hosea meant us to believe that under divine command he married a woman whom he knew from the first to be of profligate character. But the point of the allegory is that Gomer's infidelity after marriage is a figure of Israel's departure from the covenant God, and the struggle of Hosea's affection with the burning sense of shame and grief when he found his wife unfaithful is altogether inconceivable unless his first love had been pure, and full of trust in the purity of its object. Hosea did not understand in advance the deep prophetic lesson which Jehovah desired to teach him by these sad experiences. It was in the struggle and bitterness of his spirit in the midst of his great unhappiness that he learned to comprehend the secret of Jehovah's heart in his dealings with faithless Israel, and recognised the unhappiness of his married life as no meaningless calamity, but the ordinance of Jehovah, which called him to the work of a prophet. This he expresses by saying that it was in directing him to marry Gomer that Jehovah first spoke to him (comp. Jer. xxxii. 8, where in like manner the prophet tells us that he recognised an incident in his life as embodying a divine word *after the event*). It was through the experience of his own life, which gave him so deep an insight into the spiritual aspect of the marriage tie, that Hosea was able to develop with inmost sympathy his doctrine of the moral union of Jehovah to Israel, and to transform a conception which in its current form seemed the very negation of spiritual faith, full of associations of the merest nature worship, into a doctrine of holy love, freed from all carnal alloy, and separating Jehovah for ever from the idols with which His name had till then been associated.

The possession of a single true thought about Jehovah, not derived from current religious teaching, but springing up in the soul as a word from Jehovah Himself, is enough to constitute a prophet, and lay on him the duty of speaking to Israel what he has learned of Israel's God. But the truth made known to Hosea could not be exhausted in a single message, like that delivered to Amos. As the prophet's own love to his wife shaped and coloured his whole life, so Jehovah's love to faithless Israel contained within itself the key to all Israel's history. The past, the present, and the future took a new aspect to the prophet in the light of his great spiritual discovery. Hosea had become a prophet, not for a moment, but for all his life.

We have already seen that the greater part of the book of Hosea, from chap. iv. onwards—the only part that has the form of direct address to his people—appears to date from the period of increasing anarchy, while the briefer prophecies in chap. i., associated with the names of Gomer's three children, belong to the reign of Jeroboam II. It would seem, therefore, that Hosea was conscious of his prophetic calling for some years before he appeared as a public preacher; and this fact we can well understand in a nature so poetically sensitive, and in connection with the personal circumstances that first made him a prophet. But it was impossible for him to be altogether silent. He felt that he and his family were living lessons of Jehovah to Israel, and in this feeling he gave to the three children symbolical names, to each of which a short prophetic lesson was attached. In this he was followed by Isaiah, whose sons, Mahar-shalal-hash-baz and Shear-jashub, also bore names expressive of fundamental points in the prophet's teaching.

The eldest of Gomer's sons was named Jezreel. "For yet a little while," saith Jehovah, "and I will punish the house of Jehu for the sin of Jezreel, and will cause to cease the kingdom of the house of Israel. And in that day I will break the bow of Israel in the valley of Jezreel"—the natural battlefield of the land. To Hosea, as to Amos, the fall of the house of Jehu and the fall of the nation appear as one thing; both prophets, indeed, appear to have looked for the overthrow of the reigning dynasty, not by intestine conspiracy, as actually happened, but at the hand of the destroying invader. It was fitting, therefore, that the great sin of the reigning dynasty should hold the first place in the record of the nation's defection. To Hosea that sin begins with the bloodshed of Jezreel, the treacherous slaughter of the house of Ahab. The very existence of the ruling dynasty rests on a crime which cries for vengeance.

That Hosea judges thus of a revolution accomplished with the active participation of older prophets is a fact well worthy of attention. It places in the strongest light the limitations that characterise all Old Testament revelation. It shows us that we can look for no mechanical uniformity in the teaching of successive prophets. Elisha saw and approved one side of Jehu's revolution. He looked on it only as the death-blow to Baal worship; but Hosea sees another side, and condemns as emphatically as Elisha approved. In the forefront of his condemnation he places the bloodshed, still unatoned, which, according to the view that runs through all the Old Testament and was familiar to every Hebrew, continued to cry for vengeance from generation to generation. But we must not suppose that in Hosea's judgment all would have been well if the house of Omri had retained the throne. The Northern kingship in itself, and quite apart from the question of the particular dynasty, is a defection from Jehovah—"They have made kings, but not by Me; they have made princes, and I knew it not" (viii. 4); "Where now is thy king to save thee in all thy cities, and thy judges, of whom thou saidst, Give me a king and princes? I gave thee a king in Mine anger, and take him away in My wrath" (xiii. 10, 11). The kingdom of Ephraim, in all its dynasties, rests on a principle of godless anarchy. What wonder, then, that the nation devours her judges like a fiery oven :[19] all their kings are fallen (vii. 7), the monarchy of Samaria is swept away as foam upon the water (x. 7). The ideal which Hosea holds up in contrast to the unhallowed dynasties of the North is the rule of the house of David. In the days of restoration the people shall inquire after Jehovah their God, and David their king (iii. 5). Now, it is not surprising that Amos, who was himself a man of Judah, should represent the re-establishment of the ancient kingdom of David as part of the final restoration; but when Hosea, a Northern prophet, gives utterance to the same thought, he places himself in striking contrast to all his predecessors, who never dreamed of a return of Ephraim to the yoke cast off in the days of the first Jeroboam. No doubt there were many things which made such a thought natural, at least in the days of anarchy that followed the death of Jeroboam II. The stability of the Davidic throne stood in marked contrast to the civil discords and constant changes of dynasty to which the prophet so often alludes; and, though he speaks of Judah as sharing Israel's sin and Israel's fall (v. 5, 10, 13, 14 ; viii. 14), Hosea regards the corruption of the Southern kingdom as less ancient (xi. 12 ; *Heb.*, xii. 1) and deep-rooted (iv. 15), and, in his earlier prophecies at least, excludes Judah from the utter destruction of the North. When Jehovah's mercy is withdrawn from Israel He will yet save Judah, though not by war and battle as in days gone by (i. 7). Hosea is so essentially a man of feeling, and not of strict logic, that it would be fruitless to attempt to form an exact picture of his attitude to Judah, expressed as it is in a series of brief allusions scattered over a number of years. In his last picture of Israel's restoration the house of David is not mentioned at all, and images of political glory have no place in his conception of the nation's true happiness. One part of the ideal of Amos is the resubjugation of the heathen once tributary to David; he looks for a return of the ancient days of victorious warfare. But Hosea has altogether laid aside the old martial idea as we found it expressed in Deut. xxxiii. The fenced cities of Judah are a sin, and shall be destroyed by fire (viii. 14). The deliverance of Judah is not to be wrought by bow or sword (i. 7); repentant Ephraim says, "We will not ride upon horses" (xiv. 3). His picture of the future, therefore, lacks all the features that give strength to an earthly state; it reads like a return to Paradise (ii. 21 *seq.*; xiv.). In such a picture the kingship of David is little more than a figure. The return of David's kingdom, as it actually was, would by no means have corresponded with his ideal; but the name of David is the historical symbol of a united Israel.

To Hosea the unity of Israel is a thing of profound significance. His whole prophecy, as we know, is penetrated by the conception of the people of Jehovah as a moral person; the unity of Israel and the unity of God are the basis of his whole doctrine of religion as a personal bond of love and fidelity. Thus the political divisions of Israel on the one hand, and on the other the idolatry which broke up the oneness of Israel's God, are set forth by Hosea as parallel breaches of covenant ; when he mentions the one he instinctively joins the other with it (viii. 4 ; x. 1 seq.). In contrast to this twofold defection and division " Jehovah their God and David their king" appear in natural connection.

One sees from all this that in Hosea's hands the old national theory of the religion of Jehovah is on the point of breaking up, and that new hopes take its place. This was indeed inevitable. The ideal of a victorious and happy nation, dwelling apart in a goodly land and secure from invasion in Jehovah's blessing on its warlike prowess, as we find it in the prophecies of Balaam or the Blessing of Moses, was hopelessly shattered by the first contact with a great conquering empire such as Assyria. Amos was the first to realise that the advance of Assyria meant the ruin of Israel as it actually was, but he did not see that the new movements of history meant more than speedy captivity, that Israel could never again be restored on its old footing. To him it still seems possible that the remnant of the nation, purified by sifting judgment, may return to Canaan and restore the ancient kingdom of

David. His picture of the last days is no more than a glorified image of the best days of the past, when the flow of Jehovah's blessings, victory in war and prosperous seasons in time of peace, is renewed in fuller measure to a nation purged of sinners. The realism of this picture has no counterpart in Hosea's eschatology. The total dissolution of national life which he foresees is not a mere sifting judgment, but the opening of an altogether new era. Hosea never draws a distinction between the sinners who must perish in captivity and the righteous remnant which shall return. To him Ephraim is not a mingled society of the righteous and the wicked, but a single moral person which has sinned and must repent as one man. Amos does not look for national repentance; the wicked remain wicked, and perish in their sins, the righteous return in their old righteousness, and so the new Israel is just a continuation of the old. But to Hosea the repentance of the nation is a resurrection from the dead. "Come and let us return to Jehovah, for He hath torn and He will heal us; He hath smitten and He will bind us up. After two days will He revive us, in the third day He will raise us up, and we shall live before Him" (vi. 1 *seq.*; xiii. 14). Even Ephraim's hard heart cannot for ever resist Jehovah's love. "He will allure her and lead her into the wilderness" of exile "and *speak to her heart*" (ii. 14). The desolate valley of Achor shall be to her the gate of hope, and there "she shall answer as in the days of her youth and the day when she came up out of the land of Egypt" (ii. 15). When His people are scattered in exile Jehovah shall roar like a lion, and the wanderers shall come fluttering to His call like a bird from Egypt, like a dove from the land of Assyria (xi. 10, 11). The purpose of the judgment is not penal; it is meant to teach them that Jehovah alone is the husband of Israel, and the giver of those good things which in their blindness she esteemed the gifts of the Baalim (ii. 5 *seq*.). Taught by adversity, Ephraim shall acknowledge that neither the alliance of strange empires, nor his own prowess, nor his vain idols can give deliverance; "Asshur shall not save us, we will not ride upon horses, neither will we say any more to the work of our hands, Ye are our gods; for in Thee the fatherless findeth mercy." And so at length all Israel shall be saved; but in this redemption every feature of the old nation has disappeared—its state, its religion, its warlike might, its foreign policy, king and prince, sacrifice and sanctuary, images (ephod) and teraphim. The very face of nature is changed; the wild beasts of the field, the fowls of heaven, the creeping things of the earth are at peace with Jehovah's people; sword and battle are broken out of the earth that they may lie down safely (ii. 18). Jehovah alone remains overshadowing Israel and Israel's land with His infinite compassion (xiv. 7). And then the voice of Ephraim is heard, "What have I to do any more with idols? I answer and look to Him; I am as a green fir-tree, from me is Thy fruit found." [20]

It is no mere accident that Hosea in this closing picture returns to the image of the evergreen tree which played so large a part in that nature-religion which it was his chief work to contend against. In translating religion into the language of the most spiritual human affections, Hosea fixed for ever the true image of religious faith; and we still find in his book a fit expression of the profoundest feelings of repentant devotion—a delineation of Jehovah's forgiving love which touches the inmost chords of our being. But to Hosea the worshipping subject the object of God's redeeming grace is the nation in its corporate capacity, not a true person but a personified society. So long as the individual side of religion fails to receive that central place which it holds in the Gospel it is impossible to represent the highest spiritual truth without some use of physical analogies; and this shows itself in the most characteristic way when the book of Hosea closes with an image derived from mere vegetative life. The true goal of Hosea's ideas lay beyond his own horizon, in a dispensation when the relation of the redeeming God to every believing soul should have all that tenderness and depth of personal affection with which he clothes the relation of Jehovah to Israel.[21]

LECTURE V.

THE KINGDOM OF JUDAH AND THE BEGINNINGS OF ISAIAH'S WORK.[1]

WE have now reached the point in the Old Testament history at which the centre of interest is transferred from Ephraim to Judah. Under the dynasties of Omri and Jehu, the Northern Kingdom took the leading part in Israel; even to the Judæan Amos it was Israel *par excellence*. Judah was not only inferior in political power, but in the share it took in the active movements of national life and thought. In tracing the history of religion and the work of the prophets, we have been almost exclusively occupied with the North; Amos himself, when charged with a message to the whole family that Jehovah brought up out of Egypt, leaves his home to preach in a Northern sanctuary. During this whole period we have a much fuller knowledge of the life of Ephraim than of Judah; the Judæan history consists of meagre extracts from official records, except where it comes into contact with the North, through the alliance of Jehoshaphat with Ahab; through the reaction of Jehu's revolution in the fall of Athaliah, the last scion of the house of Ahab, and the accompanying abolition of Baal worship at Jerusalem, or, finally, through the presumptuous attempt of Amaziah to measure his strength with the powerful monarch of Samaria. While the house of Ephraim was engaged in the great war with Syria, Judah had seldom to deal with enemies more formidable than the Philistines or the Edomites; and the contest with these foes, renewed with varying success generation after generation, resolved itself into a succession of forays and blood-feuds such as have always been common in the lands of the Semites (Amos i.), and never assumed the character of a struggle for national existence. It was the Northern Kingdom that had the task of upholding the standard of Israel: its whole history presents greater interest and more heroic elements; its struggles, its calamities, and its glories were cast in a larger mould. It is a trite proverb that the nation which has no history is happy, and perhaps the course of Judah's existence ran more smoothly than that of its greater neighbour, in spite of the raids of the slave-dealers of the coast, and the lawless hordes of the desert. But no side of national existence is likely to find full development where there is little political activity; if the life of the North was more troubled, it was also larger and more intense. Ephraim took the lead in literature and religion as well as in politics; it was in Ephraim far more than in Judah that the traditions of past history were cherished, and new problems of religion became practical and called for solution by the word of the prophets. So long as the Northern Kingdom endured Judah was content to learn from it for evil or for good. It would be easy to show in detail that every great wave of life and thought in Ephraim was transmitted with diminished intensity to the Southern Kingdom.

In many respects the influence of Ephraim upon Judah was similar to that of England upon Scotland before the union of the crowns, but with the important difference that after the accession of Omri the two Hebrew kingdoms were seldom involved in hostilities. At the first division of North and South, upon the death of Solomon, the house of David was disposed to treat the seceding tribes as rebels, and the accumulated wealth and organised resources of the capital enabled Rehoboam for a time to press hard upon his rival.[2] The invasion of Shishak, in which Rehoboam was impoverished and severely chastised, restored the natural balance of things, and soon after we find Asa, king of Judah, reduced to the necessity of calling on the Syrians to help him against Baasha ; but the house of Omri cultivated friendly relations with the Davidic kings. Jehoshaphat was the ally of Ahab and his sons, and an ally on inferior terms, bringing a contingent to their aid in the Syrian and Moabite wars. From this time forward the North and the South seem to have felt that they had common interests and dangers ; indeed, when the power of Damascus was at its height Judah as well as Ephraim suffered from the inroads of Hazael (2 Kings

xii. 17 *seq.*). The wanton attempt of Amaziah to provoke a conflict with King Joash, about the close of the Syrian period, ended in humiliation; but Joash made no attempt to incorporate Judah in his dominions, and the popular rising which cost Amaziah his life probably expressed the dissatisfaction of his subjects with his presumptuous policy. Amaziah was succeeded by Uzziah, whose long and prosperous reign appears to have corresponded pretty exactly with that of Jeroboam II. The current chronology, which obscures this correspondence, is certainly corrupt, and we shall not be far wrong if we view Uzziah and Jotham as the contemporaries of Jeroboam II. and Menahem, while Ahaz of Judah came to the throne soon after Menahem's death, and saw the greater part of the wars which began with the invasion of Tiglath Pileser and closed with the fall of Samaria.[3] The date of Hezekiah's accession is much disputed by chronologers; but he appears to have taken the sceptre before the fall of Samaria, while the greater part of his reign certainly falls after that event. Thus, speaking broadly, we may say that in the time of Hosea and Amos, under Kings Uzziah and Jotham, Judah was at peace with Israel, and still free from implication in the stream of larger politics. Ahaz, on the contrary, was attacked by Pekah and Rezin, and to escape this danger accepted the position of an Assyrian vassal; but his land was not yet brought into direct contact with Assyria. Under Hezekiah the Assyrian armies were close to Judah, conducting operations, not only against

Samaria, but against other neighbouring states, so as to become a source of imminent danger to Judah itself, which could only hope for safety by patiently fulfilling the duties of a vassal state, and rejecting every temptation to chafe under the Assyrian yoke; but meantime it had become plain that Egypt was the ultimate goal of the Assyrian operations in Palestine. Egyptian diplomacy was busy in the Palestinian states, with tempting promises to encourage revolt against the empire of the Tigris. Judah had to choose between absolute political quietude, accepting the present situation as it stood and leaving the great struggle to be fought out by others, and the task of entering for the first time into the movements of an imperial policy, in which the principal actors were great empires altogether different from the petty states with which it had formerly had to do. The alternative was pregnant with important issues, not only for the political existence of the little nation, but for the religion of Jehovah, and to indicate the religious solution of the problems of this crisis was the work of the greatest of Judæan prophets, Isaiah the son of Amos. The famous expedition of Sennacherib, which marks the culminating point of his prophetic life, fell in the year 701 B.C., twenty years after the capture of Samaria and thirty-three after the expedition of Tiglath Pileser against Pekah and Rezin, which gave occasion to the first important series of Isaiah's prophecies. To the student of prophecy these years are the most important in the Old Testament history, and as such they claim from us a very careful study; but to understand them aright it will be necessary to go back to the epoch of prosperity running parallel to the reign of Jeroboam II., and consider the political and religious position of Judah in the reign of Uzziah. Amos, it will be remembered, flourished under this king, and the call of Isaiah, described in chapter vi. of his book, took place in the year of Uzziah's death. Our business, therefore, is to examine the state of things in the Southern Kingdom at the time when Amos and Hosea were prophesying in the North, and at the commencement of Isaiah's ministry.

From the overthrow of Athaliah to the accession of Ahaz and the acceptance by him of the position of an Assyrian vassal is something more than a century. It was, on the whole, a century of material progress, of political stability, and of successful war. Two kings indeed, Joash and Amaziah, met a violent death; but, while in the North the assassination of a monarch was always followed by a change of dynasty, the people of Judah remained constantly attached to the house of David, and the order of succession was never broken. The judgments passed upon the character of Judæan sovereigns in the book of Kings have almost exclusive reference to their actions in regard to the affairs of public worship; but the stability of the dynasty is the best proof that the generally favourable estimate of their conduct was borne out by the opinion of their contemporaries. Their religious policy, indeed, may be fairly assumed to be typical of the general principles of their rule. These principles were conservative; the son followed in the footsteps of his father (2 Kings xv. 3; xvi. 3); and so, if no high ideal was aimed at, there were at least no new and crying abuses to excite discontent. The conservative character of the Judæan state is readily explained from the history of the house of David. The earliest political unity in Israel was not the nation, but the tribe or its subdivision the clan. The heads of clans and communities were the hereditary aristocracy, the natural leaders in peace and in war; and we have already seen that this form of organisation is that which history proves to be most conducive to stability and good order among Semitic peoples (*supra*, p. 93 *seq.*). The natural aim of a strong monarchy, ruling over a confederation of tribes, is to break down the tribal system, and bring all parts of the kingdom more directly under the control of the capital; while the natural conservatism of the individual provinces opposes this process, and seeks to limit the power of the king to the supreme command in war, and the office of deciding appeals laid before him in peace. In the Northern Kingdom, as we have further seen, the overthrow of the old tribal system was already part of Solomon's policy, and the more powerful of the kings of Ephraim appear, in like manner, to have laboured in the direction of centralisation and political absolutism. Prolonged and exhausting wars naturally favoured this policy, but at the ruinous cost of breaking up old social bonds and opening a fatal gulf between the aristocracy of the court and the mass of the people. In Judah the course of events was different. In his own tribe Solomon appointed no such provincial governors or tax-gatherers as excited the discontent of Northern Israel with his rule,— moved perhaps by the example of his father David, who, after the revolt of Absalom, in which Judah was the first to rise and the last to return to obedience, appears to have deemed it necessary to treat his own tribe with special favour, and recognise its willing support as the chief prop of his throne. The Judæans remained loyal to Rehoboam, because their prejudices and ancestral usages had not been violated like those of the North; and when the kingdom was practically narrowed to a single tribe, and could no longer pretend to play the part of a great power, neither policy nor interest urged the Davidic kings to startling innovations in government. Thus the internal condition of the state was stable, though little progressive; the kings were fairly successful in war, though not sufficiently strong to maintain unbroken authority over Edom, the only vassal state of the old Davidic realm over which they still claimed suzerainty, and their civil administration must have been generally satisfactory according to the not very high standard of the East; for they retained the affections of their people, the justice and mercy of the throne of David are favourably spoken of in the old prophecy against Moab quoted in Isaiah xv. xvi., and Isaiah contrasts the disorders of his own time with the ancient reputation of Jerusalem for fidelity and justice (i. 21). This reputation hardly proves that any very ideal standard of government was reached or aimed at, but we may conclude that ancient law and usage were fairly maintained, and that administrative or judicial innovations, which irritate an Eastern people much more than individual miscarriages of justice, were seldom attempted. The religious conduct of the house of David followed the same general lines. Old abuses remained untouched, but the cultus remained much as David and Solomon had left it. Local high places were numerous, and no attempt was made to interfere with them; but the great temple on Mount Zion, which formed part of the complex of royal buildings erected by Solomon, maintained its prestige, and appears to have been a special object of solicitude to the kings, who treated its service as part of their royal state.

It is common to imagine that the religious condition of Judah was very much superior to that of the North, but there is absolutely no evidence to support this opinion. Throughout the Old Testament history the abuses of popular worship are brought into prominence mainly in connection with efforts after reform. In Judah there was no movement of reform to record between the time of Joash, when the Tyrian Baal was abolished, and the time of Hezekiah, who acted under the influence of Isaiah. Thus, in the narrative of Kings, the history of religion remains an absolute blank during the century with which we are particularly concerned, and it is only just before Hezekiah arose that the historian finds it necessary to call unfavourable attention to the fact that Ahaz sacrificed on the high places, on the hills, and under every green tree. His predecessors had undoubtedly done the same, for they accepted the high places as legitimate; the guilt of Ahaz is not measured by his deflection from the standard of his ancestors, but by his refusal to rise to the higher standard which prophets like Isaiah began to set forth. There can be no question that the worship of the Judæan sanctuaries was as little spiritual as that of the Northern shrines. Isaiah has as much to say against idols as Hosea. "Their land," he says, "is full of idols; they worship the work of their own hands" (ii. 8). And these idols were not new things; the brazen serpent, destroyed by Hezekiah, was worshipped as the work of Moses, which certainly implies a cultus of immemorial antiquity. In detail, no doubt, there was considerable difference between the idolatry of the North and the South. We read of a brazen serpent, but not of golden calves as symbols of Jehovah; nor does the name of Baalim, by which the latter were known in Ephraim, appear in Isaiah or Micah. The association of the Godhead with symbols of natural growth and reproductive power, which proved so fatal to religion and morality in the North, was not lacking: in Judah as in Israel the people worshipped under evergreen trees—the Canaanite symbol of the female side of the divine power; and the *ashera*, which has the same meaning, was found in Judæan as in Northern sanctuaries (Isa. i. 29; xvii. 8; Micah v. 14, where for *groves* read *asheras*). Other Canaanite elements were not wanting; the worship of Adonis or Tammuz, for which we have direct evidence in the last days of Jerusalem (Ezek. viii. 14), appears to be already alluded to by Isaiah. But on the whole it is probable that the popular religion was not so largely leavened with Canaanite ideas and Canaanite immorality as in the North; there is nothing in the prophecies of Isaiah and Micah corresponding to the picture of vile licentiousness under the cloak of religion drawn by Amos and Hosea. This, indeed, is what we should expect; for in the population of Judæa the fusion of Canaanite and Hebrew elements was not so great as in Ephraim and Manasseh; in Southern Judah the chief non-Hebrew element was of Arab stock; and the great sanctuaries of the South do not appear to have been to the same extent as in the North identical with Canaanite holy places. Judah, moreover, was a much poorer country than Ephraim; there was less natural wealth, and apparently the whole conditions of life were simpler and more primitive; so that we should naturally expect to find less sympathy with the luxurious Canaanite worship, but at the same time more relics of the ancient superstitions of the Hebrews before Moses. These, again, can hardly have been without affinity to the original beliefs of the incorporated Arab elements, and a variety of circumstances make it probable that a species of fetichism or totemism was largely current in Judah as in the neighbouring desert. Such ancestral superstitions are probably alluded to in Amos ii. 4, and their nature is illustrated in the worship of family gods, in the form of unclean animals, described in Ezek. viii. 10 *seq.* One of the most characteristic proofs of the prevalence of the lowest superstitions is the frequent reference made by the Judæan prophets to various forms of magic and divination, such as the consultation of familiar spirits through "wizards that peep and mutter"—a kind of ventriloquists (Isa. viii. 19, comp. xxix. 4).[4] The practice of divination was not confined to the masses. Isaiah reckons "the cunning magician and the man skilled in enchantments" alongside of the captains and counsellors as recognised props of the state (iii. 3); while Micah characterises the ordinary prophets as diviners (iii. 7, 11, comp. v. 12). Isaiah represents these superstitious practices as of foreign, in part of Philistine, character (ii. 6); and, when we take along with this the undisturbed existence of the sanctuaries built by Solomon for his foreign wives, we must conclude that the opposition to distinctively foreign elements which characterises the worship of Ephraim from the time of Elijah was not so strongly marked in the religious practices of Judah. Under the dynasty of Jehu Jehovah had nominally undivided allegiance from the house of Ephraim; foreign elements were eschewed, and the superstitions incorporated with the ritual of the sanctuaries, which led Hosea to declare that the popular religion was not Jehovah worship at all, were those indigenous to the land of Canaan. In Judah the influence of the work of Elijah had been only indirectly felt; the nation had passed through no such great crisis as the long battle of the Northern prophets with the house of Ahab; and thus the prevalent superstitions were partly of a different character from those we meet with in Ephraim, and partly indicated a less hopeless condition of religious life, because a higher ideal of Jehovah worship had never been so distinctly set before the mass of the people. All this, of course, must be understood as not excluding a great influence of the North on the minor kingdom. On the one hand it is clear that Amos had thoroughly assimilated the teaching of Elijah, while Isaiah and Micah appropriate the teaching of Hosea on the subject of idolatry. In truth, everything that we possess of the sacred literature and history of the North has been conveyed to us through Judæan channels. On the other hand, the growing corruption of Ephraim in religion and social order was full of peril to Judah. Hosea warns the Judæans against participation in the guilt of Israel (iv. 15), and Micah tells us that the transgressions of Israel were found in his own land (i. 13, comp. vi. 16).

The material prosperity of Ephraim in the last generation of the house of Jehu had its counterpart, as we have already seen, in the condition of Judah under Uzziah. Edom was again reduced to subjection, and thus the harbour of Elath on the Red Sea came into the possession of the house of David, which at the same time obtained the control of the important caravan route from Sela to Southern Arabia (2 Kings xiv. 7, 22). These successes gave Judah an important commercial position, and led to the formation of a fleet (Isa. ii. 16) and a great development of wealth (Isa. ii. 7). The resources of the monarchy were enlarged, and its warlike strength was increased by the multiplication of chariots and horses (Isa. ii. 7; Micah i. 13; v. 10; comp. Hosea i. 7; viii. 14). But to a nation situated like the Hebrews the sudden expansion of commerce brought grave social dangers. Society was constructed on the basis of a purely agricultural life, the merchants of early times were not Hebrews, but Canaanites, who had a trading quarter of their own at Jerusalem (Zeph. i. 11, where for *merchant* read *Canaanite*). The newly-developed trade could not but fall largely into the hands of the grandees and courtiers, and the wealth they accumulated changed their relations to the commonalty, and gave them opportunity for the exactions and injustice from which, in Eastern society, the wealthy seldom keep themselves pure. Hosea complains that in Ephraim commerce, deceit, and oppression went hand in hand (xii. 7), and in Judah the case was not otherwise. The centralisation of large capital in a few hands led to the formation of huge estates, the poorer landowners being either bought out when they fell into the power of their creditors, or ejected by violence and false judgment (Isa. v. 8; Micah ii. 2, 9). Judicial corruption increased; every man had his price (Micah iii. 11), and the poor in such a state of things could do nothing against the tyrants who, in the forcible phrase of Micah, "stripped the skin from off them, and their flesh from off their bones" (iii. 2). These evils, no doubt, assumed an intenser form after the calamitous war with Pekah and Rezin had spread desolation in the land, and when the burden of taxation, which in the East always falls heaviest on the poor, was increased by the tribute to Assyria; and it is to this later time that the most melancholy prophetic pictures of the state of Judah apply. But the fatal degeneracy of the higher classes, unequal distribution of wealth, oppression of the poor, corrupt luxury, and the like are dwelt on in the earliest utterances of Isaiah (chaps. ii.-v.), at a time when the external prosperity of the nation was still uninterrupted. Isaiah began his work in the year of Uzziah's death, and when he accepted the task of a prophet he already pictures his nation as so corrupt that it could be purified only by a consuming judgment.

The year of Uzziah's death cannot be determined with precision. The present chronology gives to his son Jotham a reign of sixteen years, which in all probability is a good deal too much. But at all events Isaiah began to prophesy some years before 734 B.C., and his influence was at its height during the expedition of Sennacherib in 701, so that his career covers a period of some forty years at the least. More happy in his work than Amos and Hosea, he succeeded during this long period in acquiring a commanding position in the state. In the time of Hezekiah, plans which it was known he would condemn were carefully concealed from him by the politicians he opposed (Isa. xxix. 15); and in the day of Jerusalem's sorest trouble the king and his people sought from him the help which only the word of Jehovah could supply. Though we are not expressly told so in the narrative of Kings, there can be no doubt that it was he who inspired Hezekiah's plans of reformation in the national worship, and at his death he left behind him a prophetic party so strong that the counter-reformation of Manasseh was only carried out by the aid of bloody persecution. And, though his work thus seemed for a time to be undone, its influence was not extinguished. It is the teaching of Isaiah that forms the starting-point of the book of Deuteronomy, and of the reformation of Josiah, of which that book was the programme; and thus the ideas of the great prophet continued to exercise a decisive influence on the affairs of Judah more than a century after they were first proclaimed. In truth, the whole subsequent history of the Hebrew people bears the impress of Isaiah's activity. It was through him that the word of prophecy, despised and rejected when it was spoken by Amos and Hosea, became a practical power not only in the state but in the whole life of the nation. We can readily understand that so great a work could not have been effected by an isolated mission like that of Amos, or by a man like Hosea, who stood apart from all the leaders of his nation, and had neither friend nor disciple to espouse his cause. Isaiah won his commanding position, not by a single stroke, but by long-sustained and patient effort. His work must have commenced when he was still a young man, and it was continued into old age with the same unfailing courage which marks his first appearance as a prophet. The work of a prophet was the vocation of his life, to which every energy was devoted; even his wife is called the prophetess (viii. 3); his sons bore prophetic names, not enigmatic like those given by Hosea to Gomer's children, but expressing in plain language two fundamental themes of his doctrine—the speedy approach of judgment by hostile invasion (Maher-shalal-hash-baz, viii. 3), and the hope of return to Jehovah and His grace by the remnant of the nation (Shear-jashub, vii. 3 ; the name is translated in x. 21). The truths which he proclaimed he sought to make immediately practical in the circle of disciples whom he gathered round him (viii. 16), and through them to prepare the way for national reformation. And in this work he was aided by personal relations within the highest circles of the capital. Uriah, the chief priest of the temple, was his friend, and appears associated with him as witness to a solemn act by which he attested a weighty prophecy at a time when king and people had not yet learned to give credence to his words (viii. 2). His own life seems to have been constantly spent in the capital ; but he was not without support in the provinces. The countryman Micah, who prophesied in the low country on the Philistine border near the beginning of Hezekiah's reign, was unquestionably influenced by his great contemporary, and, though his conceptions are shaped with the individual freedom characteristic of the true prophet, and by no means fit mechanically into the details of Isaiah's picture of Jehovah's approaching dealings, the essence of his teaching went all to further Isaiah's aims. Thus Isaiah ultimately became the acknowledged head of a great religious movement. It is too little to say that in his later years he was the first man in Judah, practically guiding the helm of the state, and encouraging Jerusalem to hold out against the Assyrian when all besides had lost courage. Even to the political historian Isaiah is the most notable figure after David in the whole history of Israel. He was the man of a supreme crisis, and he proved himself worthy by guiding his nation through the crisis with no other strength than the prophetic word. His commanding influence on the history of his nation naturally suggests comparison with Elisha, the author of the revolution of Jehu, and the soul of the great struggle with Syria. The comparison illustrates the extraordinary change which little more than a century had wrought in the character and aims of prophecy. Elisha effected his first object—the downfall of the house of Ahab—by entering into the sphere of ordinary political intrigue; Isaiah stood aloof from all political combinations, and his influence was simply that of his commanding character, and of the imperial word of Jehovah preached in season and out of season with unwavering constancy. Elisha in his later years was the inspiring spirit of a heroic conflict, encouraging his people to fight for freedom, and resist the invader by armed force. Isaiah well knew that Judah had no martial strength that could avail for a moment against the power of Assyria. He did not aim at national independence; and, rising above the dreams of vulgar patriotism, he was content to accept the inevitable, and mark out for Judah a course of patient submission to the foreign yoke, in order that the nation might concentrate itself on the task of internal reformation till Jehovah Himself should remove the scourge appointed for His people's sin. In this conception he seized and united in one practical aim ideas which had appeared separately in the teaching of his predecessors, Amos and Hosea. Amos had taught the salvation of a righteous remnant in a nation purified by judgment, Hosea had pointed out that warlike effort and political combinations could not help Israel, which must seek its deliverance in repentance and reliance on Jehovah's sovereignty. With Isaiah the doctrine of the remnant becomes a practical principle; the true Israel within Israel, the holy seed in the fallen stock of the nation, is the object of all his solicitude. Living in the very midst of the winnowing judgment which Amos had seen approaching from afar, he sought to give the vital elements of the nation a centre round which they could rally, and a task of internal reformation conformed to the duty of national repentance. This alone was

Israel's wisdom; Jehovah's power and Jehovah's spirit must accomplish the rest without help from the arm of flesh. In the supreme crisis of the Assyrian wars Isaiah was not less truly the bulwark of his nation than Elisha had been during the Syrian wars. But his heroism was that of patience and faith, and the deliverance came as he had foretold, not by political wisdom or warlike prowess, but by the direct intervention of Jehovah.

When we endeavour to trace the history of Isaiah's prophetic activity by the aid of his own writings, we are met by the difficulty that his book is not arranged in strict chronological order. Thus the inaugural vision in which he received his consecration as Jehovah's messenger to Judah is not the first but the sixth chapter of the book; or again chap. xx., which is dated from the year of the capture of Ashdod by the general of Sargon, *i.e.* B.C. 711, would in chronological order stand after chap. xxviii., which speaks of the kingdom of Ephraim as still in existence. It is plain, then, that the book as it stands is in a somewhat disordered state. Presumably Isaiah himself issued no collected edition of all his prophecies, but only put forth from time to time individual oracles or minor collections, which were gathered together at a later date, and on no plan which we can follow. Some of the prophecies bear a date, or even have brief notes of historical explanation; others begin without any such preface, and their date and occasion can only be inferred from the allusions they contain. We cannot even tell when or by whom the collection was made. The collection of all remains of ancient prophecy, digested into the four books named from Isaiah, Jeremiah, Ezekiel, and the Twelve Minor Prophets, was not formed till after the time of Ezra, two hundred and fifty years at least after the death of Isaiah. In one of these four books every known fragment of ancient prophecy had to take its place, and no one who knows anything of the collection and transmission of ancient books will think it reasonable to expect that the writings of each separate prophet were carefully gathered out and arranged together in such a way as to preclude all ambiguity as to their authorship.[5] If every prophecy had had a title from the first the task of the editor would have been simple; or if he did not aim at an exact arrangement we could easily have rearranged the series for ourselves. But there are some prophecies, such as those which occupy the last twenty-seven chapters of Isaiah, which have no title at all, and in some other cases there is conclusive evidence that the titles are not original, because, in point of fact, they are incorrect. In the absence of precise titles giving names and dates to each separate prophecy, an editor labouring after the time of Ezra would be quite as much at a loss as a modern critic, if he made it his task to give what is now called a critical edition of the remains that lay before him. But ancient editors did not feel the need of an edition digested according to the rules of modern literary workmanship. Their main object was to get together everything that they could find, and arrange their material in volumes convenient for private study or use in the synagogue. In those days one could not plan the number of volumes, the number of letters in a page, and the size and form of the pages, with the freedom to which the printing press has accustomed us; the cumbrous and costly materials of ancient books limited all schemes of editorial disposition. In ancient books the most various treatises are often comprised in one volume; the scribe had a certain number of skins, and he wished to fill them. Thus, even in the minor collections that fell into the hands of the editor of the prophets, a prophecy of Isaiah and one from another source might easily occupy the same roll; copies were not so numerous that it was always possible to tell by comparison of many MSS. what pieces had always stood together, and what had only come together by accident; and so, taking all in all, we need not be surprised that the arrangement is imperfect according to our literary lights, but will rather expect to find much more serious faults of order than the lack of a just chronological disposition. If the present book of Isaiah has itself been made up from several MSS., a conclusion which the lack of chronological order renders almost inevitable, we must deem it probable that at the end of some of these MSS. prophecies not by Isaiah at all may have been written in to save waste of the costly material; and so, when the several small books came to be joined together, prophecies by other hands would get to be embedded in the text of Isaiah, no longer to be distinguished except by internal evidence. That what thus appears as possible or even probable actually took place is the common opinion of modern critics. We must not accept this opinion without examination, and we cannot now pause to go over every chapter of the book in detail; but, on the other hand, we cannot hope to get a just picture of Isaiah's life and work without keeping our minds open to the possibilities now suggested. Instead of taking up his prophecies in the order in which they now stand, we must look for internal evidence to connect each oracle with one or other part of his career. Those sections of the book which cannot be read in clear connection with any part of the prophet's life and times must provisionally be set on one side. Even if they are Isaiah's they can have but secondary importance for our present business, which is to study the prophetic word in the light of the history of the prophet's own times; and in fact the more clearly we come to see that the rest of the book is full of references to present history the more shall we be disposed to ask whether these prophecies too have not an historical setting of their own, but one which belongs to a later stage of the Old Testament progress. It may be well to say at once that most parts of the book of Isaiah whose authorship is disputed have a plain connection with the Chaldæan period. Whether this connection is of a kind which justifies us in holding that they were written in that period is a question which almost every critic answers in the affirmative, but which cannot be profitably discussed in these Lectures, because the discussion involves an historical study of the age of the Exile. The critical problems of Isaiah belong to the history of prophecy under the Chaldæan empire, and even those scholars who still believe that the whole book is from the pen of Isaiah ascribe the prophecies against Babylon to his old age, after his active life was over, so that it at least can be completely studied without them. And it is further agreed that these prophecies had no part in the great influence which Isaiah exerted on the immediately subsequent age, so that for the whole study of the Old Testament religion before the Exile we lose nothing by leaving them out of account.

The period of Isaiah's ministry falls into three parts:—(1) The time previous to the Syro-Ephraitic war, when Judah enjoyed external peace and apparent prosperity; (2) The troubles under the reign of Ahaz, when the land was invaded by Pekah and Rezin, and the Judæan monarch became a vassal of Assyria to obtain the help of Tiglath Pileser; (3) The time of Assyrian suzerainty, when Judah's growing impatience of the yoke at length led the nation to intrigue with Egypt, and exposed it to the vengeance of Sennacherib. The last section of the prophet's life culminates in the great invasion and marvellous deliverance of the year 701 B.C. We may not in every case be able to give a precise chronological view of the progress of the prophet's work, but at least we may hope to distribute his prophecies under these three periods, and to gain an approximate conception of the order of those which belong to the last and longest of the three, especially by comparing the many historical allusions with the Assyrian monuments. Without going into detail at the present stage of the discussion, it may be convenient to indicate broadly some conclusions to which we are led by this method.

In the first place, then, it is plain that the general survey of the state of Judah given in chap. i. cannot belong to the first period of Isaiah's work, for it represents the land as reduced to the utmost distress by foreign invasion. It must have been chosen to open the book on account of its general character, and so displaced from its proper chronological setting. On the other hand, the prophecy which begins, with a separate title, at chap. ii. 1 belongs to the earliest part of Isaiah's ministry. Here there is no allusion to present wars, and at ii. 16 the ships of Tarshish appear as one of the glories of the nation. But Elath, the only Judæan harbour, was taken in the war of Pekah and Rezin, and the Syrians (or Edomites) continued to hold the town long after (2 Kings xvi. 6). This prophecy, or at least a connected series of prophecies which presumably were published by Isaiah in a single book, goes on to the end of chap. v., and there is great probability that ix. 8 to x. 4 originally formed part of the close of this publication. So common an accident as the displacement of part of a manuscript would sufficiently account for the transposition of these verses to their present place.

The account of the inaugural vision of the prophet in chap. vi. does not belong to Isaiah's first published work, but stands at the head of a new series of prophecies dating from the great trouble at the commencement of Ahaz's reign. There is no reason to doubt that this arrangement is due to Isaiah himself. He might have many reasons for not speaking of the vision at the time when it occurred, and its contents form a very appropriate introduction to the series of prophecies which it now precedes, extending from vii. 1 to ix. 7. The prophecy of the downfall of Damascus (xvii. 1-11) plainly belongs to the same period. All the remaining parts of the book appear to be subsequent to the Assyrian intervention (B.C. 734). Most of them refer more or less clearly to successive stages in the progress of the Assyrians, which in the present state of our knowledge must often remain obscure. They cannot have been all published at once, and probably Isaiah himself, in reducing selections of his prophecies to writing from time to time, united oracles of various date. Chap. xxviii., for example, must have been first spoken before the fall of Samaria, but as we now read it it is closely connected with several following chapters which seem to be of later composition. For our present purpose it is enough to regard all the prophecies of Isaiah's third period as one group, without attempting at this stage to arrange them more exactly. The parts of the book which do not fall under any one of the three groups now spoken of, and which, as already explained, I shall pass over altogether, are the prophecies against Babylon, xiii. 1 to xiv. 23 ; xxi. 1-10 ; [6] the very remarkable and difficult section, chaps. xxiv. to xxvii. ; the prophecy against Edom, chap. xxxiv ; and the great prophecy, chaps. xl. to lxvi., which is separated from the rest of the book by an historical section, certainly not written by Isaiah himself. There are also two lyrical chapters, xii. and xxxv., of which the latter seems to go with chap. xxxiv. Both are so unlike the style of Isaiah that it will be prudent to pass them over also.[7]

Although Isaiah did not publish the account of the vision in which he received his prophetic consecration until the second period of his work (chap. vi.), it is reasonable that we should take it first. In the year of Uzziah's death, he tells us, he saw Jehovah seated on a lofty throne, while the skirts of His kingly robes filled the palace. Jehovah's palace is the common name of the great temple at Jerusalem, and the features of the temple are reproduced in the vision. There was an altar (ver. 6), a threshold (ver. 4, where for *posts of the door* read *sockets of the thresholds*), and a cloud of smoke filling the house during the adoration of the seraphim, like the smoke of incense or sacrifice during ordinary acts of worship. In the earlier history of the temple the Debîr or Holy of Holies appears not to have been shut off by doors from the holy place (1 Kings vi. 21 as contrasted with ver. 31), and in like manner Isaiah's palace forms one great hall, so that the prophet standing at the door, where he felt the rocking of the thresholds at the thunder of the Trisagion, could see the seat of Divine majesty within. Yet the palace of Isaiah's conception is not the earthly temple but the heavenly seat of Jehovah's sovereignty. The lofty throne of Jehovah takes the place of the ark, and the ministers of the palace are not human priests but fiery beings,—the seraphim. It is plain that the very idea of the dwelling-place of Jehovah involves to human minds the aid of figure and symbol; it cannot be realised at all except under images derived from visible things. The scenery of Isaiah's vision is of necessity purely symbolical, and the form of the symbol was naturally determined by the old Hebrew conception of the sanctuary as God's palace on earth, while the additional feature of the fiery, winged seraphim appears to have been suggested by a current conception analogous to that of the cherubim. The Old Testament contains more than one trace of weird personification of atmospheric or celestial phenomena. The cherubim are possibly a personification of the thunder cloud, and the seraphim of the lightning.[8] But the origin of the scenery is immaterial for the ideal meaning of Isaiah's vision; temple and seraphim are nothing more than the necessary pictorial clothing of the supreme truth that in this vision his soul met the Infinite and Eternal face to face, and heard the secrets of Jehovah's counsel

directly from His own mouth. Nor can it be of
importance to us to determine how far the description
is conscious poetry, and how far the pictures described
passed without any effort of thought or volition before
his inward eye. Even in the highest imaginings of
poetical genius this question would be hard to answer;
much less can we expect to be able to analyse the
workings of the prophet's soul in a supreme moment of
converse with God.

In some quarters a great deal too much stress has
been laid upon the prophetic vision as a distinctive
note of supernatural revelation. People speak as if the
divine authority of the prophetic word were somehow
dependent on, or confirmed by, the fact that the prophets
enjoyed visions. That, however, is not the doctrine of
the Bible. In the New Testament Paul lays down the
principle that in true prophecy self-consciousness and
self-command are never lost—the spirits of the prophets
are subject to the prophets (1 Cor. xiv. 32). In like manner the prophets of the Old Testament never appeared
before their auditors in a state of ecstasy, being thus
clearly marked off from heathen soothsayers, who were
held to be under the influence of the godhead just in
proportion as they lost intelligent self-control. And,
as the true prophets never seek in heathen fashion to
authenticate their divine commission by showing themselves in a state of visionary ecstasy, so also they do
not record their visions as a proof that they are inspired. They knew very well that vision and ecstasy

were common in heathenism, and therefore could prove no commission from Jehovah (Jer. xxiii.); and so, as we have seen, Isaiah did not even publish his inaugural vision at the time, but reserved it till his ministry had been public for years. Moreover, the Hebrews were aware that the vision, in which spiritual truth is clothed in forms derived from the sphere of the outer senses, is not the highest method of revelation. In the twelfth chapter of Numbers, which belongs to the part of the Pentateuch composed before the rise of written prophecy, Moses, who received his revelation in plain words not involved in symbolic imagery, is placed above those prophets to whom Jehovah speaks in vision or in dream. This view is entirely conformed to the conclusions of scientific psychology. Dream and vision are nothing more than a peculiar kind of thought, in which the senses of the thinker are more or less completely shut to the outer world, so that his imagination moves more freely than in ordinary waking moments among the pictures of sensible things stored up in the memory. Thus, on the one hand, the images of fancy seem to stand out more brightly, because they are not contrasted with the sharper pictures of sense-perception, while, on the other hand, the power of the will to conduct thought in a predetermined direction is suspended, or so far subdued that the play of sensuous fancy produces new combinations, which appear to rise up of themselves before the mind like the images of real things before the physical senses. The ultimate elements of such a vision can include nothing absolutely new; the conceptions of which it is built up are exclusively such as are supplied by previous waking experience, the whole novelty lying in their combination. So far, therefore, as its structure is concerned, there is no essential difference between a vision and a parable or other creation of poetic fancy; and this is as strictly true for the visions of the prophets as for those of other men; so that it is often difficult to say whether any particular allegory set forth by a prophet is visionary or not—that is to say, we often cannot tell whether the prophet is devising an instructive figure by a deliberate act of thought, or whether the figure rose, as it were, of itself before his mind in a moment of deep abstraction, when his thoughts seemed to take their own course without a conscious effort of will.

In the experience of the greatest prophets visions were of very rare occurrence. Isaiah records but one in the course of forty years' prophetic work. As a rule, the supreme religious thought which fills the prophet's soul, and which comes to him not as the result of argument but as a direct intuition of divine truth, an immediate revelation of Jehovah, is developed by the ordinary processes of the intellect. There is nothing rhapsodical or unintelligible in the prophetic discourses; they address themselves to the understanding and the heart of every man who feels the truth of the fundamental religious conceptions on which they rest. But all thought about transcendental and spiritual things must be partly carried out by the help of analogies from human life and experience, and in the earlier stages of revelation, before the full declaration of God in His incarnate Son, the element of analogy and symbol was necessarily larger in proportion as the knowledge of God's plan was more imperfect. The prophets, as we are taught in the first verse of the Epistle to the Hebrews, saw only fragmentary parts and individual aspects of divine truth. This is not a peculiarity of early revelation alone; it applies equally to early thought about the things of nature, which in like manner reveal themselves only in isolated aspects to the primitive observer, so that all thought is in its beginnings fragmentary, and, being so, requires to bridge over gulfs by the aid of analogy and figure, in a way which in later ages is mainly confined to the poetic imagination. And for this reason early thought is less clearly self-conscious than the scientific reasonings of later time. The thinker loses himself in his thought, and seems to be swept on by his own ideas instead of ruling and guiding them. The further back we can go in the history of human ideas the more closely do we approach a stage in which all new intellectual combinations are expressed in symbol, and in which the symbol, instead of being used only for purposes of illustration, is the necessary vehicle of thought. At this stage new ideas appear, not as logical inferences, but as immediate intuitions, in which the volition of the thinker has little or no share; and when such symbolic views of abstract or spiritual things rise before the mind in a moment of deep abstraction, as they most naturally do, they may without impropriety be called *visions*, though they are not necessarily associated with the symptoms of ecstasy in the strict sense. It is thus easy to understand that vision, in the sense now defined, was a predominant characteristic of the earliest stages of prophecy, as Num. xii. seems to imply, but that it fell more and more into the background with the great prophets of the eighth century, as their conceptions of spiritual truth became more articulate and wider in range. For purposes of exposition it was still necessary to make a large use of symbol and analogy, but vision begins to merge more and more into conscious parable, till at length in the teaching of Jesus we reach a stage where vision altogether disappears in direct communion with the Father, and parable is no longer a means of thinking out religious problems, but simply a method of bringing truth home to popular understanding. At every stage, however, in the history of prophecy the spiritual value of vision is precisely the same as that of parable, and is proportioned to the measure in which the symbolic picture presents spiritual things under a true analogy. Whether the prophet merely set forth in symbolic form truths which he had reached in another way, or whether he consciously devised a symbol, in order to have the aid of analogy to bridge over gaps in his view of divine things, or whether the symbol rose up before his mind without a conscious effort of the intellect, does not affect its value as a vehicle of spiritual truth. The value of the symbol or vision depends simply on the fact that in one or other way he was guided to the use of imagery fitted to give larger and deeper views of spiritual realities.

Of the spiritual realities impressed on Isaiah's mind in his great vision, and which continued to exercise a profound influence on his whole career, the first is the *holiness* of Jehovah. The notion of holiness belongs to the ancient stock of common Semitic conceptions, being expressed in all the Semitic languages by the same root (קדש). The etymological idea of the root is obscure. If the Arabic commentaries on the Koran may be believed, it is that of distance or separation; but the word was so early appropriated to a special religious sense that its primary notion can no longer be traced with certainty.[9] The traditional etymology seems, however, to be so far justified by usage. To the Semite everything divine is also holy, and in this connection the word does not in its earliest use seem to convey any positive conception, but rather to express the distance and awful contrast between the divine and the human. The supreme Godhead of Jehovah is expressed in 1 Sam. ii. 2 by saying, "There is no holy one like Jehovah; yea, there is none beside Thee." "I am God, and not man," says Hosea; "the Holy One in the midst of thee" (xi. 9). Holiness, in fact, is the most comprehensive predicate of the Godhead, equally familiar to the Hebrews and their heathen neighbours. The "holy gods" is a standing designation of the Phœnician deities, as we learn from the monument of Eshmunazar; and so the word in its original use cannot have conveyed any idea peculiar to the religion of Jehovah. Its force lay in its very vagueness, for it included every distinctive character of Godhead, and every advance in the true knowledge of God made its significance more profound; thus the doctrine of Jehovah's holiness is simply the doctrine of His true Godhead. When the first sound that Isaiah hears in the heavenly temple is the Trisagion of the seraphim—

> "Holy, holy, holy is Jehovah of Hosts;
> All that the earth contains is His wealth,"

we see that Isaiah does not find the starting-point of his prophetic work in the contemplation of any one attribute of Jehovah—His universal justice, as it is set forth by Amos, or His love, as developed in the teaching of Hosea —but in the thought that all the predicates of true Godhead are concentrated in Jehovah, and in Him alone.

The prophets who preceded Isaiah did not preach a doctrine of abstract monotheism, they did not start from the idea that there can be only one God; but, looking at Jehovah, Israel's God, as He was actually known to His people, they interpreted His being and character in a way that placed a great gulf between Him and the nature-gods of the heathen. Thus the Godhead of Jehovah as taught by the prophets meant something quite different from the godhead or holiness attributed to idols or to heathen deities. There was no longer any meaning in applying the same terms to both; Jehovah alone was holy, or, what is practically the same thing, He alone was God in the true sense of these words. It is this truth which forms the foundation of Isaiah's teaching. The whole earth is full of the signs of Jehovah's sovereignty; He dwells on high, exalted over all (xxxiii. 5); He reigns supreme alike in the realm of nature and the sphere of human history; and the crash of kingdoms, the total dissolution of the old order of the Hebrew world, which accompanied the advance of Assyria, is to the prophet nothing else than the crowning proof of Jehovah's absolute dominion, asserting itself in the abasement of all that disputes His supremacy. The loftiness of man shall be humbled, and the haughtiness of men shall be bowed down, and Jehovah alone shall be exalted in that day (ii. 17).

But with all this Isaiah does not cease to regard Jehovah's kingship as essentially a kingship over Israel. At first sight this may seem to us a strange limitation on the part of one who declares that all that the earth contains is Jehovah's wealth; but in reality the limitation gives to his doctrine a concrete and practical force otherwise unattainable. The kingship of Jehovah is to our prophet not a mere figure but a literal truth, and so His kingdom can only consist of the nation whose affairs He administers in person, whose human rulers reign as His representatives, and which receives its law and polity from His mouth. To Isaiah, therefore, Jehovah is not simply the Holy One in an abstract sense; He is the Holy Being who reigns over Israel; or, to use the prophet's favourite phrase, "The Holy One of Israel." When the idea of holiness is thus brought into connection with Jehovah's relation to His people, it becomes at once a practical factor in religion; for in the ordinary language of the Hebrews holiness was not limited to the Deity, but could also be predicated of earthly things specially set apart for Him. The sanctuary was a holy place, the religious feasts were holy seasons, material things were consecrated or rendered holy by being appropriated to use in the worship of the Deity, or presented to the sanctuary. And in like manner holiness could be predicated of persons; the prophet who stood in a particular relation of nearness to the Godhead was "a holy man of God" (2 Kings iv. 9); the ordinary Israelite was not holy in this sense, but at least he was consecrated, or made holy, by special ceremonies before engaging in an act of sacrificial worship (1 Sam. xvi. 5); and the same expression is used of the ceremonial purification employed to purge away those impurities which excluded an Israelite from participation in holy functions (2 Sam. xi. 4).

In all this, you observe, there is nothing proper to spiritual religion, nothing that goes beyond the sphere of the primitive conceptions common to the Israelites with their heathen neighbours. Holy places, things, or times are such as are withdrawn from common use and appropriated to a religious purpose, and in like manner holiness, as ascribed to persons, is no moral attribute;

it refers only to the ritual separation from things common and unclean, without which the worshipper dare not approach the divine presence. Holiness and immorality might even go side by side; the "holy women" (*ḳedēshōt*) of the Canaanite religion, found also in the popular Hebrew shrines, were *Hierodouloi* consecrated to immoral purposes. But when the teaching of the prophets brought Jehovah's holiness into sharp contrast with the pretended godhead of the Baalim, the holiness of Jehovah's people could not but in like manner take a sense different from that which prevailed in heathenism. So already in Amos the licentious practices of the Hierodouloi are said to profane Jehovah's holy name (Amos ii. 7). But with Isaiah this transformation of the notion of Israel's holiness has a wider scope. He does not develop the idea in special connection with distinctively religious acts. The holiness of Israel rather depends on the thought that Israel, in all its functions, civil as well as religious, is Jehovah's people, Jehovah's property (His vineyard, as he puts it in chap. v.), the immediate sphere of His personal interest and activity. Thus the whole land of Judah, but more especially Jerusalem, the centre of the state, is, as it were, a great sanctuary, the holy mountain of Jehovah (xi. 9), and within this holy mountain everything ought to be ordered in conformity with His sanctity. The requisites of ceremonial sanctity fall altogether into the background; the task of Israel as a holy nation is to give practical recognition to Jehovah's holiness—that is, to acknowledge and reverence His Godhead, in those moral characters which distinguish Him from the idols and false gods (viii. 13; xxix. 23). According to Isaiah, "the knowledge and fear of Jehovah" (xi. 2) are the summary requisites for the right ordering of the state of Israel; where these are supreme the conditions of Israel's holiness are satisfied. The ideal condition of Jehovah's holy mountain is one in which the earth is full of the knowledge of Jehovah as the waters cover the sea (xi. 9). And, conversely, where these things are lacking, where the homage due to Him is shared by idols, where heathen divinations are looked to instead of "the revelation and the testimony" of Jehovah (viii. 20), where injustice and oppression flourish in defiance of the righteous king of Israel, the holiness of His people is changed to uncleanness, and cannot be restored save by fiery judgment purging away the filth of the daughters of Zion and the bloodguiltiness of Jerusalem (iv. 3, 4).

It is easy to see that in this view of the religious problem of his times, Isaiah builds on the foundations laid by his predecessors Amos and Hosea. But his treatment of the problem is more comprehensive and all-sided. The preaching of Amos was directed only to breaches of civil righteousness, and supplied no standard for the reformation of national worship—it left even the golden calves untouched. Hosea, on the other hand, has a clear insight into the right moral attitude of the religious subject to God; but that subject is to him the personified nation, sinning and repenting as one man, and therefore he has no practical suggestions applicable to the actual mixed state of society; his prophecy leaves an unexplained hiatus between Israel's present sin and its future return to Jehovah. Isaiah, on the contrary, finds in Jehovah's holiness a principle equally applicable to the amendment of the state and the elevation of religious praxis, an ideal which supplies an immediate impulse to reformation, and which, though it cannot be fully attained without the intervention of purging judgments, may at least become the practical guide of those within Israel who are striving after better things. In every question of national conduct presented by the eventful times in which he lived Isaiah was ready with clear decisive counsel, for in every crisis Israel's one duty was to concentrate itself on the task of shaping the internal order of the state in conformity with the holy character of Jehovah, and to trust the issue to His sovereignty.

In very truth the task of internal reform was more than sufficient for one generation. The whole order of the state was glaringly at variance with right conceptions of Jehovah; or, in the language now familiar to us, the actual life of the nation was not holy but unclean. A strong sense of this uncleanness was the feeling which sprang to the prophet's lips when he first saw the vision of Jehovah's holiness—"Woe is me! for I am undone; for I am a man of unclean lips, and I dwell in the midst of a people of unclean lips, for mine eyes have seen the King, Jehovah of hosts." On the old ritual view of holiness there was fatal danger in contact with holy things to any one ceremonially unclean. But the impurity of which Isaiah speaks is impurity of lips— that is, of utterance. In Hebrew idiom, a man's words (*debārīm*) include his purposes on the one hand, his actions on the other, and thus impurity of lips means inconsistency of purpose and action with the standard of divine holiness. The prophet himself supplies the translation of his metaphor at iii. 8—"Jerusalem is ruined and Judah is fallen, for their tongue and their doings are against Jehovah of hosts, to provoke the eyes of His glory," and the expansion of this sentence forms the main burden of his first great discourse to the house of Israel (chap. ii. *seq.*). There is, however, a special reason why, in this vision, the uncleanness of the people is particularised as uncleanness of lip. The vision is Isaiah's consecration as Jehovah's messenger, and for the discharge of such a function "pure lips" (Zeph. iii. 9) are necessary. But Isaiah feels himself to be personally involved in the impurity or unholiness of his people; his own lips are impure and unfit for personal converse with Jehovah. And so the act of consecration is symbolically represented as the purging of his lips by contact with a glowing stone taken from Jehovah's sacred hearth. "Lo, this hath touched thy lips," says the ministering seraph, "and thine iniquity is taken away, and thy sin purged." The form of this visionary transaction is suggested by the old familiar symbolism of ceremonial holiness. In primitive religious thought, the idea of godhead is specially connected with that of fresh unfading life, and the impurity or unholiness which must be kept aloof from the sanctuary is associated with physical corruption and death. Fire and water, the pure and life-like elements, man's chief aids in combating physical corruption, are the main agents in ceremonies of ritual sanctification (Num. xxxi. 23; this passage belongs to the later legislation, but the antiquity of the principle appears from Josh. vi. 19, 24). But fire is a more searching principle than water. Fiery brightness is of old the highest symbol of Jehovah's holiness, and purification by fire the most perfect image of the total destruction of impurity. To Isaiah, of course, the fire of Jehovah's holiness is a mere symbol. That which cannot endure the fire, which is burned up and consumed before it, is moral impurity. " Who among us shall dwell with devouring fire, who among us shall dwell with everlasting burnings ? He that walketh in righteousness and speaketh uprightly, that shaketh his hands from holding of bribes, that stoppeth his ears from hearing of blood [consenting to bloodshed], and shutteth his eyes from beholding [delighting in] evil; he shall dwell on high; his place of defence shall be the munitions of rocks, his bread shall be given him, his water shall be sure" (xxxiii. 14 *seq.*). That which can endure the fire is that which is fit to enter into communion with Jehovah's holiness, and nothing which cannot stand this test can abide in His sanctuary of Israel. Thus the fire which touches Isaiah's lips and consecrates him to prophetic communion with God has its counterpart in the fiery judgment through which impure Israel must pass till only the holy seed, the vital and indestructible elements of right national life, remain. As silver is purified by repeated smeltings, so the land of Judah must pass, not once, but again and again through the fire. "Though but a tenth remain in it, it must pass again through the fire" (vi. 13), till all that remain in Zion are holy, "even every one that is ordained to life in Jerusalem, when Jehovah shall have washed away the filth of the daughters of Zion, and purged the bloodshed of Jerusalem by the blast of judgment, and the blast of burning" (iv. 4 *seq.*).

That this is the law of Jehovah's holiness towards Israel is revealed to the prophet as soon as his own lips are purged. For the prophetic insight into Jehovah's purpose is the insight of spiritual sympathy, and thus, as soon as his sin is taken away and his own life penetrated by the power of the divine holiness, he who had before heard only the awful voice of the seraphim shaking the very threshold at which he stood, and filling his heart with terror at the unendurable majesty of the Most High, hears the voice of Jehovah Himself asking, "Whom shall I send, and who will go for us?" and replies without fear, "Here am I; send me." But from the first he is made to know that his mission cannot bear sudden fruit, that no swift and superficial repentance can correspond to Jehovah's plan. He is sent to men who shall be ever hearing, but never understand; ever seeing Jehovah's work, but never recognising its true import; whose heart (or intelligence) becomes more gross, their ears more dull, their eyes veiled with thicker clouds of spiritual blindness under the prophetic teaching, who refuse to turn and receive healing from Jehovah till cities lie waste without inhabitants, and houses without inmates, and the land is changed to a desert by invading foes. And yet Isaiah knows from the first that this consuming judgment at the hand of the Assyrians moves in the right line of Jehovah's purpose of holiness. The axe is laid at the root of the tree, and the present state, corrupt beyond the reach of partial remedies, must be hewn to the ground. But the true life of Israel cannot perish. "Like the terebinth and the oak, whose stock remains when they are hewn down," and sends forth new saplings, so "the holy seed" remains as a living stock, and a new and better Israel shall spring from the ruin of the ancient state.

Such are the first principles of Isaiah's teaching as he presents them in describing his vision of consecration. Their development and application in his public ministry must be reserved for another Lecture.

LECTURE VI.

THE EARLIER PROPHECIES OF ISAIAH.

WE found in last Lecture that the arrangement of the extant collection of Isaiah's prophecies points to the conclusion that the prophet, at different times in his life, put forth several distinct volumes embodying the sum of certain parts of his oral teaching. In the case of Amos and Hosea it is not clear that anything of this kind took place, and as regards Amos we may take it as certain that his book was not written till his whole message to Israel had been delivered and rejected. Isaiah, on the other hand, used the publication of his past prophecies as an agency supplementing his continued oral work. He was not left to the same isolation as Amos and Hosea. At an early period of his ministry we find him surrounded by a circle of disciples, to whom it would appear that his written prophecies were in the first instance committed (viii. 16) ; and in this way he was able to influence a wider circle than he could have reached by mere oral preaching. The adoption of this method of teaching by books, and even, it would seem, by placards fixed in some public place (viii. 1 ; xxx. 8),[1] implies the existence of a considerable reading public ; and it may be noticed, as an interesting illustration of this fact, that the recently-discovered inscription in the rock-cut tunnel of Siloam, probably dating from the lifetime of Isaiah, is no official record, but seems to have been carved by the workmen on their own account. Reading and writing must therefore have been pretty common accomplishments (comp. Isa. xxix. 11 *seq.*), and the well-timed publication of connected selections of prophecy, disseminated by the friends of Isaiah, had no doubt much to do with the solid and extensive influence which he gradually acquired. We must not suppose that Isaiah's publications were mere fly-sheets containing single oracles. Each of them was manifestly a well-planned digest of the substance of teaching which, in its first delivery, may have occupied several years; chaps. ii.-v., for example, with the connected passage ix. 8 to x. 4, cover all the prophet's teaching before the war of 734, and can hardly have been published till the outbreak of that war, to the first stage of which some of the allusions appear to point. The gravity of the crisis made it natural for Isaiah to make a special effort to lead his nation to form a just estimate of its religious significance, and this he could best do by recalling in summary form the substance of the lessons which year after year he had been laying before them. A book written in this way became something more than a series of skeleton sermons : it took the shape of a prophetic commentary on the political events, the social and religious phenomena, of a certain period of Judah's history, in which predictive announcements were mingled with historical retrospect. The peculiarities of Hebrew grammar and prophetic style often make it difficult to distinguish between narrative and prediction, and the difficulty is increased by the fact that predictions referring to the near future were sometimes fulfilled before they were set forth in a book. If the highest object of the prophet had been to show that he could foresee future events, he would no doubt have been careful to draw a sharp line between the predictive and retrospective parts of his writings; but in reality prediction was only one element in the work of explaining to the nation what Jehovah's present dealings meant, and how He desired them to be laid to heart. It would have been mere pedantry to sacrifice this object to that of recording each prediction exactly as it was first made. When historical events had thrown new light on any part of the prophet's argument, he used that new light in its proper place, and thus, on the whole, though many parts of Isa. ii.-v. are no doubt in the main a good deal older than the commencement of Ahaz's reign, we must take this section of Isaiah's prophecies as practically representing the stage to which his prophetic argument had advanced, after a good many years of prophetic work, about the beginning of the war with Pekah and Rezin, or, which is the same thing, about the time of the accession of Ahaz.

The situation of the kingdom when this book appeared is clearly described by the prophet in his peroration, but to the English reader the sense of this passage is somewhat obscured not only by the transposition of ix. 8-x. 4 from its proper place, but by the inaccurate translation of many of the tenses as futures instead of perfects, so that the Authorised Version puts as prediction statements which are really descriptive of the present condition of affairs. To restore the order and the sense we must read ix. 8 *seq.* immediately after v. 25, so as to form a series of four strophes, describing in ascending series the evils that had already fallen on the Hebrews, and each closing with the words,—"For all this His anger is not turned away, but His hand is stretched out still." The final judgment therefore lies still in the future, the Assyrians are the instruments destined to accomplish it, and their approach is pictured in the predictive passage, v. 26-30, with which the book closes.

King Jotham, the last of a series of strong and generally successful princes, had died at a critical moment, when Pekah and Rezin were maturing their plans against his kingdom. The opposing parties in Northern Israel suspended their feuds to make common cause against Judah (ix. 21), and the proud inhabitants of Samaria hoped by this policy to more than restore the prestige forfeited in previous years of calamity (ix. 9, 10). At the same time the Syrians began to operate in the eastern dependencies of Judah, their aim being to possess themselves of the harbour of Elath on the

Red Sea, while the Philistines attacked the Judæans in the rear, and ravaged the fertile lowlands (ix. 12 ; 2 Kings xvi. 6). A heavy and sudden disaster had already fallen on the Judæan arms, a defeat in which head and tail, palm-branch and rush—that is, the highest officers and the common multitude of the host—had been mowed down in indiscriminate slaughter (ix. 14).[2] Ahaz was no fit leader in so critical a time ; his character was petulant and childish, his policy was dictated in the harem (iii. 12). Nor was the internal order of the state calculated to inspire confidence. Wealth, indeed, had greatly accumulated in the preceding time of prosperity, but its distribution, as we saw in last Lecture, had been such that it weakened rather than added strength to the nation. The rich nobles were steeped in sensual luxury (v. 11 *seq.*), the Court was full of gallantry, and feminine extravagance and vanity gave the tone to aristocratic society (iii. 16 *seq.* ; comp. iii. 12, iv. 4), which, like the *noblesse* of France on the eve of the Revolution, was absorbed in gaiety and pleasure, while the masses were ground down by oppression, and the cry of their distress filled the land (iii. 15 ; v. 7). All social bonds were loosed in the universal reign of injustice, every man was for himself and no man for his brother (ix. 19 *seq.*). The subordination of classes was undermined (iii. 4, 5), things were tending to a pass when ere long none would be found willing to accept a post of authority, or to risk his own substance for the good of the state (iii. 6 *seq.*).

We must not suppose that to ordinary political observers at the time these internal wounds of the state appeared so aggravated and so patent as Isaiah represents them. The best Oriental administrations permit abuses which we would think intolerable, and in particular the wrongs and sufferings of the poor make little noise, and find no ready access to the supreme seat of government. The attention of the rulers was doubtless directed almost exclusively to the dangers that menaced from without; their schemes of deliverance took the shape of warlike preparations, or were already turned to the project of an alliance with Assyria. As yet they saw no cause for despondency; the accumulated resources of the nation were not exhausted, and the characteristic Hebrew obstinacy, which in later times more than once plunged the Jews into hopeless struggle with irresistible antagonists, was backed up by false religious confidence. The idols of which the land was full had not lost their reputation; Isaiah alone foresaw the approach of the hour of despair when these vain deliverers should be confronted with stern realities (x. 10, 11), when the nations and their gods, from the Euphrates to the Mediterranean, should go down before the brute force of the Assyrian hosts, when men should cast their idols to the moles and to the bats, before the terror of Jehovah when He cometh to shake the earth (ii. 21). To the mass of Israel, the contrast which Isaiah draws between Jehovah and the idols did not exist; the idols themselves were associated with the sanctuaries of the national Deity, and men fancied, as the house of Ephraim fancied in the days of Amos, that Jehovah had no part in the calamities that befell His land; that though He was inactive for the moment, He must soon interpose, and could only interpose on behalf of Judah. But to Isaiah, these supposed tokens of Jehovah's temporary inactivity had quite an opposite sense: they proved that the King of Israel had risen for judgment, and would no longer pass by the sins of the state. "Jehovah setteth Himself to plead, and standeth up to judge His people; Jehovah will enter into judgment with the elders of His people, and the princes thereof, for *ye* have eaten up the vineyard, the spoil of the poor is in your houses. What mean ye that ye beat my people to pieces, and grind the faces of the poor? saith the Lord Jehovah of hosts" (iii. 13 *seq.*). "The vineyard of Jehovah of hosts is the house of Israel, and the men of Judah His pleasant planting: and He looked for judgment, but behold bloodshed; for righteousness, but behold a cry" (v. 7). Once and again does Isaiah expose the strange delusion which could see no connection between the sins of the state and the threatening conjunction of foreign powers, the insensate conduct of the nobles who went on their course of lawlessness and riot without turning their eyes to the work of Jehovah or regarding the operation of His hands (v. 12). The whole perceptions of these men were radically perverted: they called evil good and good evil, they put darkness for light and light for darkness, bitter for sweet and sweet for bitter (v. 20). Far from reading the lesson of Jehovah's displeasure, written so plainly on the page of contemporary events, they longed for His interposition as the cure for all their troubles. "Let Him make speed," they said, "and hasten His work that we may see it, and let the purpose of the Holy One of Israel draw nigh that we may know it." Thus, in their blindness to all moral distinctions and to all the signs of the times, they went on courting destruction, "drawing guilt upon themselves with the cords of their vain policy, and sin as it were with a cart rope." In their own conceit they were full of political wisdom (v. 21), but they had no eyes for the cardinal truth which Isaiah saw to outweigh every principle of earthly politics—that Jehovah was the one dispenser of good and evil to Israel, and that the law of His rule was the law of holiness and righteousness; "They had cast away the revelation of Jehovah of hosts, and despised the word of the Holy One of Israel" (v. 24). And now this whole fabric of sin and self-delusion must perish in a moment utterly, like chaff and stubble at the touch of fire (v. 24). "Sheol [the under world] hath enlarged its maw and opened its mouth without measure, and her glory and her multitude and her pomp and the joyous ones of Zion shall descend into it. And the mean man shall be brought down, and the mighty man shall be humbled, and the eyes of the lofty shall be humbled. And Jehovah of hosts shall be exalted in judgment, and the Holy God shall be sanctified in righteousness" (v. 14 *seq.*). Jehovah shall be exalted, for it is at His call that the messengers of destruction are hastening towards the doomed nation. Past and present warnings have been alike despised. What Israel has already suffered has brought no fruit of repentance, and Jehovah's wrath is still unappeased. And now "He lifts up a standard to far nations and hisses to them from the ends of the earth, and behold they come with speed swiftly. None is weary, and none stumbleth among them; they slumber not nor sleep; the girdle of their loins is not loosed, nor the latchet of their shoe broken. Their arrows are sharp, and all their bows bent; their horses' hoofs are like the flint, and their chariot wheels like the whirlwind. Their roar is like the lioness, they roar like young lions, moaning and seizing the prey and carrying it off safe, and none can deliver." The roar of the lion marks the moment of his spring, the sullen moaning that follows shows that the prey is secured. Judah lies prostrate in the grasp of the Assyrian, and over all the land no sound is heard but the deep growl of brutal ferocity as he crouches over the helpless victim. "In that day he shall moan over Judah like the moaning of the sea, when the mariner looks for land, but lo, darkness hems him in, and light is turned to darkness by the clouds" (v. 26-30).

This picture of judgment, you observe, has all the precision due to the fact that Isaiah is not describing an unknown danger, but one very real and imminent—the same danger which Amos had seen so clearly a generation before. The intervention of Assyria in the affairs of the Palestinian states could not in the nature of things involve anything less than a complete dissolution of the old balance of power, and of the whole political system. There was nothing in the circle of the nations round about Judah which could offer successful resistance to the well-directed force of a great and disciplined martial power, and the smallest acquaintance with the politics of Assyria was sufficient to prove that the absorption of the Mediterranean seaboard by that empire was only a question of time, and could in no case be very remote. The politicians of Judah were blinded to this truth by their characteristic Semitic vanity, by the truly Oriental indolence which refuses to look beyond the moment, but above all by a false religious confidence. The kind of Jehovah worship which had not learned to separate the God of Israel from idols, which left men to seek help from the work of their own hands, was only possible to those who knew as little about the world as about God. A just estimate even of the natural factors of the world's history would have shown them that the Assyrian was stronger than the idols, though it needed a prophet's faith to perceive that there was a God in Israel to whose commands Assyria itself was constrained to yield unconscious obedience. But, in truth, the leaders of Judah dared not face the realities of a situation which broke through all their established ideas, which offered no prospect but despair. Isaiah had courage to see and proclaim the truth, because he was assured that amidst the crash of nations Jehovah's throne stood unmoved, and He was exalted when all was abased.

The whole meaning of the impending crisis is summed up by the prophet in a sentence already quoted : "Jehovah of hosts shall be exalted in judgment, and the Holy God shall be sanctified in righteousness." But to understand the scope of the judgment, the plan of the righteousness here spoken of, we must be on our guard against taking these terms in such a technical sense as they bear in modern theology. When Isaiah speaks of Jehovah's righteousness, he does so because he thinks of Jehovah as the King of Israel, discharging for His people, either directly or through His human vicegerent, all the ordinary functions of civil government. Jehovah's righteousness is nothing else than kingly righteousness in the ordinary sense of the word, and its sphere is the sphere of His literal sovereignty— that is, the land of Israel. Jehovah's great work of judgment by the hand of the Assyrians has for its object precisely the same things as a good and strong human judge aims at—not the transformation of the hearts of men, but the removal of injustice in the state, the punishment of offenders, the re-establishment of law and order, and the ultimate felicity of an obedient nation. " I will again bring my hand upon thee," says Jehovah, " smelting out thy dross as with lye, and taking away all thine alloy ; and I will make thy judges to be again as aforetime, and thy counsellors as at the beginning ; thereafter thou shalt be called the city of righteousness, the faithful city" (i. 25, 26). No doubt when Isaiah limits the divine purpose to the restitution of Jerusalem as it had once been, we must remember that the days of David were idealised in the nation's memory. It is the virtues of ancient Jerusalem that are to be reproduced without its long-forgotten faults; but for all that it is plain that the ideal is simply a state perfectly well ordered—not a heavenly state, in which every individual is free from all sin in the New Testament sense of the word. It is such an ideal as would be actually realised if the judges and counsellors of the nation again were what they ought to be in a land whose king is the Holy One of Israel.[3]

The limitation of Isaiah's conception of the divine judgment leads us at once to observe the corresponding limitation in his use of the words sin, sinners, and the like. Sin, as we have seen in a former Lecture (p. 102 *seq.*), is to the Hebrew any action that puts a man in the wrong with one who has the power to make him rue it. Sin against Jehovah, therefore, is such conduct as He must take cognisance of in His quality of king and supreme judge in Israel, not sin in the New Testament sense, but on the one hand offences against social righteousness and equity, and on the other hand idolatry, which is the denial of Jehovah's true kingship. Hence the prophet has no doctrine of universal sinfulness. The Israelites are divided into two classes—the righteous, who have nothing to fear from Jehovah, and the wicked, whom His presence fills with terror (xxxiii.

14). Weal to the righteous, who shall eat the fruit of their doings; woe to the wicked, because the deserving of his hands shall be rendered to him—is the law of Jehovah's justice (iii. 10, 11); and when it is executed in all its fulness the ideal of His sovereignty is fully realised. The redemption of Zion is conceived in the same plain sense: "Zion shall be redeemed by judgment, and those in her that return by righteousness" (i. 27). The redemption is not the spiritual deliverance of the individual but the deliverance of the state, which can only be accomplished by purging out the sinners and their sin, and bringing back the remnant of the nation to obedience and right worship. If more than this were meant there would be no truth in Isaiah's representation of the fall of the might and independence of the state before Assyria as the means of redemption. But when we take the prophet's doctrine as he sets it forth himself, without complicating it by importing ideas from a later stage of revelation, the force of his argument at once becomes plain. The first condition of social reformation was the downfall of the corrupt rulers. While they held the reins there could be no hope of amendment, and in the approach of the Assyrians Isaiah sees the appointed means to level their pride and tyranny with the dust. And in like manner the first condition of true worship and homage to Jehovah was that men should recognise the nothingness of the idols, which the Assyrians in all their campaigns broke down or carried away captive.

Thus Isaiah looks forward without fear to the day when all the might of Judah shall be brought low, when great and fair houses shall be without inhabitant (v. 9), when wandering shepherds shall range at will over the rich corn-land and fertile vineyards of Judah (v. 17). He does so because Jehovah rules as Israel's king in the midst of judgment, and rules in grace for the remnant of Israel (iv. 2). In the day of utmost distress, when the land is shorn of all the artificial glories of man's making, "the spring of Jehovah[4] shall be the beauty and the wealth, the fruit of the land shall be the pride and the ornament of them that are escaped of Israel" (iv. 2). Once more, as in the old days, the Hebrews shall recognise the fruits of the land of Canaan, the simple blessings of agricultural life, as the best tokens of Jehovah's goodness, the best basis of a happy and God-fearing life, and shall cease to regret the lost splendours of the time when the land was full of silver and gold, of horses and chariots, and all the apparatus of human luxury and grandeur. All that remain in Zion shall be holy, for the filth of the daughters of Zion and the blood-guiltiness of Jerusalem have been purged away by the fiery blast of judgment. Jehovah Himself shall overshadow His people, protecting them from all ill. His glory, manifested in smoke and cloud by day, in flaming fire by night, shall rest like a canopy over Mount Zion. He shall be their shadow by daytime from the heat, their hiding-place and covert from storm and from rain (iv. 3 *seq.*).

The picture of Israel's restoration, we observe, has none of that full precision of detail with which the prophet describes the present, or delineates the approaching judgment. The method of Jehovah's ideal government is as yet all vague; the grand but undefined image of overshadowing glory expresses no more than the constant presence and all-sufficient help of the King of Israel. And this is the law of all prophecy. It is a great fallacy to suppose that the seers of Israel looked into the far future with the same clear perception of detail which belongs to their contemplation of present events. The substance of Messianic prophecy is ideal, not literal; the business of the prophet is not to anticipate history, but to signalise the principles of divine grace which rule the future, because they are eternal as Jehovah's purpose. True faith asks nothing more than this: it is only unbelief that inquires after times and seasons, that claims to know not only what Jehovah's purpose is as it bears on the practical questions of the present, but how it will shape itself to needs and circumstances still remote. The law of prophetic revelation is that already laid down by Amos; the Lord Jehovah does nothing without revealing His secret to His servants the prophets. He deals with them as a prudent king does with a trusty counsellor. He never leaves them in the dark as to the scope and meaning of His present action, and He opens the future as far as is requisite to this end, but not further.

The vain confidence of the rulers of Judah described by Isaiah in his first prophetic book, was rudely shaken by the progress of the war with Pekah and Rezin. " It was told the house of David, saying, Syria is confederate [5] with Damascus. And the heart of the king and the hearts of his people were moved as the trees of the wood are moved by the wind" (vii. 2). The plan of the confederates was directed to the entire destruction of the Davidic dynasty, and a new king of Judah had already been selected in the person of a certain " son of Tabeel" (vii. 6). The allies obtained important successes, the Syrians in particular making themselves masters of the port of Elath. But an attempt to take Jerusalem failed, and though Ahaz was hard pressed on every side, his position could not be called desperate while he still held the strongest fortress of Palestine. On the part of the king and his princes, however, unreasoning confidence had given place to equally unreasoning panic. They saw only one way of escape, namely, to throw themselves on the protection of Assyria. They were well aware that the only conditions on which this protection would be vouchsafed were acceptance of the Assyrian suzerainty with the payment of a huge tribute, and an embassy was despatched laden with all the treasures of the palace and the temple, to announce that the king of Judah regarded himself as " the servant and the son " of Tiglath Pileser (2 Kings xvi. 7 *seq.*). The ambassadors had no difficulty in attaining their object, which perfectly fell in with the schemes of the

Great King. The invincible army was set in motion, Damascus was taken and its inhabitants led captive, and Gilead and Galilee suffered the same fate. At Damascus Tiglath Pileser received the personal homage of Ahaz, whose frivolous character was so little capable of appreciating the dangers involved in his new obligations that he returned to Jerusalem with his head full of the artistic and religious curiosities he had seen on his journey. In a national crisis of the first magnitude he found no more pressing concern than the erection of a new altar in the temple on a pattern brought from Damascus (2 Kings xvi. 10 *seq.*). The sundial of Ahaz (2 Kings xx. 11), and an erection on the roof of the temple, with altars apparently designed for the worship of the host of heaven (2 Kings xxiii. 12),[6] were works equally characteristic of the trifling and superstitious *virtuoso*, who imagined that the introduction of a few foreign novelties gave lustre to a reign which had fooled away the independence of Judah, and sought a momentary deliverance by accepting a service the burden of which was fast becoming intolerable. The Assyrians had no regard to the welfare of their vassals. The principle of the monarchy was plunder; and Ahaz, whose treasures had been exhausted by his first tribute, was soon driven by the repeated demands of his masters to strip the temple even of its ancient bronze-work and other fixed ornaments (2 Kings xvi. 17 *seq.*). The incidental mention of this fact in a fragment of the history of the temple incorporated in the book of Kings is sufficient indication of the straits to which the Kingdom of Judah was reduced. The time was not far off when the rapacity of the Assyrian could no longer be satisfied, and his plundering hordes would be let loose upon the land.

At the moment when Ahaz and his panic-stricken counsellors were framing the desperate resolution of entrusting the state to the tender mercies of the Great King, Isaiah was the only man in Judah who retained his composure and his faith. He had long foreseen that judgment was inevitable, and he knew that the disasters of the Syro-Ephraitic war were only the prelude of a greater catastrophe in which the scourge of Assyria must fall on Judah and Ephraim alike. He had proclaimed these truths when no one else perceived the danger, and the publication of the first volume of his prophecies was almost coincident with the sudden collapse of national confidence. But to Isaiah the downfall of the sinners of Judah was not more certain than the indestructibility of the holy seed, the deliverance of those who were ordained to life in Jerusalem. In the moment of panic it was this side of prophetic truth that asserted its supremacy, and it did so in the form of absolute assurance that the scheme of Pekah and Rezin, which aimed at nothing less than the dissolution of the Judæan monarchy, could not succeed. "Take heed," he said to Ahaz, "and be still; fear not because of these two smoking ends of firebrands, in the hot rage of Rezin with Syria and the son of Remaliah. Whereas they plot mischief against thee, saying, Let us go up against

Judah, and strike terror into it, and conquer it for ourselves, and set up the son of Tabeel as king in it; thus saith the Lord Jehovah, It shall not stand, and it shall not come to pass. For the head of Syria is Damascus, and the head of Damascus is Rezin, and the head of Ephraim is Samaria, and the head of Samaria is the son of Remaliah. If ye will not believe, ye shall not be established" (vii. 4-9).

In translating this prophecy I follow the best recent commentators in rejecting as irrelevant the clause which in the Hebrew text stands at the end of verse 8, breaking the parallelism and weakening the force of the contemptuous allusion to Rezin and Pekah. The historical reference of the interpolated clause has become clear to us from the Assyrian monuments. When the Kingdom of Ephraim fell before Shalmaneser and Sargon, the Assyrians set up a vassal kingdom in Samaria (*supra*, p. 153), which is mentioned on the monuments for the last time a little less than sixty-five years after the date of Isaiah's prophecy to Ahaz. After that time we find the district of Samaria administered by an Assyrian prefect. It is plain that a reference to this change—which had no bearing on the fortunes of Judah or the history of Israel's religion—is quite out of place in the prophet's argument; it could afford no ground for his confidence, no consolation to Ahaz's fears. When Isaiah bids Ahaz consider that the whole strength of his enemies has no better front than the two half-consumed and smouldering firebrands, Pekah and Rezin, and then adds,

"If ye will not have faith ye shall not be established," he plainly contrasts the mere human leaders of Ephraim and Damascus with the strength of Jehovah, the King of Israel. The same thought recurs at viii. 12, "Speak not of conspiracy [or formidable alliance] when this people speaks of conspiracy; and fear not what they fear, neither be ye afraid. Sanctify Jehovah of hosts, and let Him be your fear and let Him be your dread." The strength of Judah lies in its divine king, against whom man can do nothing; and lack of faith in Him can alone imperil the continuance of the state.

The delivery of this divine message to Ahaz marks an epoch in the work of Isaiah and in the history of Old Testament prophecy. In it Isaiah first appears as a practical statesman, no longer speaking of sin, judgment, and deliverance in broad general terms, but approaching the rulers of the state with a precise direction as to the course they should hold in a particular political juncture. The older prophets of Israel down to the time of Amos were habitually consulted on affairs of state. In all matters of difficult decision "the mouth of Jehovah" was appealed to; it was not doubted that He was with His people, that the cause of Jehovah was the cause of the nation, and that He was ever ready with prophetic counsel when man's wisdom failed. The influence of a great prophet like Elisha was therefore an influence directly political; in the period of the Syrian wars Elisha was the very soul of the struggle for independence. Jehovah and His people were still allied in a common cause, and the word of the prophet was accepted and obeyed accordingly. The doctrine of Amos and Hosea broke through the ancient faith in the unity of Jehovah's will with the immediate political interests of the nation. As the God of righteousness, they taught, Jehovah had nothing but chastisement to offer to an unrighteous nation; as a God of holy and jealous love He could not accord the privileges of a true spouse to a faithless people. The cause of Jehovah was for the present entirely divorced from the interests of Israel's political prosperity; the sinners of His people must be destroyed, or, on Hosea's view, Israel must pass through a moral resurrection before the union of the God with His nation could be restored and the felicity of the Hebrew state again become the central object of Jehovah's solicitude. The picture of a nation victorious and happy in Jehovah, which in the Blessing of Moses appears as realised, or at least in the course of realisation, in the events of present history, becomes to Amos and Hosea an ideal of the future, between which and the sin and misery of the present there yawns a great gulf, bridged over only by faith in the ultimate victory of righteousness and love. The breach between Jehovah and His people brings with it the suspension of prophetic guidance in the present difficulties of the state. The new prophecy has no counsel or comfort to offer to the corrupt rulers, whom Jehovah has not appointed and whose acts He does not recognise. When the people go with their flocks and herds to seek Jehovah they shall not find Him, He hath withdrawn Himself from them (Hosea v. 6). In the day of judgment "they shall wander from sea to sea, and run to and fro from north to south to seek the word of Jehovah, but they shall not find it" (Amos viii. 11 *seq.*). There were still prophets enough in Israel and in Judah who were ready with pretended divine counsel, but the prophets of the new spiritual school do not recognise them; they are not true prophets but diviners (Micah iii.). The disseverance of true prophecy from the political questions of the day is absolute; the faith that looks forward to a future redemption casts no light upon the affairs of the present; of them it can only be said that Jehovah has rejected His people (Isa. ii. 6), and that the cup of judgment must be filled up before brighter days dawn.

The position of Amos and Hosea is also the position of Isaiah in the prophecies that precede the campaign of Pekah and Rezin. Like his predecessors, he speaks both of mercy and of judgment; but the vision of judgment fills the immediate horizon, the picture of mercy lies all in the future, and its purely ideal outlines stand in the sharpest contrast with the historical realities of the present. The assurance of Israel's redemption rests on an act of pure faith; there is nothing to bear it out in Jehovah's present relations to His people. The work of mercy is not yet seen to be going on side by side with the work of judgment.

This complete dissociation of the two sides of Jehovah's dealings with Israel belongs, it is plain, to the fragmentary and imperfect character which in the Epistle to the Hebrews is attributed to all Old Testament prophecy. There is a want of unity in the prophetic argument. When we are told by Amos that the overthrow of the Hebrew state by the Assyrians has for its purpose the destruction of the sinners of Jehovah's people, in order that the righteous may remain and form a new and better Israel, we naturally ask how this separation of the righteous from the wicked can be effected in accordance with the ordinary laws of history. Or when Hosea predicts that the remnant of Israel scattered in Egypt and Assyria shall hear and answer the call of Jehovah in the day of restoration, the question forces itself upon us how that measure of the knowledge of Jehovah which the possibility of such a return implies can be kept alive in the midst of exile. To such questions Amos and Hosea supply no answer; they never tell us how the work of judgment is to be limited in order that the subsequent redemption may remain an historical possibility. And yet it is plain that there must be a continuity in Jehovah's work, and that in the midst of judgment the course of events must be so shaped as to give a basis and starting-point for the future work of grace. Provision must be made for the unbroken preservation of God's cause in Israel. The new Israel has its roots in the old; the new work of grace rests on the same principles with the great things which Jehovah did for His people in the past, and the work of judgment cannot sever this connection.

It is this principle which comes to the front in that second great group of Isaiah's prophecies to which chap. vi. serves as a preface, and which contains in chaps. vii.-ix. 7 the summary account of his teaching in the crisis of the Syro-Ephraitic war. The question which Isaiah proposes in vi. 11 is the key-note of this teaching. What are the limits prescribed to the impending judgment by the purpose that underlies it? The certainty of Jehovah's plan of grace involves the certainty that He will preserve to Judah in the coming disaster all that is necessary to make its realisation a practical possibility, and in this certainty the limits and measure of the judgment are prescribed. Hence the fundamental thesis expressed in vi. 13; the stock of the people of Jehovah is imperishable, the holy seed retains its vitality through all the work of judgment. In other words, the community of God's grace in Israel can never be extinguished. Within the corrupt mass of Judah there ever remains a seed of true life, a precious remnant, the preservation of which is certain. Beyond this the prophet sets no limit to the severity of the troubles through which the land must pass. In the first years of Isaiah's ministry this principle seemed to slumber; it was not wholly forgotten, for in chap. iv. it is the remnant ordained to life in Jerusalem that appears as constituting the commonwealth of the redeemed in the final glory; but it is not brought into practical connection with the events of the present. But in the day of Judah's calamity, when kings and princes trembled for the endurance of the state, the doctrine of the remnant became immediately practical in the prophetic argument that, *because the community of Jehovah is indestructible, the state of Judah and the kingdom of the house of David cannot be utterly overthrown.*

We shall best understand the bearings of this proposition, and the validity of the argument on which it rests, by comparing it with the prophecy of total captivity made by Jeremiah a century later. Both prophets start from the same inflexible conviction of the sovereignty of Jehovah's purpose; both are persuaded that the sphere of that purpose is the nation of Israel, and its goal the establishment in the land of Canaan of a nation conformed to Jehovah's holiness. But at this point the teaching of the two prophets diverges. Isaiah is convinced that the dissolution of the political existence of Judah is inconsistent with the accomplishment of the divine purpose. Jeremiah, on the other hand, regards the temporary suspension of the national existence in the land of Canaan as the necessary path to the future glory. According to Isaiah, the holy seed must remain rooted in Canaan, and must remain under the headship of the house of David. According to Jeremiah, Jerusalem and the cities of Judah shall be desolate, without inhabitant, and the kingdom of the house of David shall come to an end, not for ever, but till the day when Jehovah again gathers His captives. Each prophet was borne out by the events of the immediate future. Isaiah continued to affirm the inviolability of Jerusalem through all the dangers of the Assyrian invasion, and the event justified his confidence. Jeremiah foretold the captivity of Jerusalem, and Nebuchadnezzar accomplished his prediction. But we should do little justice to the sacred wisdom of the prophets if we regarded the fulfilment of their predictions as relieving us from all further inquiry into the reason why they took such widely divergent views of the method of Jehovah's sovereignty. When we look at Isaiah's prophecies more closely we see that in every one of them he directly connects the Assyrian judgment with the inbringing of the final glory. The maintenance of the continuity of Judah's political existence appears to him the necessary condition of the future redemption. To Jeremiah this necessity no longer exists; to him it appears possible, while to Isaiah it seems impossible, that the religion of Jehovah can survive the fall of the state. This difference of view is not arbitrary, and is not to be referred to an unintelligible secret of divine providence; it rests on a difference in the religious condition of Israel at the times of the two prophets.

We have already seen, in speaking of the fall of Northern Israel (*supra*, p. 154), how the history of the Ten Tribes, after the fall of Samaria, proves that the religion of Jehovah, as it existed in Ephraim in the eighth century, was not able to survive in exile from the land of Canaan. The continued existence of a religion implies the maintenance of a religious community, united by acts of worship, and handing down the knowledge of God from father to son by inculcation not only of religious doctrine but of religious praxis. At the time when Samaria fell these conditions could not be fulfilled beyond the limits of the land of Canaan. Hosea expressly states that all religious observances were necessarily suspended in the exile of Israel. The feasts, the sacrifices, and all the other recognised elements of the worship of Jehovah demanded access to the sanctuary. When this was denied the whole life of the nation became unclean (Hosea ix. 3 *seq.*); and Israel was divorced from Jehovah (chap. iii.). The relapse of the Ten Tribes into heathenism was the inevitable consequence of their exile; nay, even the remnant that remained in Canaan was unable to maintain any consistent tradition of Jehovah worship in the dissolution of the independent monarchy, which had till then been universally regarded as the visible representation of Jehovah's sovereignty. The national religion of Judah was not more advanced than that of Ephraim. There, also, the ideas of the state and the religious community were inseparable; and, though isolated prophets could see that the elements of religion were independent of the traditional sanctuaries and their ritual, there was no community of men confirmed in these ideas, who could have held together in captivity, and nurtured their faith in Jehovah by spiritual exercises, unsupported by those visible ordinances which demanded regular access to the holy places of Canaan. In Judah as in Ephraim captivity and the dissolution of the state could have meant nothing else than relapse into heathenism, and the total obliteration of faith in Jehovah's kingship. In the time of Jeremiah all this was changed, and changed mainly by the work in which Isaiah was the chief instrument. The abolition of the provincial high places had taught religion to dispense with constant opportunity of access to the sanctuary; the formation of a consolidated prophetic party, which was the great work of Isaiah's life, provided a community of true faith able to hold together even in times of persecution, and conscious that its religion rested on a different basis from that of the idolatrous masses; and the accumulation of a sacred literature, of which only the first beginnings existed when Isaiah rose, kept the knowledge of Jehovah alive in the Exile, supplied materials for religious instruction, and permitted the development of the synagogue service, in which the captives found opportunity for those visible acts of united worship without which no religion can subsist. Thus the faith of Jehovah survived the Exile, and was handed down from father to son in the Chaldæan dispersion in a way that would have been impossible in the Assyrian period; and so we see that Isaiah and Jeremiah measured the conditions, each of his own time, with equal accuracy, when the older prophet taught that the preservation of the community of Jehovah's religion involved the preservation of the Judæan state, and his successor looked forward to captivity as the only means of liberating the true faith from entanglement with a merely political Jehovah-worship.

I have asked you to consider the bearings of Isaiah's doctrine of the indestructibility of the Jewish state in the light of later history and prophecy, because in this way we not only see why the doctrine was true and necessary in the prophet's own time, but also learn that, as the divine purpose moved onwards, the community of grace came to exist under new conditions, which made the preservation of the kingdom of Judah no longer a matter of religious necessity, or, in other words, no longer a matter of faith. This, however, is a view of the case which goes beyond what was revealed to Isaiah. His faith in the preservation of Jerusalem and the Davidic kingdom amidst the troubles of the Syrian and Assyrian wars was not the special application of a general principle of religious truth, which he had grasped, and was able to express, in a form independent of the concrete circumstances of his age and nation. The prophets, as we have once and again had occasion to observe, saw only individual aspects and particular phases of divine truth; they apprehended the laws of Jehovah's dealings with men, not in their universal form, but in the particular shape applicable to present circumstances; and therefore they were altogether unconscious of the limitations of the principles of faith which they proclaimed. When we should say that, in order to preserve alive the knowledge and fear of the true God and maintain the continuity of Jehovah's pur-

pose on earth, it was necessary that the kingdom of
Judah should be saved through the Assyrian troubles,
till the spiritual preaching of the prophets had formed
a society within Israel in which true religion could be
preserved even in exile, Isaiah says simply and without
limitation that the sphere of Jehovah's purpose and
the Kingdom of Judah are identical. Jehovah sits as
King in Zion (viii. 18). His supreme purpose is to
remodel the kingdom of Judah as a holy kingdom, and
He will not suffer the hostile efforts of any nation to
impede the development of this design. This view is
altogether remote from the theory of the popular religion
that the political interests of Israel and the interests
of Jehovah's kingdom are always identical, that the
mere fact that Jehovah is Israel's God secures His
help in every emergency. On the contrary, all the evils
that have befallen and are still to befall the state are
Jehovah's work, but amidst these it remains true that
Jehovah has a purpose of grace towards His nation, and
that He will not suffer the enemies whose attacks He
himself directs to do anything inconsistent with that
purpose. And therefore the first duty of the rulers of
Judah is to make no vain attempt to resist Jehovah's
chastisement, but to submit to it with patience, and in
the faith that He will bring the troubles of the nation
to an end in His own way and in His own good
time. The true policy of Judah is "to take heed
and be quiet" (vii. 4). The safety of the kingdom
depends on the maintenance of an attitude of faith :

"If ye will not have faith, ye shall not endure" (vii. 9).

The chief practical object of Isaiah at this time was to prevent the scheme of alliance with Assyria. He saw plainly that Assyria was the real danger to all the Palestinian states; Damascus and Ephraim were mere smouldering firebrands. Confident upon grounds of faith that their immediate enterprise could not lead to the dissolution of the Judæan Kingdom, Isaiah also saw that Pekah and Rezin were not likely to trouble Judah in the future. It was indeed as clear as day that the Assyrians would not suffer extensive schemes of conquest to be carried on by their own rebellious vassals. If Ahaz had not called in the aid of Tiglath Pileser, his own interests would soon have compelled the Assyrian to strike at Damascus; and so, if the Judæan king had had faith to accept the prophet's assurance that the immediate danger could not prove fatal, he would have reaped all the advantages of the Assyrian alliance without finding himself in the perilous position of a vassal to the robber empire. As yet the schemes of Assyria hardly reached as far as Southern Palestine. Even Pekah was left upon his throne when Damascus was led captive, and so, if Isaiah had been followed, Judah would at all events have had twelve years of respite before she met Assyria face to face; and what might not have been accomplished in these years in a nation once more obedient to the prophetic word? The advice of Isaiah, therefore, displayed no less political sagacity than elevation of faith; but it could not approve itself to a king who had neither courage nor faith to accept the prophet's assurance that Jehovah would secure the defeat of Pekah and Rezin without the aid of the politicians of Judah. In vain did Isaiah seek to convey to the pusillanimous monarch some part of his own confidence by encouraging him to ask from Jehovah a sign or pledge of His help. Ahaz would ask nothing; he would not put Jehovah to the proof (vii. 12). The Assyrian alliance was finally determined on, and Judah was at once hopelessly involved in the toils of the empire of the Tigris.

Isaiah received the refusal of Ahaz as the loss of a great opportunity, a deliberate thwarting of Jehovah's counsel. The house of David, he says, are not content to try the patience of man by their silly obstinacy; they must, forsooth, try God's patience too. The phrase is characteristic of the intense realism with which he conceived the religious situation. Never for a moment doubting the final execution of Jehovah's purpose, he yet saw quite clearly that that purpose must be realised along the lines of the historical movement of the time, and that the conduct of Ahaz interposed a new difficulty, and must of necessity lead to new and perilous complications. The first result of the Assyrian intervention must be the fall of Pekah and Rezin, and this could not be delayed more than two or three years. Before a child born in the following spring was of age to say, "My father," and "My mother," or to distinguish good and evil (vii. 16 ; viii. 4), the land whose two kings had filled Ahaz with terror should be forsaken, the riches of Damascus and the spoil of Samaria should be taken away before the king of Assyria. And then Judah's turn must come. "Jehovah shall bring upon thee and upon thy father's house such days as have not been since the time when Ephraim broke off from Judah" (vii. 17). For with the fall of Northern Israel, and the acceptance by Judah of the position of a vassal, the last barrier interposed between the empires of the Tigris and the Nile would have disappeared. . A prolonged conflict must ensue between the two great powers, and their hosts shall swarm over the land of Judah like clouds of noxious insects (vii. 18 *seq.*), and lay the whole country utterly waste. The strongholds of Judah shall lie in ruins like the old hill-forts of the Amorites after the Hebrew conquest (xvii. 9).[7] Even the operations of agriculture shall become impossible : briers and thorns shall cover the whole face of the land, and the fair hill-sides now crowned with terraced vineyards or blooming under careful tillage shall fall back into jungle, where sheep and oxen roam unchecked, where no human foot penetrates save that of the archer pursuing the gazelle or the mountain partridge. Bread shall be hardly known to the scanty remnant of the Judæans (vii. 22), honey and sour milk shall be the chief articles of diet, and human life shall be reduced to its most primitive elements.[8]

Thus far Isaiah does no more than describe the

natural consequences of Ahaz's foolish policy. His anticipations of evil show a clear appreciation of the dangers of the situation; but they are of the nature of a shrewd political forecast rather than of exceptional prediction, and as the future actually shaped itself his worst anticipations were not realised. The fall of Samaria did not come so soon as he expected (viii. 4), the conflict of Assyria and Egypt was deferred, and when it actually took place, thirty years later, the field of battle was in the extreme south of Palestine, and more in Philistine than in Judæan territory. The land suffered grievously from the armies which the Assyrian directed against Egypt, but the distress never reached the pitch which Isaiah feared. It is well to note these facts, for they show us that the prophetic predictions, even when they applied to the near future, were not always fulfilled in that literal way for which some theologians think it necessary to contend. And, as Isaiah did not lose his credit as a true prophet when it became plain that he had overstated the immediate danger, we are justified in believing that, in the age when prophecy was a living power, the hard-and-fast rule of literal interpretation which is the basis of so much modern speculation about the prophetic books was not recognised. It was understood that the prophets speak in broad poetically effective images, the essential justice of which is not affected by the consideration that they are not exactly reproduced in the future, so long as they embody true principles and indicate right points of view for the direction of conduct. In the case before us the practical object of Isaiah was to inspire new faith where all trust in the God of Israel seemed to be paralysed by terror. Ahaz had refused to put Jehovah to the proof; the oracles of the sanctuary and the vulgar herd of prophets were silent. Men knew no better counsel than to turn, as Saul had done in the moment of his despair, to the lowest forms of divination, to the peeping and muttering wizards, the ventriloquists who pretended to raise the shades of the dead that they, forsooth, might give help to the living. But to Isaiah it appeared that Jehovah had never been more clearly manifested as the living King of Israel. In the days of false prosperity it could be said with truth that He had cast off His people (ii. 6); then indeed there was no present token of the sovereignty of the holy God in a nation where everything that was inconsistent with His rule was suffered to run its course unchecked. But now the signs of Jehovah's presence and personal activity were plain. He had risen to shake the earth, and the lethargy that had so long covered the circle of Palestinian states was dispelled. On all sides the nations were astir, girding themselves for battle, knitting secret alliances, forging plans of defence against the approach of the Assyrian; and above all this turmoil Jehovah sat supreme. As the might of the heathen went down before the irresistible conqueror, as their plans were broken and their proud words of confidence brought to nought, each day made it more clear that there was no god but the God of Israel. The religions of the world were on their trial, and the verdict is pronounced by Isaiah in the words, "With *us* is God" (Isa. viii. 10).

What is the evidence on which Isaiah bases this verdict? We are all, I suppose, more or less accustomed to fancy that in Bible times the truths of religion were brought home to men's minds by evidence of a more tangible kind than in the present day. The ordinary method of dealing with the historical evidences of Christianity encourages the notion that the most serious difficulty of belief lies in the fact that we are separated by so many centuries from the time when God actually proved Himself a living God and the God of salvation; and we fancy that, if we had lived in the days of the prophets and seen with our own eyes the things that Jehovah wrought then, it would have been easy to believe, or rather impossible not to do so, because the supernatural in those days was as palpable to the senses as natural phenomena are now. An examination of the grounds which led Isaiah to declare that God was with Israel shows how erroneous this idea is. The events that gave him assurance of a present God were the same events that filled Ahaz with despair. It was indeed abundantly clear that the gods of the nations were naught, for none of them could save his worshippers from the Assyrian. But where was the proof that Israel was in a better case? The men of Judah might well say, as Gideon had said in the days of Midianite oppression, "If Jehovah be with us, why then is all this befallen us, and where be all His miracles which our fathers told us of, saying, Did not Jehovah bring us up from Egypt? but now Jehovah hath cast us off." To the spirit that will not believe except it see signs and wonders the natural inference from the Assyrian victory was that Asshur and not Jehovah was the God who ruled on earth. But to Isaiah divine rule means the rule of holiness. Judgment and mercy are equally valid proofs of the sovereignty of Jehovah in Israel. Where Amos had said, Jehovah knows Israel alone of all nations, therefore He punishes their sins, Isaiah inverts the argument and says, Because Jehovah punishes His people's sins there is verily a living God in Israel. Ahaz had refused to ask a pledge of Jehovah's interest in His people; but Jehovah Himself supplies that pledge in the swift approach of the calamity which Ahaz's rebellion entails.

The circumstance that Isa. vii. 14 *seq.* is applied in Mat. i. 23 to the birth of our Saviour has too often served to divert attention from the plain meaning of the sign or pledge which the prophet sets before the men of Judah. It is perfectly certain that the New Testament writers, in citing passages from the Old, do not always confine themselves to the original reference of the words they quote. The Old Testament Scriptures were an abiding possession of the Church. Their meaning was not held to have been exhausted in the events of past history; they all pointed to Christ, and every passage that could be brought into relation with the Gospel history might, it was felt, be legitimately adduced in that connection. The New Testament writers therefore do not help us to understand what a text of Isaiah meant to the prophet himself, or to those whom he personally addressed. They tell us only what it meant to the first generation of Christianity. The discussion of this secondary sense lies altogether beyond our present purpose. As historical students of prophecy, we have only to ask what the prophet designed to convey to his own contemporaries; and to them, it is clear, he offered a present token of Jehovah's presence, and of the truth of the prophetic word in its reference to current events. That token was not a miraculous conception. The word which the English version renders "virgin" means, strictly speaking, nothing else than a young woman of age to be a mother. On the person of the future mother Isaiah lays no stress; it does not appear that he pointed his hearers to any individual. He says only that a young woman who shall become a mother within a year may name her child "God with us." For, before the babe begins to develop into intelligent childhood, the lands of Pekah and Rezin shall be laid waste, and Judah as well as Israel shall be stripped of all its artificial wealth, and reduced to wild pasture ground, whose inhabitants feed on sour milk and honey.[9] In the collapse of all human resources, in the return of the nation to that elemental form of life in which the creations of human skill and industry no longer come between man and his Maker, it will become plain that there is a God in Israel. "In that day man shall look unto his Maker, and his eyes shall be turned to the Holy One of Israel. And they shall not look to the altars, the work of their hands, neither shall they turn to that which their own fingers have made, to the *ashērim* and the sun-pillars" (xvii. 7, 8). To put the thought in modern language, the proof that God is with Israel, and with Israel alone, lies in this, that no other conception of godhead than that of the Holy God preached by Israel's prophets can justify itself as consistent with the course of the Assyrian calamity. The world is divided between two religions, the religion that worships things of man's making, and the religion of the Holy One of Israel. Judah is called to choose between these faiths, and its rulers have chosen the former. Their trust is in earthly things ;— be these chariots and horses, strong cities and munitions of war, commercial wealth and agricultural prosperity, carnal alliances and schemes of human policy, or idols, altars, and sun-pillars, is alike to Isaiah's argument. When Jehovah rises in judgment all these vain helpers are swept away, and the Holy One of Israel alone remains. The plans of earthly policy which Ahaz and his counsellors had matured with so much care are likened by the prophet to the Adonis gardens [10] or pots of quickly withering flowers, which the ancients used to set at their doors or in the courts of temples: "Because thou hast forgotten the God of thy salvation, and hast not been mindful of the rock of thy strength, therefore thou shalt plant Adonis gardens, and set them with strange slips. In the day that thou hedgest in thy plants, in the morning that thou makest thy seed to bud, the harvest is vanished in a day of grief and of hopeless sorrow" (xvii. 10 *seq.*).

Meantime, the duty of the prophet and his disciples is to hold themselves aloof from the rest of the nation, to take their stand on the sure word of revelation, and patiently await the issue. " Jehovah hath laid His strong hand on me, and taught me not to walk in the way of this people, saying, Speak not of confederacy where this people speaketh of confederacy, and fear not what they fear, neither be ye afraid. Sanctify Jehovah of hosts Himself, and let Him be your fear, and let Him be your dread. And He shall prove a sanctuary [asylum], but a stone of stumbling, and a rock of offence to both the houses of Israel, a gin and a snare to the inhabitants of Jerusalem." " Bind up God's testimony, seal the revelation among my disciples. And I will wait for Jehovah that hideth His face from the house of Jacob, and I will look for Him" (viii. 11 *seq.*). The circle that gathered round Isaiah and his household in these evil days, holding themselves apart from their countrymen, treasuring the word of revelation, and waiting for Jehovah, were indeed, as Isaiah describes them, " signs and tokens in Israel from Jehovah of hosts that dwelleth in Mount Zion." The formation of this little community was a new thing in the history of religion. Till then no one had dreamed of a fellowship of faith dissociated from all national forms, maintained without the exercise of ritual services, bound together by faith in the divine word alone. It was the birth of a new era in the Old Testament religion, for it was the birth of the conception of the *Church*, the first step in the emancipation of spiritual religion from the forms of political life,—a step not less significant that all its consequences were not seen till centuries had passed away. The community of true religion and the political community of Israel had never before been separated even in thought; now they stood side by side, conscious of their mutual antagonism, and never again fully to fall back into their old identity.

Isaiah, indeed, and the prophets who followed him were still far from seeing how deep was the breach between the physical Israel and the spiritual community of faith. To them the dissociation of these two qualities appeared to be merely temporary; they pictured the redemption of Israel as the vindication of the true remnant in a day of national repentance, when the state should accept the prophetic word as its divine rule. For the order of salvation is first light and then deliverance. In the depth of Israel's despair, when men walk in darkness, hardly bested and hungry, "they shall curse their king and their god, and look upward" (viii. 21). As their eyes turn to Him whom they cast off for the things they now curse as false helpers, the darkness is lifted from the land. "She who is in anguish shall not be in darkness." The work of redemption begins where the desolation of Israel by Assyria began, in the northern lands of Galilee by the shores of the Lake of Tiberias (ix. 1). But all Israel shares the great deliverance, in which the yoke of Assyria is broken, and Jehovah's zeal for His people manifested in a glorious redintegration of the Davidic kingdom. "The people that walk in darkness have seen a great light: they that dwell in the land of deep shade, upon them hath the light shined. Thou hast made the gladness great,[11] Thou hast increased their joy; they joy before Thee according to the joy in harvest, as men are glad when they divide the spoil. For Thou hast broken the yoke of his burden, the rod of his back, the staff of his oppressor, as in the day of [battle with] Midian. For the greaves of the warrior that stampeth in the fray, and the garments rolled in blood, shall be cast into the fire as fuel for the flame. For to us a child is born, unto us a son is given; and the government shall be on his shoulder, and his name shall be called Wonderful Counsellor—God, the mighty One—Everlasting Father—Prince of Peace, for the increase of the government, and for peace without end, upon the throne of David, and upon his kingdom; to confirm it and to establish it in judgment and in righteousness, from henceforth even for ever. The zeal of Jehovah of hosts will perform this" (ix. 2-7).

In these words the picture of Israel's final glory assumes a much preciser form than in the earlier prophecy of chap. iv. There is still a large element of figure and symbol, so used as to show that the prophet does not possess a detailed revelation of the process of the work of salvation, but is guided, as was the case in the earlier predictions, by general principles of faith, too large to be immediately translated into the language of literality. But he has now gained a clearer view of the nature and limits of the work of judgment than was expressed in chaps. ii. and iii., and the new light shed on the present casts its rays into the future. The turning-point of Israel's history is the destruction of the power of the Assyrian oppressor, and with this deliverance the Messianic days begin. To Isaiah, therefore, the law of Jehovah's kingship is still the same as in ancient days. The new salvation is parallel to the great things which God did for His people in times of old, when the victories of Israel over such enemies as Midian were recognised as victories of Jehovah, and proved the chief means of confirming the national faith. But now the deliverance is no temporary victory over a mere Arab horde, but the final and complete discomfiture of the great power which represented all that man could do against the kingdom of Jehovah. The blood-stained relics of the struggle are cast into the fire. War has ceased for ever, and the reign of perpetual peace begins under a child of the seed of David, whose throne is established in righteousness and for evermore. In this last conception we meet for the first time with the idea of a personal Messiah. In chap. iv. it was Jehovah's glory, manifested in fire and cloud, that overshadowed and protected the ransomed nation. Now this image is translated into a new and more concrete form. The establishment and enlargement of the divine kingdom is committed to a human representative of Jehovah's sovereignty, and it is in a fresh scion of the house of David that Israel finds the embodiment of more than human wisdom, divine strength, and an everlasting reign of fatherly protection and peace. The further examination of these Messianic ideas must, however, be deferred till we can compare the prediction now before us with the later prophecies in which Isaiah recurs to the same subject.

LECTURE VII.

ISAIAH AND MICAH IN THE REIGN OF HEZEKIAH.[1]

THE reign of Ahaz was not a very long one; he did not live to see the revolt of Hoshea and the fall of Samaria. The last rebellion of Northern Israel was not an isolated rising; it was accompanied or followed by a general revolt of all the Syrian principalities from Philistia in the south to Hamath and Arpad in the north. Hoshea, as we know, was encouraged by the hope of support from So (Sewe), king of Egypt (2 Kings xvii. 4), and this monarch, the Sebech of the Assyrian monuments, was in fact concerned with the whole movement that threatened the Assyrian supremacy in the districts west of the Euphrates. The interference of Egypt at this juncture is explained by the fact that, for some time before, that country had been much divided and weakened by contests between an Ethiopian dynasty in the upper country and the princes of the Delta. But the Ethiopians at last prevailed, and under Sebech Egypt and Ethiopia formed a single power, able to devote itself to foreign affairs. After taking Samaria, Sargon in B.C. 720 reduced the Philistine cities, and, advancing to

Raphia (now Rafaḥ) on the border of the desert on the short caravan road from Egypt to Gaza, encountered and defeated Sebech.² The victory was not pursued into Egypt itself, but it secured the subjection of Syria, and for some years the only operations of Sargon in the west of which we hear were directed against Arab tribes. But in B.C. 711, nine years after the battle of Raphia, Ashdod was once more in revolt under a king named Yaman. The Egyptians of course were again pulling the strings, and the affair must have been regarded as serious, for Sargon speaks of it at length in several of his inscriptions. He acted with great promptitude, crossing the Tigris and Euphrates while the waters were still in flood, and advancing with the characteristic rapidity which forms a chief feature in Isaiah's description of the Assyrian armies (Isa. v.) "In the anger of my heart," says Sargon, according to Oppert's translation (*R.P.* vii. 40 ; ix. 11), " I marched against Ashdod with my warriors, who did not leave the trace of my feet." The Egyptians were far from exhibiting equal energy. All through the history of this period their policy was made up of large promises and small performance ; they were always stirring up plots against their Eastern rivals, but never ready when the moment for action came ; and Isaiah fitly sums up their conduct in the two words "turbulence and inactivity " (xxx. 7). In the present instance, they left Ashdod to its fate, and Pharaoh was glad to make his peace with Sargon by surrendering Yaman, who had taken refuge in Egypt.

This campaign has a special interest for us, because it is referred to in the first prophecy of Isaiah after the Syro-Ephraitic war, the date of which is altogether undisputed. In the year of the siege and capture of Ashdod, so we are told in chap. xx., Isaiah, under Divine command, put off the sackcloth from his loins and the shoe from his foot, and continued for three years to walk naked and barefoot, as a sign and token upon Egypt and Ethiopia. Even so, he explained, Egypt and Ethiopia shall be led captive by the king of Assyria, naked and barefoot, to the shame of all who looked to them for help. . "Then the inhabitants of this coast shall say, So have they fared to whom we looked and to whom we fled for help to be delivered from the king of Assyria; and how can we escape?" The only point in this chapter that demands explanation is the three years' continuance of the prophet's symbolic action, which plainly implies that for three years the lesson still required to be enforced. Here the annals of Sargon come to our help. The siege of Ashdod, as we have seen, fell in 711, and for the next two years Sargon was wholly engrossed by a revolt of the Babylonians under Merodach Baladan. It was this, perhaps, that prevented him from pressing forward against Egypt as Isaiah had expected him to do on the fall of Ashdod. At all events, the revolt of Babylon gave hopes of independence to Assyria's western vassals, for we are told in the *Annals* that the kings of Cyprus, who had previously refused tribute, voluntarily submitted themselves when they heard of the humiliation of Merodach Baladan. Cyprus, the Phœnicians, and the Philistines were closely connected in trade and politics; so it appears that in the third year of Isaiah's symbolical conduct the Palestinian nations gave up all further hope of escape from the Assyrian yoke. It is true that this result had not come about in the way that Isaiah anticipated; but his assurance that their efforts after independence were hopeless had none the less justified itself, and there was no further motive for continuing the sign by which he had confirmed it.

From this date to the death of Sargon (B.C. 705) things appear to have remained quiet in Palestine; but before we pass on to the reign of Sennacherib, we are called to examine more closely the attitude and fortunes of Judah and the activity of the prophets during the events already described. In the wars of 722-720 against Samaria and the Philistines, the Judæans seem to have had no direct part; they still adhered to Assyria, as was natural enough, since Philistia and Ephraim had been dangerous enemies but a few years before. To this date Isa. xxviii. can most naturally be assigned. The prophet looks forward to the fall of Samaria, when the proud crown of the drunkards of Ephraim shall be trodden under foot, and the glory of Samaria pass as a fading flower; and still he sees in the near catastrophe but a fresh pledge of the approach of the day when Jehovah shall be the crown and pride of the remnant of His people, giving "the spirit of justice to him who sitteth for justice, and of valour to them that turn back battle from the gate." He at least has not lost faith or changed his hope during the ten years that have elapsed since he withdrew from public life with his disciples, to wait for better days ; the purpose of Jehovah has been deferred, but not abandoned, and in the new crisis Isaiah sees Him rising up to accomplish it in His ancient might, as that was displayed at Baal-Perazim and Gibeon (2 Sam. v. 20 *seq.*; Josh. x.). Thus, in spite of the threatening aspect of the present, Jehovah's purpose appears to Isaiah as a purpose of grace to Israel—but of grace that can only be realised by those who are willing to yield obedience to the Divine precepts. The condition of deliverance is still national repentance, and from this the rulers of Judah and the official heads of Judah's religion (ver. 7) are far removed. The chiefs of the people are like men in the last stage of a drunken debauch (vers. 7, 8), incapable of listening to sane counsel, deaf to Jehovah's words when He declares to them by His prophet where rest for the weary and refreshing for the exhausted nation are to be found (ver. 12). In this prophecy Isaiah does not again detail, what he had explained at length before, the course in which these blessings are to be found. But throughout life he pointed steadily to the establishment of civil justice and the abolition of the idols as the things most necessary, and we may safely conclude that in these respects there was as yet no real amendment. The "scornful men" who guided the helm of the state were absorbed in schemes which left no room for the thought that the fate of kingdoms is governed by Jehovah's providence and by the supremacy of His holy will. They had made lies their refuge, and hid themselves under falsehood. They had made their covenant with death and Sheol—that is, with the fatal power of the Assyrian—and trusted that when the "overflowing scourge," the all-destroying invasion, passed through it should not reach them. Isaiah had no share in this illusion. He saw that the present state of things was intolerable and could not last; "the bed was too short for a man to stretch himself on it, the coverlet too narrow for a man to wrap himself in it" (ver. 20). The Assyrian alliance must soon be dissolved. "Your covenant with death shall be annulled, your agreement with Sheol shall not stand; when the overflowing scourge passeth through, ye shall be trodden down by it." Once and again the invading host shall pass through the land and smite its inhabitants (ver. 19). So long as the policy of irreligion lasts, it can only serve to prolong the bondage of the nation (ver. 22). Jehovah's purpose is now decisive and final (ver. 22); the measure of strict justice shall be applied to those who have mocked at judgment and righteousness (ver. 17). In the universal overthrow there is but one thing fixed and immutable: "Jehovah hath laid in Zion a stone, a stone of proof, a precious corner-stone of sure foundation; he that believeth shall not make haste" (ver. 16). Those who have faith in the sovereign providence that rules in Israel, and is surely working out Jehovah's counsel, can await the future with patience; they, and they alone, for " hail shall sweep away the refuge of lies, and the waters shall overflow the hiding-place." It is still the old faith in the inviolability of Zion, the prophetic confidence in the continuity of Jehovah's purpose, that forms the root of Isaiah's hope ; but now more clearly than before the prophet lays the basis of this faith in the doctrine of an all-embracing divine ordinance, the same ordinance that rules the actions of every-day industry. The wisdom that tells the husbandman how to plough and sow, which directs the daily labours of agricultural life, is also a part of Jehovah's teaching (vers. 24-29). And the same God, "wonderful in counsel and excellent in practical wisdom," who prescribes the order of common toil, rules in the affairs of the state and lays down the inviolable laws of Israel's happiness.

The argument from the operations of husbandry with which Isaiah closes this prophecy is too characteristic to be passed over without further remark. To recognise its full force we must remember that all such operations were guided by traditional rules which no one dreamed of violating. These rules were the law of the husbandman, and like all traditional laws among ancient nations they had a sacred character. Every one understood that it was part of religion to observe them, and that it would be in the highest degree unlucky to set them aside. The modern mind is disposed to laugh at such ideas, but Isaiah takes them in all seriousness. In the sedulous observance of the traditional lore which expressed the whole wisdom of the peasant, and was reverently accepted as a divine teaching, the husbandman brought his religion into the daily duties of his humble toil, and every operation became an act of obedience to God. And thus his life appears to the prophet as a pattern for the scornful rulers of Judah. They too in their seat of judgment and government have a divine law set before them, in the observance of which the felicity of the nation lies. But they refuse to learn. The incessant prophetic inculcation of " command upon command, rule upon rule, here a little and there a little"—in brief, the attempt to make the word of God the practical guide of every action—seems to them only fit for babes (ver. 9). But Jehovah will not suffer His lessons to remain unlearned. What they refuse to hear at the mouth of the prophet they must learn from the harsher accents of the Assyrian tyrant. "With barbarous lips and in a strange tongue will He speak to this people" (ver. 11). Thus the doctrines of divine chastisement and divine grace are gathered up into one larger doctrine of Jehovah's teaching to Israel. The word of the prophet and the rod of the Assyrian are conjoint agencies, working together for the in-bringing of a time when, as the prophet elsewhere expresses it, the land shall be full of the knowledge of Jehovah, when the practical rules of conduct which He dictates shall be as supreme in the administration of the state as in the ordering of the daily tasks of the husbandman.

The way in which the rulers of Judah are addressed in this prophecy appears to show that, in spite of the increasing sufferings which the Assyrian exactions imposed on the poorer classes—for these in the East are the taxpayers—the princes still found their account in the maintenance of the settlement effected by Ahaz. Isaiah does not blame them for their acquiescence in a position of political nonentity; he certainly would not have encouraged them to cast in their lot with Samaria; but he urges that the sins which have proved the ruin of Samaria will be their ruin too. The accession of Hezekiah, it is plain, had done nothing for the cure of the internal wounds of the state; all social disorders were as rampant as at the outbreak of the Syro-Ephraitic war; the Assyrian suzerainty was tolerated for no other reason than that it maintained the governing classes in their positions, and enabled them to continue their course of riot and oppression. This picture of the state of Judah receives independent confirmation from the earlier part of the book of Micah,[3] which also dates from the days of the last struggle of Samaria, as we learn from a comparison of Micah i. with Jer. xxvi. 18. Micah was a man of Moresheth Gath, a small place, as Jerome tells us, near Eleutheropolis on the Philistine frontier, and the proximity of his home to one part of the field of war helps to explain his keen interest in the progress of the Assyrian arms. At all events, the crisis which drew Isaiah from his retirement to proclaim to Judah the lesson preached by the impending ruin of Ephraim, called forth the countryman Micah to give a like warning. In the storm that was ready to burst upon Samaria he beheld Jehovah going forth from His heavenly palace, and marching over the mountains of Palestine in righteous indignation to visit the sins of Jacob. Samaria shall become a heap of the field; the stones of her fortifications shall be rolled down into the valley, her graven images dashed to pieces. But Judah too has shared the sin of Samaria, and the same judgment menaces Zion (i. 1-9). It is the cities of his own district that are in immediate danger (i. 10-15)—a natural thought, since they lay next to the scene of war in Philistia; but the centre of Judah's sin is the capital; and the evil that has come down from Jehovah already stands at the gate of Jerusalem (i. 5, 9, 12). The sins which Micah has in view are the same as those signalised by Isaiah: on the one hand, a religion full of idolatry and heathenish sorceries (iii. 7; v. 12 *seq.*), a spurious confidence in Jehovah, which has no regard to His moral attributes, and is bolstered up by lying oracles (ii. 11; iii. 5, 11, comp. Isa. xxviii. 7), while it refuses to hear the warnings of true prophecy (ii. 6; iii. 8, comp. Isa. xxviii. 9 *seq.*); on the other hand, the gross corruption and oppressions of the ruling classes, who "build up Zion with bloodshed, and Jerusalem with iniquity" (iii. 10). But Micah depicts the sufferings of the peasantry at the hands of their lords from much closer personal observation than was possible to Isaiah as a resident in the capital. He speaks as a man of the people, and reveals to us, as no other prophet does, the feelings of the commonalty towards their oppressors. To the peasantry the nobles seem to have no object but plunder (ii. 1 seq.). The poorer agriculturists are daily stripped of their houses and holdings by violence or false judgment. The true enemies of the people are their own rulers (ii. 8),[4] and the prophet contemplates with a stern satisfaction, which doubtless found an echo in many breasts, the approach of the destroyer who shall carry into exile "the luxurious sons" (i. 16) of this race of petty tyrants, and leave them none "to stretch the measuring line on a lot in the congregation of Jehovah" (ii. 5). "Arise," he cries, "and depart, for this is not your place of rest."

The strong personal feeling which Micah displays towards the governing classes gives a peculiar turn to his whole prophecy. Isaiah speaks as severely of the sins of the nobles, but never, as Micah does, from the standpoint of a man of the people. Isaiah's own circle belonged to the upper classes; the chief priest of the temple was his friend; and an aristocratic habit of thought appears in more than one of his prophecies. His doctrine of the indestructibility of Zion as the condition of the continuity of the national existence of Judah seems to indicate that the capital and the Court appeared to him as the natural centre of the true remnant. There is nothing democratic in his picture of

Israel's restoration; he looks for the amendment of the ruling classes (i. 26), who retain their old place in the reconstruction of the state (chap. xxxii.). Micah, on the contrary, conceives the work of judgment essentially as a destruction of the government and the nobles. The race of the unjust aristocrats shall be rooted out of the land (ii. 5); the proud and guilty capital shall be ploughed as a field; Jerusalem shall become as heaps and the mountain of the temple as the heights of the forest (iii. 12); the judge or king of Israel shall suffer the last indignities at the hand of the enemy (v. 1; Heb., iv. 14). It has often been supposed from these predictions that Micah, unlike Isaiah, looked forward to a total captivity; and that his words were referred by the Jews themselves to the Babylonian exile, appears from the fact that at an early date the gloss, "and shalt come even to Babylon," was inserted in iv. 10.[5] But a closer examination does not bear out this view. When the aristocrats are carried captive "the congregation of Jehovah" remains in the land (ii. 5). The glory of Israel is not banished from Canaan, but takes refuge in Adullam, as in the old days, when a band of freebooters and broken men contained the true hope of the nation (i. 15). The days of David, when the ruler of Israel came forth from Bethlehem, a town too small to be reckoned as a canton in Judah (v. 2), the times of "the first kingdom," when Jerusalem itself was but a hill fort, "a tower of the flock" (iv. 8), appear to Micah as the true model of national well-being; the acquisitions of later civilisation and political development, horses and chariots and fenced cities—always associated with tyranny in the minds of the common people—are stamped by him as sins, and shall be utterly abolished in the days of restoration (i. 13; v. 10, 11).[6] Hence, though Micah no less than Isaiah recognises Zion as the centre of Jehovah's sovereignty, from which divine instruction and decisions shall go forth in the days to come to all the surrounding nations, who shall lay aside their weapons of war and make Jehovah the arbiter of their strifes (iv. 1 *seq.*), the fall of the Zion of the present, the city built up by bloodshed and guilt, the strong fortress of Israel's oppressors, appears to our prophet as a necessary step in the redemption of the nation. The daughter (or population) of Zion must pass through the pangs of labour before her true king is born; she must come forth from the city and dwell in the open field; there, and not within her proud ramparts, Jehovah will grant her deliverance from her enemies. For a time the land shall be given up to the foe, but only for a time. Once more, as in the days of David, guerilla bands gather together to avenge the wrongs of their nation (v. 1). A new David comes forth from little Bethlehem, and the rest of his brethren return to the children of Israel— that is, the kindred Hebrew nations again accept the sway of the new king, who stands and feeds his flock in the strength of Jehovah, in the majesty of the name of Jehovah his God. Then Assyria shall no longer insult Jehovah's land with impunity. The national militia, again numerous and warlike as of old, has no lack of captains to meet the invader, and the tide of battle shall be rolled back into the land of Nimrod, which the sword of Israel shall lay waste. The remnant of Judah shall flourish in the midst of the surrounding peoples, like grass fertilised by the waters of heaven, that tarry not for man nor wait for the sons of men. Judah shall be among the nations irresistible as a lion among flocks of sheep ; for its strength comes down from Jehovah, like dew from the skies, and all false helpers, strongholds and chariots, enchantments and graven images, *asherim* and *maççeboth*, are swept away. And Jehovah will execute judgment in wrath and fury on the nations that refuse obedience (v. 2-15).

It is interesting to observe that according to Jer. xxvi. 19 the prophecy of Micah produced a great impression on his contemporaries. And this is not strange ; for he spoke to the masses of the people as one of themselves, and his whole picture of judgment and deliverance was constructed of familiar elements, and appealed to the most cherished traditions of the past. David, as it is easy to recognise from the narrative of the books of Samuel, was the hero of the common people ; and no more effective method of popular teaching could have been devised than the presentation of the antique simplicity of his kingdom in contrast to the corruptions of the present. Thus Micah's teaching went straighter to the hearts of the masses than the doctrine of Isaiah, which at this time was still working only as a leaven in a small circle. Isaiah's work, in truth, was the higher as it was the more difficult; it was a greater task to consolidate the party of spiritual faith, and by slow degrees to establish its influence in the governing circle, than to arouse the masses to a sense of the incongruity of the present state of things with the old ideal of Jehovah's nation. But both prophets had their share in the great transformation of Israel's religion which began in the reign of Hezekiah and found definite expression in the reformation of Josiah. It is Micah's conception of the Davidic king which is reproduced in the Deuteronomic law of the kingdom (Deut. xvii. 14 *seq.*), and his prophecy of the destruction of the high places (v. 13), more directly than anything in Isaiah's book, underlies the principle of the one sanctuary, the establishment of which, in Deuteronomy, and by Josiah, was the chief visible mark of the religious revolution which the teaching of the prophets had effected.

These remarks, however, threaten to carry us too far out of the course of the history which we are pursuing. Let us return to Judah and its rulers as they were on the eve of Samaria's calamity, when Micah was preaching the fall of the corrupt nobles, and Isaiah was appealing to the grandees of the capital to be warned by the fate of their compeers in Samaria. At the time, we may well suppose, the words of Micah found no audience beyond his own district, and the prophecy of Isaiah xxviii. was little heeded, so that, if we may judge from the present arrangement of his book, he deemed it fitting to republish it many years later as a seasonable introduction to a collection of prophecies o. the time of Sennacherib. But the events that followed proved that Isaiah's foresight was sound. The sum of his warning had been, "Be ye not mockers, lest your fetters be made strong." Judah refused his admonition, and the Assyrian bondage became every year more grievous. The tone of chap. xx. makes it hardly questionable that ten years later, in 711 B.C., the Judæans took a lively and favourable interest in the uprising of Philistia, which, by its close connection with Egypt on the one hand and Phœnicia on the other, as well as by the physical advantages of its position in the rich Mediterranean coast-land, was marked out as the natural focus of Palestinian revolt. The pressure of the foreign yoke caused ancestral enmities to be forgotten, and Judah leaned more and more to the scheme of an Egyptian alliance embracing all the Syrian states. Sargon himself, on a cylinder which repeats the main facts of the war of 711, already described from his *Annals*, tells us that the tributary states of Judah, Edom, and Moab, were speaking treason and beseeching the alliance of Egypt, and many recent inquirers have supposed that at this time Hezekiah and his people broke out into open revolt, and shared the miseries of the war that ensued. This conjecture has considerable interest for the interpretation of Isaiah's prophecies. The prophet was not an ordinary preacher; his voice was mainly heard in great political crises, and in uneventful times he might well be silent for years. But in the day of danger, when Jehovah was pre-eminently at work, the fundamental law of prophecy came into play: "The Lord Jehovah doeth nothing, without revealing his secret to his servants the prophets." If Judah was actively engaged in the war of 711, and was reduced by force, it is scarcely doubtful that the book of Isaiah must preserve some record of the fact; and so the latest English commentator, Mr. Cheyne, developing the suggestions of Professor Sayce and other Assyriologists, proposes to ascribe to this period, not only chaps. x. 5 to xi. 16, but chaps. i., xiv. 29-32, xxii., xxix.-xxxii. If we accept this view we must conclude that Judah had a very large share in the campaign of 711, that the whole land was overrun by the enemy and the provincial cities taken and burned (i. 7), that Jerusalem itself was besieged (xxii.) —in short, that Judah suffered precisely in the same way and to the same extent as under the invasion of Sennacherib ten years later. But, more than this, we must conclude that Isaiah held precisely similar language in the two cases,—that under Sargon, as under Sennacherib, he taught that the Assyrian might indeed approach and lay siege to Jerusalem, but Jehovah in the last extremity would Himself protect His holy mountain and strike down the invader, and that he did this in the second invasion without making any reference back to the events of the siege which had called forth similar predictions ten years before.

The mere statement of this hypothesis is, I think, sufficient to show its extreme improbability. History does not repeat itself exactly, and even if the two invasions of the hypothesis ran a similar course, as up to a certain point they might well do, they must have had very different issues. If Jerusalem was besieged in 711 the issue certainly was the submission of Hezekiah and his return to obedience. And if this were so, it is highly improbable that he would have been allowed to restore the Judæan fortresses, and regain so large a measure of military strength as is implied in the fact that ten years later he was the most important member of the rebel confederation. On the contrary, the fact that the campaign of 711 was essentially a campaign against Ashdod, Judæa not being so much as named in the account of it in the *Annals*, while that of 701 was as essentially a campaign against Judæa, in which the Philistines played quite a subordinate part, seems to be clear evidence that, though Hezekiah may for a moment have thought of revolt on the earlier occasion, he did not take an active part in the war. The extraordinary rapidity of Sargon's movements, specially emphasised on the monuments, enabled him to crush Ashdod before the Egyptians could send aid to their allies, and no doubt nipped in the bud all schemes of revolt on the part of the neighbouring states. That this was the actual course of events is further clear from Isa. xx. The language of the prophet must have been very different if at this time Judah had been actively engaged on the side of Ashdod. And finally, it can hardly be supposed that the book of Kings would have been altogether silent on the subject, if Sargon as well as Sennacherib had besieged Jerusalem and captured the cities of Judah. But the attempt of the Assyriologists to find in 2 Kings xviii. 13 *seq.* some trace of an earlier invasion which has got mixed up with that of Sennacherib is altogether chimerical. Everything in the narrative of Kings is either borne out by the monuments of Sennacherib, or is altogether inapplicable to the expedition of Sargon. Sennacherib tells only of his successes, not of his ultimate retreat and the escape of Hezekiah, and so his account corresponds only with 2 Kings xviii. 13-17*a*. But everything spoken of in these verses agrees exactly with the Assyrian record.[7]

If we are compelled to reject the theory of an invasion of Judæa under Sargon, the only prophecy in Mr. Cheyne's list which can be held to be earlier than the reign of Sennacherib appears to be that extending from x. 5 to xi. 16, which sets forth with greater completeness than any other single discourse preserved to us the whole views of Isaiah concerning the mission of Assyria as an instrument of Jehovah's anger, the ultimate fate of the robber empire, and the future glory of Jehovah's people. The destruction of Samaria, the final captivity of Northern Israel—which the prophet does not seem to have contemplated in the discourses of the reign of Ahaz—and the thorough subjugation of all Syria and Northern Palestine, which were stripped by Sargon of the last shadow of independence, were events that could not fail to produce a deep impression in Judah; and, while others stood aghast at the terrible portent which had changed the whole face of the Hebrew world, Isaiah—who had not lost confidence in the ultimate victory of Jehovah's cause, or ceased to associate that victory with the preservation through all trouble of the visible kingdom of Jehovah in Israel, which had its centre on Mount Zion—could hardly fail to feel it necessary to restate his view of the future of Judah in a form that took account of recent events. The great prophecy of chaps. x. and xi. corresponds to this description. The cardinal thoughts are the same as in chap. xxviii.;[8] but the date is after the fall of Samaria, the destruction of the principalities of Syria, such as Hamath and Arpad, which we know to have taken place at the same time with the final subjugation of Ephraim, is alluded to as a recent event (x. 9), and the immediate historical background of the prophecy is the total revolution which the successes of Assyria and the policy of captivities *en masse* (x. 13) had worked in all the countries between Judæa and the Euphrates. It is difficult for us to conceive the terror which these events must have inspired among the petty nations of Palestine, who for centuries past had gone on their way, each walking in the name of its god (Micah iv. 5), and fancying itself secure in his help from any greater danger than was involved in the usual feuds with its neighbours. To Isaiah, however, the progress of the

Assyrian had no terrors and brought no surprise. There was neither strength nor permanency in the idolatrous kingdoms, which one after another had fallen before the all-conquering power. So far as they were concerned, Assyria was irresistible; its mission upon earth, confided to it by Jehovah Himself, was to prove that there was no God but the Holy One of Israel. But Jehovah's kingdom and Jehovah's citadel of Zion stood in a very different position. The Assyrian in his greatest might is but the rod of Jehovah's anger; and though he knows not this, but deems that the strength of his own hand has gotten him the victory, and that he can deal with Jerusalem and her idols at his will as he has done with Samaria and her idols, it is as impossible for him to lift himself up against Jehovah as for the axe to boast itself against him that heweth therewith, or for the rod to shake the hand that wields it. It is indeed plain that the pride of the Assyrian will not acknowledge this limitation of his might, and that his all-devouring greed will soon carry him onwards to open assault on Judah, which as yet is itself unconscious of its high destiny, still "leaning on him who smites it"—that is, as appeared in chap. xxviii., still depending on that treaty of tributary alliance which, Isaiah saw, could not be long observed. But when the crisis comes, when Jehovah has accomplished His whole work on Mount Zion and on Jerusalem, He will punish the proud heart and stout looks of the king of Assyria, and it shall be seen that the conqueror who has removed the bounds of nations and gathered all the earth as a man gathers eggs from a deserted nest, where there is none that moves a wing or opens the mouth or peeps, is powerless before the walls of Jehovah's citadel. Thus, as King Sargon continued his career of universal conquest, the history of the world appeared to Isaiah to converge towards one great decision, when all other nations should have disappeared from the struggle, and the supreme world-power should come face to face with the God who has founded Zion as His inexpugnable sanctuary. This thought shaped itself to the prophet's mind in the picture of a great invasion, in which the Assyrian advances through the pass of Michmash, in the fulness of his arrogancy and might, sweeping the helpless inhabitants before him till he stands upon the broad ridge of Scopus looking down upon Jerusalem from the north, and shakes his hand in contemptuous menace at the mount of the daughter of Zion. Then Jehovah arises in His might and prostrates the proud host, as a mighty forest falls before the axe of the woodman. Compare xiv. 24-27.

The fall of the Assyrian closes the first act of the divine drama as it unfolds itself before the spiritual eyes of the prophet, and this great deliverance seals the repentance of Jehovah's people. "In that day the remnant of Israel and the survivors of the house of Jacob shall no more again stay upon him that smote them; but shall stay upon Jehovah the Holy One of Israel in truth" (x. 20). The judgment is past, and days of blessing begin. The Davidic kingdom starts into new life, or, as the prophet expresses it, a new sapling springs from the old stock of Jesse, on whom the spirit of Jehovah rests in full measure, as a spirit of wisdom, heroism, and true religion, who rules in the fear of Jehovah, his loins girt about with righteousness and faithfulness, doing justice to the poor without respect of persons, and consuming the evildoers out of the land by the sovereign sentence of his lips, till crime and violence are no longer known in Jehovah's holy mountain, and the land of Israel is full of the knowledge of Jehovah as the waters cover the sea. No figure is too strong to paint this reign of peace and order. The wolf shall dwell with the lamb, and the leopard shall lie down with the kid, and the sucking child shall play on the hole of the asp. It would be puerile to take these expressions literally, and the prophet himself interprets his figure when he represents the abolition of all hurt and harm as the fruit of just judgment and pure government.

The blessings of this Messianic time belong, in the first instance, to Israel alone; the other nations share in them only in so far as they seek arbitration and guidance from the kingly house of Jesse, which stands forth as a beacon to the surrounding peoples. But the restoration of Israel is complete. Jehovah will gather back the remnant of His people, scattered in Egypt and Assyria and all the four corners of the earth, opening a way before the returning exiles by drying up seas and rivers, as in the day when Israel came up out of Egypt. Judah and Ephraim shall no more be foes, and their united armies shall restore the ancient conquests of David. On the west they shall swoop down victoriously on Philistia; to the east they shall spoil the children of the desert; and Edom, Ammon, and Moab shall return to their old obedience.

The connection of ideas in this prophecy is so clear, and it sets forth with so much completeness Isaiah's whole view of Jehovah's purpose towards Judah, that we may regard it as a typical example of what is usually called Messianic prediction. The name Messiah is never used in the Old Testament in that special sense which we are accustomed to associate with it. *The Messiah* (with the article and no other word in apposition) is not an Old Testament phrase at all, and the word Messiah (Māshîᵃh) or "anointed one" in the connection "Jehovah's anointed one" is no theological term, but an ordinary title of the human king whom Jehovah has set over Israel. Thus the usual way in which the time of Israel's redemption and final glory is called the Messianic time is incorrect and misleading. So long as the Hebrew kingdom lasted, every king was " Jehovah's anointed," and it was only after the Jews lost their independence that the future restoration could be spoken of in contrast to the present as the days of the Messiah. To Isaiah the restoration of Israel is not the commencement but the continuation of that personal sovereignty of Jehovah over His people of which the

Davidic king was the recognised representative. As the holy seed which repeoples the land after the work of judgment is done is a fresh growth from the ancient stock of the nation (vi. 13), so too the new Davidic kingship is a fresh outgrowth of the old stem of Jesse. We are apt to think of the days of the Messiah as an altogether new and miraculous dispensation. That was not Isaiah's view. The restoration of Jerusalem is a return to an old state of things, interrupted by national sin. "I will restore thy judges as at the first, and thy councillors as at the beginning; afterward thou shalt be called the city of righteousness, the faithful city" (i. 26). And so when we examine the picture presented in chap. xi. with care, and make allowance for traits so plainly figurative as the lion which eats straw like the ox, the seas and rivers dried up to facilitate the return of the exiles of Judah, we find but one fundamental difference between the old and the new Israel: the land shall be full of the knowledge of Jehovah, and shall enjoy the happiness which in all ages, past as well as future, has accompanied obedience to the laws of its Divine King. And this obedience again is not taken in a New Testament sense, as if it rested on a new birth in every heart. Obedience to Jehovah as a King is not the affair of the individual conscience, but of the nation in its national organisation; the righteousness of Israel which Isaiah contemplates is such righteousness as is secured by a perfectly wise and firm application of the laws of civil justice and equity. It is this which gives so much importance to the person of the future king. It is the exercise of his functions that abolishes crime and violence, and makes the land which he governs worthy to be called Jehovah's holy mountain. Thus the cardinal point in the prophecy is the equipment of the Davidic king for the perfect exercise of his task by the spirit of Jehovah which rests upon him. But even here the prophet does not bring in any absolutely novel element, marking off the future felicity of Israel as a new dispensation. That good and strong government was the fruit of Jehovah's spirit poured upon the king of Israel was the ancient faith of the Hebrews. So we read that a divine spirit, or the spirit of Jehovah, descended first on Saul and afterwards on David at their respective anointings (1 Sam. x. 6, 10; xvi. 13, 14), as in earlier times the same spirit came upon the judges of Israel and strengthened them for their deeds of heroism (Judges iii. 10; vi. 34; xi. 29). Isaiah himself does not confine this operation of the spirit to the king of the future. In the day of deliverance Jehovah shall be for a spirit of judgment to him that sits for judgment, and of might to them that turn back the battle in the gate (xxviii. 6). All power to do right and noble deeds is Jehovah's gift, and the operations of His spirit are everywhere seen where men do great things in the strength of true faith. And so the indwelling of this spirit in the Davidic king does not constitute an absolutely new departure in the kingship, or offer anything inconsistent with the conception that

Jehovah will restore the judges of Jerusalem as they were in the beginning. The new thing is the completeness with which this divine equipment is bestowed, so that the king's whole delight is set on the fear of Jehovah, and his rule is wise and just, without error or defect of any kind.

But does not such an indwelling of the divine spirit, it may be asked, imply that the new king must be more than human? Does not Isaiah himself regard his rule as eternal, and bestow upon him in ix. 6 names that imply that he is God as well as man? In looking at this question, we must not allow ourselves to be influenced by the fuller light of the Christian dispensation which we possess, but which Isaiah had not. To us it is clear that the ideal of a kingdom of God upon earth could not be fully realised under the forms of the Old Testament. The dispensation of the New Testament is not a mere renewal of the days of David in more perfect form. The kingdom of God means now something very different from a restoration of the realm of Judah, and a resubjugation of Philistia and Edom, Ammon and Moab, under a sovereign reigning visibly on Zion ; and its establishment on earth was not, and could not be, the fruit of any such outward event as the destruction of the Assyrian monarchy. The very fact that Isaiah did not foresee this, that it was still possible for him immediately to connect the glory of the latter days with the fall of Assyria, and to speak of it as a restoration of the peace, the independence, the political supremacy of the land of Judah, is enough to show that the lineaments of his future king are not yet identical with the image of the New Testament Christ. The question, then, which we have to consider is whether Isaiah looked forward to a time when an immortal God-man should sit on the earthly Zion and use his divine strength and wisdom to make the Hebrew race happy and victorious over their neighbours. And to this question I think the answer must be in the negative. We believe in a divine and eternal Saviour, because the work of salvation, as we understand it in the light of the New Testament, is essentially different from the work of the wisest and best earthly king. Isaiah's ideal is only the perfect performance of the ordinary duties of monarchy : for this end he sees a king to be required who reigns in Jehovah's name, and in the strength of His Spirit, but there is no proof and no likelihood that he thought of more than this. It is by no means clear that he looks for an everlasting reign of one king, or indeed that he ever put to himself the question whether the new offshoot from the root of Jesse is to be one person or a race of sovereigns. It is the function and equipment of the kingship, not the person of the king, that absorbs all his attention. And though the names of the child who is to be born to Israel wonderfully foreshadow New Testament ideas, there is no reason to think that they denote anything metaphysical. The king of Israel reigns in Jehovah's name. In him Jehovah's rule becomes visible in Israel, and his great fourfold name speaks rather of the divine attributes that shine forth in his sovereignty, than of the transcendency of a person that is God as well as man. The prophet does not say that the king *is* the mighty God and the everlasting Father, but that his *name* is divine and eternal, that is, that the divine might and everlasting fatherhood of Jehovah are displayed in his rule.[9] That the person of the Messiah has not that foremost place in Isaiah's theology which has often been supposed appears most clearly from the fact that in his later utterances he ceases to speak of the rise of a new king. In the prophecies of the time of the war with Sennacherib he says only that the king shall reign for righteousness and princes rule for justice, that the churl shall no more be called princely, and the man of guiles a gracious lord. The right men shall be at the head of the state, and their authority shall bring protection and refreshing to the distressed (xxxii. 1 *seq.*) ; Jerusalem's princes and judges shall be such as they were in the good old days (i. 26). So long as the throne was filled by a king like Ahaz, or while his successor was still in the hands of a corrupt nobility, the contrast of the present and future kingship was a point to be specially emphasised ; but when there was promise of better days, when a vizier like Shebna had to give way to a man whom Isaiah esteemed so highly as Eliakim (xxii. 15 *seq.*), and the king himself began to rule on sounder principles, the sharpness of this contrast disappeared, and the prophet spoke rather of the glorious Jehovah Himself, who, above and through the earthly sovereign, was the true Judge, Lawgiver, King, and Saviour of Israel.

To realise what Isaiah looked to when he described a state of things in which the land of Israel should be full of true religion, or, as he expresses it, of practical knowledge of Jehovah, it is well to remember how in chap. xxviii. he presents the daily toil of the husbandman as itself regulated by divine revelation. The Hebrew state consisted essentially of two classes, the peasants and the governors or nobles. Husbandry on the one side, good government and justice on the other, are the twin pillars of the state, and for prince and peasant alike the knowledge of Jehovah means the knowledge of the duties of his vocation as sacred rules enforced by divine sanction and blessed by divine grace. Well-ordered and peaceful industry on the one hand, strict and impartial justice on the other, are the marks by which it is known that Jehovah's law is supreme in Israel; and He Himself crowns such obedience by blessing the fruits of the land, by giving unfailing direction in every time of need, and protecting the righteous nation from every enemy. Compare xxx. 18 *seq*.

Such is Isaiah's conception of the ideal of the internal order of the state, and his view of the foreign relations of Israel is not less plain and practical. It contains, as we have seen, two elements, the subjugation of the vassal nations which in old days did homage to

David, and the establishment of a kind of informal headship over more distant tribes who seek arbitration and direction from Jerusalem. The first of these elements is easy to understand. The new kingdom cannot fall short of the glories of David's reign, and Amos had already predicted that, in the last days, the house of Israel should possess the remnant of Edom and all the nations that in doing homage to Israel had acknowledged the sovereignty of Jehovah. Less than this, indeed, could not be regarded as sufficient to establish the peace and security of the Hebrews, who in every generation had been harassed by the enmity of Philistia and Edom, of Ammonites and Moabites. The other element in like manner contains no new thought. It is expressed in a passage which is now read in the books both of Isaiah and Micah (Isa. ii. 2 seq.; Micah iv. 2), and which, if it has a right to stand in both places, and has not rather been transferred from Micah to the text of Isaiah, must be a quotation from an older prophet. For Isaiah ii. was written long before Micah i.-v.; and Micah, on the other hand, is certainly not quoting Isaiah.[10] But, in truth, the thought that when justice and mercy rule on the throne of David foreign nations shall willingly bring their feuds before it for arbitration is expressed in the old prophecy, Isa. xvi. (*supra*, p. 92). This is far from implying a world-wide sovereignty of Israel; the thought covers no more than that kind of influence which a just and strong government always obtains among Semitic populations in its neighbourhood, which we ourselves, for example, exercise at the present day among the Arabs in the vicinity of Aden. The interminable feuds of tribes, conducted on the theory of blood-revenge, which makes no conclusive peace possible while either side has an outstanding score against the other, can seldom be durably healed without the intervention of a third party who is called in as arbiter, and in this way an impartial and wise power acquires of necessity a great and beneficent influence over all around it. Such an influence Israel must obtain when the knowledge and fear of Jehovah are established in the midst of the land.

And now, in conclusion, the practical simplicity and apparently restricted scope of Isaiah's ideal must not cause us to undervalue the pure and lofty faith on which it rests. A too prevalent way of thinking, which is certainly not Biblical, but which leavens almost the whole life of modern times, has accustomed us to regard religion as a thing by itself, which ought indeed to influence daily life, but nevertheless occupies a separate place in our hearts and actions. To us the exercises of religion belong to a different region from the avocations of daily life; God seems to us to stand outside and above the world, which has laws and an order of its own, in which it costs us a distinct effort to recognise the evidence of a personal providence. When we are dealing with the world we seem to have turned our backs upon God, and when we look to Him in the proper exercises of religion we strive to leave the world behind us. Hence our whole thoughts of God are dominated by the contrast of the natural and the supernatural; the miracles by which God approves Himself as God seem to us to have evidential force only in so far as they break through the laws of nature. To us, therefore, the ideal of an existence in full converse with God is apt to present itself as that of a new world in which everything is supernatural, a heaven in which the tasks of common life have no more place, and the natural limitations of earthly being have disappeared. The time when faith shall have passed into sight seems to us to be necessarily a time in which everything is miraculous, in which life is a dream of the fruition of God. To such a habit of thought the ideal of Isaiah is necessarily disappointing, and that not so much on account of the unquestionable imperfection of the Old Testament standpoint which considers the Divine Kingship only in reference to the nation of Israel, as on account of the realism which represents the state of perfected religion as consistent with the continuance of earthly conditions and the common order of actual life. But in reality it is just this realism which is the greatest triumph of Isaiah's faith. For him that contrast of the natural and supernatural which narrows all the religion of the present has no existence. He knows nothing of laws of nature, of an order of the world which can be separated even in thought from the constant personal activity of Jehovah. The natural life of Israel is already, if I may use terms which the prophet would have refused to recognise, as thoroughly penetrated by the supernatural as any heavenly state can be. It is not in the future alone that the Holy One of Israel is to become a living member in the daily life of His people. To him who has eyes to see and ears to hear the presence and voice of Jehovah are already manifested with absolute and unmistakable clearness. It requires no argument to rise from nature to nature's God; the workings of Jehovah are as palpable as those of an ordinary man. In the time of future glory His presence cannot become more actual than it is now; it is only the eyes and ears of Israel that require to be opened to see and hear what to the prophet is even now a present reality.

With all its faults, the old popular religion of Israel had one great excellence: it made religion an inseparable part of common life. The Hebrew saw God's hand and acknowledged His presence in his sowing and his reaping, in his sorrows and his joys. The rules of husbandry were Jehovah's teaching, the harvest gladness was Jehovah's feast, the thunderstorm Jehovah's voice. It was the armies of Jehovah that went forth to battle, the spirit of Jehovah that inspired the king, the oracle of Jehovah that gave forth law and judgment. This simple faith was obscured and threatened with utter extinction by the intrusion into the life of the nation of new and heterogeneous elements, by the gradual dissolution of the ancient balance of society, and above all by the advent of the Assyrian, who swept away in the tide of conquest the whole traditional life of the conquered nations. Then it was that the prophets arose to preach a kingdom of Jehovah supreme even in the crash of nations and the dissolution of the whole fabric of society. But the very cardinal point of their faith, which alone gave it value and power, was the doctrine that the God who reigned in the storm that raged round Israel was no new deity, but the ancient God of Jacob ; the kingdom of the future was one with the kingdom of the past, and the task of that divine grace in which they never ceased to trust was not to set a new religion in the place of the old, but to re-establish the ancient harmony of religion and daily experience, and make common life as full of Jehovah's presence as it had been in times gone by. To this end a work of judgment must sweep away all that comes between man and his Maker. The sins of Israel are the things that hide Jehovah from its eyes, and from this point of view idols and idolatrous sanctuaries stand on one line with wealth and luxury, fortresses and chariots, everything that can hold man's heart and prevent it from turning in every concern directly to the Holy One of Israel. To the prophet all these things are emptiness and vanity. The one thing real on earth is the work of Jehovah in relation to His people. To Isaiah, therefore, the supernatural is not something added to and differing from the common course of things. Everything real is supernatural, and supernatural in the same degree. Where we contrast the supernatural and the natural, Isaiah contrasts Jehovah and the things of nought. To him the fall of Assyria by the stroke of the Holy One of Israel is just as supernatural and just as natural as the previous conquests of the Great King; he sees the hand of Jehovah working alike in both, and both exemplify the same principle of the absolute sovereignty of the King who reigns in Zion. From our point of view the picture drawn in chaps. x. and xi. is apt to seem a strange mixture of the most surprising miracle and the most prosaic matter of fact. The Assyrian falls by no human sword, and presently the men of Judah are engaged in the petty conquest of Philistia or Edom. Or again, in chap. xxx., the light of the Holy One of Israel flashes forth from Zion, Jehovah causes His glorious voice to be heard and scatters His enemies with flame of a devouring fire, with crashing storm and hail; and when the tempest is past we see the cattle feeding in large pastures, the oxen and the asses that plough the ground eating savoury provender winnowed with the shovel and the fork. But to Isaiah the miracles of history and the providences of common life bring Jehovah alike near to faith. His religion is the religion of the God without whose will not even a sparrow can fall upon the ground, the God whose greatness lies in His equal sovereignty in things small and vast.

The first requisite to a better understanding of the religion of the Bible is that we should learn to enter with simplicity into this point of view, and to this end we must remember above all things that the Bible knows nothing of that narrow definition of miracle which we have inherited from mediæval metaphysics. When Isaiah draws a distinction between Jehovah's *wonders* and the things of daily life he thinks of something quite different from what we call miracle. "Forasmuch as this people draw near Me with their mouth, and with their lips do honour Me, but have removed their heart far from Me, and their fear towards Me is a precept of men learned by rote: therefore behold I will proceed to do a marvellous work among this people, even a marvellous work and a miracle, and the wisdom of their wise men shall perish, and the understanding of their prudent men shall be hid" (xxix. 13, 14). A marvel or miracle is a work of Jehovah directed to confound the religion of formalism, to teach men that Jehovah's rule is a real thing and not a traditional convention to be acknowledged in formulas learned by rote. And the mark of such a work is not that it breaks through laws of nature—a conception which had no existence for Isaiah—but that all man's wisdom and foresight stand abashed before it. The whole career of Assyria is part of the marvel that confounds the hypocrisy and formalism of Judah; even as the prophet speaks the work is already begun and proceeding to its completion. And therefore it was of no moment to Isaiah's faith whether his picture of the sudden downfall of the enemy before the gates of Jerusalem was fulfilled, as we say, literally. The point of his prophecy was not that the deliverance of Judah should take place in any one way, or with those dramatic circumstances of the so-called supernatural which a vulgar faith demands as the proof that God is at work. In truth the crisis came, as we shall see in next Lecture, in a form far less visibly startling than is pictured in chap. x.; but it was none the less true that Jehovah so worked His supreme will that man's wisdom was confounded before it, that it was made manifest to the eyes of Israel that Jehovah reigns supreme and that there is no help or salvation save in Him. And in this sense the age of miracle is not past. All history is full of like proofs of divine sovereignty and divine grace, when in ways incalculable, and through combinations that mocked the foresight and policy of human counsellors, God's cause has been proved indestructible, and the faith in a very present God and Saviour which Isaiah preached has come forth in new life from the wreck of societies in which religion had become a mere tradition of men.

LECTURE VIII.

THE DELIVERANCE FROM ASSYRIA.[1]

BETWEEN the Syro-Ephraitic war and the accession of Sennacherib to the throne of Nineveh the power of Assyria had been steadily on the increase. The energy and talent of Sargon, devoted to the consolidation rather than the unlimited extension of his empire, effectually put down every movement of independence on the part of subjects and tributaries, and even the united realm of Egypt and Ethiopia no longer ventured to measure its strength with his. The nations groaned under a tyranny that knew no pity, but they had learned by repeated experience that revolt was hopeless while the reins of empire were held by so firm a hand. At length, in the year 705, Sargon died, and the crown passed to his son, Sennacherib. A thrill of joy ran through the nations at the fall of the great oppressor (Isa. xiv. 29). In a few months Babylon was in full revolt, the Assyrian vassal king was overthrown, Merodach Baladan—either the old adversary of Sargon, or a son of the same name—assumed the sovereignty, and for two years (704-3), according to the canon of Ptolemy, the Assyrian kingship in Chaldæa was interrupted. The rebel king sought alliances far and wide; the monuments tell us that he found support in Elam (the region to the east of the lower Tigris, now part of Khuzistan), among the Aramæans of Mesopotamia, and among the Arab tribes, and that two campaigns were occupied in reducing the revolt in these districts. But the plan of Merodach Baladan had not been limited to Chaldæa and the neighbouring regions. The far West was equally impatient of Assyrian rule with the eastern provinces, and the first hope of the Babylonian leader was to raise the whole empire in simultaneous insurrection from the shores of the Mediterranean to the Persian Gulf. It is to this date that we must refer his embassy to Hezekiah spoken of in 2 Kings xx. (Isa. xxxix), for which the sickness of the king of Judah can have been no more than the formal pretext, since we are told that Hezekiah "hearkened to the ambassadors," and displayed before them the resources of his kingdom. Such a reception given to a declared rebel against Assyria could have but one meaning. It meant that the king of Judah was more than half inclined to join the revolt. Merodach Baladan, in fact, had not misjudged the feelings of the Palestinian nations. The Philistine states especially, the old hotbed of revolt, were in a ferment of exultation at the news of Sargon's death, and already committed to war, and the contagion of their enthusiasm had reached Judah. Hezekiah, however, does not seem to have engaged himself to immediate action. He was not disposed to advance without the aid of Egypt, and the diplomacy of the Pharaohs moved slowly. But while the king hesitated, Isaiah had at once taken up his position. At the first news of the attitude of the Philistines he had sounded a note of warning in the brief prophecy preserved in xiv. 29-32. "Rejoice not, O all Philistia, that the rod that smote thee is broken; for from the root of the serpent shall come forth a basilisk, and its fruit shall be a flying dragon." Sennacherib, that is to say, will prove an enemy still more dangerous than his father. The cities of Philistia are doomed, " for a smoke cometh out of the north "—the cloud that marks the approach of the Assyrian host—" and there is no straggler in his bands." But if Judah hold the safe course, and eschew all connection with foreign schemes of liberation, the destruction shall not be suffered to affect Hezekiah, or disturb the peace of the poorest in his land (xiv. 30). What answer then should be made to the ambassadors of the nation which solicits the Judæan alliance? "That Jehovah hath founded Zion, and in it His afflicted people shall find shelter."[2]

Thirty years had passed since Isaiah first struck this very note of warning and of hope in his famous interview with Ahaz, at a time when the leaders of Judah were as eager to commit themselves to the Assyrian tutelage as they now were impatient to throw it off. The new generation which had grown up in the interval, and now held the reins of the state, had seen greater changes take place in their own lifetime than had passed before all the generations of their fathers from the time of Solomon downwards. Judah was like a ship that had lost its rudder, drifting at the mercy of shifting winds. Every ancient principle of national policy had disappeared or been reversed. No one knew whither the state was tending, or what results might flow from the new alliance with Philistia and Egypt, so contrary to all the traditions of past history, which the king and his counsellors were disposed to welcome as offering at least a hope of momentary relief from a bondage that had become intolerable. During these thirty years Isaiah alone had remained ever constant to himself, alike free from panic and flattering self-delusion, unshaken by the successes of Assyria, assured that no political combination which lay within the horizon of Judæan statesmanship could stem the tide of conquest, but not less assured that Jehovah's kingdom stood immovable, the one sure rock in the midst of the surging waters. An attitude so imposing in its calm and steadfast faith, and justified by so many proofs of true insight and sound political judgment, could not fail to secure for Isaiah a deep and growing influence. He no longer, as in the days of Ahaz, confronted the king as a mere isolated individual, whose counsels could be contemptuously brushed aside. The prophetic word had become a power in Jerusalem, and though the "scornful men," who despised Jehovah's word and trusted in oppression and crooked ways (xxx. 9-12), were still predominant in the counsels of state, they were afraid openly to challenge the opposition of Isaiah until the nation was too deeply committed to draw back. Their plans of revolt were matured in all secrecy ; they hid their counsel deep from Jehovah and kept their actions in the dark—so Isaiah complains — saying, Who seeth us and who knoweth us ? (xxix. 15). The prolonged wars of Sennacherib in the east gave them time to ripen their plans in private negotiation with Egypt. An embassy was sent to Zoan with a train of camels and asses bearing a rich treasure as the best argument to secure the assistance of Pharaoh (xxx. 1-6). The delay which attended these negotiations was in itself sufficient to ruin the prospects of the conspirators, for it gave Sennacherib time to crush the Babylonians and their allies in detail, before the flame of war broke out in the west. Even the common political judgment must justify Isaiah when he pointed out that the strength of the Assyrian was in no sense broken by the death of Sargon, and that the inertness of the Egyptians gave no promise of effectual help (xxx. 7). When Sennacherib had secured his eastern provinces, and at last moved westward (701 B.C.), the allies had effected as good as nothing. No Egyptian army was yet in the field. The Philistines had risen in conjunction with Hezekiah, and King Padi of Ekron, the vassal of Sennacherib, had been laid in chains in Jerusalem ; the Phœnician cities were also in revolt, but no scheme of joint action was prepared, and the Great King advanced victoriously along the Mediterranean coast. The first blow fell upon Tyre, Zidon, and the minor Phœnician ports, and, when they were reduced, the Samaritans,* Ammonites, Moabites, Edomites, and even a part of the Philistines, hastened to bring gifts and do homage to the conqueror. Still continuing his march along the coast, Sennacherib successively reduced Ashkelon and the other maritime cities of Philistia; and, having thus thrown his force between the Palestinian rebels and their tardy allies of Egypt, he was able to turn his arms inland against Ekron and Judæa without fear of their forces effecting a junction with Tirhakah. Tirhakah, in fact, had already begun to move, and sent an army to the relief of Ekron, but it was defeated at Eltekeh,³ and compelled to retire without effecting its purpose. From this moment the fall of Ekron was assured, and the Judæans, who had been the soul of the revolt in Southern Palestine, had no human hope of deliverance from the Great King. The crisis had arrived which Isaiah had so long foreseen; the last act of the Divine judgment had opened, and all eyes could now see the madness of a policy which had sought help and counsel from man and not from God.

During the three years of suspense that intervened between the embassy of Merodach Baladan to Hezekiah and the defeat of the forces of Egypt and Ethiopia at Eltekeh, Isaiah had never wavered in his judgment on the insensate folly of the rulers of Judah. When the secret of the negotiations with Egypt, so long hid with care from Jehovah and His prophet, was at length
* See page 439.

divulged, and the whole nation was carried away by a tide of patriotic enthusiasm, his indignation found utterance in burning words. The political folly of the scheme was palpable; the enthusiasm with which it was greeted was mere intoxication (xxix. 9). Yet it was not for miscalculating the relative strength and readiness of Egypt and Assyria that Isaiah blamed his countrymen, but for entering at all into a calculation which left Jehovah out of the reckoning. "Woe to them that go down to Egypt for help, and stay on horses and trust in chariots because they are many, and on horsemen because they are a great host; but they look not to the Holy One of Israel, neither do they consult Jehovah. Yet He is wise, and bringeth evil, and will not call back His words, but will rise against the house of evildoers and the help of them that work iniquity. The Egyptians are men and not God, and their horses flesh and not spirit: Jehovah stretcheth forth His hand, and the helper stumbleth, and he that is holpen falls, yea, all of them shall fail together" (xxxi. 1 *seq.*). Their plans had left out of account the one factor that really makes history, the supreme purpose and will of the Holy One of Israel. A judicial blindness seemed to cover the eyes of Judah. Jehovah had poured upon them a spirit of deep sleep; His revelation had become a sealed and illegible book to the nation which called itself Jehovah's people, but refused to hear His counsel (xxix. 10 *seq.*). He had long since set before His people the path of true deliverance. "Thus saith the Lord Jehovah, By returning and rest ye shall be saved ; in quietness and confidence shall be your strength : but ye would not." The rest and quietness which Isaiah prescribes are not the rest of indolence ; he calls on Israel to abjure the vain bustle of foreign politics and put their trust in Jehovah ; but faith in Jehovah brings its own obligations,—conformity to Jehovah's law, the establishment of religion as a practical power in daily life, and not as a mere precept of men learned by rote. To think that the divine wrath expressed in the continuance of Assyrian oppression can be escaped where these conditions are ignored is to reduce Jehovah to the level of man ; it is not against Assyria but against Jehovah Himself that the plans of Judah are directed. " Out on your perversity," he cries ; "shall the potter be esteemed as the clay, that the thing made should say of him that made it, He made me not ? or the thing framed of him that framed it, He hath no understanding ?" (xxix. 16). Not by such vain rebellion against the Maker of Israel can peace and help be found. Jehovah's salvation must be sought in His own way, and when it comes it shall sweep away not only the foreign tyrant, but the idolatry and traditional formalism of the masses, the oppressive and untruthful rule of the godless nobles (xxxi. 7 ; xxxii. 1 *seq.*).

To a superficial view the teaching of Isaiah in this juncture may seem to present the aspect of political fatalism. The apparent patriotism of his opponents enlists a ready sympathy, and the prophet's declaration that it was vain to attempt anything against the

Assyrian till Jehovah Himself rose to bring deliverance is very apt to be confounded with the vulgar type of Oriental indolence, which identifies submission to the divine will with a neglect of the natural means to a desired end, leaving the means and the end alike to the sovereignty of fate. Such a view altogether mistakes the true point of Isaiah's argument. He does not refuse the use of means, but condemns the choice of means that are necessarily inadequate because they ignore the conditions of Jehovah's sovereignty. If the plans of Hezekiah and his princes had succeeded, they would still have contributed nothing to the true deliverance of Judah. To be freed from Assyria only that the rulers of the land might continue their oppressions uncontrolled, that religion might go on in its old round of formal observances which had no influence on conduct, that the credit of the idols might be re-established, and the true word of Jehovah still treated with contumely, would have been no benefit to the land. Isaiah was not the enemy of patriotic effort, but only of the spurious patriotism that identifies national prosperity with the undisturbed persistence of cherished abuses; he did not value political freedom less than his countrymen did, but he valued it only when it meant freedom from internal disorders as well as from foreign domination, the substitution for Assyrian bondage of the effective sovereignty of Jehovah's holiness.

And so the criticism which Isaiah directed against the policy of Egyptian alliance was not merely negative.

As a true prophet he could not preach the vanity of mere human helpers without at the same time unfolding the all-sufficiency of the divine Saviour. The crisis which the folly of the rulers had brought upon the nation had to Isaiah a meaning of mercy as well as of judgment, for mercy and judgment meet in those supreme moments of history when the wisdom of the wise and the understanding of the prudent are confounded before Jehovah's counsel, when the arm of flesh is broken, and the might of Jehovah stands revealed to every eye. The impending destruction of the human helpers of Judah, the confusion that awaits those who put their trust in idols and in that religion learned by rote (xxix. 13) of which the idols were a part (xxxi. 7), the disasters which are prepared for the armies of Hezekiah (xxx. 17), the overthrow of citadel and fortress, and the desolation of the fruitful land (xxxii. 9 *seq.*), are so many steps towards the great turning-point of Israel's history, when all the delusive things of earth that blind men's eyes to spiritual realities are swept away, and Jehovah alone remains as the supreme reality and the one help of His people. "In that day shall the deaf hear the words of the book [of revelation, xxix. 11], and the eyes of the blind shall see out of darkness and out of obscurity. And the afflicted ones shall renew their joy in Jehovah, and the poor among men shall rejoice in the Holy One of Israel. For the tyrant is brought to nought, and the scorner is consumed, and all that watched for iniquity are cut off, that make men to sin by their words, and lay a snare for him that judgeth in the gate, and undo him that is in the right by empty guiles." Jehovah's deliverance, you observe, is not limited to the overthrow of the Assyrian; its goal is the establishment of His revelation as the law of Israel, and especially as a law that restores justice in the land and enables the poor and oppressed to rejoice in their divine King. "Therefore, thus saith Jehovah, who redeemed Abraham, unto the house of Jacob, Jacob shall not now be ashamed, neither shall his face now wax pale; for when his children see it, even the work of My hands in the midst of him, they shall sanctify My name and sanctify the Holy One of Jacob, and shall fear the God of Israel. And they that erred in spirit shall come to understanding, and they that murmured shall learn instruction" (xxix. 18-24).

Thus the words of stern rebuke which Isaiah continued to direct against the princes and their carnal policy (chaps. xxix.-xxxii.) are mingled with pictures of salvation, in which the main ideas are those already developed in earlier prophecies, but set forth with a depth of sympathy and tender feeling to which none of the earlier prophecies attain. The prophet's fire had not been quenched, but his spirit was chastened and his faith mellowed by the experience of forty years spent in waiting for the salvation which Judah's unbelief had so long deferred. One can see that the old man had begun to live much in the future, that he was glad to look beyond the present, and delight himself in the images of peace and holiness that lay on the other side of the last and crowning trouble which the nation had so wantonly drawn upon itself. Jehovah is ready with grace and help at the first voice of repentant supplication. "He waiteth long that He may be gracious unto you; He lifteth Himself on high that He may have compassion upon you, for Jehovah is the God of judgment; blessed are all they that wait for Him. Nay! weep no more, O people of Zion, that dwellest in Jerusalem; He will surely be gracious to thee at the voice of thy cry, even as He heareth it He will answer thee. And when the Lord giveth you the bread of adversity and the water of affliction, yet shall not thy Revealer be hidden any more, but thine eyes shall see thy Revealer; and thine ears shall hear a word behind thee saying, This is the way, walk ye in it, when ye turn to the right hand or to the left. Then ye shall defile the silver plating of your graven images, and the golden overlaying of your molten images; thou shalt cast them away as a foul thing; thou shalt say to it, Get thee hence. Thus He shall give the rain of thy seed that thou sowest the ground withal, and bread of the increase of the earth, and it shall be rich and full; in that day shall the cattle feed in large pastures. . . . Moreover, the light of the moon shall be as the light of the sun, and the light of the sun shall be sevenfold, in the day that Jehovah bindeth up the hurt of His people and healeth the stroke of their wound" (xxx. 18, *seq.*). In these pictures of assured prosperity in a nation that has cast aside its idols to seek deliverance and continual guidance from the true Teacher, Isaiah dwells again and again, and with a fulness which we are apt to think disproportionate, on images of fertility and natural abundance, of plenty and contentment for man and beast, when streams flow on every mountain (xxx. 25), when Lebanon is changed to a fruitful field, and the fruitful field of to-day shall be esteemed as a forest (xxix. 17). There is true poetical pathos in these images of rural peace and felicity, drawn by an old man whose life had been spent in the turmoil of the capital, in the midst of the creations of earthly pride, where the works of man's hands disguised the simple tokens of Jehovah's goodness. But the emphasis which Isaiah lays on the gifts of natural fertility has more than a poetic motive. From the days of his earliest prophecies he had pointed to the "spring of Jehovah," the God-given fruits of the earth, as the true glory of the remnant of Israel, — the best of blessings, because they come straight from heaven, and are the true basis of a peaceful and God-fearing life (chap. iv.). And so he draws once more the old contrast between the immediate prospect of a land desolated by invading hosts, when the pleasant fields and the fruitful vineyards lie waste, when the gladsome houses of the joyous cities of Judah are covered with thorns and briers, when the citadel is forsaken and the turmoil of the city changed to silence, when ruined fortress and tower are the haunt of the wild asses, a pasture for flocks, and the days of Israel's restoration, " when the spirit is poured upon us from on high, and the wilderness shall be a fruitful field, and the fruitful field be counted for a forest." To Isaiah the fertility of the land is a spiritual blessing, the token of acceptance with Jehovah, the seal of the return of the nation to the paths of righteousness and true obedience. The desert is transformed to fertility, for judgment dwells in it, and righteousness abides in the fruitful field. "And the effect of righteousness shall be peace, and the reward of righteousness quietness and security for ever. And My people shall dwell in a peaceable habitation and in sure dwellings and in quiet resting-places." "Blessed are ye that sow beside all waters, sending forth the feet of the ox and the ass" to tread in the seed. Blessed is Israel, when the turmoil of the present has passed away for ever, and all corners of the land are again the scene of the yearly routine of simple husbandry (xxxii. 12, *seq.*).

There is a tinge of weariness, an earnest longing after rest, in these idyllic pictures, but Isaiah did not suffer them to withdraw his attention from the pressing questions of the present. Step by step he watched the progress of events. While all around him were still steeped in careless security, while the feasts still ran their round, and more than one year passed by and brought no tidings of the approach of Sennacherib, he continued to send forth words of warning. Jehovah Himself is preparing the onslaught. He will camp against Zion round about, and build siege-works and forts against the city of David, and the deliverance shall not come till Jerusalem is humbled to the dust, and her plaintive cry seems to rise from the depths of the earth like the voice of a ghost. But in the last extremity her help is sure, and her adversaries vanish as chaff before the wind. " She shall be visited of Jehovah of hosts with thunder, and with earthquake, and great noise, with storm and tempest, and the flame of devouring fire. And the multitude of all the nations that fight against Ariel—the hearth of God—even all that fight against her and her munition, and they that distress her, shall be as a dream, a vision of the night" (xxix. 1 *seq.*). Thus assured of the limits of the appointed judgment, Isaiah follows with calmness the gradual evolution of Jehovah's purpose. The Assyrian is drawing nigh to discharge his last commission, to complete the work of judgment, and then to disappear for ever. The greatness of the crisis and the lofty eminence of faith from which Isaiah looks down upon it declare themselves in an expansion of the prophetic horizon. The impending decision is not merely the turning-point of Israel's history, it is the crisis of the history of the world; the future not of Judah alone, but of all the nations, from Tarshish in the Mediterranean West, and Meroe in the distant South, to the far Eastern lands of Elam, hangs upon the approaching conflict. On every side the nations are mustering to battle; Assyria, on its part, is gathering the peoples of the East (xvii. 12; xxii. 6; xxix. 7); on the Nile swift messengers are hurrying to and fro betwixt Ethiopia and Egypt (xviii. 2); and the centre of all this turmoil is Jehovah's mountain land of Judah. For Jehovah hath sworn that in His land the Assyrian shall be broken, and on His mountains He will tread him under foot. "This is the purpose that is purposed upon the whole earth, and this is the hand that is stretched out upon all nations" (xiv. 24-27). And so the prophet calls upon all the inhabitants of the world to watch for the decisive moment, the signal of Jehovah's visible intervention, when the ensign is lifted up on the mountains, and the trumpet blast proclaims the great catastrophe. Meanwhile Jehovah in His heavenly dwelling-place looks down at ease upon the gradual ripening of His purpose, as the skies seem lazily to watch the ripening grapes on a clear bright day in the hot autumn. "For before the vintage, when the blossom is over and the flower gives place to the ripening grape, He shall cut off the sprigs with pruning-hooks, and the branches shall He hew away." Thus surely and without interruption shall the Assyrian mature his plans of universal conquest, till Jehovah Himself strikes in, and the invincible armies of Nineveh are left together to the fowls of the mountains and to the beasts of the earth; and the vultures shall summer upon their carcasses, and all the beasts of the earth shall winter upon them. Then shall Mount Zion, the place of the name of Jehovah of hosts, be known to all the ends of the earth, and from far Ethiopia tribute and homage shall flow to Jehovah's shrine (xviii. 4-7).

Thus, while Isaiah does not cease to concentrate his chief attention on Israel, or to regard the restoration and true redemption of the ancient people of Jehovah as the central feature of the Divine purpose, the largeness of the historical issues involved in the downfall of the supreme world-power carries the prophetic vision far beyond the narrow limits of Judah, and in the destruction of the Assyrian tyrant the King of Israel declares Himself Lord of all the earth. And so when Babylon had fallen (xxiii. 13), and Sennacherib at length began his destroying march upon the western provinces, Isaiah followed his progress with absorbing and almost sympathetic interest. First he announces the speedy discomfiture of the Arab tribes; within a short year all the glory of Kedar shall be consumed, and the remnant of the bowmen of the desert shall be few (xxi. 13 *seq.*). And next, as we know was the actual course of events, the stroke shall fall on the proud city of Tyre, the mart of nations, whose merchants are princes, and her traffickers the honourable of the earth; for Jehovah of hosts hath purposed to stain the pride of all glory, and to bring into contempt all the honourable of the earth (chap. xxiii.). And still the career of the destroyer has not reached its end: " Behold Jehovah rideth upon a swift cloud, and cometh unto Egypt, and the idols of Egypt shall be moved at His presence, and the heart of Egypt shall melt in the midst thereof." The strength of Pharaoh is brought to nought, and the wisdom of his counsellors is changed to folly; the land is divided against itself and passes under the hand of a cruel Lord —the merciless king of Assyria (chap. xix.). It is Jehovah Himself that leads the armies of Nineveh in this career of universal conquest, paralysing the arms of their enemies; all the nations must be abased before Him, the strength of the world must be laid low, that His majesty may be exalted and every land do homage to Him. The crowning decision has assumed proportions so vast that its issue can be nothing less than the subjugation of the inhabited world to Jehovah's throne. For the desolation of the kingdoms is no longer, as it had appeared to earlier prophecy, a mere work of judgment on a godless world. To them as well as to Judah, if not in so exalted a sense, the judgment is the prelude to a great conversion. Tyre shall be forgotten for seventy years—the period, as the prophet explains it, of a single reign—and then Jehovah shall visit her in mercy, and she shall return to her merchandise and her gains, no longer to heap up treasure in the temple of Melkarth, but to consecrate her wealth to Jehovah, and supply abundance of food and princely clothing to the people of Israel that dwell in His presence.

We see from this detail that Isaiah still pictures the conversion of the nations under the limitations prescribed by the national idea of religion, which the Old Testament never wholly laid aside, which could not indeed be superseded in an age to which all cosmopolitan ideas were utterly foreign. But, while Isaiah was unable to conceive of the conversion of foreign nations to Jehovah in any other form than that of homage done to the Divine King that reigned on Zion, and tribute paid to His court, we should greatly err if we imagined that this conception sprang, as has sometimes been supposed, from mere national vanity. The subjection of the nations to Jehovah's throne, and the share which they thus obtain in the blessings of peace and good governance that are ministered by His sovereign word of revelation (ii. 2 *seq.*) is no grievous bondage, but their best privilege and happiness, their redemption from the cruel yoke which pressed so heavily on all the earth. This appears most clearly in the prophecy of the conversion of Egypt in chap. xix. On no land do the evils of a selfish and oppressive government weigh so grievously as on the valley of the Nile, where the very conditions of life and the maintenance of the fertility of the soil depend on a continual attention to the canals and other public works, the condition of which has, in all ages, been the best criterion of a strong and considerate administration.[4] This characteristic feature of the economy of the nation does not escape Isaiah, for the lofty spirituality of his aims is always combined with a penetrating insight into actual historical conditions. Under the cruel king whose advent dissolves the government of the Pharaohs, and sets free the intestine jealousies of the Egyptian nomes, the prophet describes the canals as dried up, and all the industries that depended on them as paralysed. Then the Egyptians shall cry unto Jehovah because of their oppressors, and He shall send them a saviour and a prince, and He shall deliver them. "And Jehovah shall be known to Egypt, and the Egyptians shall know Jehovah on that day, and shall do worship with sacrifice and oblation, and shall vow vows to Jehovah, and perform them." Then all the lands of the known world from Egypt to Assyria shall serve the God of Jacob. "Israel shall be the third with Egypt and Assyria, even a blessing in the midst of the earth, whom Jehovah of hosts shall bless, saying, Blessed be Egypt my people, and Assyria the work of my hands, and Israel mine inheritance." Never had the faith of prophet soared so high, or approached so near to the conception of a universal religion, set free from every trammel of national individuality. For now the history of the world had narrowed itself to a single issue; the fate of all nations turned on the decisive contest between the Assyrian and the God of Zion; and it was plain that Jehovah's kingship in Israel was naught unless it could approve itself by arguments that spoke to all the earth.[5]

If the vindication of the divine mission of the prophets of Israel must be sought in the precision of detail with which they related beforehand the course of coming events, the hopes which Isaiah continued to preach during the victorious advance of Sennacherib must be reckoned as vain imaginations. The great decision which shall call back the earth to the service of the true God is still an object of faith, and not an accomplished reality. The Assyrians passed away, and new powers rose upon the ruins of their greatness to repeat in other forms the battle of earthly empire against the Kingdom of God. As Babylonia and Persia, Greece and Rome, successively rose and fell, the sphere of the great movements of history continually enlarged, till at length a new world went forth from the dissolution of ancient society, the centre of human history was shifted to lands unknown to the Hebrews, and its fortunes were committed to nations still unborn when Isaiah preached. Not only have Isaiah's predictions received no literal fulfilment, but it is impossible that the evolution of the divine purpose can ever again be narrowed within the limits of the petty world of which Judah was the centre and Egypt and Assyria the extremes. Fanciful theorists who use the Old Testament as a book of curious mysteries, and profane its grandeur by adapting it to their idle visions at the sacrifice of every law of sound hermeneutics and sober historical judgment, may still dream of future political conjunctions which shall restore to Palestine the position of central importance which it once held as the meeting-place of the lands of ancient civilisation; but no sane thinker can seriously imagine for a moment that Tyre will again become the emporium of the world's commerce or Jerusalem the seat of universal sovereignty. The forms in which Isaiah enshrined his spiritual hopes are broken, and cannot be restored; they belong to an epoch of history that can never return, and the same line of argument which leads us reverently to admire the divine wisdom that chose the mountains of Palestine as the cradle of true religion at a time when Palestine was, in a very real sense, the physical centre of those movements of history from which the modern world has grown, refutes the idea that the Kingdom of the living God can again in any special sense be identified with the nation of the Jews and the land of Canaan. These indeed are considerations which have long been obvious to all but a few fantastic Millenarians, whose visions deserve no elaborate refutation. But even serious students of Scripture do not always clearly realise the full import of the failure of the literalistic view of prophecy; and the doctrine of literal fulfilment, rejected in principle, is still apt to exercise a fatal influence on the details of prophetic exegesis. If we repudiate the dream of an earthly Millennium, with Jerusalem and a Jewish restoration as its centre, we have no right to reserve for literal fulfilment such details of the prophecies as seem more capable of being reconciled with the actual march of history, or to rest the proof of the prophets' inspiration on the literal realisation of isolated parts of their pictures of the future, while it is yet certain that as a whole these pictures can never be translated into actuality—nay, that there is boundless variety and discrepancy of detail between the pictures contained in the various prophetic books, or even between those drawn by the same prophet at different periods of his career.

The perception of these difficulties, which can escape

no thoughtful reader of the prophecies, has therefore long formed the chief support of the figurative or allegorical school of exegesis, which, not only in the Old Catholic and Mediæval Churches, but in modern Protestantism, may claim to be viewed as the official type of prophetic exegesis. It is plain, however, that this method of exegesis labours under precisely the same difficulties when applied to prophecy with those which have caused its general abandonment as regards other parts of Scripture. The general law of allegorical interpretation, as developed in the ancient Church, is that everything which in its literal sense seems impossible, untrue, or unworthy of God must be rescued from this condemnation by the hypothesis of a hidden sense, which was the real meaning of the inspiring Spirit, and even of the prophet himself, except in so far as he was a mere unintelligent machine in the hand of the revealer. Now, it is certainly true, as we saw in a former Lecture (*supra*, p. 221 *seq.*), that all early thought about abstract and transcendental ideas is largely carried out by the aid of figure and analogy, and that general truths are apprehended and expressed in particular and even accidental forms. But this is something very different from the doctrine of a spiritual sense in the traditional meaning of the word. It means that the early thinker has apprehended only germs of universal truth, that he expresses these as clearly as he can, and that the figurative or imperfect form of his utterance corresponds to a real limitation of vision. That is not the principle of current allegorical exegesis, which holds rather that the obscurity of form is intentional, at least on the part of the revealing Spirit, and so that the true meaning of each prophecy is the maximum of New Testament truth that can be taken out of it by any use of allegory which the Christian reader can devise. Such a method of exegesis is purely arbitrary; it enables each man to prove his own dogmas at will from the Old Testament, and leaves us altogether uncertain what the prophets themselves believed, and what work they wrought for God in their own age. All this uncertainty disappears when we read the words of the prophets in their natural sense. The teaching of Isaiah, the greater part of which has now fallen under our survey, is the very reverse of unintelligible, if we consent to understand it by the plain rules of ordinary human speech, and in connection with the life of his own age. We do not need to carry with us to the study of the prophet any formulated principles of prophetic interpretation; the true meaning of his words unfolds itself clearly enough as soon as we realise the historical surroundings of his ministry, and the principles of spiritual faith, or, in other words, the conception of Jehovah and the laws of His working, which dominated all Isaiah's life. The kingship of Jehovah, the holy majesty of the one true God, the eternal validity of His law of righteousness, the certainty that His cause on earth is imperishable and must triumph over all the wrath of man, that His word of grace cannot be without avail, and that the community of His grace is the one thing on earth that cannot be brought to nought,—these are the spiritual certainties the possession of which constituted Isaiah a true prophet. Everything else in his teaching is nothing more than an attempt to give these principles concrete shape and tangible form in relation to the problems of his own day. The practical lessons which he drew from them for the conduct of Israel were in all respects absolutely justified. At every point his insight into the actual position of affairs, his judgment on the sin of Judah and the right path of amendment, his perception of the true sources of danger and the true way of deliverance, had that certainty and clear decisiveness which belong only to a vision purged from the delusions of sense by communion with things eternal and invisible. But when he embodied his faith and hope in concrete pictures of the future, these pictures were, from the necessity of the case, not literal forecasts of history, but poetic and ideal constructions. Their very object was to gather up the laws of God's working into a single dramatic action,—to present in one image, and within the limited scene of action that lay before the Hebrews, the operation of those divine forces of which Isaiah had only apprehended the simplest elements, and which since his day have expanded themselves, in new and more complex workings, through all the widening cycles of history. In such dramatic pictures it is only artistic or poetical truth that can be looked for. The insight of the prophet, like that of the unprophetic dramatist, vindicates itself in the delineation of true motives,—in the representation of the actual forces that rule the evolution of human affairs,—not in the exact reproduction of any one stage of past or future history. Actual history, as we know, is far too complex a thing to make it possible to isolate any one part of its action and delineate it literally in perfectly dramatic form ; and just as every drama of human life maintains its ideal truth and perfection, as an exhibition of historical motives, only by abstracting from many things that the literal historian must take account of, so the drama of divine salvation, as it is set forth by the prophets, gives a just and comprehensive image of God's working only by gathering into one focus what is actually spread over the course of long ages, and picturing the realisation of the divine plan as completed in relation to a single historical crisis.

The supreme art with which the great prophets of Israel apply these laws of poetic or ideal truth to the dramatic representation of the divine motives that govern the history of Israel was no doubt in great measure the unconscious and childlike art of an age in which all lofty thought was still essentially poetical, and the reason was not yet divorced from the imagination. And yet I think it is plain from the very freedom with which Isaiah recasts the details of his predictions from time to time,—adapting them to new circumstances, introducing fresh historical or poetic motives, and cancelling obsolete features in his older imagery,—that he himself drew a clear distinction between mere accidental and dramatic details, which he knew might be modified or wholly superseded by the march of history, and the unchanging principles of faith, which he received as a direct revelation of Jehovah Himself, and knew to be eternal and invariable truth. Jehovah and Jehovah's purpose were absolute and immutable. Through all the variations of history He was the true asylum of His people, and in Him the victory of faith over the world was assured. The proof that this faith was true and all-sufficient was not dependent on the completeness or finality of the divine manifestation that vindicated it in any one crisis of history. Isaiah's faith was already victorious over the world, and had proved itself a source of invincible steadfastness, of peace and joy which the world could not take away, when it raised him high above the terrors and miseries of the present, and filled his mouth with triumphant praises of Jehovah's salvation in the depth of Judah's anguish and abasement. There was no self-delusion in the confidence with which he proclaimed Jehovah's victory amidst the crash of the Palestinian cities and the advance of Sennacherib from conquest to conquest. For, though the victory of divine righteousness came not at once in that complete and final form which Isaiah pictured, it was none the less a real victory. When the storm rolled away, the word of Jehovah and the community of the faith of Jehovah still remained established on Mount Zion, a pledge of better things to come, a living proof that Jehovah's kingdom ruleth over all, and that though His grace tarry long it can never come to nought, and must yet go forth triumphant to all the ends of the earth.

When we learn to seek the true significance of the work of the prophets, not in the variable details of their predictions, but in the principles of faith which are common to all spiritual religion, and differ from the faith of the New Testament only as the unexpanded germ differs from the full growth, we see also that the complete proof of their divine mission can only be found in the efficacy of their work towards the maintenance and progressive growth of the community of spiritual faith. It is the mark of God's word that it does not return to Him void, that in every generation it is not only true but fruitful, that by its instrumentality things spiritual and eternal become a power on earth, and an efficient factor in human history. Thus we have seen how the ministry of Elijah was taken up and continued by Amos, how the word of Amos and Hosea, despised and rejected by the men of Ephraim, yet formed the basis of the teaching of the Judæan prophets, Isaiah and Micah. But it was the special privilege of Isaiah that, unlike his immediate predecessors, he was permitted to enter in no small degree into the fruit of his own labours, and that the patient endurance of forty years was at last crowned by his personal participation in a victory of faith which produced wide and lasting effects on the subsequent course of Old Testament history.

As soon as he had secured his position on the coast,

Sennacherib felt himself free to direct part of his forces against King Hezekiah.[6] One by one the fortresses of Judah yielded to the foe (2 Kings xviii. 13). Sennacherib claims on his monuments to have taken forty-six strong cities and 200,000 captives. "Your country," says Isaiah,[7] "is desolate, your cities burned with fire : your land, strangers devour it in your presence, and it is desolate, as in the overthrow of Sodom. And the daughter of Zion is left as a hut in a vineyard, as a lodge in a garden of cucumbers, as a besieged city" (Isa. i. 7). As yet, however, there was no movement of true repentance. There was indeed a great external display of eagerness for Jehovah's help : solemn assemblies were convened in the courts of the temple, the blood of sacrifices flowed in streams, the altars groaned under the fat of fed beasts, and the blood-stained hands of Jerusalem's guilty rulers were stretched forth to the sanctuary with many prayers (i. 11 *seq.*). Against these outward signs of devotion, accompanied by no thought of obedience and amendment, Isaiah thundered forth the words of his first chapter. Jehovah's soul hates the vain religion of empty formalism. "When ye spread forth your hands, I will hide mine eyes from you : yea, when ye make many prayers, I will not hear : your hands are full of blood. Wash you, make you clean ; turn away the evil of your doings from before mine eyes ; cease to do evil ; learn to do well ; follow judgment, correct the oppressor, give justice to the fatherless, plead for the widow." Even now it is not too late to repent. "If ye be willing

to obey, ye shall eat the fruit of the land. But if ye refuse
and rebel, ye shall be devoured with the sword : for the
mouth of Jehovah hath spoken it." Always practical
and direct in his admonitions, Isaiah concentrates his
indignation on the guilty rulers, and announces their
speedy fall as the first step to restoration (i. 23 *seq.*) ;
one in especial, the vizier Shebna, he singles out by
name, and declares that he shall be hurled from his post
and dragged captive to a distant land (xxii. 15 *seq.*).
For the moment these denunciations had no recognised
effect; but already Isaiah felt himself master of the
situation, and so sure was he that the march of events
would set his party at the helm of the state that he
even proceeded to nominate "Jehovah's servant," Eliakim, the son of Hilkiah, as the successor of the wicked
minister (xxii. 20 *seq.*). Meantime a strong Assyrian
column advanced against the capital, and the affrighted
inhabitants found the city in no fit state of defence.
Some hasty preparations were made, which are graphi-
cally described in Isaiah xxii. The armoury was examined, the walls of the city of David were found to be
full of breaches, and houses were pulled down that the
material for needful repairs might be quickly available,
and a store of water was accumulated in a new reservoir
between the two walls at the lowest part of the town.
But no confidence was felt in these provisions ; there
was no calm and deliberate courage to abide the issue.
Many of the nobles fled from the danger. (xxii. 3), and
those who remained knew no better counsel than to

drown their cares in wine, and spend in riot the few days of respite that remained to them. "Jehovah of hosts called to weeping, and to mourning, and to baldness, and to girding with sackcloth : and behold joy and gladness, slaying oxen and killing sheep, eating flesh and drinking wine: let us eat and drink, for tomorrow we die." Nevertheless, it would appear from the monuments of Sennacherib that Hezekiah resolved to stand the siege ; and it was not till the operations of the assailants had made some progress that he made his submission as recorded in 2 Kings xviii. 14. All his treasures were surrendered to the Assyrian, the captive Padi of Ekron was delivered up, and large portions of Judæan territory were detached and given over to Philistine princes of the Assyrian party ; but Hezekiah was left upon his throne ; perhaps, indeed, Sennacherib thought this the safest course to adopt, as it is very clear from the whole tenor of Isaiah's prophecies that Hezekiah was not a man of much personal strength of character, and had during the previous years been little more than a passive instrument in the hand of Shebna and the other princes. No doubt, provision was made for a change of administration, and the party of war was effectually superseded ; for a little later we actually find Eliakim in place of Shebna in the possession of the dignity for which Isaiah had marked him out (2 Kings xviii. 37).

Notwithstanding the hard conditions laid upon Hezekiah, these changes were, in a certain sense, of good omen for the future of the state. The party which had so long resisted all internal reformation had been hurled from power, the delusive visions of a brilliant foreign policy were dissipated, and the influence of the prophetic party, which took for its maxim the reform of religion, the abolition of idolatry, and the administration of equal justice to rich and poor, was greater than at any previous moment. But, on the other hand, the land was exhausted by the disastrous progress of the war, and by the enormous sacrifices which had been demanded as the price of peace. The Assyrian yoke pressed more heavily than ever upon Judah; and, though the nation was at length convinced that Isaiah's words were not to be despised, the course of events which had justified his foresight was by no means calculated to inspire that buoyancy and confidence of faith which were necessary to unite all classes in a vigorous and successful effort to reorganise the shattered life of the nation on higher principles than had been followed in time past. True religion cannot live without the experience of grace, and as yet Jehovah had shown all the severity of His judgment, but little or nothing of His forgiving love. This onesidedness, if I may so call it, of the historical demonstration of His effective sovereignty in Israel was fraught with special danger in a community like that of Judah. Where religion was so intimately bound up with the idea of nationality, the depression of all the energies of national life, involved in the abject humiliation of the land before the

Assyrian, could not fail to prove a great stumbling-block to living faith; and to this must be added the marked tendency to a brooding melancholy which characterises the Hebrew race, and in later ages of oppression exercised a stifling influence on the religion of the Jews, changing its joy to gloom, and transforming the gracious Jehovah of the prophets into the pedantic taskmaster of Rabbinical theology. When we remember what Judaism became under the Persian and Western Empires, or what strange developments of cruel superstition and gloomy fanaticism displayed themselves a generation after Isaiah, in the reign of King Manasseh, we can form some conjecture as to the dangers which true religion would have run if Sennacherib had retired victorious, and Judah had been left to groan under a chastisement more grievous than had ever before fallen on its sins. But the divine wisdom decreed better things for Jehovah's land.

The submission of Hezekiah and the fall of Ekron had not completed Sennacherib's task. Some strong places on the Philistine frontier of Judah, such as Lachish and Libnah, still held out, and Tirhakah was not disabled by the defeat of the army he had sent to the relief of Ekron. On the contrary, Sennacherib now learned that the king of Ethiopia was marching against him in person (2 Kings xix. 9), and that the most serious part of the campaign was yet to come. Under these circumstances he began to feel that he had committed a grave strategical error in allowing Hezekiah to retain possession of the strongest fortress in the land. It cost the treacherous Assyrian no difficulty to devise a pretext for cancelling the newly-ratified engagement; and, while the siege of Lachish occupied the main army, a great officer was sent to Jerusalem to charge Hezekiah with complicity with Tirhakah, and to demand the surrender of the city. The troops that accompanied Rabshakeh were not sufficient to enforce submission; the Assyrians supposed that intimidation and big words would be sufficient to overawe the weak king of Judah. But Hezekiah was now in very different hands from those which had conducted his previous conduct. At this critical moment Isaiah was the real leader of Judah, and the confidence of Zion was no longer set on man but on God. At length the prophet knew that the turning-point had come, the false helpers had perished, and Jehovah was near to deliver His people. "Be not afraid," he said to Hezekiah, "of the words that thou hast heard, wherewith the servants of the king of Assyria have blasphemed Me. Behold, I will send a blast against him, and he shall hear a rumour and return to his own land, and I will cause him to fall by the sword in his own land." Against such confidence the menaces of Rabshakeh were of no avail. The populace, which he hoped to enlist on his side, stood firm by Hezekiah and Isaiah, and he returned to his master without accomplishing anything.[3]

Hezekiah's refusal was of course equivalent to a renewed declaration of war. But Sennacherib's hands were too full in the quarter where he awaited the advance of Tirhakah to allow him at once to detach a force sufficient for the reduction of a great city like Jerusalem. Again he had recourse to menaces, and again Isaiah responded in tones of confident assurance and scornful indignation against the presumption that dared to challenge Jehovah's might. "The virgin the daughter of Zion hath despised thee, and laughed thee to scorn; the daughter of Jerusalem hath shaken her head at thee. Whom hast thou reproached and blasphemed? and against whom hast thou exalted thy voice, and lifted up thine eyes on high? even against the Holy One of Israel." The Assyrian boasts that his own power has subdued the nations. "Nay," says Isaiah, "hast thou not heard that it was I that ordained it from afar, and that of old I formed it? now have I brought it to pass, that thou shouldest lay waste fenced cities into ruinous heaps. Therefore their inhabitants were of small power, they were dismayed and confounded: they were as the grass of the field or the green herb, like grass on the housetops and blasted corn. Thy rising up and thy sitting down are before Me;[9] I know thy going out and thy coming in, and thy rage against Me. Because thy rage against Me and thy tumult is come up unto Mine ears, I will put My hook in thy nose, and My bridle in thy lips, and I will turn·thee back by the way in which thou camest. . . . And the remnant that is escaped of the house of Judah shall again take root downward and bear fruit upward: for out of Jerusalem shall go forth a remnant, and they that are escaped out of Mount Zion: the zeal of Jehovah of hosts shall do this" (2 Kings xix. 21 *seq.*; Isa. xxxvii.). Isaiah's confidence was not misplaced. A great and sudden calamity overwhelmed the army of Sennacherib (2 Kings xix. 35), and he was compelled to return to his own land, leaving Jerusalem unmolested.[10] Of the details of the catastrophe, which the Bible narrative is content to characterise as the act of God, the Assyrian monuments contain no record, because the issue of the campaign gave them nothing to boast of; but an Egyptian account preserved by Herodotus (ii. 141), though full of fabulous circumstances, shows that in Egypt as well as in Judæa it was recognised as a direct intervention of divine power. The disaster did not break the power of the Great King, who continued to reign for twenty years, and waged many other victorious wars. But none the less it must have been a very grave blow, the effects of which were felt throughout the empire, and permanently modified the imperial policy; for in the following year Chaldæa was again in revolt, and to the end of his reign Sennacherib never renewed his attack on Judah.

The retreat of the Assyrian was welcomed at Jerusalem with an outburst of triumphant joy, the expression of which may be sought with great probability in more than one of the hymns of the Psalter, especially in Psalm xlvi. The deliverance was Jehovah's work. He had returned to His people as in the days of old, and the burden of Judah's song of thanksgiving was, "Jehovah of hosts is with us, the God of Israel is our high tower." And the God who had wrought such great things for His people was not the Jehovah of the corrupt popular worship, for He had refused to hear the prayers of the adversaries of the prophet, but the God of Isaiah, whose name or manifestation the prophet had seen afar off drawing near in burning wrath and thick rising smoke, his lips full of angry foam and his tongue like a devouring fire, and his breath like an overflowing torrent reaching even to the neck, to sift the nations in the sieve of destruction, to bridle the jaws of peoples, and turn them aside from their course (xxx. 27 *seq.*). The eyes of the prophet had seen the salvation for which he had been waiting through so many weary years; the demonstration of Jehovah's kingship was the public victory of Isaiah's faith, and the word of spiritual prophecy, which from the days of Amos downward had been no more than the ineffective protest of a small minority, had now vindicated its claim to be taken by king and people as an authoritative exposition of the character and will of the God of Israel.

The acknowledged victory of Isaiah's doctrine contained an immediate summons to a practical work of reformation, and prescribed the rules to be followed in the reconstitution of the shattered fabric of the state, which was the first concern of the government when the invader evacuated the land. It would be of the highest interest to know in full detail how Hezekiah addressed himself to this task, and how Isaiah employed his well-won influence in the direction of the work. Unfortunately the history of the kings of Judah is almost wholly silent as to the last years of Hezekiah, and we have no prophecy of Isaiah which serves to fill up the blank. The record of the prophet's work closes with the triumphant strains of the thirty-third chapter, written perhaps before the catastrophe of Sennacherib, but after the result was already a prophetic certainty, because Judah had at length bent its heart to obedience to Jehovah's word. In this most beautiful of all Isaiah's discourses the long conflict of Israel's sin with Jehovah's righteousness is left behind; peace, forgiveness, and holy joy breathe in every verse, and the dark colours of present and past distress serve only as a foil to the assured felicity that is ready to dawn on Jehovah's land. " Ha, thou that spoilest and thou wast not spoiled, that robbest and they robbed not thee; when thou makest an end of spoiling thou shalt be spoiled; when thou ceasest to rob they shall rob thee. Jehovah, be gracious unto us; we have waited for Thee : be Thou our arm every morning, our victory also in the time of trouble. At the noise of the tumult the peoples fled; at the lifting up of Thyself the nations are scattered. . . . Jehovah is exalted; for He dwelleth on high : He hath filled Zion with judgment and righteousness. Then shall there be stability of thy seasons, plenitude of victory, wisdom, and knowledge: the fear of Jehovah shall be thy treasure. . . . Hear, ye that are afar off, what I have done; and, ye that are near, acknowledge my might. The sinners in Zion are afraid; fearfulness hath surprised the godless men. Who among us shall dwell with devouring fire? who shall dwell with everlasting burnings? He that walketh in righteousness and speaketh upright things; he that despiseth the gain of oppressions, that shaketh his hands from holding of bribes, that stoppeth his ears from hearing of blood and shutteth his eyes from looking on evil; he shall dwell on high: his place of defence shall be the munitions of rocks: his bread shall be given him; his water shall be sure. Thine eyes shall behold the King in His beauty: they shall see a land that reaches far. Thy heart shall muse on the past terror; where is he that inscribed and weighed the tribute? where is he that counted the towers? . . . Look upon Zion, the city of our solemn feasts: thine eyes shall see Jerusalem a peaceful habitation, a tent that shall never be removed. . . . For there shall Jehovah sit in glory for us; but the place of broad rivers and streams"—that is, the place of the overflowing empires of the Tigris and the Nile—"no galley with oars shall go therein, neither shall gallant ship pass thereby. For Jehovah is our Judge, Jehovah is our Lawgiver, Jehovah is our King; He will save us. . . . And the inhabitant shall not say, I am sick: the people that dwell therein are forgiven their iniquity."

And so Jehovah's word to Isaiah ends, as it had begun, with the forgiveness of sins. "Lo, this hath touched thy lips; and thine iniquity is taken away, and thy sin purged" (vi. 7). "The people that dwell therein are forgiven their iniquity." The goal of prophetic religion is reached when Israel, as a nation, is brought nigh to God in the same assurance of forgiveness, the same freedom of access to His supreme holiness, the same joyful obedience to His moral kingship, that made Isaiah a true prophet, and sustained his courage and his faith through the long years of Israel's rebellion and chastisement.

The culminating points of the world's history are not always those which are inscribed in boldest characters in the common records of mankind. The greatest event of all history, the crucifixion and resurrection of Jesus, has scarcely left a trace in the chronicles of the Roman empire, and in like manner only a faint and distorted echo of the retreat of Sennacherib is heard beyond the narrow field of Judæan literature. The mere political historian of antiquity might almost refuse a place in his pages to a reverse which barely produced a momentary interruption in the victorious progress of the Assyrian monarchy. And yet the event, so inconsiderable in its outward consequences, has had more influence on the life of subsequent generations than all the conquests of Assyrian kings; for it assured the permanent vitality of that religion which was the cradle of Christianity. When Sennacherib's messenger approached the walls of Jerusalem with the summons of surrender, the fate of the new world, which lay in germ in Isaiah's teaching, seemed to tremble in the balance. "The children were come to the birth, and there was not strength to bring forth" (Isa. xxxvii. 3). Jehovah supplied the lacking strength, and the new community of prophetic faith came forth from the birth-throes of Zion (comp. Micah v. 3). But very soon it became manifest that this new born community of grace, the holy remnant, the fresh offshoot of the decaying stock of Israel, was not identical with the political state of Judah. Isaiah himself was far from suspecting this truth. All his prophecies are shaped by the assumption that in the future, as in the past, the people of Jehovah and the subjects of the Davidic monarchy must continue to be interchangeable ideas. The vindication of Jehovah's sovereignty was in his mind inseparable from such a national conversion as should stamp the impress of Jehovah's holiness on all the institutions of national life. This point of view is as plainly dominant in his latest prophecy as in his earliest discourses. The rulers of Zion, who dwell in the full blaze of Jehovah's consuming holiness, must be men whose hands are clear of bribes, who refuse to hear suggestions of crime, or to open their eyes to plans of iniquity. The salvation of God's people is manifested in the stability of national welfare, the regular succession of the natural seasons and unbroken victory going side by side with wisdom and knowledge and the fear of Jehovah. Hence the prophetic ideal of a redeemed nation contained, as has been already indicated, the outlines of a scheme for the reorganisation of national life, but of a scheme which, even at the outset, was found to be encompassed with unsurmountable practical difficulties. A radical renovation of society cannot be effected through the organs of national action, for a nation has no personal identity or invariable fixity of purpose ; and the momentary impression of the great deliverance, when, for an instant, all Israel seemed to bend as one man before Jehovah's will, could not secure a permanent and unfailing concentration of every class, in its own place in society, towards the realisation of the prophetic ideal. The effective regeneration of society, as the gospel teaches us, must necessarily begin with the individual heart, and the true analogy of the workings of the kingdom of God is not found in the forms of earthly government, but in the hidden operations of a pervading leaven. Such a leaven did indeed exist in Isaiah's day, but it was not co-extensive with the nation of Judah ; it consisted of the comparatively few whose adherence to spiritual religion was an affair of settled conviction, and not a passing impulse determined by one of those rare junctures when the power of spiritual things shows itself for an instant with all the palpable reality of a phenomenon of sense. It is not the law of divine providence that such visible manifestations of the hand of God, vouchsafed as they are only in supreme crises, should continue permanently, and supersede the exercise of the faith that endures as seeing that which is invisible ; and nothing short of a continued miracle could have held the nation as a nation in that frame of repentance and new obedience which seemed to be universal in the first burst of exultation at Jehovah's victory.

The reforms which Hezekiah was able to introduce touched only the surface of national life; a radical amendment of social life, even as regarded the administration of equal and impartial justice, and the establishment of kindlier relations between the rich and poor,—points which Isaiah had always emphasised as fundamental,—lay altogether beyond their scope. In this respect the utmost that was accomplished was a temporary mitigation of crying abuses. It was less difficult to work a change in those parts of the visible ordinances of religion which were plainly inconsistent with prophetic teaching. The abolition of idolatry, or at least of its more public and flagrant manifestations, was undoubtedly attempted; indeed we might be led to infer from the prominence assigned to Hezekiah's religious reforms in the history of Kings that some movement in this direction may have been made in the earlier part of his reign. But it is quite clear from the prophecies of Isaiah that Hezekiah was wholly in the hands of the adversaries of the prophetic party till the last period of the Assyrian war; not till after his first surrender and the discomfiture of the politicians of whom Shebna was the leader could it be said of Hezekiah, in the language of 2 Kings xviii, 5, 6, that he trusted in Jehovah and clave to Him. Even in the discourses of the reign of Sennacherib Isaiah speaks of the abolition of the idols as a thing still in the future (xxx. 22; xxxi. 7), so that any earlier work of reformation, such as may possibly have been suggested by the lesson of Samaria's fall, as it was enforced by the contemporary prophecies of Isaiah and Micah, can at best have been only imperfect and transitory. The character which Hezekiah bears in history and the reforms connected with his name really refer to the years that followed the victory of Isaiah.

Isaiah had never ceased to declare that the rejection of the idols must be one of the first-fruits of Judah's repentance, but he did not attempt to indicate a scheme of reformed worship to take their place. The idols shall be cast away when the eyes of the nation are turned to the Holy One of Israel, and His voice is heard behind them to guide all their goings. To Isaiah, in truth, ritual worship had very little significance. He certainly did not distinctly look forward to its complete abolition, for he speaks of the Egyptians as serving Jehovah by sacrifice, and even of altar and *maççeba*, such as characterised the common provincial shrines of Judah, erected within Egypt in token of homage to Jehovah (xix. 19, 21). And in like manner the solemn feasts at Jerusalem—from which a figure is derived in xxx. 29—are assumed to continue in the days of Israel's redemption (xxxiii. 20). But, on the other hand, he not only represents the sacrifice of guilty hands as unacceptable to Jehovah (chap. i.), but there is never the slightest indication that repentance and obedience require to be embodied in acts of ritual worship in order to find acceptance with God. There is not a line in all the prophecies that have come before us which gives the slightest weight to priesthood or sacrifice. Nay, in xvii. 8 the altars as well as the *asherim* and the sun-pillars appear as things of man's making that come between Israel and its God. It is not the temple that is the glory of the new Jerusalem and the seat of Jehovah's presence; the true meaning of Jehovah's residence on Zion lies in the fact that the capital is the centre of His effectual kingship in Judah; and even the name of the "hearth of God," which Isaiah bestows on the holy city, and not on the sanctuary alone, has rather reference to the consuming fire of the divine holiness than to altar or sacrificial flame. If Jerusalem appears to Isaiah as the centre of that sanctity which belongs to all Jehovah's "holy mountain land," and as the point of assembly where His people meet before Him, the meaning of this conception is that in Jerusalem Jehovah holds His kingly court, and that from Zion His prophetic word goes forth to guide His subjects. Thus, while Isaiah insists on the removal from religion of things that hide the true character of Jehovah, he has no positive views as to the institution of a reformed worship: the positive task on which he always lays stress is the purification of the organs of judgment and administration, so that the leaders of the state may be able to dwell safely in the consuming fire of Jehovah's holiness.

Isaiah had looked for the spontaneous repudiation of the idols in an impulse of national repentance which needed no official decree to guide it; the reforms of

Hezekiah were the act of the government in a nation not wholly converted to Jehovah; and, in the absence of that pure spontaneity which the prophets regard as the true spring of right religion, they must have been directed to an external aim, the establishment of a fixed type of official worship. The attempt was confronted from the first by a formidable difficulty: the idols, the sun-pillars, the asherim, the sacred trees, and all the other pagan or half-pagan symbols, so plainly inconsistent with the prophetic faith, were of the very substance of Israel's worship in the popular sanctuaries. So much was this the case that Isaiah, as we have just seen, was practically indifferent to all forms of cultus: the social exercises of his faith as described in Isa. viii. 16 *seq.* were altogether of another kind, anticipating the worship of the New Testament Church. Hezekiah could not propose to himself, and Isaiah had never formally contemplated, the entire abolition of the traditional ritual; and yet it was scarcely possible to introduce any effective reform without a great limitation, an almost radical subversion, of the ancient shrines. But at this point the zeal of Hezekiah was powerfully aided, and the plan of reformation practically determined, by the fact that almost every considerable provincial town of Judah had been ruined by the armies of Sennacherib. The local Baalim of the high places had been of no avail to save their worshippers; their shrines were burned or laid waste, and in many cases, no doubt, in accordance with the common practice of the Assyrians, the idols had been carried away to grace the triumph of Sennacherib. This destruction of the strongholds and sanctuaries of the land corresponded in the most marked way with the predictions of Micah, the influence of which on the conduct of Hezekiah is expressly attested in the book of Jeremiah. Micah, it is true, had not exempted the fortress and sanctuary of Zion from the universal destruction; his picture of the future left no room for any vestige of the ancient ritual; to him the Zion of the latter days is a religious centre, not as a place of worship, but as the seat of Jehovah's throne and of a revelation of law and judgment. But for the mass of the people the temple of Zion had received a new importance in connection with the effectual proof of the inviolability of Jehovah's holy mountain. They were unable to separate the idea of holiness from its traditional association with observances of ritual service, and the natural or even inevitable interpretation of the lesson written on the blackened ruins of the provincial holy places was that the "mountain of the house" was the true sanctuary of Judah's worship.[11] Thus the scheme of Hezekiah necessarily assumed, with more or less explicitness, the form of a superseding of the provincial shrines and the centralisation of worship in the temple of Jerusalem, purged from heathenish corruptions. At first this change would not appear very startling or difficult to carry out, for Sennacherib had left the provinces a desert (Isa. i. 7; xxxiii. 8, 9), and his monuments aver that 200,000 of their inhabitants were carried off as slaves. Judah and Jerusalem were for the moment almost identical ideas, and the sphere of Hezekiah's reforms was perhaps confined to the immediate vicinity of the capital. Even here there was one strange omission in his work. The shrines of foreign deities which had stood around Jerusalem since the days of Solomon were for some reason left untouched —probably because of privileges of worship that could not be refused to the Phœnicians and other aliens, who occupied in the capital a quarter or suburb called the Maktesh (Zeph. i. 11); and in the sequel these shrines exercised more influence on Judæan religion than they had ever done before.[12]

Thus the visible impulse of the great victory of Isaiah's faith appeared to have exhausted itself in a scheme of external reform which fell far short of giving full expression to the spirituality of prophetic teaching, and, carried out as it was by the authority of the government rather than by the spontaneous impulse of the whole nation, was sure to lead to the reaction that always follows on the enforcement by external authority of principles not thoroughly understood or sympathised with. As the nation fell back into the grooves of its old existence, ancient customs began to reassert their sway. The worship which the prophets condemned and which Hezekiah had proscribed was too deeply interwoven with all parts of life to be uprooted by royal decree, and the old prejudice of the country folk against the capital, so clearly apparent in Micah, must have co-operated with superstition to bring about the strong revulsion against the new reforms which took place under Hezekiah's son, Manasseh. A bloody struggle ensued between the conservative party and the followers of the prophets, and the new king was on the side of the reaction. Perhaps in this struggle the motives of the unpopular faction were less pure, as their aims were certainly less ideal, than Isaiah's. There were worldly interests involved in the policy of religious centralisation which claimed to represent the spiritual aspirations of the prophets; and the priests of Jerusalem, whose revenues and influence were directly concerned, were at no time the most unselfish of reformers. Thus we can well suppose that the religious war which ensued had on both sides a demoralising tendency; a contest as to forms of worship and ecclesiastico-political organisation is seldom for the advantage of spiritual faith. No great prophet arose as the champion of Hezekiah's reforms; and the one voice of lofty faith which speaks to us from these disastrous days, in the last two chapters of the book of Micah,[13] is the voice of a man who belongs to neither of the contending factions, and feels himself alone in Judah, as Isaiah had never been, in a society where all moral corruption is rampant, where justice, honesty, and truth are unknown, where the good man is perished out of the earth, and there is none upright among men, where the son dishonoureth his father, and the daughter riseth up against her mother, where the nearest friend cannot be trusted, where a man dare not speak freely

even to the wife of his bosom. And yet in a certain
sense religious earnestness was deeper than before. The
reaction had brought back all the old corruptions, but
not the old lightness of heart with which Israel rejoiced
before its God in every holy place. The terrible experiences of the Assyrian wars had left behind them a
residuum of gloomy apprehension. If Jehovah's deliverance was forgotten by the men who no longer clave to
the faith of Isaiah, the terrors of his wrath, as they had
been experienced in the ravages of Sennacherib and
perhaps in subsequent calamities—for in Manasseh's
time the Assyrians again became lords of the land—
still weighed upon the nation, and gave a sombre tinge
to all religion. In this respect Judah did not stand
alone. To all the Palestinian nations the Assyrian
crisis had made careless confidence in the help of their
national deities a thing impossible. As life was em-
bittered by foreign bondage, the darker aspects of
heathenism became dominant. The wrath of the gods
seemed more real than their favour; atoning ordinances
were multiplied, human sacrifices became more frequent,
the terror which hung over all the nations that groaned
under the Assyrian yoke found habitual expression in
the ordinances of worship; and it was this aspect of
heathenism that came to the front in Manasseh's imita-
tions of foreign religion.

Thus once more, and within a few years of Isaiah's
great victory, the national ideal of Jehovah worship had
broken down, and the old controversy of Jehovah with

His people was renewed, but with other and deeper issues, in the development of which a new race of prophets was to take part. So far as appeared on the surface of Judæan society the results of the Assyrian judgment and the prophetic preaching that interpreted it had been purely negative. The old joyous religion of Israel had broken down, but the faith of Isaiah had not taken its place. The glad confidence in Jehovah, making it an easy thing to obey His precepts and a privilege to be called by His name, which Isaiah had continually set forth as the right disposition of true religion, was lost in gloomy superstition. The grace of Jehovah, so often manifested in the past history of Israel, was forgotten (Micah vi. 4 *seq.*), and His name had become a name of terror, not of hope. This was the true secret of Manasseh's polytheism. He sought other gods, not because Jehovah was powerless, but because he despaired of securing His help (comp. Jer. xliv. 18 ; Ezek. viii. 12). But beneath all this it is not difficult to see that a real advance had been made, and that the basis was laid for a new development of spiritual truth which should carry the religion of Israel another stage towards its goal in the religion of Christ.

The failure of Hezekiah's plans of reformation involved more than a merely negative result. And it did so in two ways. In the first place, it became manifest that to purge the religion of Judah from heathenish elements it was necessary that the whole notion of sacrificial worship should undergo a radical change. The code of Deuteronomy, which must be regarded as in great measure a product of reflection on the failure of Hezekiah's measures, starts from the observation that it is impossible to get rid of Canaanite elements of worship until sacrifice and ritual observances are confined to one sanctuary, and that this again is impossible till the old principle is given up that all food, and especially every animal slain for a feast, is unclean unless presented at the altar. By dissociating the ideas of slaughter and sacrifice, which till then had been absolutely indistinguishable and expressed by a single word, the law of Deuteronomy revolutionised the religion of daily life, and practically limited the sphere of ritual worship to the pilgrimage feasts and other occasions of special importance. This principle found no complete access to the mass of the people so long as the Kingdom of Judah stood; but it put in a tangible and easy shape at least one aspect of the prophetic teaching that the religion of ordinary life does not consist in ritual, but in love to God and obedience to Him, and so prepared many in Israel to maintain their faith in Jehovah in the approaching dissolution of national existence, when ritual service was not merely restricted in scope but altogether suspended. From one point of view the law of the single sanctuary seems a poor outcome for the great work of Isaiah, and yet when it was construed in the way set forth in Deuteronomy it implied a real step towards the spiritualisation of all the service of God, and the emancipation of religion from its connection with the land and holy places of Canaan (*supra*, p. 262). That the movement which finds expression in Deuteronomy became strong enough under Josiah to lead to a second and more effective suppression of the high places was not in itself a matter of great importance, for the new reformation was not more permanent in genuine results of a visible character than that of Hezekiah; but the spiritual power that lay behind the political action of Josiah is not to be measured by visible and immediate results. The book of Deuteronomy could not have touched the conscience of the nation even in a momentary and superficial way unless there had been many in Judah who sympathised with the spirit of that prophetic teaching to which the new code strove to give expression under forms which were indeed, as the sequel proved, too strait for its spiritual substance. The introduction now prefixed to the Deuteronomic code shows clearly that it was by spiritual motives, derived from the prophetic teaching, that the new system of ordinances was commended to Israel; the great limitation of visible acts of worship presented itself to thoughtful minds not as a narrowing of the sphere of religion but as a sublimation of its contents. Jehovah requires nothing of His people but "to fear Jehovah thy God, to walk in all His ways, and to love and serve Him with all thy heart and all thy soul" (Deut. x. 12).

Thus we see, in the second place, that behind the legal aspect of the movement of reformation, as it is expressed in the Deuteronomic code, there lay a larger principle, which no legal system could exhaust, and which never found full embodiment till the religion of the Old Testament passed into the religion of Christ. The failure of Hezekiah's attempt to give a political expression to the teaching of Isaiah must have thrown back the men who had received the chief share of the prophet's spirit upon those unchanging elements of religion which are independent of all political ordinances. The religious life of Judah was not wholly absorbed in the contest about visible institutions, the battle between the one and the many sanctuaries. The organised prophetic party of Isaiah, which still found its supporters in the priesthood as it had done in the first days of that prophet's ministry, may soon have begun to degenerate into that empty formalism which took for its watchword "the Temple of Jehovah," against which Jeremiah preached as Isaiah had preached against the formalism of his day (Jer. x. 4). In Jeremiah's day the doctrine of the inviolability of Zion became in fact the very axiom of mere political Jehovah-worship. That has always been the law of the history of religion. What in one generation is a living truth of faith becomes in later generations a mere dead formula, part of the religion learned by rote with which living faith has to do battle upon new issues. But even in the darkest hours of Israel's history the true faith of Jehovah was never left without witness, and the men to whom Isaiah's teaching was more than a formula, the community of those that waited for Jehovah in a higher sense than the mass even of the so-called party of pure worship, withdrew more and more from all the forms of political religion to nourish their religious life in exercises purely spiritual, and to embody their hope of Jehovah's salvation in thoughts that stretched far beyond the limits of the old dispensation to days when Jehovah's precepts should be written on every heart (Jer. xxxi.). And in this new development of prophetic thought, of which Jeremiah is the great representative, standing to the second stage of the history of prophecy in much the same relation as Amos and Hosea stood to the first, the deeper, though misdirected, sense of guilt so characteristic of the gloomy days of Judah's decadence became an important element. The sense of sin was not extenuated, but it was interpreted aright and conquered by a new and profounder conception of redeeming grace, in which the idea of the spiritual as distinguished from the natural Israel, the servant of Jehovah, whose sufferings are the path of salvation, takes the place of the older and more mechanical notion of judgment on the wicked and salvation to the righteous (Isa. xl. *seq.*).

But to develop these and all the other ideas that come before us in the great prophecies of the Chaldæan period, to trace the course of the new religious issues that shaped themselves in the decline and fall of the Judæan Kingdom, and finally in exile and restoration, would be a task as large as that which we have already accomplished, and must be reserved for a future opportunity. Meantime, the record of the first period of prophetic religion may fitly close with the words in which the solitary voice crying out of the darkness of Manasseh's reign sets forth the sum of all preceding prophetic teaching, and gathers up the whole revealed will of Jehovah in answer to the false zeal of the immoral bigotry of the age.

"O my people, what have I done unto thee? and wherewith have I wearied thee? testify against Me. For I brought thee up out of the land of Egypt, and redeemed thee out of the house of bondage, and I sent before thee Moses, Aaron, and Miriam. . . . Wherewith shall I come before Jehovah, and bow myself before the high God? Shall I come before Him with burnt-offerings, with calves of a year old? Will Jehovah be pleased with thousands of rams, or with ten thousands of rivers of oil? Shall I give my firstborn for my transgression, the fruit of my body for the sin of my soul? He hath showed thee, O man, what is good, and what doth Jehovah require of thee, but to do judgment, and to love mercy, and to walk humbly with thy God?" (Micah vi. 2 *seq.*).

It is no mere religion of legal obedience that these words proclaim. Jehovah requires of man not only to *do* but to *love* mercy. A heart that delights in acts of piety and loving-kindness, the humility that walks in lowly communion with God,—these are the things in which Jehovah takes pleasure, and this is the teaching of the law and the prophets, on which our Lord Himself has set His seal (Matt. xxii. 37 *seq.*).

Thus in the deepest darkness of that age of declension which sealed the fate of ancient Israel, when the true prophet could no longer see any other end to the degenerate nation than a consuming judgment that should leave the land of Canaan a desolation and its inhabitants a hissing and a reproach among the nations (Mic. vi. 16), the voice of spiritual faith rises high above all the limits of the dispensation that was to pass away, and sets forth the sum of true religion in words that can never die. The state of Israel perished; the kingdom of Judah and all the hopes that had been built upon it crumbled to the dust; but the word of the God of Israel endureth for ever.

NOTES AND ILLUSTRATIONS.

Lecture I.

Note 1, p. 4.—With all its defects, the Federal theology of Cocceius is the most important attempt, in the older Protestant theology, to do justice to the historical development of revelation. See Diestel's essay in *Jahrb. f. d. Theol.*, vol. x. pp. 209-276, and the briefer discussion in his *Geschichte des Alten Testamentes in der christlichen Kirche* (Jena, 1869). The first conception, however, of the Bible record as the history of true religion, of the adoption and education of the Church from age to age in a scheme of gradual advance, appears pretty distinctly in Calvin ; and the method of Calvinistic theology, in which all parts of the plan of grace are considered in dependence on the idea of the sovereign Divine Providence, made it natural for theologians of his school to busy themselves with the demonstration of the historical continuity of revelation. So long, however, as it was attempted to find the law of this continuity by speculative and dogmatic methods rather than by ordinary historical investigation, no result really satisfactory could be reached. In this connection a reference may be added to the *History of Redemption* of Jonathan Edwards.

Note 2, p. 5.—In illustration of the position taken up by the older Protestant divines, I may refer to Witsius's treatment of the *Protevangelion*, Gen. iii. 14 *seq.*, in his *Œconomia Fœderum*, lib. iv., cap. 1. After deducing from the words addressed to the serpent the principal theses of systematic theology, including the doctrines of Saving Faith, Sanctification, and the Resurrection of the body, he remarks (§ 26) that it was not unreasonable that so large a range of doctrines should be summed up in a few enigmatic words. The splendour of midday was not appropriate to the first dawn of the day of grace ; " and besides,

God did not even then withdraw revelations of Himself from our first parents, but by frequent instruction and gracious illumination of their minds expounded to them the things that concern faith and piety. And it is fair to suppose that they treasured up this promise of salvation in particular, thought over it with care, and expounded it in frequent discourse to one another and their children." In other words, they received from the Revealer, and handed down to their posterity, a traditional exposition of the words of Scripture.

NOTE 3, p. 13.—The great empires of the East overran foreign countries, reducing them to subjection, or even transplanting their inhabitants to new seats, but made no attempt to break down differences of national custom between the several parts of their realm, or to assimilate the conquered peoples to a single cosmopolitan type. The motley character of the great Persian empire, for example, is strikingly illustrated in the picture drawn by Herodotus (vii. 61 *seq.*) of the various contingents that served in the army of Xerxes, each in its own national garb. In contrast with the earlier empires the kingdom of the Greeks appears to the prophet Daniel, as "diverse from all kingdoms, devouring the whole earth, treading it down, and breaking it in pieces" (Dan. vii.). And so King Antiochus, who sought to Hellenise his subjects, is spoken of as "changing times and laws" (*Ibid.* ver. 25). But the first thoroughgoing and successful attempt to create an empire possessing an organic unity, with a cosmopolitan civilisation and institutions displacing the old varieties of local custom and law, was the monarchy of Cæsar. See Mommsen's *History*, bk. v. ch. 11.

NOTE 4, p. 19.—A large mass of translations from Assyrian and Babylonian texts is now accessible to the English reader, in numerous separate publications, such as those of the late G. Smith, in the *Transactions of the Society of Biblical Archæology*, and in the somewhat unequal but very convenient collection published by Messrs. Bagster under the title of *Records of the Past*. In this collection the volumes with odd numbers (i. to xi.) contain the Assyrian texts. There can be no question that the sense of a great many texts, especially simple historical narratives, has been determined with sufficient certainty to afford the greatest assistance in the study of the Bible history; and most fortunately the Assyrian chronology, as determined in particular by the Eponym Canon (*supra*, p. 150), is one of the most certain as it is one of the most important of the new discoveries. But, on the other hand, many details even of historical texts are too imperfectly understood to justify the large conclusions too often built on them, and, above all, the reading and identification of proper names in certain ways of writing them—for in Assyrian character the same sounds may be written in different ways, and the same character may have different sounds—are often highly precarious. The doubts that still attach to many things which have been accepted, often on the faith of a single Assyriologist who does not himself distinguish his facts from his conjectures, have been very forcibly set forth, though perhaps with an extreme of scepticism, by Prof. v. Gutschmid in his *Neue Beiträge*, Leipzig, 1876, and a more popular demonstration of the amount of uncertainty still attaching to the translations of historical texts will be found in the recent brochure of M. A. Delattre, *Les inscriptions historiques de Ninive et de Babylone* (Paris, 1879). In truth, there are few Assyriologists in Europe whose tact, caution, and general knowledge of the Semitic dialects entitle them to speak with authority upon problems far more difficult than those, for example, of the Phœnician inscriptions, where our best orientalists are often not ashamed to confess themselves at a loss. The very nature of the material often compels the translator to guess at the general import of a mutilated text or at the true sense of a word. It is fair, indeed, to remember that the vast extent of the material now available and the great sameness of style and expression which characterises Assyrian historical documents often counterbalance these difficulties. As regards the application of Assyrian results to the Old Testament, it is too often forgotten that the fruits of Assyrian study can be of no substantial use to the Biblical student except in connection with a critical study of the Hebrew sources.

As I am not able to make independent use of the cuneiform monuments, I do not venture to build upon them in the present volume except where the sense seems to be thoroughly made out by the consent of the best scholars.

NOTE 5, p. 23.—On the Hittites see Mr. Cheyne's article in the ninth edition of the *Encyclopædia Britannica*. On the identification of Carchemish with the modern Jirbâs (Yâkût ii. 688)—that is, the Syriac Agrôpôs, Greek Εὐρωπός, Ὠρωπός—see G. Hoffmann, *Syrische Akten Persischer Märtyrer* (1880), p. 161 *seq.*; Delitzsch, *Wo lag das Paradies?* (1881), p. 265 *seq.* The name

Ierabolus given by some travellers is false. The town lay on the west side of the Euphrates opposite Dêr Kinnisrê. The passage of Stephanus Byzantius, quoted by Hoffmann, which says that Oropus was formerly called Τελμησσός, presumably הל מש, not only confirms the identification with Carchemish, but shows that the latter is a Semitic word, "castle of Mîsh."

NOTE 6, p. 26.—See Wellhausen, *Jahrb. f. d. Theol.*, vol. xxi. p. 602; Meyer in Stade's *Zeitschrift*, vol. i. p. 122; Stade, *Geschichte*, p. 110. An essay by Steinthal, *Z. f. Völkerpsychologie*, vol. xii. p. 267, is referred to by the last two writers.

NOTE 7, p. 28.—See especially Wellhausen, *De Gentibus et Familiis Judæis*, Gött., 1870, and *Geschichte*, vol. i. p. 225 *seq.*, for the analysis of the genealogy of the originally nomad elements of Judah, the Hezronites. The great clan of the Kalibbites (Caleb) belonged to this branch of the population of Southern Judæa. For the Amalekites and their original connection with Mt. Ephraim, see Judges v. 14; xii. 15; Nöldeke, *Ueber die Amalekiter*, u.s.w., Gött., 1864.

NOTE 8, p. 29.—As we shall hear of these routes again in connection with the history of Judah, I may here refer to Pliny's account of the great incense road from Thomna to Gaza (*H. N.* xii. 14), and the discussion in Sprenger's *Alte Geographie Arabiens*, Bern, 1875, p. 141 *seq.* On this inland route the Edomite capital of Petra was a station. The incense trade, it must be remembered, was of enormous importance in ancient times from the use of frankincense in all temples.

NOTE 9, p. 29.—The land of Goshen did not belong to the Delta proper, which never can have been given up to a shepherd tribe, and would not have suited their way of life. In all ages nomadic or half nomadic tribes, quite distinct from the Egyptians proper, have pastured their flocks on the verge of the rich lands of the Delta. The Eastern shepherd or herdsman does not base his conception of good pasture ground on anything like an English meadow, and it is not necessary to suppose that the south-eastern borders of the Delta were much more fertile in the days of Moses than they are now. That the Israelites at this time came under any considerable influence of Egyptian civilisation must appear highly improbable to any one who knows the life of the nomads of Egypt even in the present day, when there is a large Arab element in the settled population. It is impossible here to enter into details on the supposed traces of Egyptian culture and religion in the institutions of Israel ; but it may safely be affirmed that they are far fewer than is often stated, and that those which are beyond question cannot be traced back to the oldest times, and may with great probability be held to have come in for the most part, not from Egypt direct, but through the Phœnicians.

NOTE 10, p. 29.—The important assistance rendered to Israel by the Kenites comes out clearly in the oldest parts of the Pentateuchal narrative. Compare Exod. xviii. and Num. x. 29 seq., with Judges i. 16 ; iv. 11 ; 1 Sam. xv. 6.

NOTE 11, p. 29.—The classical passage in this connection is Judges i. ; comp. Josh. xviii. 14 seq. ; Judges xvii. 1 seq. See especially Graf, *Der Stamm Simeon*, Meissen, 1866.

NOTE 12, p. 30.—On the stone of Dibon, which records the victories of King Mesha (2 Kings iii.) over the Israelites, we read that he slew the whole inhabitants of Nebo, seven thousand in number, for they were devoted by the ban to Ashtar-Kamosh —a deity related to the god Chemosh, who is repeatedly mentioned in the Bible.

NOTE 13, p. 34. — See *The Old Testament in the Jewish Church* (1881), especially Lectures xi. and xii. It may be convenient to repeat that the three main masses of legislation still distinguishable in the Pentateuch are—(1) The Book of the Covenant, as it is generally called, Exod. xxi.-xxiii., a primitive legislation designed for a very simple state of agricultural society, and corresponding in its precepts with the traces of the actual usage and law of Israel found in the history of the age of the Judges and the earlier monarchy. (2) The Deuteronomic Code, Deut. xii.-xxvi., in which the laws of the Book of the Covenant are recast with special reference to the limitation of ritual worship to a single sanctuary. This limitation is introduced as a new thing. It was unknown up to the time of Isaiah and Hezekiah, but was formally accepted as law when the Deuteronomic code was promulgated as binding in the great reformation of the reign of Josiah. The code must have been written between this date (B.C. 621 or 622) and the reforms which Hezekiah adopted after the retreat of Sennacherib in B.C. 701 (see Lect. viii.). (3) The Priestly or Levitical Legislation, composed after the book of Ezekiel and adopted as the law of the New Jerusalem (in conjunction with the rest of the Pentateuch) under Ezra, B.C. 445. See Neh. viii. seq.

NOTE 14, p. 35.—The main passage for the way in which Moses organised the administration of justice in Israel is Exod. xviii. Compare *O. T. in Jewish Church*, p. 334.

NOTE 15, p. 36.—"Every Arab tribe," says Burckhardt, "has its chief sheikh, and every camp is headed by a sheikh, or at least by an Arab of some consideration ; but the sheikh has no actual authority over the individuals of his tribe. . . . Should a dispute happen between two individuals the sheikh will endeavour to settle the matter ; but if either party be dissatisfied with his advice he cannot insist upon obedience. The Arab can only be persuaded by his own relations ; and if they fail war commences between the two families and all their kindred respectively. . . . In fact the most powerful Aeneze chief dares not inflict a trifling punishment on the poorest man of his tribe without incurring the risk of mortal vengeance from the individual and his relations. . . . . . . The prerogative of the sheikhs consists in leading their tribe against the enemy ; in conducting negotiations for peace or war; in fixing the spot for encampments; in entertaining strangers of note, etc., and even these privileges are much limited." —*Bedouins and Wahabys*, 8vo ed., p. 115 seq.

NOTE 16, p. 39.—See *O. T. in Jewish Church*, p. 225 seq., p. 257 and *note* (Shechem in the time of Abimelech was a Canaanite town), p. 78 seq. ; and *infra*, Lect ii. note 6.

LECTURE II.

NOTE 1, p. 47.—On the one hand, the great Phœnician trading cities, with the usual jealousy of commercial monopolists, were little disposed to form a close and equal union with any outside their own circle. Nor were they disposed to warlike operations to extend their territory. Carthage, it will be remembered, neither made the natives Carthaginians nor even sought to make them subjects till a comparatively late date. See Mommsen's *History of Rome*, bk. iii. chap. 1. The jealousy and political inertness of the Phœnicians had two results. It long prevented the Hebrews from becoming a trading people, and so saved them from rapid social changes which would greatly have endangered their old life and religion ; and, on the other hand, it left them free to deal as they could with the Canaanites of the interior. Even in the interior the Canaanites continued to be the trading class, and, as the Hebrews occupied the land, became more and more exclusively traders. Between traders and cultivators of the soil there was a natural class-antagonism, which no doubt helped to maintain the distinct character of Israel. On the other hand, the Israelites of the frontier, in Judah and beyond the Jordan in Gilead, evidently retained not a little of the ancient nomad habits, and in part were closely allied with other tribes of the wilderness. Thus we find from time to time expressions of that characteristic distaste for the ease and luxuries of settled life which belongs to the genuine Bedouin. The Nazarite vow against drinking wine and the laws of the Rechabites are cases in point. And the Rechabites, like the Nazarites, were on the side of the old Jehovah worship, and against the Canaanite Baal.

NOTE 2, p. 47.—That the institution of the kingship was a necessary step in the development of national unity, and therefore also in the progress of the religion of Jehovah, is often overlooked under the too exclusive influence of 1 Sam. viii.; x. 17-27; xii. But it is always a mistake to estimate the real significance of events in ancient history by the speeches — never literally reported and often used as a convenient and, on ancient literary methods, legitimate vehicle for reflections of a later age influenced by changed circumstances—which are now interwoven with the context of the narrative, instead of allowing ourselves to be guided by the historical context of events; and as a matter of fact no one can doubt that the institution of the kingship was a great blessing to Israel, putting an end to the state of anarchy which the book of Judges justly represents as most unfavourable to religious progress. Nor is it less clear that Israel from the first recognised this blessing as a special gift of Jehovah, who sanctioned the kingship by bestowing His spirit on the king (1 Sam. x. 6; xvi. 13). In the Blessing of Moses the kingship is represented as the crowning gift of Jehovah, by which the branches of the nation and the tribes of Jacob were united together (Deut. xxxiii. 5). Modern criticism has made all this much more plain by pointing out that there are two distinct but parallel accounts of the choice of Saul, the older version being preserved in 1 Sam. ix.; x. 1-16; xi. (omitting v. 14). After his unction Saul returns to his father's house, awaiting the opportunity indicated in x. 7; after about a month (so the LXX. in xi. 1), this opportunity arises in the invasion of Nahash, and the sovereignty which Saul had assumed on this occasion in virtue of a divine impulse (xi. 6), is solemnly confirmed after the victory. The detailed proof of the separate character and greater antiquity of this form of the narrative may be found in Bleek's *Einleitung*, 4th ed., by Wellhausen, p. 210 *seq.*, with which compare the corresponding discussion in Wellhausen's *Text der Bücher Samuelis*. It is to be noted that the attacks on Samuel so current in the older sceptical school (see, for example, Volney's *Histoire de Samuel*), derive their whole plausibility from the onesidedness of the current uncritical treatment of the history.

NOTE 3, p. 50.—The English reader will find an account of this celebrated monument, now in the Louvre, and the translation of the inscription which it bears, in an article [by Professor W. Wright of Cambridge], printed in the *North British Review*, October 1870, or in Dr. Ginsburg's *Moabite Stone* (2d ed. 1871), where an account is also given of the literature of the subject. Dr. Ginsburg's version is reprinted in *Records of the Past*, vol. xi. p. 165. See also Dr. A. B. Davidson in the *B. and F. Ev. Review*, 1871.

NOTE 4, p. 51.—The history of this celebrated monument and a list of the literature connected with it are to be found in the *Corpus Inscriptionum Semiticarum*, pars I., tom. i., p. 1 *seq.* (Paris 1881). The inscription dates from the Persian period.

NOTE 5, p. 53.—On tithes in antiquity outside Israel see the essays of Selden and Hottinger, Spencer, *Leg. Rit. Heb.*, lib. iii. c. 10; Winer, *s.v.* "Zehnten," Ewald, *Alterthümer*, p. 398 (Eng. tr., p. 300); Knobel on Lev. xxvii. 30 *seq.* The practice of paying tithes to the gods was widely diffused, both in the form in which it appears in Gen. xiv. 20, where tithes are paid from booty (which in Greece was the commonest case), and in the shape of a regular tribute on the products of agriculture, trade, or the like. It is sufficient for the present purpose to indicate the prevalence and scope of tithes among Semitic nations or in regions of Semitic influence. Here it is to be noted first that tithes were paid to the king (as in 1 Sam. viii.) according to the ancient Babylonian law revived under Alexander (Aristot. *Œcon.*, ii. p. 1352 *b* of the Berlin ed.; comp. p. 1345 *seq.*). Next, as regards tithes to the gods, it is attested by Diodorus, xx. 14, that the Carthaginians as a Tyrian colony paid tithes to the Tyrian sun-god Melkarth or Herakles, the divine king of the city; and in like manner Hercules was the god to whom the Romans paid tithes (Diodor., iv. 21; Plut., *Mor.* ii. 267 E; compare the

authorities collected by Wyttenbach in his index to Plut., *Mor.*
s.v. ʽHρακλῆς). Among the Arabs of the frankincense country
tithes of this product were paid to the priests of the sun-god
Sabis (Pl'n. xii. 32). Among the Arabs, says the scholiast to
Harith (*Moal.*, ed. Arnold, p. 186), " men used to vow "—just as
Jacob vowed at Bethel — " If God gives me a hundred sheep I
will sacrifice one in every ten." The discharge of this vow was not
enforced, and often " his soul grudged what he had vowed, and
he would hunt a gazelle and substitute it for the sheep that
were due" (cf. Mal. i. 14). The tax on the produce of their mines
paid by the Siphnians at Delphi (Hdt. iii. 57 ; Pausan. x. 11.2)
may be plausibly ascribed to Phœnician influence, and tithes
are also an institution in various parts of Asia Minor, where we
know the influence of Semitic religion to have been very great;
e.g., in Lydia there was a tithe on cattle (Nic. Damasc. in Müller's
Fragm. Hist. Gr., iii. 371). The mention of the Kabiri also
speaks for a Semitic element in the sacrifice of tithes or first-
fruits—note the connection of the two ideas—by the Pelasgi
mentioned by Dion. Hal., *A. R.* i. 23.

NOTE 6, p. 56.—In the oldest legislation (Exod. xxiii. 14
seq.; xxxiv. 18 *seq.*) the three annual feasts are (1) the feast of
unleavened bread, (2) the feast of harvest, (3) the feast of ingathering (of autumn fruits). The two first mark the beginning
and end of the corn-harvest ; compare Deut. xvi. 9 ; Lev.
xxiii. 10. Thus the agricultural reference of all these feasts is
clear, and they are to be compared with similar agricultural
festivals and offerings of first-fruits among other ancient nations.
Pliny, for example, says of the ancient Romans that they would
not even taste the new corn or wine till the priests had tasted
the first-fruits (*H. N.* xviii. 2) and—to take an instance from
Semitic races—a feast of first-fruits in the month of May was
celebrated according to En-Nedîm by the heathen Harranians
(Chwolson, *Ssabier*, ii. 25 ; *Fihrist*, ed. Flügel, p. 322). See Spencer,
Op. cit., lib. iii. cap. 8, 9. To trace correspondences in detail
between the Hebrew feasts and those of the surrounding nations
is not so easy. The occasions of the Hebrew festivals are those
naturally suggested by the course of the seasons of husbandry,
while at an early date we find among their neighbours feasts
determined rather by astronomical considerations, and having
reference to the worship of the heavenly bodies ; such, for
example, as the Tyrian feast of the awakening of the sun

(Herakles), Jos. *Ant.*, viii. 5, 3. This feast, however, is said to have been first instituted by Hiram, and it is probable that in general agricultural festivals were older than astronomical ones. Thus, in Judges ix. 27 we find a Canaanite vintage feast corresponding to the Hebrew feast of ingathering, which in the early books appears as the principal yearly feast, or at least as the pilgrimage feast, when men had leisure to visit distant shrines (1 Kings xii. 32). Ewald (*Ant.*, E. T. p. 351, comp. *Z. f. d. Kunde des Morgenlandes*, iii. 419), who conjectures that a spring and an autumn feast were known to the Hebrews before the time of Moses, points to the fact that according to the scholion cited in last note, the Arabs paid tithes in the month Rajab, and that the Arabs had of old two sacred months —Moharram, the first month from autumn, and Rajab, the seventh. See, however, Sprenger in *Z. D. M. G.*, 1859, p. 134 *seq.*; *Leben Mohammed's*, iii. 516 *seq.*; Dozy, *Israëliten te Mekka*, p. 138, from which it will be seen that there is still considerable obscurity about the holy seasons of the heathen Arabs. The ancient holiness of Rajab as a sacrificial season (see Lane *s. v.*) is the best established point, and as this month corresponds to the Hebrew Nisan, the sacrifices then offered may be taken as a probable parallel to the paschal sacrifices of the Hebrews.

That there were great similarities in the method of celebration between the feasts of the Hebrews and their heathen neighbours is clear from the Bible, especially from the undoubted fact of the admixture of elements of Baal worship with the service of Jehovah. The custom of holding feasts in tents or booths (Hosea xii. 9) reappears in the Babylonian *Sacaea* and elsewhere in the East; see Movers, *Phœnizier*, i. 483 *seq*. Again, the Hebrew technical term עצרה reappears in the worship of the Tyrian Baal, 2 Kings x. 20. The description of Syrian festivals given by Posidonius (Müller, *Fragmenta*, iii. 258), the copious eating and drinking, the portions carried home, the noisy music, recalls forcibly what we read of the Hebrew feasts (1 Sam. i. 14; 2 Sam. vi. 19; Lam. ii. 7, etc.).

In addition to the great yearly feasts, Hosea ii. 13 specially designates the Sabbath and the New Moon as occasions of festal joy. The latter of these was also a sacred season among the Phœnicians celebrated by special offerings, *Corp. Inscr. Sem.*, pars i. cap. 2, No. 86. The Sabbath, on the other hand, as a day of joy, stands in marked contrast to the unlucky seventh day of the

Babylonians, on which see Sayce in *Records of the Past*, i. 164 ; vii. 157 *seq*. The relation of the Hebrew Sabbath to the planetary week of the Babylonians, in which the seventh day is connected with Saturn, is still far from clear. The week is perhaps originally nothing else than the fourth part of a lunation. Thus among the Harranians, if we may believe En-Nedim, four days in each month were suitable for sacrifices, and to these belonged the new moon, the first quarter, and the twenty-eighth day. (Chwolson, ii. 8 ; *Fihrist*, ed. Fl., 319.)

NOTE 7, p. 56.—The literature of the sacrificial tablet of Marseilles is cited, and the inscription itself published with a commentary in Schröder's *Phönizische Sprache*, p. 237 *seq*. It contains an account of the dues in money or in parts of the victim to be paid to the priest for every kind of sacrifice. A fragment of a similar tablet from Carthage may be found in the same work, or in Davis, *Carthage and her Remains*, p. 296 *seq*.

NOTE 8, p. 57.—See in particular the inscription of Iehawmelek (*C. I. S.*, p. i. cap. 1. Art. 1, where the king records the erection of a brazen altar, of golden chased work, and of a portico and columns. The aspect of a Phœnician temple, with its court and portico and a lofty obelisk or sun-pillar, is best seen on the coin of Byblus, figured *ibid.* p. 6, and in Renan's *Miss. de Phénicie*, p. 177. The brazen altar recurs in the Sardo trilinguis (Schröder, p. 249 ; Levy, *Phön. Stud.*, iii. 40). The palm-tree or palm-branch found among the temple ornaments is one of the commonest of Phœnician symbols. See, for example, the woodcuts in Renan's *Mission*, p. 651 *seq*.; the woodcut from Yârûn, *Survey of Western Palestine*, i. 259, and the coins figured by Schröder, Plate xviii. 10-14. Compare further *Old Test. in J. Ch.*, p. 248 and *note* 2 there. For the classes of ministers in a Phœnician sanctuary, see *C. I. S.*, No. 86.

NOTE 9, p. 57.—See *Old Test. in J. Ch.*, p. 285 and *note* 4 there.

NOTE 10, p. 62.—The ancient exegesis of Exod. iii. 14 flowed in two main channels. The Hellenistic tradition, attaching itself to the rendering of the LXX., ἐγώ εἰμι ὁ ὤν . . . ὁ ὤν ἀπέσταλκέ με, finds the meaning of the ineffable name in the absolute being and *aseity* of God ; the Palestinian tradition, on the other hand, understands the name of God's eternity and immutability. The former view is untenable on linguistic grounds, for the Hebrew substantive verb has not the sense of metaphysical entity, and the imperfect אהיה does not mean *I am*, but *I will be* [something]. This the Palestinian exegesis recognised (Aq., Theod.), and, taking the verb, not in the abstract metaphysical sense of the Hellenistic interpretation, but in the simpler sense of actuality (*Daseyn*), which it certainly has, at least in later Biblical Hebrew, they seem to have got the notion of eternity by rendering *I will be in existence, I will not cease to be.* In that case the whole clause must be rendered [*My name is*] *I will be,* [that is] *I who will be.* As A. ben Ezra puts it, אשר אהיה is an explanatory apposition to אהיה. This view of the grammatical structure of the clause has been recently supported by Mr. W. A. Wright (*Jour. Phil.*, iv. 70) and Wellhausen (*Z. f. d. Th.*, xxi. 540), who, however, do not object to retain the present tense, which I think is impossible in such a connection and with the substantive verb. For my own part, I doubt if even the notion of actuality, as we find it in the Hebrew of Ecclesiastes, can be given to the substantive verb in such an early passage. The sense of אהיה is not so much *I exist* or *I will exist* as *I will be it*—an incomplete predication. On this view the predication, incomplete in the simple יהוה or אהיה, is completed in the fuller אהיה אשר אהיה. This clause may certainly be grammatically rendered *Be I what I may*—a view adopted and grammatically justified with his usual wealth of illustration by Lagarde, *Psalt. Hieron.*, p. 156 *seq.* To the passages from various languages which he cites—the Biblical ones are Gen. xliii. 14; 1 Sam. i. 24; xxiii. 13; 2 Sam. xv. 20; Zech. x. 8; Ezek. xii. 25—I add in illustration of the idiom, Deut. ix. 25; Exod. iv. 13; xvi. 23; xxxiii. 19; Esther iv. 16; Mishna, *Shab.* xiv. 4 אם נתרפא נתרפא; Freytag, *Prov. Ar.*, i. 339, No. 212, *Ujlus heith tajlus;* Tabary, iii. 93, l. 3, *qataltu man qataltu.* The great difficulty in the view of Professor Lagarde, and indeed in almost every view except that of A. ben Ezra, is that the meaning of the full אהיה אשר אהיה disappears in the shorter form אהיה or יהוה, the whole clause being essential to the sense. In a paper in *Brit. and For. Ev. Rev.*, Jan. 1876, I proposed to meet this difficulty by following out the hint given by R. Jehuda Hallevy (*Kusari*, ed. Cassel, p. 304), who explains אהיה to mean "I will be present to them when they seek me," and appeals to ver. 12, "I will be with thee," in support of this interpretation. In truth this divine *I will be* rings through the whole Bible in varying form (Gen. xxvi. 3; Josh. i. 5;

Judges vi. 16 ; Jer. xxiv. 7; Zech. ii. 5[9]; viii. 8, etc.) Is there not a presumption that this oft-repeated *I will be* is akin to the אהיה of ver. 14, and that the latter must also mean, not *I will exist*, but *I will be—something* which lies implicitly on the mind of him who uses the name ? In this case it is possible with R. Jehuda and A. ben Ezra to take the אשר אהיה as an apposition, but it seems more reasonable to think that the added אשר אהיה, *I will be what I will be*, expresses more distinctly the fact that the predicate is vague. The construction, in fact, is in principle analogous to the well-known idiom שְׁמַע הַשֹּׁמֵעַ to express the indefinite subject. The relative clause is without emphasis—as appears from the parallels cited above, and the sense is not that God reserves for His own arbitrium to determine what He will be, but simply that what He will be to His people He will be, will approve Himself to be, without fail. The vagueness is inevitable, for no words can sum up all that Jehovah will be to His people ; it is enough for them to know that He will be it (comp. Isa. lxiv. 3 ; Lam. iii. 23). On this view the clause is exactly parallel to Exod. xxxiii. 19, which does not mean that God will choose the objects of His grace arbitrarily, but that to those to whom He is gracious—who they are is left vague—He *will* be gracious. I am disposed to think that this exegesis of the passage is as old as Hosea iii. 9, where the words, " I will not be for you," seem to be chosen in direct contrast to the promise, " I will save Judah in the quality of Iahwè their God." It must of course be remembered that Exod. iii. 14 does not give the original sense of the name Iahwè, which is still obscure (*O. T. in J. Ch.*, p. 423 ; compare Delitzsch, *Wo lag das Paradies?* p. 158 *seq.*, and the reply of Tiele, *Theol. Tijd.*, 1882, p. 262 *seq.*), but an adaptation of the name, so that we need not be surprised to find a little awkwardness in the expression.

NOTE 11, p. 64.—This monument may now be seen in the Louvre. " Let them," says Eshmunazar, " have no bed with the shades, and let them not be buried in a grave, nor let there be to them son or seed in their stead, and let the holy gods deliver them into the hand of a powerful kingdom . . . let them have no root downward or fruit upward (comp. Isa. xxxvii. 31), nor any comeliness among the living under the sun." —*C. I. S., ut supra*, No. 3. The Authorised Version of the Bible unfortunately obliterates the characteristic ideas of the " underworld " (Sheól) and the " shades " (Rephāim). In Isa. xiv. 9, for example, the former word is rendered "hell," and the latter "dead."

NOTE 12, p. 72.—A reference may here be added to the latest discussion of the derivatives of the root ÇDK by Prof. Kautzsch of Tübingen (*Festeinladung*, 6 *März* 1881), who concludes that the fundamental idea of the root is *conformity to a norm*. Even this, perhaps, is too wide, and does not lay sufficient weight on the distinctly forensic element which the author recognises as preponderant in the earlier Hebrew writings. The roots צדק and רשע are correlatives, and ought to be taken together. All the other uses of the derivatives of ÇDK may, I think, be traced from the primitive forensic sense; but the more complex developments belong to a later period than that covered by the present volume. Prof. Kautzsch is certainly right in declining to start from the very doubtful considerations of etymology often put in the front, and especially from the obscure Arabic phrase *rumḥ çadq*.

NOTE 13, p. 75.—The Biblical narrative is here supplemented by the "Moabite Stone" erected by King Mesha.

NOTE 14, p. 79.—The sources for the history of Elijah are not all of one date, and do not all reproduce with equal immediacy the aspect in which his work presented itself to his contemporaries. See Wellhausen's edition of Bleek's *Einleitung*, and the article KINGS, BOOKS OF, in the forthcoming volume of the *Encyclopædia Britannica*.

NOTE 15, p. 81.—In Hosea vi. 5 for אור משפטיך read with LXX. משפטי כאור.

NOTE 16, p. 84.—On wine and wine-drinking among the Arabs before Islam, see especially I. Guidi, *Della Sede primitiva dei popoli Semitici* (Rome, 1879), p. 43 *seq*. Like all barbarians, the Arabs were fond enough of getting drunk, but wine was a foreign and costly luxury, and the opposition to its use found distinguished advocates before Mohammed. Among the Nabatæans of the Syrian desert, according to Diodorus (xix. 94, 3), it was a law neither to sow nor to plant any fruit-bearing plant, nor to use wine, nor to construct a house, and death was the penalty of disobedience. See also Ammianus, xiv. 4.

NOTE 17, p. 85.—See G. Hoffmann, *Verhandlungen der Kirchenversammlung zu Ephesus, etc.*, Kiel, 1873, p. 89; "*bar naggârê* is not the son of a carpenter, but a carpenter as member of the incorporation." The current notion that the prophets were not a guild is derived from too exclusive attention to the prophets of the school that arose with Amos and expressly disclaimed connection with the established guilds. In Jerusalem, as we see from Jeremiah, the prophets were under a certain official control on the part of the priests.

NOTE 18, p. 86.—The etymological sense of the Hebrew *nābî* is much disputed. It must be observed that there is nothing in extant Hebrew literature by which it can be determined, for Exod. iv. 16 ; vii. 1 ; Jer. xv. 19, cannot be taken as giving the meaning of the word, or as proving that it ever meant a speaker or interpreter in general, but only as evidence how the function of the prophet in relation to God was conceived among the Israelites. *Nābî*, in the Old Testament, always has the technical sense of a prophet, and the other derivatives of the root (*nibbā* and *hithnabbē*, prophesy) are denominatives formed from *nābî*. The word, in short, has no root in Hebrew of the historical period, and we must suppose either that it has survived from very remote antiquity or that it is a loan word. It is not, however, like *kōhēn*, "priest," a common Semitic term ; the other Semitic dialects have certainly borrowed it from the Hebrews (Nöldeke, *Gesch. d. Qorans*, p. 1). Thus it belongs to an isolated sphere of Semitic religious life ; and as the Nebî'îm were common to Israel and the worshippers of Baal, while according to 1 Sam. ix. 9 *nābî* superseded the old Hebrew term *rō'eh* after the time of Samuel, it is hardly likely that the word is older than the settlement of the Hebrews in Canaan. This circumstance, taken with the fact that the root is not otherwise found in Hebrew, certainly favours the view of several recent inquirers that the name is of Canaanite origin. In this case the etymology becomes comparatively unimportant, and in any case the origin of the name lies too remote from the historical development of Hebrew prophecy to be of value in illustration of the conception of a prophet among the Israelites.

As regards the meaning of the root, it is hardly doubtful that the ultimate stem is NB with the notion of *protrusion* (Fleischer in Delitzsch's *Genesis*, 4th ed. p. 552), and so the *Tâj el ʿArûs* (i. 131) remarks that *naba'a ʿala*, in the sense of *hajama watalaʿa*, is interchangeable with *nabaha* and *nabaʿa*. But this fundamental idea not only divided itself under a variety of triliteral roots ; the root *nabaʿa* itself, according to the Arabic lexicographers, has very various meanings, among which it is difficult to find one that can be regarded as central. Thus, when Kuenen (*Onderzoek*, ii. 3 ; comp. *Godsdienst*, chap. iii. *note*, and *Prophets*, p. 42) selects the notion of *bubbling up*, and regards the prophet as one who bubbles up under inspiration, this hypothesis has no more value than that of a guess guided by the particular development of the root idea found in נבך and נבע. The most interesting etymological question is whether *nâbî* may not originally mean simply a "speaker" or "herald" of God. This view is supported mainly from the Arabic by Ewald (*Propheten*, i. 7), Fleischer (*ut supra*), and many others, while Hupfeld (*Z. f. d. K. des Morgenl.*, iii. 40) and Riehm (*Mess. Weiss.*, p. 21), also starting from the Arabic, take the view, less accordant with the grammatical form of the word, that the *nâbî* is one to whom God whispers His revelation. Kuenen (*Prophets*, p. 42), in opposing the argument from the Arabic, goes so far as to say that the Arabic verb is probably derived from *nâbî*, and so is a Hebrew loan word. I presume that he does not mean to deny that there is a real Arabic root *naba'a* with the sense of *prominence, impetus*, etc., but only refers to the use of Conjugations II., IV., in the sense of "tell" (*akhbara*), and to the *nom. act.* of Conj. I. explained by *khabar*, news. And no doubt the usage of the Korân is to reserve these words for divine or supernatural communications, and Ragheb, cited at length in the *Tâj el 'Arûs*, explains that *nab'* is not to be used of any *khabar*, but is confined to announcements that are valuable and promote knowledge and are certain truth, like the word of God and His prophet. Yet it seems impossible to treat Conj. II. as a mere theological term derived from the Hebrew. Even in the Koran (lxvi. 3) it is used in a wider sense, and, what is more important, it is so found in old Arabic, *e.g.* in 'Antara (*Moall.*, l. 61 of Arnold's ed., or l. 68 of Ahlwardt's *Divans*, p. 48). This circumstance adds importance to the fact that in Assyrian *nabû* means to "announce," Delitzsch, *Ass. Lesestücke*, 2d ed. (1878), p. 3. *Nab'at*, "a gentle sound" (Harith, *Moall.*, l. 11, and *Tâj el 'Arûs* i. 131, *foot*), is also an old word. It cannot, however, be said that the sense "speaker," or "newsbringer," is as yet established as the etymological meaning of *nâbî*.

NOTE 19, p. 86.—From 1 Sam. x. 5, 10 *seq.* ; xix. 20 *seq.*, we see that the *nebî'îm* at their first appearance in Israel formed bands or companies. Their "prophesying" was a joint act ;

Samuel, in xix. 20, stands presiding over them, precisely like the sheikh in a *zikr* of Dervishes. Further, these exercises were sometimes gone through in sacred processions, sometimes at a fixed place, as at the *Naioth* at Ramah, which ought probably to be rendered "dwellings"— a sort of cœnobium. They were accompanied by music of a somewhat noisy character, in which the hand-drum and pipe played a part, as was otherwise the case in festal processions to the sanctuary (2 Sam. vi. 5 ; Isa. xxx. 29). Thus the religious exercises of the prophets seem to be a development in a peculiar direction of the ordinary forms of Hebrew worship at the time, and the fact that the "prophesying" was contagious establishes its analogy to other contagious forms of religious excitement. That Saul under the influence of these exercises stripped off his clothes, and so joined in the prophesying, is precisely identical with what Ibn Khallikân (ed. Slane, p. 610 ; Eng. Tr. ii. 538) relates of Kûkubûry, that he used, under the influence of religious music, to become so excited as to pull off part of his clothes. It does not seem that at this early time the prophetic exercises necessarily involved any gift of prophecy in the ordinary sense of the word, but it was recognised that "a divine spirit" (*rû"ḥ ĕlōhîm*) came upon those who participated in them ; Saul was, as an Arab would now say, *malbûs*. The connection of music with the prophetic inspiration is still found in the time of Elisha (2 Kings iii. 15).

The exercises of the prophets of Baal, as described in 1 Kings xviii., were much more violent and ecstatic. They correspond exactly with the later descriptions of the fantastic enthusiasm of the wandering priests of the Syrian goddess given by Apuleius, *Metam.* lib. viii., and Lucian, *Asinus*, c. 37. These priests correspond to the *kelābîm* (literally "dogs") of the Phœnician sanctuaries (*C. I. S.*, No. 86), and of Deut. xxiii. 18, who again are the same with the *kedēshîm* of 1 Kings xv. 12 ; 2 Kings xxiii. 7. At the time of Josiah's reformation these wretched creatures had dwellings in the temple.

Lecture III.

Note 1, p. 91.—The vagueness of 2 Kings xiii. 5 is not an isolated phenomenon. Amos never mentions the Assyrians by name, though he plainly alludes to them, as at vi. 14. So, too,

Wellhausen (Bleek's *Einl.*, 4th ed. p. 251 *seq.*) remarks that the cause of the sudden raising of the siege of Samaria (2 Kings vii. 6) can have been nothing else than an invasion of the Damascene territory by the Assyrians ; but the Hebrew narrator plainly did not know this.

NOTE 2, p. 91.—The "torrent of the 'Arabah," in Amos vi. 14, is identical with the brook of the 'Arabîm, or willows (Arabic *gharab;* Celsius, *Hierobot.*, i. 304 *seq.* ; I can testify from personal observation that a tree of this name is still common in the Zôr of the Jordan valley), the southern boundary between Moab and Ammon. The sea of the 'Arabah in 2 Kings xiv. 25 is, of course, the Dead Sea, the 'Arabah (A. V. "Wilderness") being the great depressed trough in which the Jordan flows and the Dead Sea lies.

NOTE 3, p. 92.—Isaiah closes his citation with the words: "This is the word that Jehovah spake concerning Moab long ago. And now within three short years [comp. xxi. 16] the glory of Moab shall be brought to contempt," etc. Isaiah presumably cited the old prophecy at some period of revolt against Assyria, most likely in the great rising against Sennacherib, when, however, Moab made voluntary submission after the fall of the Phœnician cities (*supra*, p. 322 ; G. Smith, *Hist. of Sennacherib*, p. 55). That the prophet quoted by Isaiah is Jonah is a conjecture of Hitzig (*Des proph. Jonas Orakel über Moab*, u.s.w., 1831 ; *Der Prophet Jesaia*, 1833, p. 178 *seq.*). See also Cheyne's *Prophecies of Isaiah.*

NOTE 4, p. 94.—I transcribe, by way of illustration, a passage from Sprenger's *Alte Geographie Arabiens*, p. 213, referring to the Druses. "The government is a patriarchal aristocracy. The common people are distinguished by industry, the hereditary aristocracy by chivalry and disinterestedness, and both by a frugality bordering on asceticism. The individual is lost in the tribe, and within the community a rigid observance of the laws of morality is enforced. . . . The people have the most absolute confidence in their leaders, who are not without education, and obey their smallest sign. . . . By such institutions the Druses have been able to effect brilliant military successes, and fill their neighbours with a sort of superstitious belief that they are invincible. . . . There have always been such tribes with military organisation in Arabia, and such are still the Dhu Mohammed and Dhu Hoseyn spoken of by Maltzan." See Maltzan, *Reisen in Arabien*, ii. 404 *seq.*

NOTE 5, p. 95.—Saul governed essentially as a Benjamite, and his court consisted, at least mainly, of men of his own tribe (1 Sam. xxii. 7). David's original policy was more enlarged. He chose a capital with no tribal connection, formed a foreign bodyguard, and showed no exceptional favour to his own tribe, as is clear from the fact that the men of Judah were the first to rebel under Absalom, and the last to return to obedience. In fact, David had to win them over by a promise that he would in future recognise their position as his brethren (2 Sam. xix. 12, 13). Under Solomon the Judæans continued to enjoy special favour. They did not share the discontent of Northern Israel, and the chief mark of their favoured position is that, in 1 Kings iv. 7 *seq.*, Judah is exempted from the system of non-tribal government—essentially for purposes of taxation—applied in the other parts of Canaan. It is quite clear, too, from 1 Kings v. 13 ; xi. 28 (where for *charge* read *burden*, with reference to the forced labour employed in the repair of the city of David) that Solomon did not exempt Israelites from forced labour, as 2 Chron. viii. 9 supposes. The system of government by rulers of provinces—that is, the system of centralisation, destructive of old tribal organisation—reappears in the time of Ahab (1 Kings xx. 14 *seq.*). The word "provinces" is rather Aramaic than Hebrew, which may point to an influence of foreign models on the organisation of the state.

NOTE 6, p. 98.—See on all these points *Old Test. in J. Ch.*, Lect. viii., p. 223 *seq.*

NOTE 7, p. 110.—See *O. T. in J. Ch.*, Lect. xi., p. 336 *seq.* It is strange that a sound Hebraist like Prof. W. H. Green (*Presb. Rev.*, iii. 123) should still maintain that Exod. xx. 24 refers, not to co-existing sanctuaries in Canaan, but to altars successively reared at different places in the wilderness, and even assert that the Authorised Version "in all places" does not accurately represent the Hebrew. The Authorised Version is perfectly accurate, and the idiom quite common, Exod. i. 22 ; Deut. iv. 3 ; 1 Sam. iii. 17 ; Jer. iv. 29 ; Ewald, *Lehrb.*, 290 c. But the climax of absurdity is reached when Prof. Green regards this law, with its express provision that if an altar is built of stone it shall not be of hewn stone, as referring to the earth with which the frame of the brazen altar was filled. So, again, it is suggested that Exod. xxii. 30 may have been a law only for the wilderness journey, when all Israel was encamped in the vicinity of the tabernacle. But it is certain that there was no regular sacrificial observance in the wilderness (Amos v. 25 ; Jer. vii. 22), and the whole law to which Exod. xxii. 30 belongs is on the face of it a law for Canaan ; the offering of the firstlings on the eighth day is only part of an ordinance embracing also the first-fruits of cereals and liquors (ver. 29). How Prof. Green can possibly deny that the asylum in Exod. xxi. 12-14 is the altar, and that in Deuteronomy the idea of asylum-cities is separated from connection with the sanctuary, I do not understand.

NOTE 8, p. 119.—For the interpretation of this most important chapter see especially, in addition to the commentaries on Deuteronomy, Graf, *Der Segen Mose's*, Leipzig, 1857 ; Wellhausen, *Geschichte*, i. 266, 376. In verse 2 the text must be corrected as suggested by Ewald, *Gesch.*, ii. 280, so as to read, "came to (from ?) Meribath Kadesh."

NOTE 9, p. 120.—With the exception of Vater's *Amos* (Halle, 1810) and the lengthy work of G. Baur (Giessen, 1847), the recent commentaries on Amos are incorporated in books on the prophets in general or on the minor prophets. Among modern English works Prof. Gandell's *Amos* in the *Speaker's Commentary* closely follows Dr. Pusey's *Minor Prophets*. The prophet is also included in the second volume of Heilprin's *Historical Poetry of the Ancient Hebrews* (New York, 1880). Of German commentaries those of Ewald, Keil, and Schmoller (in Lange's *Bibelwerk*) are translated. The most influential modern commentaries have been those of Ewald (*Propheten*, vol. i.), and Hitzig in his *Kleine Propheten*, of which the last edition by Steiner (1881) contains little new matter of consequence. Of the older commentaries that of Le Mercier (Mercerus) is the most valuable. There have been a good many recent discussions of individual questions, especially of the difficult passage, v. 26, which will be alluded to below. See also the section on Amos in Duhm's *Theologie der Propheten* (Bonn, 1875) ; an essay, containing a great deal that is arbitrary, by Oort, *Theol. Tijdsch.*, 1880, p. 114 *seq.* ; Nöldeke's valuable article in Schenkel's *Bibellexikon*; and the excellent remarks of Wellhausen, *Encyc. Brit.*, xiii. 410. I have not seen Juynboll, *Disp. de Amoso*, 1828.

NOTE 10, p. 120.—If we could venture to suppose that 1 Chron. ii. 24, iv. 5 refer to the settlement of Judah before the Exile, we should gather that the ancient inhabitants of Tekoa were not pure Hebrews, but belonged to the Hezronites, nomads from the desert who had settled down in the southern part of the land of Judah. In this case we should have an interesting line of connection between the kinship of Amos and the Kenite family of the Rechabites, who gave their support to Jehu in the interests of ancient nomadic simplicity. The analysis of Wellhausen, however, *De Gentibus et Familiis Judæis*, 1870, makes it probable that the connection of the Hezronites with the district of Bethlehem began after the Exile, when their older seats in the south had been occupied by the Edomites. On Tekoa and the surrounding district see especially the preface to Jerome's *Comm. in Amos;* Reland, *Palæstina*, vol. ii. p. 1028; Tobler, *Denkblätter aus Jerusalem*, 682 *seq.*; Robinson, *Biblical Researches*, 2d ed. p. 486; Stickel, *Das Buch Hiob*, p. 269 *seq.*, whose remarks on the active movements of commerce in this district serve, as Kuenen has pointed out (*Onderzoek*, ii. 335), to throw light on the range of the prophet's historical and geographical knowledge. The idea that Amos belonged to the Northern Kingdom and to some other and unknown Tekoa (Grätz, Oort, *ut supra*) is quite arbitrary. That Amos has a thorough knowledge of the Northern Kingdom proves nothing. Oort's most striking argument is derived from the mention of sycamore culture as the prophet's occupation. The chief home of this tree was certainly in the plains, especially in the low country on the Mediterranean coast (1 Kings x. 27; compare the notice of a great sycamore grove between Rafaḥ and Gaza in Yâḳût, ii. 796); and Jerome (on Amos vii.) already remarks that it did not exist in the wilderness of Tekoa, and conjectures that the bramble is meant. According to Tristram (*Land of Israel*, p. 34), it seems only to be found " on the sea-coast, where frost is unknown, or in the still warmer Jordan valley." It is, however, rather daring to affirm that the sycamore can never have grown in the vicinity of Tekoa or between Tekoa and the Dead Sea, as it was certainly widely distributed in Palestine. Compare on the whole subject Celsius, *Hierob.*, i. 310; Gesenius, *Thes.*, s.v.; Winer, s.v. "Maulbeerfeigenbaum"; and especially Warnekros in Eichhorn's *Repertorium*, xi. 224 *seq.* That Amos was a Judæan is clear from the way in which he alludes to the sanctuary of Zion, i. 2.

NOTE 11, p. 124.—The phrase "eat bread" for "earn one's bread" is common to Hebrew and Arabic. See De Goeje's glossary to the *Bib. Geog. Arab.* (vol. iv. p. 180). Moḳaddasy says, "I am not one of those who eat their loaf by their knowledge." Thus Amaziah distinctly treats prophecy as a trade by which men live.

NOTE 12, p. 125.—That the text in both these passages is corrupt hardly admits of doubt. With regard to iv. 3 this is generally admitted; for ix. 1 see Lagarde, *Anm. zur Gr. Ueb. d. Proverbien*, p. v. In some other places there are irregular spellings (vi. 8; viii. 8; v. 11; comp. Wellh. in Bleek, p. 633), which must rather be put to the account of transcribers than taken as indications of dialectic peculiarities of the prophet, and probably there may be one or two other passages where LXX. has preserved better readings, but Oort (*ut supra*) goes too far in the numerous corrections he introduces. The text is on the whole in an unusually good state, nor can I see that there is evidence of such extensive interpolations as Duhm, Oort, and even Wellhausen assume (*infra, note* 18).

NOTE 13, p. 126.—An interesting example of this will be found in Ibn Khallikân's article on Ibn al-Kirrîya (p. 121, or i. 236 *seq.* of the English translation).

NOTE 14, p. 128.—On the origin and date of the several parts of this tableau of the geography (not the ethnography) of the Hebrews see, in addition to the commentaries, De Goeje in the *Theol. Tijdschrift*, 1870, p. 233 *seq.*, and Wellhausen in *Jahrb. f. D. Theol.*, 1876, p. 395 *seq.* The problems of the chapter are still far from being conclusively solved, and De Goeje, for example, is disposed to regard the parts of the chapter which are not from the hand of the main author as later additions. But it is more probable that Wellhausen is right in assigning them to the earlier history JE. The verses which he regards as most ancient are 8-19, 21, 25-30. The distant northern nations of Japhet mentioned in the later part of Gen. x. are not known to Amos.

NOTE 15, p. 132.—The current idea that the day of Jehovah is primarily a day of judgment, or assize-day, is connected with the opinion that the earliest prophecy in which the idea occurs is that of Joel. See, for example, Ewald, *Propheten*, i. 90 *seq.* But if the book of Joel, as there is reason to believe (see *Encyc. Brit.* s.v.), is really one of the latest prophetical books, Amos v. 18 is the fundamental passage, and here the idea appears, not as peculiar to the prophet, but as a current popular notion, which Amos criticises and, so to speak, turns upside down.

The popular idea in question cannot have been that of a day of judicial retribution; the day which the men of Ephraim expected must have been a day of national deliverance, and, from the whole traditions of the warlike religion of old Israel, presumably a day of victory like the "day of Midian" (Isa. ix. 4). The last cited passage shows that among the Hebrews, as among the Arabs, the word "day" is used in the definite sense of "day of battle." Illustrations of the Arabic idiom have been collected by Gesenius on Isa. ix. and Schultens on Job, p. 54, to which may be added a reference to the section on the "Days of the Arabs" in the '*Ikd* of Ibn'Abd Rabbih, Egyptian ed., iii. 60 *seq*. The "days" of the Arabs often derive their name from a place, but may equally be named from the combatants, *e.g.*, "the days of Tamîm against Bekr" (*'Ikd*, p. 80). By taking the day of Jehovah to mean His day of battle and victory we gain for the conception a natural basis in Hebrew idiom. The same idea seems still to preponderate in Isa. ii., and is quite clearly seen in many later prophecies. That the day of Jehovah's might is not necessarily a day of victory to Israel over foreign powers, but a day in which His righteousness is vindicated against the sinners of Israel as well as of the nations, is the characteristic prophetic idea due to Amos, and from this thought the notion of the day of judgment was gradually developed.

NOTE 16, p. 135.— Offences against the dead appear to antiquity as among the gravest breaches of natural piety, as is well known from the story of Antigone. The same feeling finds frequent expression in the Old Testament (Deut. xxi. 23; Josh. x. 27; Ps. lxxix. 2, 3; Jer. xxxvi. 30). The feeling is connected with the doctrine of the Underworld—"All the kings of the nations lie in glory, every one in his own house; but thou art cast out of thy grave like a worthless sapling—the slain are thy covering, pierced through with the sword, who go down to the stones of the pit—like a carcase trodden under feet" (Isa. xiv. 19). The curse of Eshmunazar on those who disturb his grave (*supra*, p. 387) is a pertinent illustration. Compare also the account in Jos. *Ant.*, xvi. 7, of the portents which deterred Herod from his attempt to violate the grave of David, and of the costly monument that he erected by way of expiation. The attempt was deemed so unseemly that the eulogist of Herod, Nicolaus of Damascus, omitted to record it in his history.

NOTE 17, p. 135.—The tablet of Marseilles seems to show

that among the Phœnicians the whole burnt-offering was used especially in supplicating the favour of the deity, or as an exceptional thankoffering (Schroeder, *op. cit.*). So it appears also in old Israel (Judges xi. 31 ; 1 Sam. vii. 9 ; 2 Sam. xxiv. 25). Thus Amos means that Jehovah will not pay regard even to those offerings which were regarded as of special importance and efficacy.

NOTE 18, p. 136.—Duhm, *Theologie der Propheten*, p. 119, followed by Oort, *ut supra*, p. 116, proposes to reject Amos ii. 4, 5, as a Deuteronomistic interpolation. But it is plain that Amos could not have excepted Judah from the universal ruin which he saw to threaten the whole land, or at all events such exception would have required to be expressly made on special grounds. Such grounds did not exist ; for in vi. 1 the nobles of Judah and Samaria are classed together, and both kingdoms are mentioned in vi. 2. Comp. iii. 1, where all who came up from Egypt are included. Nor is there anything suspicious in the language used about Judah. "To reject the Torah of Jehovah" is a pre-Deuteronomic phrase, Isa. v. 24, comp. Hosea ii. 4, "thou hast rejected knowledge;" and "the statutes of God and His Torah" appear together just as in our passage in the undoubtedly ancient narrative, Exod. xviii. 16. See also Deut. xxx. 10. In all these parallel passages the reference is to ordinances of civil righteousness, and such, probably, are meant by Amos. It is therefore a second, though not unconnected, offence that the men of Judah have been led astray by the deceitful superstitions practised by their ancestors. This again is quite a natural accusation, for in Josh. xxiv. ancestral superstition appears as one of the two great temptations leading the people away from Jehovah. The worship of the brazen serpent is an instance in point, and Ezek. viii. 10, 11 is a clear proof of the survival of primitive totemism in the last days of the kingdom. The connection makes it probable that Amos views these superstitions as producing moral obliquity. That, however, is in the highest degree natural. Observations in all parts of the world show that totemism is directly connected with peculiar systems of social ethic, and particularly with such practices as are condemned in Lev. xviii., and were still common in the time of Ezekiel (xxii. 10, 11). Comp. *Journ. of Philology*, vol. ix. pp. 94, 97. Duhm further proposes to reject as later additions iv. 13 ; v. 8 *seq.* ; ix. 5, 6, and in this he is followed not only by Oort, but by Wellhausen, *Geschichte*, i. 349 *seq.*, who compares these passages to the lyrical *intermezzi* celebrating Jehovah as Lord of the Universe, which characterise Isa. xl.-lxvi., and argues that Jehovah's all-creating power acquires a sudden prominence in the Exilic literature ; Jehovah becomes Lord of the World when the realm of Israel falls to pieces. It may be conceded that these verses are not closely connected with the movement of the prophet's argument in detail ; but they are thoroughly appropriate to its general purport. To Amos Jehovah is not merely the God of Israel, and Wellhausen has himself observed that the prophet studiously avoids the use of this familiar title. It is true that the universal Godhead of Jehovah appears to Amos rather as a sovereignty over all mankind than as a sovereignty over the mere powers of nature. He uses nature as a factor in history as a means of dealing with man ; and this agrees with the older account of creation in Gen. ii. But undoubtedly Amos teaches that all nature is at Jehovah's command for the execution of His moral purpose (vii. 4 ; ix. 2 *seq.*, etc.), and thus it is natural that the prophet should make occasional direct appeal to that lordship over nature which is the clearest proof that Jehovah's purpose is wider and higher than the mass of Israel supposed. That such appeal takes an ejaculatory form is not surprising under the general conditions of prophetic oratory, and in each case the appeal comes in to relieve the strain of intense feeling at a critical point in the argument. It is certainly possible that v. 8, 9 originally stood in direct connection with iv. 13 ; but even this transposition rests too much on merely subjective arguments to claim general acceptance.

NOTE 19, p. 140.—In this verse there are two disputed points. The first is with reference to the tense of ונשאתם. See, besides the commentaries, Merx in the *Bibel-lex.* s. v. " Chiun " ; Graf in Merx's *Archiv*, ii. 93 *seq.* ; Kleinert, *Das Deuteronomium* (1872), p. 111; Smend, *Moses apud Prophetas*, p. 23 *seq.*; Driver, *Hebrew Tenses*, 2d ed. p. 167 ; and references to discussions of the point in Holland in Oort, *ut supra*, p. 145. The question is whether (*a*) Amos in this verse describes the idolatry of the wilderness (so Hitzig, De Goeje, Kuenen, Merx, Keil, and others), or (*b*) describes the present services of the Israelites as consisting of a carrying about of certain idolatrous objects in sacred procession (so Kamphausen, Schultz, etc.), or (*c*) predicts that they shall have to carry these things away into captivity (so Rashi, Ewald, etc.). The question of the consecution of tenses is complicated by the fact that the preceding verb is an interrogative, and thus De Goeje in support of his view appeals to Job xxviii. 21, וְנֶעֶלְמָה, which, however, is no exact parallel. An allusion to the sins of Israel in the wilderness would be singularly out of place in this connection. Amos, like the other older prophets, regards the wilderness journey as a time when Jehovah's favour was specially manifested (ii. 10), and his argument is that this favour was enjoyed without sacrifice. Compare the argument of the *Clementine Homilies* (iii. 45), that "God did not desire sacrifices, for He slew those who lusted after the taste of flesh in the wilderness." (Lightfoot, *Colossians*, p. 373.) In point of fact there is no close syntactical connection between v. 26 and v. 25, and the force of the consecutive Waw is rather to be determined by וְהִגְלֵיתִי following, which is a true future. Thus the captivity of the idols seems to be alluded to, as in Isa. xlvi. 1, 2. It was a known practice of the Assyrians to carry off the *palladia* of vanquished cities, and the captives are here represented as compelled to bear them.

If, now, the allusion is to religious institutions of the prophet's own time, it is still a difficult question what these were. What is plain is that the allusion is to astral worship, and to idols, the work of man's hands. The verse contains two unique words סִכּוּת (A. V. *tabernacle*), and כִּיּוּן (A. V. *Chiun*). Are these common or proper names? As regards the first the whole weight of the early versions supports the English version, and, as the form in ות from סכך may be an abstract used as a concrete, there is no difficulty in supposing a reference to the well-known portable chapels or tabernacles of Phœnician worship (Diod. xx. 14, 65 ; comp. 2 Kings xxiii. 7, where we read of women who wove tents for the Ashēra), and it is not necessary with Ewald to compare the Syriac *sekkitha*, "post." With regard to the second word, however, where the Septuagint introduces a problematic Raiphan, or Rephan, there is an early variation of the tradition. Whether the Raiphan of the oldest version is a synonym of Saturn, borrowed from the Egyptians, is highly doubtful ; it may be a mere error, and Theodotion does not take the word as a proper name. But the Syriac and perhaps the Tgm. do take it so, and both Jewish and Syriac expositors identify it with *Keiwân*, Saturn. According to Abulwalîd, most Jewish interpreters took this view, though he himself prefers the opinion, essentially that of most recent commentators, that the word is like מכונה, a pedestal. The great difficulty is that the name Keiwân is not Semitic (see Fleischer in Levy, *Chald. Wört.,* i. 428), but probably Persian. So too, when Schrader (*Stud. und Krit.*, 1874, p. 324 *seq.;* Riehm's *Handw.*, i. 234 *seq.*) will have it that סכות is Sakkuth, an epithet of the god Adar, we are met by the difficulty that this also is no Semitic name, but so-called Accadian (Delitzsch in the German transl. of Smith's *Genesis*, p. 274). It is hardly credible that elements of Eastern religion not common to all Semites could have been established in Israel at the time of Amos, or that the Adrammelech (Adar), the introduction of whose worship is recorded in 2 Kings xvii. 31, was known before that time under a non-Semitic name; while, on the other hand, the identification of כיון with Keiwân naturally suggested itself when that name of Saturn became current; but this interpretation can hardly have existed when the pronunciation expressed by the Massorets was adopted. That our word may be the source of the Greek κίων is suggested by Hitz. *in loc.* and Lagarde, *Abhandlungen*, p. 13.

NOTE 20, p. 140.—See *O. T. in J. Ch.*, Lect. xi. p. 341, and note 7.

LECTURE IV.

NOTE 1, p. 145.—The chronological discussions which I have felt it necessary to introduce in one or two places in these Lectures start chiefly from the results obtained by Nöldeke, *Untersuchungen zur Kritik des Alten Testaments:* " 4, Die Chronologie der Richterzeit," and Wellhausen, *Jahrbb. f. Deutsche Theologie*, 1875, p. 607 *seq.* (compare Bleek's *Einleitung*, 4th edition, p. 264 *seq.* ; *Geschichte*, i. 287 ; and Krey, *Zeitsch. f. Wiss. Theol.*, 1877, p. 404 *seq.*). The observation of the trisection of the 480 and 240 periods of Judah and Ephraim, by which I confirm the systematic character of the chronology already pointed out by these scholars, was first published in the *Journal of Philology*, x. 209 *seq.*, to which I refer for various details. In several notes to the present volume I have endeavoured to carry further the argument there opened. The material for the Assyrian synchronisms is excellently brought together by G. Smith, *The Assyrian Eponym Canon*, where also an account will be found of various proposals for harmonising the dates. Another attempt is that of Oppert, *Salomon et ses successeurs*, 1877. I do not accumulate references to other works, because it appears certain that the first basis of a sound treatment of the problem is the recognition of the fact long ago pointed out by Ewald, that the synchronisms of Judah and Israel are not independent chronological data (*infra*, note 2). The first chronologer who has used the Assyrian data in a thoroughly critical spirit is therefore Ewald's scholar Wellhausen. The ordinary schemes of harmonists are mere guesswork. For students who desire to look into the subject for themselves, and are not yet familiar with the literature, I may add a reference to Scaliger's *Thesaurus Temporum;* Ussher's *Annals of the World*, 1658 (preceded by the Latin *Annales*, 1650-54) ; and G. Syncellus, Bonn ed., i. 388 *seq.*, where the famous Canon of Ptolemy is preserved.

NOTE 2, p. 146.—In fixing on this particular means of harmonising the two lines chronologers were guided by the so-called synchronisms or cross references which in the present text of the books of Kings occur as the beginning of each reign, to the effect that A, king of Judah, came to the throne in such a year of B, king of Israel, or *vice versa*. Jeroboam II. is said to have begun his reign in the 15th year of Amaziah, and his son Zachariah succeeded in the 38th year of Azariah. Thus the interval between the two accessions is 52 years, instead of 41, which is explained by assuming an interregnum of 11 years. On the other hand, we are told that Amaziah lived 15 years after the death of Jehoash or the accession of Jeroboam, and yet the accession of Amaziah's son Azariah is placed in the 27th year of Jeroboam (2 Kings xv. 1). In other words, the synchronisms themselves are not exact, and the right to use them as a key to the chronology becomes doubtful. In fact, when we go over the whole series of synchronisms, as has been done at length by Wellhausen (*Jahrb. f. D. Theol.*, 1875, pp. 607 *seq*), we are forced to the conclusion that they are not independent data, furnishing additional material for the chronological scheme, but have simply been added by a later hand, who calculated them out so as to harmonise as he best could the already discrepant lines of the Judæan and Northern chronology. This view was expressed by Ewald (*Geschichte*, iii. 464), and subsequent inquiry has fully confirmed its correctness ; for not only are the synchronisms full of such inconsistencies as were inseparable from the task of harmonising two sets of data that do not agree, but an exact examination of the text shows that they are inserted in such a way as to disturb the natural construction of the sentences in which they occur. See Wellhausen, *ut supra*, p. 611. For chronological purposes, therefore, it is not only legitimate, but imperative, to ignore these synchronisms, and for simplicity's sake I have passed them by in the text of my Lecture. There are only two synchronisms of which account must be taken, viz. the contemporaneous accession of Jehu and Athaliah, and the siege of Samaria from the fourth to the sixth year of Hezekiah.

NOTE, 3, p. 148.—On forty as a round number see Gesenius, *Thesaurus*, p. 1258 *seq.*; Lepsius, *Chr. der Aegypt.*, i.

NOTE 4, p. 151.—The precise year of the fall of Samaria is still open to dispute. The siege began under Shalmaneser, while the conquest is claimed by Sargon. The data which determine Sargon's first year have given rise to considerable discussion, and are difficult to harmonise. See Schrader, *K. A. T.*, p. 158 *seq.*; Oppert in *Records of the Past*, vii. 22, 28, Smith; *Assyrian Eponym Canon*, pp. 125, 129, 174; the criticism of v. Gutschmid, *Neue Beiträge*, 101 *seq.*; and Schrader again in *K. G. F.*, p. 313 *seq.* It seems pretty certain, however, that Sargon came to the throne in 722, and reckoned 721 as his first year. He records the siege and capture of Samaria together, as happening in the beginning of his reign, apparently distinguishing this from his first year, when he was occupied with a revolt in Babylonia. This leaves it uncertain whether he records the capture in the first year of the siege or the siege in the year of capture, but the extreme limits for the commencement of the siege are 724 and 722, assuming always that the latter year is that of Shalmaneser's death. Now, it is noteworthy that in 720 Sargon was in Syria and Palestine meeting a revolt supported by the Egyptians, in which Samaria is mentioned as taking part, and, on the other hand, that 2 Kings xvii. 4 *seq.* seems to place the defeat and capture of Hoshea before the three years' siege. This would fit very well with the hypothesis that the fall of Samaria took place in two acts, the first falling in 722 and the second in 720. If we do not accept this solution we must suppose that a revolt broke out in Samaria immediately after its capture, of which the Bible tells us nothing. Were it possible to go by a tablet in the Louvre, aided by a conjecture of v. Gutschmid (*ut supra*), based on the variations which Assyriologists themselves have given in the rendering of an obscure word, we might even place Shalmaneser's death and the commencement of the siege in 721; but this seems hardly possible in view of the line, indicating a change of rule, placed in the Eponym Canon before 722. The year 721 would lend itself to the theory of Sayce and others, that 2 Kings xviii. 9, 13 are to be harmonised by making the latter verse refer to an expedition in 711 ; but that theory has so many other difficulties that it cannot be allowed to influence the dates with which we are now concerned.

NOTE 5, p. 153.—See Schrader in *Jahrbb. f. prot. Theol.*, 1875, p. 329 *seq.*, and in particular A. v. Gutschmidt, *Neue Beiträge*, p. 143 *seq.*

NOTE 6, p. 154.—The literature upon the book of Hosea is in large part the same with that upon Amos, but there are several special German commentaries of recent date, by Simson (1851), Wünsche (1868), and Nowack (1880). The last-named gives a very complete view of recent discussions. There is also a very excellent old commentary by Pococke (1685). Further references to books are given in *Encyc. Brit.*, xii. 298, where also some notices of the traditions about the prophet may be found. Many parts of the book of Hosea are very imperfectly understood, and this not merely from the intrinsic difficulties of the prophet's style, but from the fact that the text is often manifestly corrupt.

NOTE 7, p. 156.—In the title to Hosea's prophecy i. 1, his date is given by the reigning kings of Judah and Israel. He prophesied, we are told, (1) in the days of Uzziah, Jotham, Ahaz, and Hezekiah; (2) in the days of Jeroboam, the son of Joash, king of Israel. As Jeroboam died probably in the lifetime of Uzziah, and certainly long before the accession of Ahaz, these two periods do not coincide, and it can hardly be thought that they are both from the same hand or of equal authority. As the first part of the book was certainly written under Jeroboam II., and Hosea himself would not date by the kings of a foreign realm, it seems natural to suppose with Ewald and other scholars that the date by Jeroboam is original, but stood at first as a special title to chaps. i. ii., or to these chapters along with chap. iii., and that the special title was generalised by a later hand, which inserted the words, "Uzziah, etc., kings of Judah and in the days of." The later editor or scribe cannot have been a man of Ephraim, and perhaps was the same who penned the identical date prefixed to the book of Isaiah. In this case he must have lived a considerable time after Hosea, for the title of Isa. i. 1 can hardly be older than the collection of Isaiah's prophecies in their present form (see p. 215 *seq.*), and we are hardly entitled to accept his statement as proving more than that he knew Hosea to have been a contemporary of Isaiah. If the title were correct, Hosea, on the common chronology, must be held to have continued to prophesy for a period of some sixty years. This difficulty, indeed, is now removed by the shortening of the last period of the history of Ephraim, which we have seen to be demanded by the Assyrian synchronisms. But the fact still remains that there is nothing in the book of Hosea that points to the reigns of Ahaz and Hezekiah, or justifies the later title. Some writers indeed, including Dr. Pusey, suppose that the Shalman of x. 14 is Shalmaneser IV., the successor of Tiglath Pileser. But of this there is no proof. Dr. Pusey's theory is that Beth Arbel is the Arbela in the plain of Jezreel known to Eusebius, and that it was sacked by Shalmaneser when he first received Hoshea's submission at the beginning of his reign. But a town in this quarter, important enough to be used to supply a figure for the fall of Samaria, could hardly have remained without mention in the historical books, and it does not appear that Hoshea ventured to resist Shalmaneser at the time referred to. Hosea is fond of historical allusions, and does not confine himself to such as lie near at hand. There was another Arbela known to Eusebius (*Onom.*, ed. Lagarde, p. 214), east of the Jordan near Pella, which might conceivably have been reached by Shalmaneser III. This combination has been suggested by Schrader (*K. A. T.*, p. 283), who, however, himself admits its very problematic character, and offers the more plausible alternative that Shalman may have been a Moabite king, a sovereign of Moab of that name (Salamann), actually appearing on the monuments (comp. Smith, *Eponym Canon*, p. 124). An episode in the ferocious wars of Gilead, spoken of by Amos, may indeed very well be referred to, and in any case the allusion is too obscure to be used to fix the date of any part of Hosea's prophecies.

NOTE 8, p. 156.—The general sense of this passage has been best illustrated by Wellhausen, *Geschichte*, i. 141, who is certainly right in saying that the direct address to the priests does not begin with verse 6, but must include verse 5. In spite of the objection taken by Nowack, there is no difficulty in understanding אם (A. V. *mother*) of the stock or race of the priests, 2 Sam. xx. 19 ; Ezek. xix. 2 ; Arabic, *ummah*. But to gain a proper connection between ver. 5 and ver. 4 is more difficult, and seems to require a slight readjustment of the text. The lines on which this must proceed have been clearly laid down by Wellhausen. Hosea in ver. 4 suddenly breaks off in his rebuke of the nation at large, "Yet let no man accuse and no man rebuke for ..." What follows must be to the effect that the real blame in the matter lies with the priests, whose destruction is then announced in ver. 5 following. It is they who, by rejecting the knowledge of Jehovah which they were set to teach, have banished that knowledge from the land. But the reading which Wellhausen accepts, ועמי ככמריו, "for my people is like its priests," is not satisfactory: כהנים and כמרים are not synonyms, and the conjectured reading not only leaves an unexplained יבה at the end, but does not do justice to the circumstance that, in order to get a natural transition to ver. 5, the clause must be addressed to the priests and the concluding word a vocative. This requisite of a plausible conjecture is in so far met by Heilprin's ועמך כמריבו, "thy people are like its accusers, O priest." But the priests were judges, not accusers, and the people at large could hardly be called the priest's people. Rather the people of the priest must be the priestly caste or clan, and this points to the very slight correction מרו בי for כמריבי, "thy people have rebelled against me, O priest." The corruption might easily arise, especially with *scriptio defectiva*, under the influence of the preceding ירב. Perhaps, indeed, it would be enough to change the pointing and simply read, "Thy people are as mine enemies, O priest" (1 Sam. ii. 10).

NOTE 9, p. 160.—The etymological relations of חסד are obscure. In Syriac we find two words ḥesda: the first, written according to Bar Hebræus with hard d, means "reproach," the latter with *rukkakha*, ḥesdha, is the Hebrew חסד. The aspiration is exactly the opposite of what we should expect, especially as the hard form seems to correspond with Arabic ḥasad, envy. The sense "reproach" or "shame" in Hebrew (Lev. xx. 17 ; Prov. xiv. 34) may safely be regarded as an Aramaism; and in all probability the two like-sounding words are etymologically distinct ; the one corresponds to the Arabic root HSD, the other to IISHD, in which the idea of friendly combination appears to lie, in correspondence with the fact that in Hebrew חסד is the virtue that knits together society. It is noteworthy that *hashada* has a special application, in the phrase ḥashadû lahu, to the joint exercise of hospitality to a guest.

It ought never to be forgotten that in Hebrew thought there is no contrast such as is drawn in certain schools of theology between justice, equity, and kindness. Kindness and truth are the basis of society, and righteousness—even forensic righteousness—involves these, for it is the part of good government not to administer a hard-and-fast rule, but to insist on considerate and brotherly conduct. If we forget this we shall not do justice to the emphasis laid by the prophets on civil righteousness. Compare, for example, 2 Sam. xiv.

NOTE 10, p. 166.—The difficulties which surround the literal interpretation of Gen. xxxiv. are in part so obvious that they were felt even by the old interpreters. The latest stage of inquiry into the meaning of the chapter may be studied in Wellhausen's *Composition des Hexateuchs* (*Jahrb. f. Deutsche Theol.*, vol. xxi. p. 435 *seq.*), Dillmann's *Genesis*, and Kuenen's essay in *Theol. Tijdschrift*, 1880, p. 257 *seq.*, and leads to the result that the narrative, as it now stands, has passed through a complicated history which need not occupy us here. It is plain that the two individuals Simeon and Levi could not take and destroy a city ; that in verse 30 Jacob speaks of himself, not as an individual, but as a community, " I am a few men ;" and that in Gen. xlix. 6 he speaks of his sons as tribes, for two men do not form an "assembly" (קהל). As regards what is said of Reuben in Gen. xxxv. 22 ; xlix. 4, it is to be observed that the Hebrews undoubtedly were accustomed to state facts as to the relationships and fusion of clans or communities under the figures of paternity and marriage ; and this plan inevitably led in certain cases to the figurative supposition of very strange connections. A clear instance of such figurative use of marriage with a father's wife is found in 1 Chron. ii. 24, as the text has been restored by Wellhausen after the LXX. (*De Gentibus*, etc., p. 14) ; and the story of the birth of Moab and Ammon, as well as of the elements of the tribe of Judah spoken of in Gen. xxxviii. (see *Encyc. Brit.*, 9th ed., article JUDAH), may be probably explained in a similar way. The form of the figure was probably not repulsive when first adopted, as marriage with a stepmother is a Semitic practice of great antiquity, and at one time was known to the Israelites (*Journ. of Phil.*, vol. ix. pp. 86, 94 ; *O. T. in J. Church*, p. 438). The precise meaning of the deed of Reuben is, however, obscure. The tribes of Bilhah were subordinate branches of the house of Joseph, and perhaps some combination against the unity of Israel and the hegemony of Joseph may be alluded to. That these historical allegories turn largely on marriage and fathership is not unworthy of note in connection with Hosea.

NOTE 11, p. 167.—That אהי in Hosea xiii. 10 either stands for or must be corrected into איה is the almost unanimous opinion of ancient and modern interpreters, from the LXX. downwards. The prophet, therefore, does not say, "I will be thy king," but "Where now is thy king?"

NOTE 12, p. 171.—Compare Nöldeke in Z.D.M.G., xv. 809, Wellhausen, *Text der Bücher Samuelis*, p. 30 *seq.* Beeliada of 1 Chron. xiv. 7 is the same as Eliada of 2 Sam. v. 16 or as Jehoiada.

NOTE 13, p. 171.—For the meaning of the word *mohar*, dowry, and the corresponding verb, see Hoffmann's *Bar Ali*, 5504, where the corresponding Syriac word denotes "what the son-in-law gives to the parents of the bride." In the same sense the Syrians say מכר מנה ברתה, he espoused his daughter, *lit.* bought her from him (Bernstein, *Chrest.*, p. 37). The Hebrew word *ērēs*, "betroth" (Exod. xxii. 15, Hosea ii. 16), properly means to barter or hire, so that *ērīs* in Palestinian Syriac is a farmer (Lagarde, *Semitica*, i. 50). In Exod. xxii. the primitive sense is still felt, as also in 2 Sam. iii. 14, where *ērēs* is construed as a verb of buying with the preposition ב. Note also the law of Exod. xxi. referring to a secondary wife, where the provision that the marriage is not dissolved at the close of seven years may be directed against the principle of temporary marriages as practised among the Arabs (*nikaḥu 'l mutʿati: Mowatta*, iii. 24; Bokhâri, Bûlâk ed., vi. 124; Ibn Khallikân, Slane's transl. iv. 36). For our present purpose it is important to note that this view of marriage explains how Hosea had to buy back his wife (iii. 2). This would constitute a new betrothal, and so Jehovah betroths Israel to Himself anew (ii. 19).

NOTE 14, p. 171.—The variation of the form of the metaphor, in which the spouse of Jehovah is now the land (Hosea i. 2), now the stock of the nation (ii. 2 *seq.*), belongs to the region of natural symbolism, in which land and nation form a natural unity. The nation, as it were, grows out of the land on which it is planted (Hosea ii. 23; Amos ix. 15); the living stock of the race has its roots in the land, and is figured as a tree (Isa. vi. 13; xvi. 8; Hosea xiv. 5, 6; Num. xxiv. 6, etc.). From this point of view the multiplication of the nation is just one aspect of the productivity of the land, and it is indifferent whether we say that the deity marries the land and so makes it productive, or marries the stock of the nation. In Semitic heathenism, in fact, ʻAshtoreth the spouse of Baal is not so much connected with the earth as with the stock of the earth's vegetation. Her symbol is the sacred tree, the Arabic ʻ*athary* is the palm tree planted on the *baʻl* land, and the same conception of the sacred tree was found in the popular worship of Israel (Hosea iv. 13). The heathenish element in these conceptions is the constant reference to natural productivity, the identification of the godhead with a natural fertilising principle. Hosea entirely strips off this conception. The heaven-watered land of Israel and its goodly growth are Jehovah's gift (Hos. ii. 8, 22, 23), not his offspring. But all analogy leads us to believe that the physical use of the symbolism of marriage was the earlier, and without this supposition the details of the allegory can hardly be explained. Even in Isaiah (iv. 2) the spring of Jehovah is analogous to the Arabic *baʻl* (Lagarde, *Semitica*, i. 8), and must be interpreted, not in a moral sense, but of the natural products of Jehovah's land.

NOTE 15, p. 172.—In Euting, *Punische Steine* (1871) p. 15, we find a woman's name אשׁתבעל, "the espoused of Baal." For Babylon and parallel examples from other nations see Herodot. i. 181 *seq.* See also Jos., *Ant.*, xviii. 3 § 4.

NOTE 16, p. 172.—On the Arabic *baʻl* see Wetzstein in *Z. D. M. G.*, xi. 489; Sprenger, *ibid.* xviii. 300 *seq.*; Lagarde, *Semitica*, i. p. 8. The glossaries to De Goeje's Belâdsori and to the *Bib. Geog. Ar.* supply examples. The term is also Talmudic. But for the illustration of the conception of the marriage of the deity with his land, it is more important to look at the term ʻ*athary* or ʻ*aththary*, for which see Lane *s. v.*; Prof. W. Wright in *Trans. Bib. Arch.*, vi. 439; Lagarde in *Nachr. K.G.W. Gött.* 1881, p. 396 *seq.*; and in particular the glossary to Belâdsori s. v. *baʻl*. The connection of ʻ*athary* with ʻAshtoreth seems to have been first observed by G. Hoffmann. The land of Baal, or the growth springing from such land, fertilised by the rains of Baal, bears a name derived from ʻAshtoreth, and this appears to be a clear enough indication of the ancient prevalence of the ideas touched on in the text.

NOTE 17, p. 179.—One or two corrections are necessary in the English version of Hosea iii. in order to bring out the full sense. In verse 1, read "Go and love once more a woman beloved of a paramour, and an adulteress." It is the same faithless wife to whom Hosea is still invited to show his affection. The עוֹד qualifies the main verb, not the לָךְ; comp. for this construction Cant. iv. 8. The grape cakes in the end of the verse (not "flagons of wine") are a feature of Dionysiac Baal-worship (*O. T. in J. Ch.*, p. 434). In ver. 3 the sense seems to be that for many days she must sit still, not finding a husband (Jer. iii. 1)—not merely as A. V., not marrying another, but not enjoying the rights of a lawful wife at all—while at the same time Hosea is "towards her," watching over and waiting for her (the phrase is as 2 Kings vi. 11 ; Jer. xv. 1 ; comp. Hosea i. 9).

NOTE 18, p. 181.—The true sense of this narrative was, I believe, first explained by Ewald. The older literal interpretation, in the form still maintained by Dr. Pusey, was offensive to every sound moral sense. The idea that a divine command could justify a marriage otherwise highly improper, and that the offensive circumstances magnify the obedience of the prophet, substitutes the nominalistic notion of God for that of Scripture. In addition to Ewald's exposition, the remarks of Wellhausen in Bleek, *Einl.*, p. 406 *seq.*, well deserve perusal. See also *Encyc. Brit.*, xii. 297, for an indication of the various interpretations that have been offered, and Nowack, *op. cit.*, p. xxxvi., for a catalogue of recent Continental literature on the question.

NOTE 19, p. 185.—A remark may here be offered on the difficult passage, vii. 5 *seq.* The prophet is describing the wickedness of the king, princes, and people as a hot fever, an eager and consuming passion, which burns up the leaders of the nation, and makes Ephraim like a cake not turned, and so spoiled by the fire. In v. 5 this figure is mingled with that of the heat of intoxication. "In the day of our king the princes were sick with the heat of wine, they stretched out their hands with scorners" or reckless despisers of right. The figure here is quite similar to Isa. xxviii. 1 *seq.* In the following verse we must plainly read קֵרְבוֹ, "For their inward parts are as a furnace," with the same *enallage numeri* as in מֹשֵׁךְ for מֹשְׁבוּ in ver. 5 ; or, as is suggested by Schorr (in Heilprin, ii. 145), we may read קרבם (many supposed enallages are probably corruptions of text, and מֹשֵׁךְ in old writing can as well be plural as singular). The following words לבם בארבם may be defended from Jer. ix. 8 [Heb. ix. 7] אֲרֻבּוֹ בְּקִרְבּוֹ יָשִׂים, to which the construction stands related as שׂים לב על דבר to שׂים דבר על לב. It will then be a circumstantial clause. The prophet is speaking of a wicked project of king and princes in which they join hands with impious men in the intoxication of their evil passions, and proceeds, "for their inward part is as a furnace, when their heart is in their guiles." [There is, however, a good deal that is attractive in Schorr's proposal to read בער בם, "their heart burns within them."] In what follows, Houbigant long ago thought of עֵשׁ (perfect) for יְשִׁי, but neither he, nor Wünsche, who follows him, saw that יְשִׁי is simply an obsolete orthography for the imperfect יָעֵשׁ, like לָמוֹ for לְעָמוֹ, Psalm, xxviii. 8, so that the passage is to be explained by Deut. xxix. 20 [*Heb.* 19]. Thus the verse goes on, "their anger אַפָּהֶם as Tgm. Syr.) smokes all the night, in the morning it flames forth like blazing fire."

NOTE 20, p. 189.—I adhere, though not without some hesitation, to the לִי of the Massoretic text of Hosea xiv. 8 and the traditional view that the prefixed אפרים indicates Ephraim as the speaker, as against the לֹי of the LXX., which has found favour with many recent writers. The elliptical indication of the change of speaker, though unique, is not incredible, for it causes no insuperable obscurity. But in this view I think it is quite necessary to regard the whole verse as spoken by Ephraim. The first אני, indeed, on this view, marks an emphasis which we would not express in English; but precisely in the pronominal expression or suppression of emphasis Hebrew and English differ greatly. The main difficulty in the LXX. reading seems to me to be much greater than any that attaches to the other view. The comparison of Jehovah to a fir-tree is not only without parallel, but in strange contrast to all prophetic thought. The evergreen tree is in Semitic symbolism the image of receptivity, of divinely nourished life, not of quickening power. Ephraim bears fruit to Jehovah, not Jehovah to Ephraim. Moreover, the "answering" in our verse corresponds to that of ii. 15.

Although the rendering "cypress" for "fir-tree" has of late become so common, I hesitate to adopt it for two reasons. (1) Ebusus, the modern Iviza, is according to the coins אי בשם = אי ברשים, and what this means appears from the Greek Πιτυοῦσαι (see Schröder, *Phön. Spr.*, p. 99). (2) The *Bĕrôsh* is according to Scripture the characteristic tree of Lebanon along with the cedar. Now it is true that the cypress occurs on

Lebanon in association with the cedar, but a species of *Abies* is equally characteristic of these mountains, at a lower altitude, and to judge from its present frequency must have always been a prominent feature in the forests.

NOTE 21, p. 190.—According to most recent critics, the prophecy in Zechariah ix.-xi. ought to come in here to close the prophetic record of the Northern Kingdom; but Stade, in his essay on "Deuterozecharia," in the *Zeitschrift für alttestamentliche Wissenschaft* (not yet completely published), and in the *Giessner Ludwigstag Programm*, 1880, following Vatke and a few others, has put this question in a new light, and assigns Zech. ix.-xiv. to a very late date. That Ewald's view of Zech. xii.-xiv. is untenable, and that these chapters at least are post-Exilic, has been my conviction for many years. Stade seems to have shown that the same thing holds good for ix.-xi.

LECTURE V.

NOTE 1, p. 191.—The literature of the book of Isaiah, with which we shall be mainly occupied in the next four Lectures, is enormous; for an account and estimate of the commentators it is enough to refer to Mr. Cheyne's tenth essay appended to his *Prophecies of Isaiah*, 1881. This exceedingly useful book gives the English reader so complete a view of the present state of the exegetical questions connected with Isaiah that a general reference to it may take the place of many notes on individual points which would otherwise have called for remark. The book is indispensable to every one who has not access to a full library of Continental exegesis, while, on the other hand, those who have themselves worked in the same field will best appreciate the exhaustive studies witnessed to on every page. In addition to other help which these Lectures derive from it, I ought here to acknowledge repeated obligations to the translation for felicitous phrases. On the other hand, it will appear by and by that I am in very many cases at variance with Mr. Cheyne as regards the order and date of the several prophecies, a point on which he seems to have been misled by the Assyriologists. Of modern foreign commentaries, those of Gesenius, Ewald, Hitzig, and Delitzsch may be chiefly recommended to the student. The learned commentary of Dr. Kay offers little assistance in the mainly historical objects contemplated in the present Lectures. For the historical exegesis of the Prophet, the labours of Ewald are the necessary starting-point of every student, though in part now antiquated by Assyrian researches. The student should not overlook the contributions of Lagarde in his *Prophetæ Chaldaicæ*, p. il., and in his *Semitica*, I.

NOTE 2, p. 193.—This is the natural inference from the fact that for a time Jeroboam retired from Shechem to Penuel beyond the Jordan (1 Kings xii. 25).

NOTE 3, p. 194.—For the chronology of Ahaz's predecessors we must take as our point of departure the campaign of Tiglath Pileser against Pekah and Rezin B.C. 734. At this time Ahaz was king of Judah. Further we know that Menahem was still alive B.C. 738 (*supra*, p. 150), while 2 Kings xv. 37 shows that Pekah was king and had begun to attack Judah before the death of Ahaz's father Jotham. Ahaz, therefore, must have come to the throne between 738 and 734; and, as it is hardly to be supposed that the Syro-Ephraitic war was prolonged more than one or two years before the Assyrians interfered, the date of Jotham's death may be taken approximately as B.C. 735, so that 734 would count as the first year of Ahaz. Now reckoning backwards we find that the Judæan chronology assigns to the reigns from Athaliah to Jotham inclusive, $6 + 40 + 29 + 52 + 16 = 143$. The northern chronology gives for the same period 102 years of the dynasty of Jehu, 10 of Menahem, and some 3 years more up to the expedition of Tiglath Pileser—in all about 115 years. The Assyrian monuments (*supra*, p. 150) show that this reckoning is right within a few years, but if anything is rather too long than too short, so that the Judæan chronology of the period is out by about 30 years. The discrepancy may be so far reduced by assuming that part of Jotham's reign fell in his father's lifetime, as we know that he acted as vizier while Uzziah was a leper (2 Kings xv. 5). But even this does not put all right, and is at best a mere hypothesis, which finds a very uncertain stay in the supposed Assyrian reference to Azariah or Uzziah B.C. 740. In reality it seems probable that the necessary shortening of Judæan reigns must be sought at more than one part of the period with which we are dealing, and that the error is distributed between the 69 years of Joash and Amaziah and the 68 of Uzziah and Jotham. For Amaziah, Uzziah's father, was contemporary with King Joash of Israel, and his defeat by that monarch seems to have fallen near the close of Amaziah's reign. At least it is a highly plausible conjecture of Wellhausen (Z. f. d. Theol., 1875, p. 634) that Amaziah's murder in a popular rising was due to the discontent produced by his absurd challenge to Joash and the misfortunes that followed. In this case the first year of Uzziah cannot have fallen anything like so late as the 15th year of Jeroboam II., to which the present Judæan chronology appears to assign it ($6 + 40 + 29 = 75 = 28 + 17 + 16 + 14$). But, on the other hand, the campaign of Joash against Jerusalem must have fallen in his later prosperous years. [The three campaigns of Joash against Syria must be at the end of his reign, since it was left to his son to improve his victories.] Thus we are led to conclude that Uzziah came to the throne about the same time with Jeroboam II. The rest of the error belongs to the prosperous days of Uzziah and Jotham, which may very well be reduced by 15 or 16 years, and yet leave time for the great internal changes alluded to in the early chapters of Isaiah.

The chronology from B.C. 734 downwards offers a much more complicated problem, for here we have to deal with a multitude of discordant data. According to the present chronology of the book of Kings, Manasseh's accession opens the last third of the second 480 years of Israel's history, and so falls 160 years before the return or 110 before the destruction of the temple in the 11th year of Zedekiah (B.C. 586). For the last part of these 110 years we have a sure guide in the chronology of the book of Jeremiah, in which the reckoning by years of kings of Judah is adopted, and checked by another reckoning by years of Jeremiah's ministry, and by a third by years of Nebuchadnezzar, whose dates are known by the Canon of Ptolemy (Syncellus, p. 388). Now, the book of Kings divides the 110 years as follows :—

Manasseh	55
Amon	2
Josiah	31
Jehoiakim	11
Zedekiah	11

The 11 years of Zedekiah are certain from Jer. xxxii. 1 ; 2 Kings xxv. 8. Further,

4 Jehoiakim = 23 Jeremiah (Jer. xxv. 1).
13 Josiah = 1 Jeremiah (Jer. xxv. 3).

Therefore 1 Jehoiakim = 20 Jeremiah = 32 Josiah; that is, Josiah reigned 31 years as stated in Kings. But now, if Jehoiakim really reigned 11 years, 21 Jehoiakim = 10 Zedekiah = 18 Nebuchadnezzar (Jer. xxxii. 1), and so 4 Jehoiakim = 1 Nebuchadnezzar, an equation actually given in the Hebrew text of Jer. xxv. 1, but rightly wanting in the Septuagint. For in reality 4 Jehoiakim is, according to Jer. xlvi. 2, the year of the battle of Carchemish, when Nabopolassar was still on the throne, but in his last year (Berosus ap. Jos., c. 'Apion. i. 19). Hence we must conclude that the first year of Nebuchadnezzar—that is, the first year which began in his reign—was really the fifth of Jehoiakim, and that the latter reigned not 11 but 12 years.[1] The 12 years of Jehoiakim seem also to be confirmed by Ezek. i. 1 seq., which Wellhausen uses to support the current chronology. According to Ezekiel, the fifth year of Jehoiachin's captivity (i. 2) is the 30th year of another unnamed era. It appears from xxiv. 1, where the ninth year is the ninth of Zedekiah, that Ezekiel counts as the first year of captivity the first year of Zedekiah—that is, the first year that began in exile. Thus the first year of the anonymous era will be the 18th of Josiah if Jehoiakim reigned 11 years, but the 19th if he reigned 12. As the 18th year of Josiah is that of his great reformation, it would appear that Ezekiel reckons from that event. His era is the era of reformed worship. But in that case it seems a mistake to assume, as Wellhausen does (*ut supra*, p. 623), that the 18th year would be the first of the reformed era. If the first year of captivity is the first that began in captivity, the first year of reformation must be that which began after the reformation, or the 19th of Josiah. It is indeed probable, since Ezekiel reckons by Babylonian months, and so begins the year in the spring, that his

---

[1] It will not do to get over this argument by supposing that the fourth year of Jehoiakim was reckoned from autumn, and that thus, if the battle of Carchemish fell in late autumn, part of that year on the Judæan reckoning might still coincide with Nebuchadnezzar's first year reckoned from the following Easter. For the ninth month of Jeremiah's calendar is a winter month, Jer. xxxvi. 9, 22, showing that he reckons by Babylonian years, beginning in spring. To suppose that Jeremiah habitually mixed up two calendars is altogether out of the question. Besides, it is highly improbable that the encounter of Necho and Nebuchadnezzar on the Euphrates took place in late autumn, as the river can be forded in summer.

first year begins with Josiah's reformed passover. But if so, the spring era was already in use in Josiah's time in priestly circles (comp. 2 Kings xxii. 3, LXX.), and so, in spite of 2 Kings xxiii. 23, which belongs to the editor, not to the sources, and therefore has no chronological authority, that passover must have fallen in the 19th year of the king. For it is to be noted that it is always in priestly circles or in connection with events of the temple that a reckoning by years of the king is found. The assignation of 11 years to Jehoiakim instead of 12 may be a mere oversight, the Hebrew chronicler supposing that Nebuchadnezzar commanded at Carchemish as king. It may, however, be systematic, as the number 11 is the key to the last 110 years of the kingdom (Manasseh, 55; Amon + Josiah = 33). In any case it would have the effect of disordering by one year any calculations as to earlier dates.

Let us now go back to the time of Hezekiah. Taking the reigns from Manasseh to Zedekiah inclusive at 110 years, and that of Hezekiah at 29, we get 1 Hezekiah = B.C. 724; but allowing one more year for Jehoiakim the date is 725. But for the reign of Hezekiah we have the following synchronisms:—

(1) 2 Kings xviii. 9; 4 Hezekiah = the year of the commencement of the siege of Samaria = B.C. 724-722 by the Assyrian monuments.

(2) 2 Kings xviii. 13; 14 Hezekiah = the year of Sennacherib's invasion = B.C. 701 by the monuments.

These dates are quite inconsistent with one another, and the question arises which we shall take as our guide. Let us begin with (1). It is plain that, according to the received chronology, this date is at least one year out; but if we introduce the correction already found requisite for Jehoiakim it is probably exact (*supra*, p. 403). In other words, if this date is original and accurate, the book of Kings is probably right—certainly not more than two years wrong — in assigning $29 + 55 + 2 = 86$ years to Hezekiah, Manasseh, and Amon taken together. There is therefore high probability that (1) is an independent and valuable datum, and that the sum of the years of Hezekiah, Manasseh, and Amon is also accurately known. And in general this result is borne out by the statement of Jer. xxvi. 18, that Micah, who predicts the fall of Samaria, prophesied under Hezekiah, a statement inconsistent with synchronism (2), which makes Ahaz be still on the throne when Samaria was captured.

When we pass now to (2) we are encountered by a very complex problem; for the statement that Sennacherib attacked Samaria in Hezekiah's fourteenth year is closely connected with the assignation to that prince of a total reign of 29 years. The connection is as follows:—At 2 Kings xx. 1 we learn that Hezekiah's sickness took place about the time of the Assyrian invasion, and at verse 6 we find that after this sickness Hezekiah lived 15 years. Now $29 = 14 + 15$, which at first sight seems to bear out (2). A closer examination, however, shows that there is something wrong. Merodach Baladan, whose embassy is placed after Hezekiah's sickness, was no longer king in B.C. 701, and the history contains internal evidence (ver. 6) that Hezekiah's sickness fell before the expedition of Sennacherib. One, therefore, of the numbers 14, 15, 29 is certainly false, and has been calculated from the other two. In that case we have three possibilities. (a) 14 and 29 are right and the 15 is wrong. If so, Manasseh came to the throne in 686, and not in 695 as the received chronology states. In this there is no intrinsic improbability, for to make that king begin the third section of the 480 years from Solomon's temple seems to be certainly a part of the artificial chronology. But in that case it is very singular that the artificial chronology should have found its end served by a date for Manasseh which is indeed false, but combined with 29 and with 2 Kings xviii. 9 gives a date almost, if not quite, exact for the fall of Samaria. Such a coincidence could only be the result of design, and the design is an incredible one, for it implies knowledge of the true Assyrian chronology and a determination to fix the fall of Samaria (a non-Judæan date) correctly, at the expense of the date 701, which directly affected Judah. (b) 14 is right and 29 is wrong, and derived from a combination of the 14 with 15. In this case a similar argument applies. The false 29, and the artificial (but independent) date for Manasseh combine to give the true date for the fall of Samaria. And neither (a) nor (b) gives the least clue to the reason of the discordant data (1) and (2). (c) There remains a third hypothesis, viz. that 15 and 29 are the dates from which the 14 has been derived, and this view, I think, enables us to give a tenable hypothesis for the whole system of numbers.

To develop it, I return to the assumptions already found probable, that the fourth year of Hezekiah coincides with the first year of the siege of Samaria, and that Hezekiah, Manasseh, and Amon together reigned 86 years. I do not assume that the years of each king are truly known, for the accession of Manasseh seems to be an artificial date. But it is highly probable that the true reign of each of these kings was once known. For in the time of Uzziah dates were not yet popularly reckoned by years of kings (Amos i. 1), while this reckoning appears under Hezekiah. This does not seem to be accident. The sundial of Ahaz, as well as his interest in star worship, point to the fact that astronomy (combined, of course, with superstition) was one of his foreign tastes, and it is impossible that he could have dealt with astronomy without feeling the need for a more exact calendar on the Assyrian model. It seems also that the reckoning by years of kings really went by the Assyrian Calendar from the time of Josiah downwards. If so, the time of Ahaz or Hezekiah is almost the only one at which it could have been introduced. I apprehend, then, that from the time of Ahaz downwards there was an exact record of years reigned, such as there is no trace of at an earlier date, except in concerns of the temple (the latter probably reckoned by the Phœnician Calendar; see Dillmann's essay in *Monatb. Berl. Ac.*, 27 Oct. 1881). Again, though the book of Kings in its present form dates from the Exile, or indeed, as regards the schematised chronology, from after the restoration, the main stock of it is certainly earlier even in its redaction, and so might well contain the true years for Hezekiah and his successors. If so, the schematiser of the chronology would not change more than was necessary, and if he lengthened Manasseh's reign would correspondingly shorten Hezekiah's. Thus it is intelligible that the fourth year of Hezekiah comes in at the true date, or, at least, within a year or two. We may assume, therefore, that the choice of the number 29 was not arbitrary. But now again it is the independent judgment of critics that, in its present form, 2 Kings xviii. 13-xx. 19, with the exception of the remarkable verses xviii. 14-16 (not found in the parallel passage in Isaiah), belongs to a pretty late date (Wellhausen, in Bleek, § 131), or at least was retouched after the fall of the kingdom. In that case it is easy to understand how the fourteenth year of Hezekiah may be an insertion or correction made on the presupposition that Hezekiah's sickness corresponded with the year of Sennacherib's invasion. It is not quite certain that this even requires us to hold the 15 to be part of the original tradition, for Jerome gives an interpretation of Isa. xxxviii. 10 which makes the sickness fall at the bisection of Hezekiah's days, and it is probable that this explanation was traditional.

The foregoing argument is undoubtedly of a very hypothetical character, but it seems to show that at all events it is possible to explain (2) from (1), but not *vice versa;* and this, combined with the argument from the date of Micah, and the fact that (1) gives a date for the siege of Samaria as accordant with the monuments as we can possibly expect, seems to entitle us to give it the preference. Hezekiah's first year is thus fixed for 725 (724). It does not follow that Manasseh's first year was 695, for that is a schematised date, and there is force in Wellhausen's argument that the strength of the prophetic party in Judah at the time of the reaction under Manasseh makes it probable that Hezekiah reigned some considerable time after the defeat of Sennacherib.

If the first year of Hezekiah was 725, Ahaz's reign is shortened to some ten years. But his 16 years will not fit with either (1) or (2); and, though the ages given to him and Hezekiah at their accessions rather demand a lengthening than a shortening of his reign, it is difficult to assign much value to these, when numbers so much more essential to be remembered are indubitably most corrupt.

NOTE 4, p. 202.—The nature of this divination by means of familiar spirits, as the wizard or *Ba'al Ob* pretended, is seen from the narrative of the witch of Endor. In reality, the performance was a form of ventriloquism, and the *Ob* or familiar spirit seemed to speak from beneath the ground or out of the stomach of the diviner. The Greeks called such diviners ἐγγαστρίμυθοι, ἐγγαστρῖται, στερνομάντεις, Εὐρυκλεῖς or Εὐρυκλεῖδαι, and their father Eurycles was said to prophesy truly " by the *dæmon* that was within him," Schol. on Arist., *Vespæ*, 984 (1019); Iamblichus cited by Lagarde, *Abhandlungen*, p. 189. In Syriac these subterranean spirits are called *Zakkûrê*, and the conception is well illustrated in the second Syriac romance of Julian the Apostate, published by Hoffmann (*Julianos der abtrünnige*, Leyden, 1880, p. 247), translated by Nöldeke, *Z. D. M. G.*, xxviii. 666 *seq*. See also Nöldeke's note.

NOTE 5, p. 211.—Compare *O. T. in J. Ch.*, Lect. iv. p. 109 *seq.*; Lect. vi. p. 159 *seq*.

NOTE 6, p. 217.—Mr. Cheyne, mainly following Kleinert in *Theol. Stud. u. Krit.*, 1877, p. 174 *seq.*, defends the authorship of Isa. xxi. 1-10 by Isaiah, arguing that the ideas and phraseology are Isaiah's, that the second part of the prophecy seems to have been written at a distance from Babylon, with the fate of which the prophet expresses a certain sympathy, and that the reference may therefore be to the siege of Babylon by Sargon in 709, to which date Mr. Cheyne assigns the expedition of Merodach Baladan to Hezekiah. I do not think that these arguments have all the weight claimed for them. There is good reason for holding that the embassy of Merodach Baladan fell in the reign of Sennacherib (*infra*, Lect. VIII.), and it seems impossible to question that the destruction of Babylon, spoken of in ver. 2 as effected by Elam and Media, must be the capture of the city by Cyrus. The prophecy, therefore, belongs to the Chaldæan cycle.

NOTE 7, p. 217.—It may here be convenient to give in connected form the chronological order of the chief prophecies, according to the results of the following Lectures. Of course, there is necessarily a large element of hypothesis in the details.

FIRST PERIOD.—From the year of Uzziah's death to the outbreak of the Syro-Ephraitic war. Chaps. ii.-v., and probably (as Ewald conjectures), ix. 8—x. 4, the latest part of this collection dating apparently from the first epoch of the war, *circa* 735 B.C.

SECOND PERIOD.—Prophecies at the time of Ahaz's resolution to do homage to Assyria, and during the ensuing campaign of Tiglath Pileser (734 B.C.). Chaps. vii. 1—ix. 7 (chap. vi., recording Isaiah's first vision, seems to have been published as a preface to this collection). Chap. xvii. 1-11 seems also to date from the same period.

THIRD PERIOD.—The time of Assyrian domination.
(*a*) Prophecies apparently occasioned by the impending fall of Samaria, 722-720 B.C., or restating the prophet's position after that event. Chap. xxviii. (before the fall of Samaria); chap. x. 5—xi. (after that event).

(*b*) At the time of the revolt of Ashdod, 711 B.C. Chap. xx.

(*c*) Under Sennacherib :—(1) During the first movements of revolt in Philistia, 704 B.C. Chap. xiv. 29-32. (2) Prophecies addressed to Judah while the plan of revolt was ripening, 704-701 B.C. Chaps. xxix.-xxxii. (3) Against the other nations in revolt against

Assyria. Chap. xxi. 11-17, Duma and the nomads of the Syro-Arabian desert; chap. xxiii., Tyre; chap. xviii., Ethiopia; chap. xix., Egypt, The reissue of the old prophecy against Moab, chaps. xv. xvi., may belong to the same period. (4) During the campaign in Judæa, 701 B.C. Chaps. i., xxii. (5) In the last stage of the campaign, after the fall of the party opposed to Isaiah. Chaps. xxxvii. 6, 7; xxxvii. 21-35; xxxiii. (6) Chaps. xiv. 24-27; xvii. 12-14, seem to belong to this period, but their exact position in it is uncertain.

Irregular as the arrangement of these prophecies seems to be, it is not without a principle. Chap. i. seems to have been prefixed as a general introduction to the whole book, for which its contents well fit it. With this exception, the part of the book that precedes the large Babylonian prophecy of chaps. xiii. xiv. is well arranged, apart at least from the transposition of ix. 8—x. 4. It contains two sections which Isaiah himself may have published very much as they stand, followed by a great and self-contained prophecy against Assyria, which might well be chosen as the close of a first attempt at a collected edition of some of Isaiah's principal pieces. Again, from chap. xiii. to chap. xxiii. we have a collection of prophecies which, with the exception of chap. xxii., are all directed against foreign nations. As it now stands, this collection contains also Babylonian prophecies, and so must be of Exilic or post-Exilic date. But the main part of it may well be of earlier collection, and chaps. xiii., xiv. 1-23, perhaps do not properly belong to it at all. Finally, from chap. xxix. onward we have prophecies of the time of Sennacherib addressed to Judah. That xxviii., which dates from an earlier period, is associated with these is explicable from the subject, and it is not unlikely that Isaiah himself may have published it as a preface to the later prophecies with which it is now associated. The chief breaches of chronological order are entirely due to the plan adopted of putting the prophecies against foreign nations together, as was also done in the collection of the oracles of Jeremiah. A study of the varying order of the several parts of the last-named book in the Hebrew and LXX. respectively is the best exercise by which one can convince oneself that the order in which a collection now stands cannot be held to afford any sure clue to the chronological order.

NOTE 8, p. 218.—See Cheyne on the passage, and, as regards the Cherubim, his article in *Encyc. Brit.*, s.v., where references to the relevant literature are collected. If the Seraphim are a personification of the lightning flash they have some analogy to the Phœnician רשף (*C. I. S.*, p. 38).

NOTE 9, p. 224.—On the idea of holiness a great deal has been written. I need only refer to two of the most recent discussions. Duhm (*Theologie der Propheten*, p. 169 *seq.*) lays particular emphasis on the relation of the idea to the worship of God. The idea is *æsthetic;* Jehovah's majesty presents itself as holiness to the worshipper in the act of worship. It would be more correct to say that the idea of consecration to God is a religious or æsthetic and not strictly an ethical idea; it becomes ethical in the prophets because religion becomes ethical. In the elaborate article on the notion of holiness in the Old Testament in Baudissin's *Studien*, part ii. (1878), there is a useful collection of material. The most important thing in it, as Nöldeke observes in his review of the book (*Lit. Centralbl.*, 1879, No. 12), is the part devoted to show that the notion of holiness has not the primary sense of purity. It may be now held as agreed among scholars that the Arabic words on which this idea was based are taken from the Greek κάδος. That the word is old Arabic in the sense of holy seems clear from Ḳuds as the name of two mountains in Arabia (Yâḳût iv. 38, *seq.*; see also Nöldeke, *l. c.*); but its use in the Korân is influenced by Judaism; the word seems almost to have disappeared from the ordinary Arabic vocabulary, and the explanation of the commentators on Sur. ii. 28 that *ḳadasa fi 'l arḍ*, like *sabaḥa fi 'l arḍ*, means "to go far off" (Ibn Sa'ûd, Egn. ed., i. 59), does not go for much. So Nöldeke judges that the arguments from Arabic for the sense of "depart" require confirmation. The Aramaic *Ḳdâshâ*, an earring, literally a "holy thing," that is, no doubt, an amulet (comp. the *lĕḥâshîm* or amulets as articles of finery, Isa. iii. 20), is noteworthy. The remarks on the idea of holiness in the text of this Lecture are exclusively based on the earlier parts of the Old Testament down to the time of Isaiah.

LECTURE VI.

NOTE 1, p. 236.—In viii. 1 for *roll* read *tablet*. That a tablet inscribed in large letters to catch the eye of every one is meant is the plausible explanation of Ewald, *Propheten*, i. 8. A facsimile of the Siloam inscription, with commentary, etc., will appear in the forthcoming part of the *Oriental series* of the Palæographical Society.

NOTE 2, p. 239.—The explanation of ix. 14 given in the following verse is regarded as a later and inaccurate gloss by most recent critics.

NOTE 3, p. 246.—On this topic, and in general on Isaiah's theocratic ideal, see Wellhausen, *Geschichte*, i. 431 *seq*.

NOTE 4, p. 248.—The צמח (A. V. *Branch*) of Isa. iv. 2 is not, as in Jer. xxiii. 5, xxxiii. 15, a sprout from the stock of David, but, more generally, that which Jehovah causes to spring forth, viz. from the land, as appears from the parallel "the fruit of the land." This, I think, excludes all reference to the king of chap. xi., such as is still thought of by Lagarde, *Semitica*, i. 8 *seq.*, in spite of his apt illustration from Semitic heathenism, where Baal's land is, like the land of Canaan, such as derives fertility from the rains of heaven, not from irrigation (comp. Hosea ii. 21). The word צמח is best rendered, I think, by "spring" in the old English sense of young, fresh growth (as in Shakspeare's poems). This enables us to keep up the connection with the cognate verb, as in Zech. vi. 12 ("the man whose name is Spring and from under him it shall spring up," that is, wherever he treads fresh life and growth follow), as well as to feel the identity of the word in such a passage as Psalm lxv. 10, "Thou blessest the springing thereof."

NOTE 5, p. 250.—In justification of the Authorised Version in this rendering see Lagarde, *Semitica*, i. 13.

NOTE 6, p, 251.—Compare Ewald, *Geschichte*, iii. 664 ; and on 2 Kings xvi. 18, to which allusion is made a few lines down the page, see *ibid.*, p. 667.

NOTE 7, p. 267.—This verse, certainly mistranslated in the Authorised Version, may run, " In that day shall his strong cities be like the deserted places of forest and hill-top, which were left desert before the children of Israel." Possibly, however, we should correct by the aid of the Septuagint (Lagarde, *Semitica*, i. 31) "the deserted places of the Hivite and the Amorite."

NOTE 8, p. 267.—Flesh is never a common article of food with the peasantry of Syria. Bread and other cereal preparations with milk, generally eaten sour, and *dibs*, or grape honey, are the ordinary diet, as Seetzen, for example, found in the Hauran (*Reisen*, i. 48; comp. Prov. xxvii. 27; Burckhardt, *Travels in Syria*, 1822, p. 293). Where there is much cultivation of cereals the supply of milk is of course correspondingly limited. According to Isaiah vii. 22, the whole land of Judah shall become free pasture ground, with the result that the kine and ewes shall yield abundance of milk, and the man who has a young cow and two sheep shall have abundance of milk for his family, but no bread or wine. As the vineyards are the first thing to be destroyed, requiring as they do the most sedulous cultivation, the honey mentioned by Isaiah is doubtless natural honey, such as John the Baptist found in the desert, or Jonathan in the woods. As the wild bee frequents desert places, swarming in the woods or in the rocky sides of deep watercourses, the abundance of honey is another indication of the desolation of the land. At vii. 15 the true rendering is that the child whose infancy falls at the time of the destruction of Damascus shall eat butter and honey when he is of age to distinguish the good from the bad. That is, when his infancy begins to pass into rational childhood the land shall be already reduced to the state of depopulation described in verses 21 *seq*.

NOTE 9, p. 272.—The view that the sign given by Isaiah refers in its original sense to the birth of our Lord is still upheld by Dr. Kay, and some remarks on the subject, with reference to his argument, may not be out of place. The first point is the meaning of the word עַלְמָה, '*almah*, rendered παρθένος by the oldest version, and "virgin" in the A. V. The word is not a very common one, though rather commoner than the masculine '*elem*, a young man or lad, of which it is the regular feminine. This fact is alone sufficient to show that virginity is not the radical idea, and a comparison with the Arabic and Aramaic leaves no doubt that both in the masculine and the feminine the meaning is a young person of marriageable age. There is in fact another and common word for a virgin (*bethûlah*). Even the latter word can be used of a young bride (Joel i. 8), and when the idea of virginity is to be made prominent it is not out of place to express it more directly (Gen. xxiv. 16; Judges xxi. 12). But is it then at least the case that usage limits the word '*almah* to a virgin? The word only occurs six times apart from our passage; twice it is used of a grown-up girl still unmarried (Gen. xxiv. 43; Exod. ii. 8), twice it seems to be used of the slave girls of Solomon's harem (Cant. i. 3 ; vi. 8). In Prov. xxx. 19 Dr. Kay feels the force of the argument against his view so much that he backs up his appeal to Hengstenberg by the suggestion that the passage is allegorical ; Ps. lxviii. 25 may be fairly taken with the two passages first quoted. On the whole the evidence does not bear out the supposition that virginity is an essential in the notion ; though a marriageable girl naturally stands distinguished from a married woman, and thus Isaiah probably means a young woman who has not yet been a mother. But this suits the acceptation of the passage which we have adopted. The prophet's point is that before a woman presently to be married can have a child emerging from babyhood certain things will occur. That this is at all events the correct determination of the date which he has in view (viz. the following year) is absolutely clear. For the same date is given again in the parallel prophecy viii. 3, 4, by a similar and quite unambiguous sign.

The objection to all this is mainly that the sign offered by Jehovah must be of a grander and miraculous character. But what is the nature of a prophetic "sign"? Another "sign" given by Isaiah is his walking naked and barefoot for three years (xx. 3) ; he and his children are living signs to Israel (viii. 18). So, too, in Ezek. iv. 3 ; xii. 6, 11 ; xxiv. 24, 27, the signs are mere symbolic actions or God-given pledges for the fulfilment of His word. They are, as it were, seals set to prophecy, by which its truth can be put to the test in the future. What Dr. Kay further urges for the Messianic references from combination with Isa. ix. 7, Micah v. 3, is plainly not demonstrative, for the combination is not indicated in the Bible itself.

NOTE 10, p. 273.—See Ewald on the passage, and Lagarde, *Semitica*, i. 31 *seq.*, where the identity of Na'âman with Adonis is ably maintained. Note further that the river now called the Nahr Na'mân is the ancient Belus, which seems to confirm the view that Na'mân is a divine name.

NOTE 11, p. 276.—I here follow what I may call the certain correction made independently by Selwyn and Studer.

LECTURE VII.

NOTE 1, p. 279.—At this point the Assyrian records begin to be of the highest service for the history of Israel and of

Isaiah's work. I shall not refer to them at each point, but it will be convenient to indicate where English translations of them may be found. The *Annals* of Sargon, translated by M. Oppert, are given in *Rec. of the Past*, vol. vii., the inscription on his palace at Khorsabad, *ibid.*, vol. ix., and other inscriptions of the same reign in vol. xi. The Koyunjik cylinder, chiefly relied upon by those who refer several prophecies of Isaiah to a supposed invasion and siege of Jerusalem by Sargon, is translated by George Smith, *Eponym Canon*, p. 129 (*Assyrian Discoveries*, p. 289). It is, unhappily, in a very fragmentary condition. For the whole question of the relations of Judah with Sargon, as reflected in the prophecies of Isaiah, it is enough to refer to Mr. Cheyne's *Prophecies of Isaiah*, under chaps. i., x. xx., but especially in his introduction to chaps. xxxvi.-xxxix., where the literature of the subject is fully cited. It will be seen in the text of this Lecture that I am unable to follow the conclusion which has recommended itself to Mr. Cheyne on the basis of suggestions by Dr. Hincks, Prof. Sayce, and other Assyriologists. Mr. Cheyne's commentary should be taken along with his article ISAIAH, in the *Encyc. Brit.*, ninth ed., vol. xiii. In regard to the bearing of the narrative of Kings on this question, the most satisfactory discussion is that of Wellhausen in his edition of Bleek's *Einleitung* (1878), p. 254 *seq.*, and again in *Encyc. Brit.*, vol. xiii. p. 414.

NOTE 2, p. 280.—Rafia is called Râfeh by Mr. Chester (*Palestine Survey ; Special Papers*, p. 111), and Bîr Refâ in Baedeker's *Handbook to Palestine*, Route 11. The true Arabic name, however, is Rafaḥ (Yâḳût, ii. 796 ; Iṣṭakhry and Moḳaddasy *sæpius*; Makrîzy, *Ḥiṭaṭ wa-Athâr*, i. 189). Yâḳût places it eighteen miles from Gaza, at the termination of the sandy desert, with a great sycamore grove three miles on the Gaza side of it. It was, and still is, regarded as the frontier between Egypt and Syria (Iṣṭakhry, p. 45). The latest notice of the place is in the Archduke Ludwig Salvator's *Caravan Route* (Eng. Tr. 1881, p. 54), with a view of the columns that mark the site of an ancient temple.

NOTE 3, p. 287.—The difficulties of interpretation that encompass the book of Micah, and the very corrupt state of some parts of the text, are well known, and have received special attention from various critics since the publication of the *Commentarius in Vaticinium Michæ* of Taco Roorda (1869). Notwithstanding the discussion by Stade in his *Zeitschrift* for 1881, I still think that chaps. i.-v. form a single well-connected book. The question of chaps. vi.-vii. does not belong to the subject of the present Lecture. At the same time, it will be seen in Note 5 that the text of Micah i.-v. has suffered from interpolation, and it is an open question whether, besides the passages there spoken of, ii. 12, 13 does not break the connection and at least require to be transposed. There is, however, nothing in the thought of these verses which is not perfectly congruous with chap. v., and Ewald's suggestion that they are inserted as a specimen of false prophecy is therefore untenable. The false prophets of Micah's time flattered the rulers and supported the *status quo*, while the verses in question give precisely Micah's idea of a rejuvenescence of the mass of the nation under Jehovah and Jehovah's king—a popular, not an aristocratic conception.

NOTE 4, p. 289.—In Micah ii. 8, and similarly in Isa. xxx. 33, the punctuation אֶתְמוּל is not meant to be a variation of אֶתְמוֹל, but expresses a different exegetical tradition, in which the phrase is explained from מוּל, "over against." In Isaiah both traditions (and so both pronunciations) are ancient, but that with *ô* probably more ancient (LXX., Aq., Sym., Theod., Syr.). The conflate rendering of the Targum expresses both. In Micah the weight of tradition is for *û* (Aq., Hieron., Tgm., as against Sym. and perhaps LXX.; Syr. thinking of the root מוּכ). The variation can be traced down into the time of the pointed text; see *Cod. Petrop.*, edited by Strack, where in each place a later hand has put *ô* for *û*. The passage, then, is one in which there was an early divergence of tradition, and in which therefore we are thrown back on the consonantal text, which probably had originally no ו. But the opposition of vers. 7, 8 is that of sharp contrast, which suggests that we should begin with a pronoun וְאַתֶּם. Combining this conjecture with Roorda's שַׁלְמֹה for שַׂלְמָה, the latter of which gives no good sense, and omitting one of the four consecutive *mems* (יָקִם for יְקוֹמֵם) or reading יְקוֹמֵם for יְתְקוֹמֵם (which, though less likely, is certainly possible, Ols. § 68, h), we get the sense, "But ye are to My people as a foe rising up against one that is at peace with him; ye strip off the cloak from them that pass by securely, averse from [not thinking of] war." For אֶדֶר we probably should read אַדֶּרֶת, the final

ת having disappeared in that following, and the garment meant is probably the hairy mantle which, as worn by the prophets, was doubtless the garment of the simpler classes. Of interpretations retaining the present text the most ingenious is certainly that of Abulwalîd (col. 764), who anticipates Roorda in taking אֲתְמוּל as "against." The almost total neglect of this greatest of mediæval Hebraists by expositors subsequent to Gesenius is much to be deplored.

NOTE 5, p. 290.—The words ובאת עד־בבל are rejected as a gloss by Nöldeke in Schenkel's *Bibel-Lexikon*, iv. 214 (1872), and by Kuenen, *Theol. Tijdsch.*, 1872, p. 291. Kuenen forcibly points out that a precisely similar gloss has been introduced by the LXX. in ver. 8. That the words are no part of the original context appears, I think, very clearly from the sense. To say that the daughter of Zion shall be delivered in Babylon from the hand of all her enemies gives no good sense. We can speak of deliverance from captivity, but not of deliverance in it. On the other hand, to say that the population of Zion shall be delivered in the field, *i.e.* in the open country, agrees, as is shown in the text of the Lecture, with the context and the general tenor of Micah's thought. The words "And thou shalt come unto Babylon" cannot, however, be the only interpolation in chap. iv., for the impossibility of reconciling vers. 11-13 with ver. 10 is plain. According to ver. 10 Zion shall be captured by the enemy, and this agrees with iii. 12. But in the following verses the besieging hosts of many nations are broken beneath the walls of Jerusalem. The force of this difficulty has been recognised by most recent writers on the question, by Oort (*Theol. Tijdsch.*, 1872, p. 507); Kuenen (*ibid.*, 1872, p. 62—in the later paper already cited he endeavours to meet the difficulty); Wellhausen (Bleek's *Einl.*, 4th ed., p. 426); Stade (*Z. f. AT. W.*, 1881, p. 167); and Steiner (*ad l.*). The solutions proposed are various, but the simplest seems to be that of Oort, who treats vers. 11-13 as an interpolation. In accepting Oort's view thus far, I by no means agree with his general treatment of the passage, which, as Kuenen has remarked (*l. c.*), has no necessary connection with the genuineness of the verses in question. Stade, who separates out the whole pericope, iv. 11-v. 4 (*Heb.*, v. 3) as a separate prophecy, seems to me to miss the point of the prophet's thought.

NOTE 6, p. 291.—The sinfulness of these things is elsewhere

emphasised by the prophets, inasmuch as they are earthly things which come between man and Jehovah (Isa. ii.). But the thought of Micah goes further than this. Hosea had taught that Judah shall not be delivered by horses and horsemen, but also not by weapons of human war (i. 7 ; ii. 18). Micah, though he looks forward to a reign of peace among the nations, thinks of Judah as delivered by the sword (v. 6). His objection to fortresses and horses is not an objection to war. Nor is it a mere objection to the misuse of these things. They are themselves out of place in restored Israel. This is parallel to Deut. xvii. 16, where the multiplication of horses is spoken of as a fault in the king. Horses and chariots were in fact in ancient times the counterpart of the standing armies and artillery of which free peoples in modern times have been naturally jealous as dangerous to liberty. And the maintenance of the royal establishment of horses was accompanied by oppressive exactions, as we see from 1 Kings xviii. 5, and the mention of the first grass crop as the "king's mowings" in Amos vii. 7.

NOTE 7, p. 297.—A few words may here be added on the special points in the prophecies assigned by Mr. Cheyne to the invasion of Sargon, which he lays stress on as hardly consistent with a reference to the wars of 701. On chap. i. the argument that there are no points of contact between this prophecy and those composed with reference to Sennacherib's invasion is not valid if we distinguish in that campaign two periods, one before Hezekiah's submission, and another after the shameless breach of faith of which Sennacherib was guilty, in demanding the surrender of the fortress of Zion, after he had come to terms with Hezekiah. That the sketch of the moral and religious condition of Judah will not apply to Hezekiah's time is also an assumption based on the view that the reforms of that king preceded the repulse of Sennacherib, which is, at all events, very doubtful (see Lect. VIII.). In chap. xxii. " the severe tone of the prophecy" is again to be explained by referring it to the siege in the first part of the campaign, when Hezekiah made submission to Sennacherib. In chaps. xxix.-xxxii. Mr. Cheyne himself does not seem to reject the reference to Sennacherib, in spite of his remark at p. 155, that they "were evidently delivered at various stages of the Assyrian intervention under Sargon." See his notes on xxx. 29, 33.

NOTE 8, p. 298.—Several points of contact between Isa. x. xi.

and Isa. xxviii. (x. 12 : xxviii. 21 ; x. 23 : xxviii. 22 ; x. 26 : xxviii. 15, 18) have been pointed out by Ewald and Cheyne, and to these may be added x. 20 : xxviii. 15 ; xi. 2 : xxviii. 6. In their whole conception, indeed, the two chapters are most closely allied, the essential points of difference being (*a*) that in the one Samaria has fallen, in the other is only about to fall ; (*b*) that chap. xxviii. is mainly addressed to the godless rulers, while chaps. x. xi., in which very little reference is made to the sin of Judah, seem rather to be a word of comfort to the true remnant —primarily we may suppose to Isaiah's own circle. The thought that Judah and Assyria cannot long remain on terms appears already in xxviii. 20, and, taken with the lesson of the fall of Samaria, would easily lead to the thought of the decisive contest of chap. x., without the intervention of any actual war between Judah and Israel. Further, that chap. xi. was written at a considerably earlier date than the prophecies of the reign of Sennacherib seems probable from the prominence given in the former chapter to the new Davidic kingship, in that contrast to the old monarchy which disappears in later prophecies. The chief reason why many commentators feel themselves obliged to refer x. xi. to a time of actual war is the extraordinary vividness and detail of the description of the approach of the Assyrian through the pass of Michmash. We know, however, that Sennacherib's advance was not made by this road, which disposes at all events of the still not quite abandoned theory of a *vaticinium ex eventu*. Moreover, if Isaiah wrote this prophecy, as has also been supposed by some, when the Assyrian was already close at hand, he could not have chosen this route for his description, for it must have been plain from the beginning of the campaign that Sennacherib's plan was to advance by the sea-coast. In any case, therefore, the picture is an ideal one, and Isaiah gives it the most impressive form possible by depicting an advance from the North by way of Scopus. His thought is that from the conquered land of Samaria the Assyrian will move on against Jerusalem ; his progress is southwards in steady course, and this determines the details.

NOTE 9, p. 307.—The first and last of the four names bestowed on the child of Isa. ix. 6 certainly do not imply anything that involves a transcendental personality. The king who is equipped as is described in chap. xi. may well be called "Wonderful Counsellor" (these words are to be united in a single idea as in פרא אדם, Gen. xvi. 12), and "Prince of Peace." The interpretation of the third name is disputed. It is sometimes taken to mean "Father of booty," but at all events the phrase "everlasting mountains" (Hab. iii. 6) shows that it has not the transcendental idea of eternity. The words in Hebrew which we render by eternity mean only a duration the commencement or completion of which lies in the mist of extreme remoteness, or is not contemplated by the speaker. "God the mighty one," construed as an apposition, is a quite unique name, such appositional forms not occurring in pure Hebrew names of persons (Olshausen, *Sprachlehrbuch*, p. 613). If we rendered it "God is the mighty one," it would be parallel to such names as Elnaam, "God is graciousness;" Eliphelet or Elphelet, "God is deliverance;" Joah, "Jehovah is a brother." But, according to Hebrew idiom, a being in whom is God's name is one through which God manifests Himself to men, and so the prophet probably means this wondrous name to describe the manifestation of Jehovah's kingship through His human representative. It is through the New Testament that we learn that a complete and adequate manifestation of God to man can only be made through a God-man.

NOTE 10, p. 309.—The relation of these two passages has been so often and fully discussed that it is needless to go into it again. It seems to be quite clearly made out that Micah does not quote from Isaiah, but also there are no indications in the context that he quotes from any one at all, while the idea that the passage stands in Isaiah as the text for the remarks that follow is somewhat arbitrary and hardly borne out by the context. The opening words at Isa. ii. 2 show that the passage as it stands in Isaiah is divorced from its original connection, and it has just enough of apparent bearing on ii. 5 to make it possible that a copyist inserted it at that place.

LECTURE VIII.

NOTE 1, p. 317.—The Assyrian inscriptions bearing on this revolt are given in G. Smith's posthumous *History of Sennacherib*, 1878; *Eponym Canon*, p. 131. See also Alexander Polyhistor, *ap.* Euseb., *Chron.*, ed. Schoene, vol. i. p. 27; G. Syncellus (Bonn ed.), vol. i. p. 391. The Assyrians ruled Babylon by means of a vassal king, and so the two years "without a king" in the

Canon given by Syncellus are those of Merodach Baladan's revolt. His embassy to Judah can hardly fall later than 704.

NOTE 2, p. 319.—The title prefixed to this prophecy (xiv. 28) refers it to the year of Ahaz's death. In that case Ahaz must be the fallen oppressor of the Philistines, and Hezekiah the new and more terrible conqueror, and this view is supported by those who accept the title (*e.g.*, Delitzsch, *ad loc.*), by reference to the victories of Hezekiah over the Philistines, 2 Kings xviii. 8. But in ver. 31 the destroying force is unquestionably the Assyrian, as Delitzsch himself admits, and thus the title breaks the unity of the oracle. If Hezekiah continued a dominion over the Philistines commenced in the reign of his father, both must have done so as agents of the Assyrian. There is no trace of this, and in any case such a supremacy could hardly have afforded the motive for our prophecy. It is possible that Hezekiah's operations in Philistia were connected with the rising against Sennacherib, when he seems to have been accepted as head of the Philistine revolt, and held Padi the Assyrian vassal-king of Ekron as a captive. Or more probably the reference in Kings is to operations undertaken after the defeat of Sennacherib to recover the districts which, as we learn from the monuments, Sennacherib in the first prosperous part of his expedition detached from Judah and handed over to the sovereigns of Ashdod, Ekron, and Gaza. Before the war with Sennacherib, at all events, it was with Assyria, not with Hezekiah, that the Philistines had to reckon, and it is to Assyria that the prophecy clearly points. The titles of prophecies have by no means the same authority as the text; they are often demonstrably incorrect and mere late conjectures. In the present case the conjecture may have been founded on the Rabbinical exegesis expressed, as Bochart has noticed, in the Targum, which makes the root of the serpent (Nahash) mean the stock of Jesse, according to the well-known identification of Jesse with the Nahash of 2 Sam. xvii. 25. If the prophecy refers to the death of an Assyrian monarch, it is Sargon, not Shalmaneser, who must naturally be thought of.

NOTE 3, p. 322.—The Altaku of the monuments (in the neighbourhood of Tamna or Timnath) is generally and plausibly identified with the Eltekeh of Josh. xix. 44; xxi. 23, of which nothing further is known, except that it lay like Timnath in Danite territory.

NOTE 4, p. 335.—It was, I think, a saying of Napoleon, that under a good government the Delta encroaches on the desert, while under a bad government the desert encroaches on the Delta. Not only are the public works, the great canals, apt to fall into ruin under a bad government, but the peasantry, having no security for the enjoyment of the fruit of their labour, will not do their part. Thus every traveller by the overland route to India must have been struck with the small amount of cultivation along the banks of the great freshwater canal. The water was there, provided at the cost of many thousand lives, but there was not such confidence in the equity of Ismail Pasha as to encourage cultivators to risk their capital in improvements which might be rendered worthless in a moment by a rise in the water-rate or by the water being cut off. The real cure for the miseries of Egypt is still a government in which the people can have sufficient confidence to venture to help themselves, and to utilise the vast number of small hoards now lying buried in the earth or in holes in the walls of houses. It is not free institutions, but a just and firm administration that is beneficial to the East.

NOTE 5, p. 336.—On the discussion as to the authorship of Isa. xix. 16-25 see Cheyne's introduction to the chapter; Kuenen, *Onderzoek*, ii. 74. The passage may have been retouched, and at least the variants on the name of the city in ver. 18 (city of destruction, city of the sun, city of righteousness) may have something to do with the Onias temple at Leontopolis; but that an interpolation in favour of this sanctuary could have entered the Hebrew text, as Hitzig and Geiger suppose, is hardly possible. And the allusion to the consecrated maççeba, ver. 19, is quite inconsistent with a date subsequent to the reformation of Josiah and the acceptance of the Deuteronomic law of worship.

NOTE 6, p. 345.—The variety of opinion as to the history of the relations of Assyria to Judah, to which reference has been made in the notes on last Lecture, is nowhere more remarkable than in the accounts given by different historians and expositors of Sennacherib's campaign in Judah. The opinion which distinguishes two invasions under Sargon and Sennacherib respectively has been already discussed and rejected. On the other hand, the theory of Professor Rawlinson that Sennacherib was twice in Judæa (B.C. 701, and again B.C. 699), that Hezekiah's surrender and tribute belong to the first occasion and the great deliverance to the second (*Ancient Monarchies*, ii. 165), has no basis whatever except pure conjecture. Sennacherib seems to have been in quite a different quarter in the latter year (Smith, *History of Sennacherib*, p. 87). It is therefore necessary to place both the surrender and the deliverance of Jerusalem, as recorded in Kings, in the campaign of 701. The first part of the campaign, in which the Assyrians were victorious, is described in Kings exactly as on the monuments (see *Encyc. Brit.*, xiii. 414). That Sennacherib does not relate the calamity which subsequently befell his host and compelled him to retire is quite what we should expect from the exclusively boastful style of the Assyrian monuments, and his record is manifestly imperfect, for it does not tell how Sennacherib settled matters with Tirhakah or mention the conclusion of peace with him. Further, the immediate outbreak of a fresh rebellion in Babylon and the fact that Sennacherib did not again appear to make war on Egypt are clear proofs that his retreat was inglorious, in spite of the spoil he carried home from Judah. But it is arbitrary in Schrader and Duncker to suppose that the battle of Eltekeh was really the last event in the campaign, and was a virtual defeat. That battle was merely due to an attempt to raise the siege of Ekron, and the operations farther south at Libnah and Lachish must have occurred subsequently. It is plain, too, from the Egyptian tradition given in Herodotus that the Egyptians had a knowledge of the campaign and defeat of the Assyrians, but did not ascribe it to their own prowess. It is very probable that the mice which figure in the legend in Herodotus are a symbol of pestilence (Hitzig, *Gesch. d. V. Israel*, p. 125, 222; *Urgeschichte der Philistäer*, p. 201; Wellhausen on 1 Sam. vi. 4), in which case the Egyptian mythus points to the true account as given in the Bible.

NOTE 7, p. 345.—The first chapter of Isaiah must have been written at this time. It cannot well belong to the Syro-Ephraitic war, which, when the theory of invasion under Sargon is rejected, is the only other date that comes into consideration; for then the distress had not reached such a pitch as Isaiah describes. The points of contact with the contemporary chap. xxii. are manifest. The wicked rulers of chap. i. are the associates of Shebna in chap. xxii. Even the many sacrifices of i. 11 *seq*. reappear at xxii. 13, for at that time feast and sacrifice were identical; and the comparison of the two texts throws an instructive light on the popular worship as it displayed itself among Isaiah's opponents. The reading which I have adopted in i. 7 is that of Ewald, Lagarde, Cheyne, and others.

NOTE 8, p. 350.—Rabshakeh's attempt to gain the populace to his side was perhaps suggested by the course of the previous siege when, as Sennacherib relates, the garrison of Jerusalem "inclined to submission" (Smith, *Sennacherib*, p. 63; Duncker, ii. 365).

NOTE 9, p. 351.—I here follow the brilliant correction of Wellhausen (Bleek's *Einleitung*, p. 257), which has found general acceptance.

NOTE 10, p. 352.—I cannot see that the Bible narrative, as Mr. Cheyne supposes, implies that the calamity attacked a part of Sennacherib's army lying before Jerusalem. It seems to have been the main body of the host that suffered, presumably on the borders of Egypt, as we learn from the monuments that Sennacherib took Lachish, from the siege of which he sent his last summons to Hezekiah.

NOTE 11, p. 363.—The idea of the one sanctuary, the place chosen by Jehovah out of all the tribes of Israel to put His name there, and at which alone Israel's homage can be acceptably offered, is formulated in the book of Deuteronomy—especially in chap. xii.—and is presupposed in the Priestly Legislation. In the latter it appears as a fixed idea, traditionally established, and no longer requiring explanation or justification. Indeed, it is hardly too much to say that the fundamental idea of the Priestly Legislation is not the unity of the sanctuary but the prerogative of the Aaronic priesthood and ritual. The sanctuary at which these are found is the only true sanctuary, because only at it can Jehovah be approached through the mediators, and under the ceremonial forms, apart from which He is either altogether inaccessible, or manifests Himself only in wrath. Of this point of view there is absolutely no trace in the history before the Exile; it appears exclusively in the priestly parts of the Hexateuch and in the Chronicles, and this is one of the most notable general facts which combine with a multitude of special arguments to establish the post-Exile date of the Priestly Legislation. For nothing is historically more certain than that the doctrine of the exclusive privilege of the priesthood of Aaron, in the sense of the Priestly Legislation, did not yet exist at the time when Josiah brought up the priests of the high places to Jerusalem and nourished them on the unleavened bread of the sanctuary along with their "brethren" of the house of Zadok, or even at the time of Ezekiel, to whom the privilege of the Zadokites is still a law for the future, not a fixed religious principle of the past. In the book of Deuteronomy, on the other hand, the unity of the sanctuary stands by itself, and rests on argument derived from the prophets of the eighth century. To the Deuteronomist, as to the prophets, it appears as an essential of true religion to maintain the separation between the worship of Israel and the worship of the Canaanite holy places. Jehovah is to be worshipped in a single sanctuary of His own choosing, in order that His service may be kept free from heathenish elements. In this argument the question of the hierarchy has no place: the law of Deuteronomy is a solution of the problem, which became practical after the victory of Isaiah, how the national worship can be reorganised so as to answer the conditions of sacrificial *cultus*, while yet excluding all danger of Canaanite influence. The lines in which the solution is sought are not, however, explicitly suggested either by Isaiah or Micah, neither of whom draws an express contrast between the legitimate altar and the provincial holy places. Between the prophetic condemnation of the popular worship and the Deuteronomic plan of worship centralised in one sanctuary a link is wanting, and that link is found in the shape assumed by Hezekiah's reforms under the special conditions of the land at the time when the provincial sanctuaries had been destroyed by Sennacherib. Hezekiah's reforms were not permanent because they were largely guided by temporary circumstances. The Deuteronomic code endeavours to develop an adequate and permanent scheme for the whole worship of Israel, in which the principle of centralisation is carried out in all its consequences, and adapted to every requirement of social life. See the argument for this in detail, *O. T. in J. Ch.*, Lect. xii.

Here, however, the question arises, how far the religious pre-eminence which was thus accorded to Zion corresponded with tendencies already at work before the catastrophe of Sennacherib, and which might have ultimately produced the same result even in other circumstances. We have first to consider the attitude taken up towards Zion by the prophets. According to Amos i. 2, Jehovah roars from Zion and sends forth His voice from Jerusalem. Zion, therefore, to this Judæan prophet is already the centre of Jehovah's self-manifestation. But the prophetic doctrine of Jehovah's manifestation in judgment has nothing to do with His appearance to His people in their acts of worship. To Amos the organs of Jehovah's intercourse with His people are not the priests, but the prophets and Nazarites (ii. 12). Jehovah's relation to "His people Israel" is that of the supreme judge : not the temple but the tent of David occupies the central place in his picture of restoration ; the future glory of Jerusalem consists in its restoration to the position of a great capital, the centre of a dominion embracing the vassal nations, "over whom Jehovah's name was called" in the days of David. The last expression shows most clearly how little the idea of worship at the sanctuary of Jerusalem has to do with Amos's notion of the religious importance of Zion ; the subjects of the house of David are, as such, subjects of Jehovah. We shall not err, then, if we say that to Amos Zion is the seat of divine manifestation because it is the seat of the Davidic kingdom. Precisely in the same way the tent of David appears in a position of central importance in the old prophecy, Isa. xvi. It is in this relation also that Zion holds a central place in the ideal of Isaiah and Micah. Jehovah manifests Himself on Zion, not at the altar but on the throne of judgment. And so in Isa. xix. the conversion of Egypt is followed by the worship of Jehovah, not at the altar of Jerusalem, but within the land of Egypt itself. The tributary homage of Tyre and Ethiopia (Isa. xviii. 7 ; xxiii. 18) is paid to the capital of Jehovah's kingdom, and enriches the inhabitants of Jerusalem, not the priests. Had the priests been meant in Isa. xxiii. 18, the prophet would have said, "them that *stand* before Jehovah." At the same time it is obvious that the temple had necessarily a great preeminence over all other holy places because it was the royal, and so in a sense the national, sanctuary. This comes out most clearly in the old war-hymn for a king of Judah, Ps. xx. Another point which doubtless had great weight with the masses was the presence of the ark in Zion. That the ark was the token of Jehovah's presence was the ancient belief of Israel, and appears in a striking way in 2 Sam. xv. 25. On the old view the ark was the sanctuary of the armies of Israel, which led them to battle, and the words of David in the passage just cited are noteworthy as forming in a certain sense the transition from this view to that embodied in Solomon's temple, that Jehovah has now taken up His permanent dwelling-place in the seat of kingship. In this there lies a real step towards religious centralisation—only, we know that no inference was practically drawn from it for the abolition or limitation of local worship. All that is historically certain is that the autumn feast at Jerusalem, and perhaps the passover there, became great pilgrimage feasts. In this sense Isaiah himself seems to recognise Jerusalem as the religious centre of the land (xxx. 29 ; xxxiii. 20), and here we must, no doubt, seek another practical facilitation of the centralisation of worship. But the prophets lay no weight on the ark as the central point of Jerusalem's holiness. To Isaiah the whole mountain land of Israel, but especially the whole plateau of Zion, is holy (xi. 9 ; iv. 5). The code, as distinguished from the framework, of Deuteronomy never mentions the ark ; according to Jeremiah the ark of the covenant of Jehovah is a thing of no consequence. In the days of Israel's repentance it shall not be sought for or repaired, but "Jerusalem shall be called Jehovah's throne" (iii. 17). Thus it is still as the seat of Jehovah's kingship that Jerusalem has central religious importance ; the political not the priestly ideal is that which prevails among all the prophets before Ezekiel.

NOTE 12, p. 364.—Ashtoreth, Moloch or Milcom, and Chemosh, in whose worship similar elements prevailed with those of Moloch worship (2 Kings iii. 27), and who was also associated with Ashtoreth, as we learn from the compound Ashtar-Kemosh of the stone of Mesha, are the deities mentioned in connection with these sanctuaries in 1 Kings xi., 2 Kings xxiii. 13. And in the time from Manasseh onwards, Moloch-worship and worship of the "queen of heaven" appear as prominent new features of Judah's idolatry. It is also probable that the local high places took on their restoration a more markedly heathenish character than before. Isaiah and Micah do not speak in detail of Canaanite abominations in Judah, such as are mentioned for Ephraim in Amos and Hosea, while the book of Deuteronomy regards the high places as purely Canaanitish. This is very natural, for Sennacherib's invasion must have led captive a larger proportion of the higher than of the lower classes, and the latter, no doubt, were more mixed with Canaanite elements, the Israelites having long been a sort of aristocracy in the land (*Ḥōrîm*, or freemen). Compare Jer. v. 4.

NOTE 13, p. 365.—Ewald is doubtless right in assigning these chapters to the reign of Manasseh. The times are worse than those of Micah i.-v., but the religion of Judah has lost its old naive, joyful character. Without any true sense of sin, there is a strong sense of Jehovah's displeasure, a readiness to make any sacrifice—even that of the firstborn son—to appease His wrath. Then, too, the statutes of the house of Omri are kept (vi. 16). These are precisely the notes of the reign of Manasseh as described in Kings. One correction, however, must be made on Ewald's view. Wellhausen's argument that the prophecy breaks off abruptly at vii. 6, and that the following verses are written from the standpoint of Babylonian exile (Bleek's *Einl.*, p. 425 *seq.*), will, I think, when carefully weighed, be found to be conclusive. The enemy of vii. 10 cannot be the heathenish party in Judah; the restoration looked forward to is not a turn of affairs in a still existing kingdom of Judah, but the recall of the nation from banishment in Egypt and Assyria. The situation is no longer, as in the previous prophecy, one of prevailing national sin, the judgment on which cannot long be delayed, but a situation of present calamity and darkness, the punishment of past sins which are acknowledged by a penitent nation.

P. 153.—The existence of a vassal kingdom of Samaria has again become doubtful, or has even been given up by Assyriologists, as it appears that the name read *Usimurun* and identified with Samaria ought to be *Samsimurun*. See Schrader, *Abh. Berl. Ak.*, 1879; Delitzsch, *Paradies*, p. 286; Nöldeke, *Z.D.M.G.*, 1882, p. 178. In consequence of this new reading, the word *Samaritans*, at p. 322, line 3, should also be omitted.

INDEX.

ADONIS, 201; gardens of, 273.
Ahab, 48, 76 seq.
Ahaz, 200, 239; alliance with Assyria, 250 seq.; his idolatrous buildings, 251; refuses to hear Isaiah, 266.
Allegorical interpretation of prophecy, 339.
Amaziah, priest of Bethel, 101, 123 seq.; king of Judah, 194.
Amorites, 26.
Amos of Tekoah, 120; at Bethel, 122 seq.; his style, 125 seq.; his range of knowledge, 127 seq.; prophecy of Assyrian conquest, 129 seq.; his doctrine of Jehovah, 132 seq.; prophecies against foreign nations, 134; against Israel, 135 seq.; duty of Israel, 138; sins of Israel, 139; eschatology, 142, 186; contrasted with Hosea, 160 seq., 163, 187; influence on Isaiah, 209; does not condemn the calf-worship, 175 seq.; commentaries on, 394; supposed interpolations in, 398 seq.; Amos v. 26 discussed, 399 seq.
Aramæans, 23 seq.
Ark and its sanctuary, 36 seq., 437.
Ashdod, 280; Isaiah's prophecy against, 281.
Ashera (sacred pole), 96, 292, 362.
Ashtoreth, 26, 172.
Assyria, war with Damascus, 91; in the book of Amos, 130; relations to Judah, 194 seq., 250 seq., 294 seq., 321 seq., 366.
Assyrian inscriptions, 19, 376 seq.; chronology, 150.

BAAL, 26, 38; Tyrian Baal (Melkarth), 48, 52 seq., 76; prophets of, 57, 391; Dionysiac worship of, 84, 140; Land of, 172; Baal=husband, 171.
Ba'l and 'Athary, 172, 409.
Byblus or Gebal, 51.

CALVES, golden, symbols of Jehovah, 175 seq.
Canaanites, 24, 26; relations to Israel, 30 seq.; in Jerusalem 204.
Carchemish, 23, 377 seq.
Cheyne, Mr., on the prophecies of the reign of Sargon, 295 seq.
Chronology of the Hebrew kingdoms, 145 seq., 402, 413 seq.
Church, birth of the idea of, 275.

DAMASCUS, wars with Israel, 90 seq., 131; with Assyria, 91, 130.
Davidic kingship, 45 seq.; in the prophecy of Amos, 137, 186; in Hosea 185 seq.; in Isaiah, 301, 309 seq., in Micah, 291.
Day of Jehovah, 131 seq., 396.
Deuteronomic law influenced by Micah, 293; relation to Hezekiah's reformation, 363 seq.
Development of revelation, 3 seq.
"Dogs," 391.

ECCLESIASTICAL tradition, 5.
Edom, 28 seq., 135, 192, 203, 322.
Egypt, 22; united to the throne of Ethiopia, 279; its part in Hebrew politics, 280 seq., 294 seq., 319, 321 seq., 349.
Ekron, siege of, by Sennacherib, 322.
Elath, 203, 215, 238, 250.
Eliakim, 307, 346 seq.
Elijah, 76 seq.

Elijah and Elisha, history of, 116.
Elisha, 85, 87, 131, 208.
Eltekeh (Altaku), battle of, 322.
Ephod (plated image), 98.
Eponym Canon, 150.

FEASTS, religious, 38, 383 *seq.*
Federal theology, 375.
Fir-trees, 411.
Forty as round number, 148, 403.
Future state, doctrine of, 63 *seq.*

GEOGRAPHICAL knowledge of the Hebrews, 21 *seq.;* of Amos, 127 *seq.*
Gomer bath Diblaim, 179 *seq.*

Hesed (pietas) explained, 160 *seq.*, 406.
Hezekiah, his early years, 287 *seq.;* receives ambassadors of Merodach Baladan, 318; intrigues with Egypt, 321; attacked by Sennacherib, 345; surrenders, 347; encouraged to resist by Isaiah, 350; his weak character, 347; his reformation, 359 *seq.*
Hierodouloi, 228.
High places, abolition of, 362 *seq.*
Historical books of O. T., 109, 114 *seq.*
Hittites, 23, 377 *seq.*
Holiness, conception of, 224, 422; as developed by Isaiah, 225 *seq.;* of the land of Israel, 228 *seq.;* symbolism of fire and water, 232.
Hosea, date of, 144, 155; belonged to Northern Kingdom, 154; attitude to the priests, 113, 156; isolation of, 157; his prophecy of judgment, 158; his doctrine of Jehovah's love, 159 *seq.;* of His covenant, 161; Fatherhoood of Jehovah, 167 *seq.;* treats Ephraim as a moral individual, 165, 190; his references to past history, 165; contrasted with Amos, 160, 163, 186; his allegory of sonship and marriage, 167 *seq.;* his attitude to the golden calves, 175 *seq.;* his personal history, 179 *seq.;* his condemnation of the revolution of Jehu, 183 *seq.;* restoration of

Davidic monarchy, 185; his eschatology, 187 *seq.;* title of his prophecy, 404.
Hosea iv., 4 *seq.*, 405; chap. vii. 5, 410; chap. xiv. 8, 411.
Hoshea, king of Samaria, 152, 279.

IMAGE-WORSHIP, 175 *seq.;* 240.
Immanuel (God with us), 270, 271 *seq.*
Inscriptions: Moabite (Mesha), 50, 382; Phœnician (Gebal), 51, (Sidon) 64, (Marseilles) 56; of Siloam, 236.
Isaiah, 205 *seq.;* his influence, 206 *seq.*, 320, 350; compared with Elisha, 208; with Amos and Hosea, 209 *seq.*, 229 *seq.*, 254 *seq.;* with Jeremiah, 259 *seq.;* with Micah, 289 *seq.;* order of his book, 210; critical questions, 213 *seq.;* periods of his ministry, 214; inaugural vision, 217 *seq.;* doctrine of Jehovah's holiness, 224 *seq.;* his lips purged, 230 *seq.;* doctrine of the remnant, 209, 234, 258; use of writing as a vehicle of teaching, 235 *seq.;* his first prophetic book, 236 *seq.;* condemnation of the unrighteous nobles, 241, 233 *seq.*, 346; doctrine of Jehovah's kingly righteousness, 226, 245; earliest eschatological ideal, 248; first appearance as a practical politician, 254; doctrine of inviolability of Jerusalem, 258 *seq.;* opposition to Assyrian alliance, 265 *seq.;* his interpretation of the Assyrian advance, 269 *seq.;* "God with us," 270 *seq.;* formation of a prophetic party, 207 *seq.*, 274; Messianic teaching, 276 *seq.*, 301 *seq.;* prophecy against Ashdod, 281; prophecies on the eve of Samaria's fall, 282 *seq.;* argument from husbandry, 285; picture of the career and fall of Assyria, 297 *seq.;* his definition of miracle, 315; prophecy upon the death of Sargon, 319; prophecies under Sennacherib, 322 *seq.;* universalism, 331 *seq.;* conversion of Ethiopia, 332; of Tyre, 334; of

INDEX. 443

Egypt and Assyria, 335 *seq.;* prophecies during the invasion of Judah, 345 *seq.;* against Shebna, 346; encourages Hezekiah, 350 *seq.;* his great victory, 352 *seq.;* last words of Isaiah, 354 *seq.*
Isaiah i., 215, 345; ii.-v., 215, 236 *seq.;* vi., 217 *seq.;* vii. 1-ix. 7, 258 *seq.;* ix. 8-x. 4, 215, 238; x. 5-xi. 16, 297 *seq.;* xiv. 24-27, 300; xiv. 29 *seq.,* 319; xv. xvi., 92; xvii., 273, 331; xviii., 331 *seq.;* xix., 333, 335; xx., 281; xxi. 1-10, 420; xxi. 13 *seq.,* 333; xxii., 346 *seq.;* xxiii., 333 *seq.;* xxviii., 282 *seq.;* xxix. - xxxii., 307, 314, 322 *seq.;* xxxiii., 354 *seq.;* xxxvii., 351 *seq.*
Israel in Egypt, 29; in Canaan, 30 *seq.;* early religion, 32 *seq.;* consolidated into a kingdom, 45, 47; division of the kingdom, 48; tribal organisation, 93; ancient life, 94; social decay, 88, 95 *seq.;* early ideal of, as a warlike kingdom victorious in Jehovah, 119; Israel Jehovah's spouse, 170 *seq.;* unfaithfulness of, 176 *seq.*

JEHOVAH (Iahwè) God of Israel, 20, 32 *seq.;* Syncretism with Baal, 38, 173; God of the armies of Israel (Iahwè Çebaoth), 39, 42, 62, 76, 131; His attributes, 62; God of righteousness, 71 *seq.,* 245 *seq.;* a jealous God, 79, 119; His love to Israel, 159 *seq.;* His covenant, 161; holiness of, 224 *seq.;* the Holy One of Israel, 227; Jehovah and the idols, 240; His spirit, 304; meaning of the name, 385 *seq.*
Jehoshaphat, 112.
Jehu, house of, 88, 95, 183 *seq.*
Jeroboam II., 89, 92 *seq.*
Jirbâs, 377.
Jonadab the Rechabite, 84.
Judah, foreign elements in, 28, 201; history of, after the schism, 191 *seq.;* inferiority to Ephraim, 192 *seq.;* in Blessing of Moses, 118; suffers from Hazael, 193; relations to Assyria, 194 *seq.;* character of the Judæan monarchy, 196 *seq.;* religious condition, 199 *seq.;* prosperity under Uzziah, 203 *seq.;* social disintegration, 204 *seq.;* sins of the nobles, 241, 287 *seq.;* under Hezekiah, 294 *seq.,* 318 *seq.*

KENITES, 29.

MANASSEH, reaction under, 206, 365.
Marriage, religious symbolism of, 171 *seq.*
Menahem, 151 *seq.*
Merodach Baladan, 281, 317 *seq.*
Messiah, 302 *seq.*
Micah, 287 *seq.;* prophecy against Samaria, 288; description of the sins of Judah, 288 *seq.;* the wrongs of the peasantry, 289; democratic character of his prophecy, 290; fall of Jerusalem, 291; the new David, 291; great influence of Micah, 292 *seq.,* 363; interpolations in Micah, 427 *seq.*
Micah ii. 8 emended, 427; Micah vi. vii., 365, 372, 439.
Miracle, 315.
Moab, 24, 28; religion of, 50; wars with Northern Israel, 75; subdued by Jeroboam II., 91; ancient prophecy against (Isa. xv. xvi), 92 *seq.;* in the prophecy of Amos, 135; in Assyrian period, 294, 322.
Monotheism, 54, 59 *seq.,* 225 *seq.*
Moresheth Gath, 287.
Moses, 32 *seq.;* his work, 35 *seq.;* as judge or lawgiver, 110 *seq.;* Blessing of (Deut. xxxiii.), 49, 117 *seq.*

NABOTH, murder of, 77, 87.
Nazarites, 84, 137 *seq.,* 437.

OMRI, house of, 75 *seq.,* 95.

PALESTINE, physical features of, 24 *seq.;* inhabitants, 26, 28; conquest by Hebrews, 29 *seq.*
Patriarchs, history of, 116, 166.
Pekah, 152, 194, 250.
Pentateuch contains strata of very

different dates, 108 *seq.*; oldest laws, 113 *seq.*
Philistines, 45, 134, 137; wars with Judah, 192, 239; with Assyria, 279 *seq.*, 294, 318, 322.
Phœnicians, 22, 25 *seq.*; their religion, 26 *seq.*; influence of their art in the Temple, 56, 385.
Priests of the northern sanctuaries, 98, 100; corruption of in eighth century, 101.
Prophetic party of Isaiah, 207 *seq.*, 274, 320; its victory, 348 *seq.*; its decadence, 370; prophetic prediction, interpretation of, 268, 336 *seq.*
Prophets, their work, 69 *seq.*; Rabbinical conception of, 82; sons of (prophetic guilds), 85 *seq.*; contrasted with diviners, 219 *seq.*; the name *nâbî*, 389 *seq.*
Psalm xlvi., 352.

RAPHIA, 280, 426.
Religion, the subject of, in O. T., is the nation of Israel, 20; religion and morality, 72 *seq.*; chief merit of the popular Hebrew religion, 312; true and false religion, 273.
Remnant, prophetic doctrine of, 106 *seq.*, 209, 234, 258.
Rephaim (shades), 64.
Revelation, development of, 3 *seq.*; objections to doctrine of special revelation in Israel, 9 *seq.*; answer to these objections, 11 *seq.*; evidence of the truth of the Bible revelation, 16.
Righteousness, 71 *seq.*, 245, 388.

SABBATH, 384.
Samaria, Ashera in, 140; siege of, 151, 403; vassal kingdom in, 153.
Samaritans, 153.
Sanctuaries, local, 37, 43; their ritual and priesthood, 97 *seq.*; places of judgment, 100 *seq.*; in Judah, 199 *seq.*; abolished, 362.

Sargon, king of Assyria, 279 *seq.*, 294 *seq.*; his death 317.
Saul, 45, 331, 391, 393.
Sebech or So, 279 *seq.*
Semitic races, 22; their religion, 50 *seq.*; characteristics of their literature, 126.
Sennacherib, 297, 317 *seq.*, 345 *seq.*
Seraphim, 213.
Shechem, 31, 99, 118.
Sin, early Hebrew conception of, 102 *seq.*; in Isaiah, 246 *seq.*
Sinai, seat of Jehovah, 34, 39; legislation at, 111.
So, king of Egypt, 279.
Solomon, heathen shrines of, 76, 111, 202, 364; despotism of, 95, 198.
Sonship, doctrine of, in Old Testament, 20, 167 *seq.*
Spirit, 60 *seq.*; of Jehovah, 304 *seq.*
Supernatural, prophetic view of the, 310 *seq.*
Sycamore, 395.
Syria or Aram, 22 *seq.*; wars with Israel, 88, 90 *seq.* *See* Damascus.

TEKOA, 120, 394.
Teraphim, 33, 98.
Theocracy, 51 *seq.*; origin of the name, 52; among heathen Semites, 52 *seq.*
Tirhakah, 322, 349.
Tithes, 53, 382 *seq.*
Tyre, Isaiah's prophecy concerning, 333, 334.

URIAH, the friend of Isaiah, 207.
Urim and Thummim, 100.
Uzziah, 194, 203 *seq.*

VISION, prophetic, 219 *seq.*

WINE, 388.

ZECHARIAH ix.-xiv., 412.

www.ingramcontent.com/pod-product-compliance
Lightning Source LLC
Chambersburg PA
CBHW032007300426
44117CB00008B/930